STRATEGIC MARKET MANAGEMENT

THE WILEY BICENTENNIAL–KNOWLEDGE FOR GENERATIONS

Each generation has its unique needs and aspirations. When Charles Wiley first opened his small printing shop in lower Manhattan in 1807, it was a generation of boundless potential searching for an identity. And we were there, helping to define a new American literary tradition. Over half a century later, in the midst of the Second Industrial Revolution, it was a generation focused on building the future. Once again, we were there, supplying the critical scientific, technical, and engineering knowledge that helped frame the world. Throughout the 20th Century, and into the new millennium, nations began to reach out beyond their own borders and a new international community was born. Wiley was there, expanding its operations around the world to enable a global exchange of ideas, opinions, and know-how.

For 200 years, Wiley has been an integral part of each generation's journey, enabling the flow of information and understanding necessary to meet their needs and fulfill their aspirations. Today, bold new technologies are changing the way we live and learn. Wiley will be there, providing you the must-have knowledge you need to imagine new worlds, new possibilities, and new opportunities.

Generations come and go, but you can always count on Wiley to provide you the knowledge you need, when and where you need it!

WILLIAM J. PESCE
PRESIDENT AND CHIEF EXECUTIVE OFFICER

PETER BOOTH WILEY
CHAIRMAN OF THE BOARD

EIGHTH EDITION

STRATEGIC MARKET MANAGEMENT

David A. Aaker

Vice-Chairman, Prophet

Professor Emeritus, University of California, at Berkeley

BICENTENNIAL
1807
WILEY
2007
BICENTENNIAL

John Wiley & Sons, Inc.

There is a tide in the affairs of men,
Which, taken at the flood, leads on to fortune;
Omitted, all the voyage of their life
Is bound in shallows and in miseries.
On such a full sea are we now afloat,
And we must take the current when it serves,
Or lose our ventures.

—*William Shakespeare, from Julius Caesar*

ASSOCIATE PUBLISHER	Judith Joseph
SENIOR ACQUISITIONS EDITOR	Jayme Heffler
ASSOCIATE EDITOR	Jennifer Conklin
SENIOR PRODUCTION EDITOR	Valerie A. Vargas
EXECUTIVE MARKETING MANAGER	Christopher Ruel
CREATIVE DIRECTOR	Harry Nolan
SENIOR DESIGNER	Madelyn Lesure
COVER DESIGNER	Michael St. Martine
PRODUCTION MANAGEMENT SERVICES	mb editorial services
EDITORIAL ASSISTANT	Carissa Marker
MEDIA EDITOR	Allison Morris
COVER PHOTO	The Image Works

This book was set in 10/12 New Caledonia by Thomson Digital. Printed and bound by Courier-Westford. The cover was printed by Courier-Westford.

This book is printed on acid free paper. ∞

To order books or for customer service please, call 1-800-CALL WILEY (225-5945).

ISBN-13 978-0-470-05623-3
ISBN-10 0-470-05623-1

Printed in the United States of America

10 9 8 7 6 5 4

PREFACE

Developing and implementing strategies is now very different than it was only a few decades ago, when the business environments were more stable and simpler. Every market can now be described as dynamic. As a result, firms need to be able to adapt strategies in order to stay relevant. It is a challenging but exciting time, full of opportunities as well as threats.

The eighth edition of *Strategic Market Management* is motivated by the strategic challenges created by the dynamic nature of markets. The premise is that all traditional strategic management tools either do not apply or need to be adapted to a more dynamic context.

Developing successful, ongoing strategies in dynamic markets involves five types of competencies that are detailed in the book—strategic analysis, stimulating and managing innovation, managing multiple businesses, creating advantage, and developing growth strategies:

- **Strategic analysis** couples internal analysis of a firm's strengths and weaknesses with external analysis to generate winning, adaptable strategies. External analysis leads to understanding of market dynamics and aims to understand the customer, the competitor, and the important trends within the external environment of the business. This book describes and illustrates a structured approach to strategic analysis, supported by a summary flow diagram, a set of agendas to help start the process, and a set of planning forms.

- **Stimulating and managing innovation**, an indispensable part of influencing and responding to marketing dynamics, involves understating the different types of innovation and dealing with organizational challenges surrounding bringing innovations to market.

- **Managing multiple businesses** involves addressing market dynamics by allocating resources toward businesses of the future and away from businesses that lack growth potential.

- **Creating advantage** that is truly sustainable in the context of dynamic markets is challenging. One approach is to develop assets and competences that endure market changes and span business units. Another is the creation and leveraging of organization synergy created by the multiple business units. The emphasis on sustainable advantage provides a long-term perspective that can act as a counterweight to the all-too-frequent dominance of short-term goals or operational problems.

- **Developing growth strategies** by energizing the business, leveraging the business, creating new businesses, or globalizing the business.

Coping with a dynamic market requires customer driven strategies. The book will emphasize a customer perspective and the fact that every strategy should have a value proposition that is meaningful to customers.

THE EIGHTH EDITION

The eighth edition, which is again compact, develops the dynamic market theme. With more focus on innovation, there are three new growth chapters. The first, on energizing the business, includes my concepts of branded energizers and branded differentiators. The second, on leveraging the business, includes brand extensions. The third, on creating new businesses, discusses disruptive innovations and how you can create new business arenas. These topics are really at the heart of innovation, which is on the front burner in most firms.

This edition also includes three additional chapters that represent a major reformation and reposition of the material in the previous edition. One chapter discusses how to allocate resources across business units and, more particularly, how to make the decisions to exit or milk a business. Another discusses the creation and management of brand equity, a key business asset. Still another provides an overview of alternative value propositions that can drive a business strategy.

In addition, this edition contains new material on:

- The relationship of the Chief Marketing Officer (CMO) and strategy
- Ethnographic research
- The green movement and its relationship to strategy
- Transformational vs. substantial vs. incremental innovation
- Strategy adaptation
- Value propositions
- Expanding the global footprint
- Prioritizing and trimming the brand portfolio
- How the new corporate CMO gets traction as he or she works to create internal growth initiatives and synergy in the context of decentralized organizations

AN OVERVIEW

This book begins with an introduction that defines a business strategy, followed by an overview of the book and a discussion of the CMO and strategy. Part I of the book, Chapters 2 to 6, covers strategic analysis, with individual chapters on customer, competitor, market, environmental, and internal analysis. Part II of the book, Chapters 7 to 15, covers the development and implementation of strategy. Chapter 7 discusses the concept of a sustainable competitive advantage (SCA) and introduces four strategy styles—strategic commitment, strategic opportunism, strategic adaptability, and strategic intent.

Chapter 8 provides an overview of the scope of strategic choices by describing several value propositions. Chapter 9 shows how brand equity can be created and leveraged. The next four chapters discuss growth options: Chapter 10 covers energizing the business, Chapter 11 leveraging the business, Chapter 12 creating new businesses, and Chapter 13 global strategies. Chapter 14 discusses setting priorities and the disinvestment option. Finally, Chapter 15 introduces organizational dimensions and their role in strategy choice and implementation.

THE AUDIENCE

This book is suitable for any course in a school of management or business that focuses on the management of strategies. In particular, it is aimed at:

- The marketing strategy course, which could be titled strategic market management, strategic market planning, strategic marketing, or marketing strategy.
- The policy or entrepreneur course, which could be titled strategic management, strategic planning, business policy, entrepreneurship, or policy administration.

The book is also designed to be used by managers who need to develop strategies in dynamic markets—those who have recently moved into general management positions or who run a small business and want to improve their strategy development and planning processes. Another intended audience are those general managers, top executives, and planning specialists who would like an overview of recent issues and methods in strategic market management.

A WORD TO INSTRUCTORS

The eighth edition contains an extensive instructor's resource guide authored by David Aaker and Jim Prost located on the book companion Web site at www.wiley.com/college/aaker. The resource guide has a PowerPoint presentation organized by chapter, a set of lecture suggestions for each chapter, a test bank, several course outlines, and a list of cases to consider.

ACKNOWLEDGMENTS

This book could not have been created without help from my friends, students, reviewers, and colleagues at the Haas School of Business and at Prophet. Their help and support are appreciated. Special thanks to the insightful reviewers who helped me make some major changes in this edition: Gilbert Frisbie, Indiana University, and Jeffrey Stoltman, Wayne State University.

I am pleased to be associated with the publisher, John Wiley, a class organization, and its superb editors—Rich Esposito (who helped give birth to the first edition), John Woods, Tim Kent, Ellen Ford, Jeff Marshall, Judith Joseph, and Jayme Heffler (who guided this edition). It is a pleasure to be supported by competent, supportive professionals who are fun to be around. Chris Kelly, a superb copy editor, helped make this edition more readable as he has on so many of my others, and Martha

Beyerlein, who guided the manuscript through production with competence and good humor.

I owe a debt to some Nestlé people who helped with the pet food example used in the planning forms. Leah Porter, John Carmichael, and Mark Brodeur helped to develop the case study and updated it through several editions.

My thanks to my friend and colleague Jim Prost, a strategy teacher extraordinaire who made numerous suggestions about the book and has helped me create a world-class teacher's resource manual. Thanks also to Stephanie Johnson for her contributions to the manual.

This book is dedicated to the women in my life—my wife, Kay, and my three girls, Jennifer, Jan, and Jolyn.

David A. Aaker
February 2007

BRIEF CONTENTS

1. Strategic Market Management—An Introduction and Overview   1

PART I   STRATEGIC ANALYSIS   17

2. External and Customer Analysis   19
3. Competitor Analysis   38
4. Market/Submarket Analysis   58
5. Environmental Analysis and Strategic Uncertainty   78
6. Internal Analysis   95

   Case Challenges for Part I   108

PART II   CREATING, ADAPTING, AND IMPLEMENTING STRATEGY   117

7. Creating Advantage, Synergy, and Strategic Philosophies   119
8. Alternative Value Propositions   138
9. Building and Managing Brand Equity   157
10. Energizing the Business   176
11. Leveraging the Business   193
12. Creating New Businesses   208
13. Global Strategies   223
14. Setting Priorities for Businesses and Brands—The Exit, Milk, and Consolidate Options   242
15. Organizational Issues   259

    Case Challenges for Part II   280

Appendix: Planning Forms   294
Index   309

CONTENTS

Chapter 1 **Strategic Market Management—An Introduction and Overview** 1
What Is a Business Strategy? 3
Strategic Market Management 10
Marketing and Its Role in Strategy 14

PART I STRATEGIC ANALYSIS 17

Chapter 2 **External and Customer Analysis** 19
External Analysis 19
The Scope of Customer Analysis 24
Segmentation 24
Customer Motivations 29
Unmet Needs 33

Chapter 3 **Competitor Analysis** 38
Identifying Competitors—Customer-Based Approaches 39
Identifying Competitors—Strategic Groups 41
Potential Competitors 44
Competitor Analysis—Understanding Competitors 44
Competitor Strengths and Weaknesses 48
Obtaining Information on Competitors 55

Chapter 4 **Market/Submarket Analysis** 58
Dimensions of a Market Analysis 59
Emerging Submarkets 59
Actual and Potential Market Size 62
Market and Submarket Growth 64
Market and Submarket Profitability Analysis 66
Cost Structure 69
Distribution Systems 70
Market Trends 70
Key Success Factors 71
Risks in High-Growth Markets 72

Chapter 5 **Environmental Analysis and Strategic Uncertainty** 78
Technology Trends 80
Consumer Trends 82
Government/Economic Trends 87
Dealing with Strategic Uncertainty 88
Impact Analysis—Assessing the Impact of Strategic Uncertainties 89
Scenario Analysis 90

xi

Chapter 6   *Internal Analysis*   95
Financial Performance—Sales and Profitability   96
Performance Measurement—Beyond Profitability   98
Strengths and Weaknesses   102
Threats and Opportunities   103
From Analysis to Strategy   105

Case Challenges for Part I   *108*
Trends in Retailing   108
The Energy Bar Industry   110
Competing Against Wal-Mart   113

PART II   CREATING, ADAPTING, AND IMPLEMENTING
STRATEGY   **117**

Chapter 7   *Creating Advantage, Synergy, and Strategic Philosophies*   *119*
The Sustainable Competitive Advantage   120
The Role of Synergy   125
Strategic Philosophies   127

Chapter 8   *Alternative Value Propositions*   *138*
Business Strategy Challenges   139
Alternative Value Propositions   141
Superior Quality   146
Value   150

Chapter 9   *Building and Managing Brand Equity*   *157*
Brand Awareness   158
Brand Loyalty   159
Brand Associations   161
The Brand Identity   168

Chapter 10   *Energizing the Business*   *176*
Energizing the Business   177
Increasing Product Usage   178
Branded Differentiators   182
Branded Energizers   185

Chapter 11   *Leveraging the Business*   *193*
Which Assets and Competencies Can Be Leveraged?   194
Brand Extensions   196
Expanding the Scope of the Offering   199
New Markets   200
Evaluating Business Leveraging Options   201
The Mirage of Synergy   203

Chapter 12   *Creating New Businesses*   *208*
The New Business   209
The Innovator's Advantage   211

	Managing Category Perceptions	213
	Creating New Business Arenas	214
	From Ideas to Market	218
Chapter 13	**Global Strategies**	**223**
	Motivations Underlying Global Strategies	224
	Expanding the Global Footprint	227
	Standardization vs. Customization	230
	Global Brand Management	233
	Strategic Alliances	236
Chapter 14	**Setting Priorities for Businesses and Brands—The Exit,**	**242**
	Milk, and Consolidate Options	
	The Business Portfolio	243
	Divestment or Liquidation	245
	The Milk Strategy	249
	Prioritizing and Trimming the Brand Portfolio	251
Chapter 15	**Organizational Issues**	**259**
	A Conceptual Framework	260
	Structure	260
	Systems	263
	People	264
	Culture	266
	Obtaining Strategic Congruence	269
	The New Corporate CMO: Getting Traction	273
	A Recap of Strategic Market Management	276
	Case Challenges for Part II	**280**
	Hobart Corporation	280
	Xerox: The Early Days	282
	Dove	286
	Transformational Innovations	289
	Samsung Electronics	291
	Intel (available at www.wiley.com/college/aaker)	
	Appendix: Planning Forms	294
	Index	309

CHAPTER ONE

Strategic Market Management—An Introduction and Overview

Plans are nothing, planning is everything.
—*Dwight D. Eisenhower*

Even if you are on the right track, you'll get run over if you just sit there.
—*Will Rodgers*

If you don't know where you're going, you might end up somewhere else.
—*Casey Stengel*

All markets today are dynamic. Change is in the air everywhere, and change affects strategy. A winning strategy today may not prevail tomorrow. It might not even be relevant tomorrow.

There was a time, not too many decades ago, when the world held still long enough for strategies to be put into place and refined with patience and discipline. The annual strategic plan guided the firm. That simply is no longer the case. New products, product modifications, subcategories, technologies, applications, market niches, segments, media, channels, and on and on are emerging faster than ever in nearly all industries—from snacks to fast food to automobiles to financial services to software. Multiple forces feed these changes, including Internet technologies, the rise of China and India, trends in healthy living, energy crises, political instability, and more. The result are markets that are not only dynamic but risky, complex, and cluttered.

Such convoluted markets make strategy creation and implementation far more challenging. Strategy has to win not only in today's marketplace but in tomorrow's, when the customer, the competitor set, and the market context may all be different.

In environments shaped by this new reality, some firms are driving change. Others are adapting to it. Still others are fading in the face of change. How do you develop successful strategies in dynamic markets? How do you stay ahead of competition? How do you stay relevant?

The task is challenging. Strategists need new and refined perspectives, tools, and concepts. In particular, they need to develop competencies around five management tasks—strategic analysis, innovation, getting control of multiple business units, developing sustainable advantages, and developing growth platforms.

Strategic analysis. The need for information about customers, competitors, and trends affecting the market is now higher than ever. Further, the information needs to be online, because a timely detection of threats, opportunities, strategic problems, or emerging weaknesses can be crucial to getting the response right. There is an enhanced premium on the ability to predict trends, project their impact, and distinguish them from mere fads. That means resources need to be invested and competencies created in terms of getting information, filtering it, and converting it into actionable analysis.

Innovation. Without question, firms are recognizing that the ability to innovate is one key to successfully competing in dynamic markets. Innovation, however, turns out to have a host of dimensions. There is the organizational challenge of creating a context that supports innovation. There is the brand portfolio challenge of making sure that the innovation is owned and not a short-lived market blip. There is the strategic challenge of developing the right kind of innovation, on a spectrum that ranges from incremental to transformational. There is the execution challenge; it is necessary to turn innovations into offerings in the marketplace. There are too many examples of firms that owned an innovation and let others bring it to market.

Multiple businesses. It is the rare firm now that does not operate multiple business units in different channels, markets, and countries in addition to product categories and subcategories. Pepsi-Cola, Toyota, Wells Fargo, and Microsoft are examples of firms that operate a wide variety of business units in a decentralized structure. Decentralization is a century-old organizational form that provides for accountability, being close to the customer, and fast response, all of which are good things. However, in its extreme form, autonomous business units can lead to the misallocation of resources and impede the development of cross-business synergies. In dynamic markets, a key lever, discussed in Chapter 14 is the ability to allow new business units to emerge and others to fade away by making strategic investment and disinvestment decisions. Autonomous business units resist such judgments. Further, the coordination needed to create synergy is not natural for decentralized structures. A challenge is to adapt the decentralization model so that it no longer inhibits strategy adaptation in dynamic markets.

Creating sustainable competitive advantages (SCAs). Creating strategic advantages that are truly sustainable in the context of dynamic markets and dispersed business units is challenging. Competitors all too quickly copy product and service improvements that are valued by customers. What leads to SCAs in dynamic markets?

One possible cornerstone is the development of assets and competencies that endure market changes and span business units. In particular, brand equities within a brand portfolio represent an asset class that often provides an SCA in combination with other assets and competencies. Another factor is leveraging the organizational synergy created by multiple business units. A unique combination of business units and resulting synergies is much more difficult to copy than a new product or service. Synergy, however, turns out to be much easier to conceptualize than actualize.

Developing growth platforms. Growth is imperative for the vitality and health of any organization. In a dynamic environment, though stretching the organization in creative ways becomes an essential element of seizing opportunities and adapting to changing circumstances. Understanding the scope of alternative avenues to growth and revitalization is one key to successful strategies. Another is to find ways to create new growth platforms without damaging or diluting the core business.

This book is concerned with helping managers identify, select, implement, and adapt market-driven business strategies that will enjoy a sustainable advantage in dynamic markets, as well as create synergy and set priorities among business units. The intent is to provide concepts, methods, and procedures that will lead to competencies in these five crucial management tasks—and, ultimately, to high-quality strategic decision making and profitable growth.

The book emphasizes customer-driven strategies, because in a dynamic market it is a customer orientation that is likely to be successful. The current, emerging, and latent motivations and unmet needs of customers need to influence strategies. Because of this, every strategy needs to have a value proposition that is meaningful and relevant to customers.

This first chapter starts with a very basic but central concept, that of a business strategy. The goal is to lend structure and clarity to a term that is widely employed but seldom defined. It continues with an overview of the balance of the book, introducing and positioning many of the subjects, concepts, and tools to be covered. Finally, the role of marketing in business strategy will be discussed. There is a significant trend for marketing to have a seat at the strategy table and to see the CMO (chief marketing officer) be empowered to create growth initiatives.

WHAT IS A BUSINESS STRATEGY?

Before discussing the process of developing sound business strategies, it is fair to address two questions. What is a business? What is a business strategy? Having groups of managers provide answers to these basic questions can be particularly interesting and useful. What you quickly learn from such an exercise is that the issues are complex and there is no consensus answer.

A Business

A business is generally an organizational unit that has (or should have) a defined strategy and a manager with sales and profit responsibility. An organization will thus have many business units that relate to each other horizontally and vertically.

For example, HP is a business that needs to set strategic directions for the many product markets in which it competes. And each product market will, in general, have its own business strategy. Thus, there may be a business strategy for the various HP product lines such as the LaserJet product group, but within that line, there may be business strategies for products such as the LaserJet printer supplies business, for segments such as large companies in the United States, or for geographies such as South America.

Ford, for example, has businesses defined by geographies like the United Kingdom and China, by the Ford Corporation itself, and by a host of brands and subbrands. Among those brands are the cars Fusion, Mustang, and Focus; the trucks F-150, Ranger, and the e-series; and the SUVs Escape, Explorer, and Escape Hybrid. In the United Kingdom it has Fiesta, Mondeo, and Galaxy. And there are the separate business units around other brands such as Jaguar with its subbrands XJ, S, and the XK sports car. There is a need for a business strategy around most of these product markets.

The realities of multiple business units often require layered business strategies. For Ford, there might be at least five. The first would be at the model level, such as the Escape Hybrid. The second would be a strategy for product markets such as Ford in the United States, Ford SUVs in the United States, and Ford cars in the United Kingdom. The third could be for a geographic aggregation, such as Ford trucks worldwide. The fourth would be for the widest product-market scope, such as Ford vehicles worldwide. The final layer would be for Ford as a corporation. These strategies will increasingly get more general as the scope increases.

There is an organizational and strategic trade-off in deciding how many businesses should be operated. On one hand, it can be compelling to have many units, because then each business will be close to its market and potentially capable of developing an optimal strategy. Thus, a strategy for each country or each region or each major segment may have some benefits. Too many business units become inefficient, however, and result in programs that lack scale economies and fail to leverage the strategic skills of the best managers. As a result, there is pressure to aggregate businesses into larger entities.

Business units can be aggregated to create a critical mass, to recognize similarities in markets and strategies, and to gain synergies. Businesses that are too small to justify a strategy will need to be aggregated so that the management structure can be supportable. (Of course, two business units can share some elements of operations, such as a sales force or a facility, to gain economies without merging.) Businesses that have similar market contexts and business strategies will be candidates for aggregation to leverage shared knowledge. Another aggregation motivation is to encourage synergies among business units when the combination is more likely to realize savings in cost or investment or create a superior value proposition.

A Business Strategy

Four dimensions define a business strategy: the product-market investment strategy, the customer value proposition, the assets and competencies, and the functional strategies and programs. The first specifies where to compete and the remaining three indicate how to compete to win, as suggested by Figure 1.1.

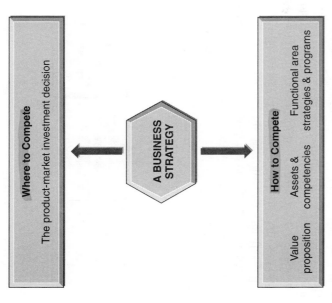

Figure 1.1 A Business Strategy

The Product-Market Investment Strategy: Where to Compete

The scope of the business, and the dynamics within that scope, represent a very basic strategy dimension. Which sectors should receive investments in resources and management attention? Which should have resources withdrawn or withheld? Even for a small organization, the allocation decision is key to strategy.

The scope of a business is defined by the products it offers and chooses not to offer, by the markets it seeks to serve and not serve, by the competitors it chooses to compete with and to avoid, and by its level of vertical integration. Sometimes the most important business scope decision is what products or segments to avoid because such a decision, if followed by discipline, can conserve resources needed to compete successfully elsewhere. Such a judgment can sometimes involve painful choices to divest or liquidate a business. Chapter 14 discusses disinvestment judgments and why they are hard to make and easy to avoid.

Many organizations have demonstrated the advantages of having a well-defined business scope. Williams-Sonoma offers products for the home and kitchen. IBM turned around its firm under the direction of Lou Gerstner in part by dialing up its service component, and more recently by expanding its software footprint. P&G provides a broad spectrum of consumer packaged goods. Wal-Mart and Amazon have a wide scope that generates both scale economies and a one-stop shopping value proposition.

More important than the scope is the scope dynamics. What product markets will be entered or exited in the coming years? As Figure 1.2 suggests, growth can be generated by bringing existing products to new markets (market expansion), bringing new products to existing markets (product expansion), or by entering new product-markets (diversification).

Expanding the business scope can help the organization achieve growth and vitality and can be a lever to cope with the changing marketplace by seizing opportunities as they emerge. During the first five years of the Jeff Immelt era, GE changed its focus and character by investing in healthcare, energy, water treatment, home mortgages, and entertainment (by buying Universal) while exiting markets for insurance, industrial diamonds, business outsourcing based in India, and a motor division. In addition, the percentage of revenue sources outside the United States grew from 40 percent to nearly 50 percent.

However, expanding the business scope poses risks as well. As the scope expansion ventures further from the core business, there will be increased risk that the firm's offering will not be distinctive, there will be problems in operations, or the firm's brands will not support the expansion. Despite similarities in manufacturing and distribution, Bausch & Lomb's attempt to move from eye care to mouthwash was a product and brand failure. An effort by a manufacturing equipment company to go into robots failed when it could not create or acquire the needed technology. Attention and resources may also be diverted from the core business, causing it to weaken.

The investment pattern will determine the future direction of the firm. Although there are obvious variations and refinements, it is useful to conceptualize the alternatives as follows:

- Invest to grow (or enter the product market)
- Invest only to maintain the existing position
- Milk the business by minimizing investment
- Recover as many of the assets as possible by liquidating or divesting the business

P&G had lost half its stock value in the six months before A. G. Lafley took over as CEO in 2000, in part because the firm invested considerable resources behind new business initiatives (such as Olay Cosmetics and Fit Wash) that disappointed or failed.[1] Two years later it had recovered most of that decline, even though the over-all stock market dropped over a third of its value during that time. A key to the

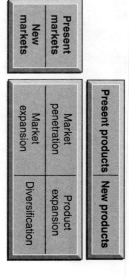

Figure 1.2   Product-Market Growth Directions

	Present products	New products
Present markets	Market penetration	Product expansion
New markets	Market expansion	Diversification

turnaround was a strategy of focusing on the twelve largest brands, each contributing over a billion dollars in sales—Tide, Arial (in Europe), Always/Whisper, Crest, Folgers, Iams, Pampers, Charmin, Bounty, Pantene, Downy/Lenor, and Pringles—and reducing investment it its other eighty or so brands. For example, with resources no longer diverted, the hair care group could focus on revitalizing Pantene. Lesser brands received less attention, and those such as Jif and Crisco, which lacked strategic fit, were jettisoned. Growth has since been obtained by expanding the list of billion-dollar brands, through both internal growth and the acquisition of Gillette.

The Customer Value Proposition

Ultimately the offering needs to appeal to new and existing customers. There needs to be a value proposition that is relevant and meaningful to the customer and is reflected in the positioning of the product or service. To support a successful strategy, it should be sustainable over time and be differentiated from competitors. The customer value proposition can involve elements such as providing to customers:

- A good value (Wal-Mart)
- Excellence on an important product or service attribute such as getting clothes clean (Tide)
- The best overall quality (Lexus)
- Product line breadth (Amazon)
- Innovative offerings (3M)
- A shared passion for an activity or a product (Harley-Davidson)
- Global connections and prestige (CitiGroup)

Home Depot and Lowe's are home improvement retailers with very different value propositions. Home Depot has very austere, functional stores that are designed to appeal to the contractor or homeowners on the basis of function and price. Lowe's strategy since 1994 was to have a softer side, a look that would be comfortable to women. Thus, their stores are well lit, the signs colorful and clear, the floors spotless, and the people friendly and helpful. Ten years later, the Lowe's strategy has traction, and Home Depot is attempting to adjust its own value proposition.

Assets and Competencies

The strategic assets or competencies that underlie the strategy often provide a sustainable competitive advantage (SCA). A *strategic competency* is what a business unit does exceptionally well—such as a customer relationship program, manufacturing, or promotion—that has strategic importance to that business. It is usually based on knowledge or a process. A *strategic asset* is a resource, such as a brand name or installed customer base that is strong relative to that of competitors. Strategy formulation must consider the cost and feasibility of generating or maintaining assets or competencies that will provide the basis for a sustainable competitive advantage.

Assets and competencies can involve a wide spectrum, from buildings and locations to R&D expertise to a symbol such as the Michelin Man. Though a strong asset or competency is often difficult to build, it can result in an advantage that is significant and enduring.

The synergies obtained from operating a business that spans product markets can be an important asset and SCA source. Synergies, which are significant because they are based on organizational characteristics that are not easily duplicated, can come in many forms. Two businesses can reduce costs by sharing a distribution system, sales force, or logistics system, as when Gillette acquired Duracell (and, later, was itself acquired by P&G). Synergy can also be based on sharing the same asset, as with the HP brand shared by the dozens of business units, or a competence such as Toyota's ability to manage manufacturing plants across business units and countries. Another source of synergy is the sharing of functional area strategies across business units. The Ford organization may be able to sponsor the World Cup, for instance, while Ford SUVs in the United Kingdom could not. Still another synergy source is the sharing of R&D. P&G aggregates brands such as Head & Shoulders, Pert, and Pantene into a hair care category not just to provide shelf space guidance of retailers and to create promotions more easily, but also to manage the use of product innovations. Finally, a combination of products can provide a value proposition. Some software firms have aggregated products in order to provide a systems solution to customers; Microsoft Office is one example.

The ability of assets and competencies to support a strategy will in part depend on their power relative to competitors. To what extent are the assets and competencies strong and in place? To what extent are they ownable because of a symbol trademark or long-standing investment in a capability? To what extent are they based on organizational synergy that others cannot duplicate?

Assets and competencies can also provide points of parity. For dimensions such as perceived quality, distribution strength, or manufacturing cost, the goal may be not to create an advantage but to avoid a disadvantage. When an asset or competency is close enough to that of a competitor to neutralize the latter's strength, then a point of parity has been achieved. Such parity can be a key to success; if the perceived quality of a Wal-Mart offering is regarded as adequate, its price perception will then win the day.

Functional Strategies and Programs

A target value proposition, or a set of assets and competencies, should mandate some strategy imperatives in the form of a supportive set of functional strategies or programs. These strategies and programs, in turn, will be implemented with a host of tactical programs with a short-term perspective.

Among the functional strategies or programs that could drive the business strategy might include a:

- Customer relationship program
- Brand-building strategy
- Communication strategy

- Information technology strategy
- Distribution strategy
- Global strategy
- Quality program
- Sourcing strategy
- Logistical strategy
- Manufacturing strategy

The need for functional strategies and programs can be determined by asking a few questions. What must happen for the firm to be able to deliver on the value proposition? Are the assets and competencies needed in place? Do they need to be created, strengthened, or supported? How?

Criteria to Select Business Strategies

The principal criteria useful for selecting alternatives can be grouped around six general questions:

- **Is the ROI attractive?** Creating a value proposition that is appealing to customers may not be worthwhile if the investment or operating cost is excessive. Starbucks opened in Japan in 1996 in the Ginza district and grew to over 400 units, many of which were in the highest-rent areas. The result was a trendy brand but one that was vulnerable to competitors, who

EXPANDING THE BUSINESS SCOPE

In his classic article "Marketing Myopia," Theodore Levitt explained how firms that define their business myopically in product terms can stagnate even though the basic customer need they serve is enjoying healthy growth.[2] Because of a myopic product focus, others gain the benefits of growth. In contrast, firms that regard themselves as being in the transportation rather than the railroad business, the energy instead of the petroleum business, or the communication rather than the telephone business are more likely to exploit opportunities.

The concept is simple. Define the business in terms of the basic customer need rather than the product. Visa has defined itself as being in the business of enabling a customer to exchange value (any asset, including cash on deposit, the cash value of life insurance, or the equity in a home) for virtually anything anywhere in the world. As the business is redefined, both the set of competitors and the range of opportunities are often radically expanded. After redefining its business, Visa estimated that it had reached only 5 percent of its potential given the new definition.

Defining a business in terms of generic need can be extremely useful for fostering creativity, in generating strategic options, and avoiding an internally oriented product focus.

matched or exceeded Starbucks' product offerings and were not handicapped with such high overhead because they developed less costly sites.

- **Is there a sustainable competitive advantage?** Unless the business unit has or can develop a real competitive advantage that is sustainable over time in the face of competitor reaction, an attractive long-term return will be unlikely. To achieve a sustainable competitive advantage, a strategy should exploit organizational assets and competencies and neutralize weaknesses.

- **Will the strategy have success in the future?** A strategy needs to be able to survive the dynamics of the market, with its emerging threats and opportunities. Either the strategy components should be expected to have a long life, or the strategy should be capable of adapting to changing conditions. In that context, future scenarios (described in Chapter 5) might be used to test the robustness of the strategy with respect to future uncertainties.

- **Is the strategy feasible?** The strategy should be within both the financial and human resources of the organization. It also should be internally consistent with other organizational characteristics, such as the firm's structure, systems, people, and culture. These organizational considerations will be covered in Chapter 15.

- **Does the strategy fit with the other strategies of the firm?** Are the sources and uses of cash flow in balance? Is organizational flexibility reduced by an investment in financial or human resources? Is potential synergy captured by the strategy?

STRATEGIC MARKET MANAGEMENT

Strategic market management is a system designed to help management create, change, or retain a business strategy and to create strategic visions. *A strategic vision is a projection of a future strategy or sets of strategies.* The realization of an optimal strategy may involve a delay because the firm is not ready, or the emerging conditions are not yet in place. A vision will provide direction and purpose for interim strategies and activities and can inspire those in the organization by providing a purpose that is worthwhile and ennobling.

Strategic market management involves decisions with a significant, long-term impact on the organization. The resulting business strategies can be costly in terms of time and resources to reverse or change. In fact, emerging strategic decisions can mean the difference between success, mediocrity, failure, or even survival.

Developing the right business strategies is a basic goal, but it is not the end of the story. With a business strategy in hand, the task is to:

- Continuously challenge the strategy in order to make sure that it remains relevant to the changing marketplace and responsive to emerging opportunities

- Ensure that the organization develops and retains the necessary skills and competencies to make the strategy succeed

- Implement the strategy with energy and focus; the best strategy badly implemented will be a failure (or worse, jeopardize the firm)

Figure 1.3 provides a structure for strategic market management and for this book. A brief overview of its principal elements and an introduction to the key concepts will be presented in this chapter.

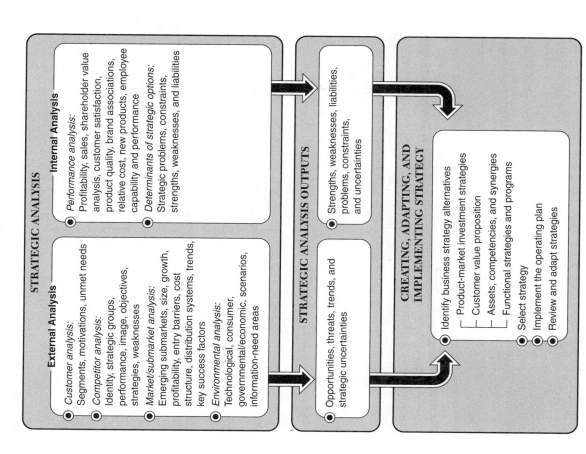

STRATEGIC ANALYSIS

External Analysis

Customer analysis:
Segments, motivations, unmet needs

Competitor analysis:
Identity, strategic groups, performance, image, objectives, strategies, weaknesses

Market/submarket analysis:
Emerging submarkets, size, growth, profitability, entry barriers, cost structure, distribution systems, trends, key success factors

Environmental analysis:
Technological, consumer, governmental/economic, scenarios, information-need areas

Internal Analysis

Performance analysis:
Profitability, sales, shareholder value analysis, customer satisfaction, product quality, brand associations, relative cost, new products, employee capability and performance

Determinants of strategic options:
Strategic problems, constraints, strengths, weaknesses, and liabilities

STRATEGIC ANALYSIS OUTPUTS

Opportunities, threats, trends, and strategic uncertainties

Strengths, weaknesses, liabilities, problems, constraints, and uncertainties

CREATING, ADAPTING, AND IMPLEMENTING STRATEGY

Identify business strategy alternatives
- Product-market investment strategies
- Customer value proposition
- Assets, competencies, and synergies
- Functional strategies and programs

Select strategy
Implement the operating plan
Review and adapt strategies

Figure 1.3 Overview of Strategic Market Management

External Analysis

External analysis, summarized in Figure 1.3, involves an examination of the relevant elements external to an organization—customers, competitors, markets and submarkets, and the environment or context outside of the market. Customer analysis, the first step of external analysis and a focus of Chapter 2, involves identifying the organization's customer segments and each segment's motivations and unmet needs. Competitor analysis, covered in Chapter 3, attempts to identify competitors (both current and potential) and describe their performance, image, strategy, and strengths and weaknesses. Market analysis, the subject of Chapter 4, aims to determine the attractiveness of the market and submarkets and to understand the dynamics of the market so that threats and opportunities can be detected and strategies adapted. Environmental analysis, the subject of Chapter 5, is the process of identifying and understanding emerging opportunities and threats created by forces in the context of the business.

The external analysis should be purposeful, focusing on key outputs: the identification of present and potential opportunities, threats, trends, strategic uncertainties, and strategic choices. There is a danger in being excessively descriptive. Because there is literally no limit to the scope of a descriptive study, the result can be a considerable expenditure of resources with little impact on strategy.

The frame of reference for an external analysis is typically a defined strategic business unit (SBU), but it is useful to conduct the analysis at several levels. External analyses of submarkets sometimes provide critical insights; for example, an external analysis of the mature beer industry might contain analyses of the import and nonalcoholic beer submarkets, which are growing and have important differences. It is also possible to conduct external analyses for groups of SBUs, such as divisions, that have characteristics in common. For instance, a food products company might consider analyses of the healthy-living segment and food trends that could span operating units within the firm.

Internal Analysis

Internal analysis, presented in Chapter 6 and also summarized in Figure 1.3, aims to provide a detailed understanding of strategically important aspects of the organization. Performance analysis looks not only at sales and return on assets but also measures of customer satisfaction/loyalty, quality, brand image, costs, and new product activity. The identification and assessment of organizational strengths and weaknesses will guide strategic priorities, including both the development of new strategies and the adaptation of existing ones.

Creating, Adapting, and Implementing Strategy

After describing strategic analysis, the book turns to the creation, adaptation, and implementation of strategy. How do you decide on the business scope? What are the alternative value propositions, and how do they guide strategy development? What assets and competencies will provide points of advantage, and which will aim for

GALLO: A CASE STUDY

Gallo, despites producing roughly one out of every four bottles of wine sold in the United States (primarily in the form of cheap wines sold under the Gallo name), felt it had to adapt to a strong market trend to premium varietals.

One vehicle was the launching of the premium Gallo of Sonoma brand, which enjoyed several significant potential SCAs. The grapes available to Gallo from Sonoma County in northern California (whose climate, some say, is superior to the famous Napa region), coupled with the company's willingness and ability to make great wine, have resulted in a product that has won some major international wine competitions. In addition, the brand gained synergies from Gallo's substantial distribution clout and operational scale efficiencies.

The decision to put the Gallo name on the new line undoubtedly created a huge liability, but it also had some compensating advantages. First, it permitted the business to leverage the credibility and personality of a third-generation family winemaker, Gina Gallo. Second, it boosted the pride of the organization and its partners in an aspect of the business (winemaking) that is at the core of its values. Finally, the seeming incongruity of Gallo making a fine wine could appeal to the wine tastemakers of the world by giving them a chance to prove that they are above labels. The success of Gallo of Sonoma emboldened Gallo to develop the Gallo Family Vineyards brand, which encompassed wines selling from $5 to $75 a bottle.

points of parity? What functional strategies and programs will lead to strategic success? What growth options will receive investment? Is the core business to be the source of growth, or is there a need to move beyond the core? What is to be the global strategy? How should the business units be prioritized? Should there be disinvestment in the business portfolio? How can the organization be adapted so that it supports rather than constrains strategy?

Chapter 7 discusses the concept of an SCA and the slippery concept of synergy before introducing four strategic philosophies—strategic commitment, strategic opportunism, strategic adaptability, and strategic intent. These strategy styles provide a good overview of alternative ways to manage strategy in the face of dynamic markets. Chapter 8 provides an overview of the scope of strategic choices by describing over a dozen possible value propositions, each of which provides an umbrella over a business strategy. Chapter 9 shows how brand equity, a key asset and adaptability lever, can be created and used. The next four chapters discuss growth options: Chapter 10 covers energizing the business, Chapter 11 leveraging the business, Chapter 12 creating new businesses, and Chapter 13 global strategies. Chapter 14 discusses the disinvestment option, an important and often overlooked dimension of the investment decision. Finally, Chapter 15 introduces organizational dimensions and their role in strategy choice and implementation.

Strategic Market Management—The Objectives

Strategic market management is intended to:

- *Precipitate the consideration of strategic choices.* What external events are creating opportunities and threats to which a timely and appropriate reaction should be generated? What strategic issues face the firm? What strategic options should be considered? The alternative to strategic market management is usually to drift strategically, becoming absorbed in day-to-day problems. Nothing is more tragic than an organization that fails because a strategic decision was not addressed until it was too late.

- *Help a business cope with change.* If a particular environment is extremely stable and the sales patterns are satisfactory, there may be little need for meaningful strategic change—either in direction or intensity. In that case, strategic market management is much less crucial. However, most organizations now exist in rapidly changing and increasingly unpredictable environments and therefore need approaches for coping strategically.

- *Force a long-range view.* The pressures to manage with a short-term focus are strong, but they frequently lead to strategic errors.

- *Make visible the resource allocation decision.* Allowing allocation of resources to be dictated by the political strengths or inertia (i.e., the same strategy as last year) is too easy. One result of this approach is that the small but promising business with "no problems" or the unborn business may suffer from a lack of resources, whereas larger business areas may absorb an excessive amount.

- *Aid strategic analysis and decision making.* Concepts, models, and methodologies are available to help a business collect and analyze information and address difficult strategic decisions.

- *Provide a strategic management and control system.* The focus on assets and competencies and the development of objectives and programs associated with strategic thrusts provide the basis for managing a business strategically.

- *Provide both horizontal and vertical communication and coordination systems.* Strategic market management provides a way to communicate problems and proposed strategies within an organization; in particular, its vocabulary adds precision.

MARKETING AND ITS ROLE IN STRATEGY

Marketing has seen its strategic role growing over the years. The question for each organization is whether the CMO (chief marketing officer) and his or her team have a seat at the strategy table or are relegated to being tactical implementers of tasks such as managing the advertising program. The view that marketing is tactical is changing; it is now more and more frequently being accepted as being part of the strategic management of the organization. Given the definition of a business strategy and the structure of strategic market management, the roles that marketing can and should play become clearer.

One marketing role is to be the primary driver of the strategic analysis. The marketing group is in the best position to understand the customers, competitors, market and submarkets, and environmental forces and trends. By managing marketing research and market data, it controls much of the information needed in the external analysis. Marketing should also take the lead in the internal analysis with respect to selected assets (such as the brand portfolio and the distribution channel) and competencies (such as new product introduction and the management of sponsorships).

A second role is to develop business strategies. The dimension of business strategy most clearly owned by marketing is the customer value proposition: What is the value that the firm will offer, now and in the future? Marketing in fact ought to be the voice of the customer in the strategic discussions, making sure that the value proposition is based on substance and is meaningful to the customer. Other components of a business strategy are also marketing-centric. The choice of market scope needs to draw on a segmentation strategy. Many assets and competencies, such as brand equity or customer relationship programs, are based in marketing. Finally, marketing programs will be among the functional area programs that are integral to strategy.

A third role is to drive growth strategy for the firm. Growth options are either based on or dependent on customer and market insights, and marketing therefore should be a key driver. In fact, a study by Booz Allen and Hamilton of some 2,000 executives found that a small (9 percent) but growing number of firms describe the CMO as a growth champion involved in all strategic levers relating to growth.[3]

A fourth role is to deal with the dysfunctions of product and geographic silos. Although all functional groups need to deal with this problem, marketing is often on the front lines. The corporate brand and major master brands usually span silos, and a failure to exercise some central control and guidance will result in inefficiencies and inconsistencies that can be damaging to one or more business strategies. Business-spanning marketing programs such as sponsorships or distribution channels need to be actively managed if opportunities are to be realized and waste and inefficiency are to be avoided.

KEY LEARNINGS

- Strategy needs to be developed and executed in the context of a dynamic market. To cope, it is important to develop competencies in strategic analysis, innovation, managing multiple business, and developing SCAs.

- A business strategy includes the determination of the product-market investment strategy, the customer value proposition, assets and competencies, and the functional area strategy.

- Strategic market management is a system designed to help management create, change, or retain a business strategy and to create strategic visions. A strategic vision is a vision of a future strategy or sets of strategies. Strategic market management includes a strategic analysis of the business to identify existing or emerging opportunities, threats, trends, strategic uncertainties, and strategic alternatives.

- The CMO role has grown over the years and is now often charged with being a partner in developing strategies and a vehicle to deal with the dysfunctions of the product-market silos.

FOR DISCUSSION

1. What is a business strategy? Do you agree with the definition proposed? Illustrate your answer with examples.

2. Consider one of the following firms. Read the description of a business strategy in the text. Go to the firm's Web site and use it to gain an understanding of the business strategy. Look at elements such as the products and services offered, the history of the firm, and its values. What is the business strategy? What are the firm's product markets? What are its value propositions? How are the value propositions delivered? What assets and competencies exist? What strategic options? Consider the scope question raised by Levitt. What would be a narrow and broad scope specification?

    a. Dell

    b. P&G (Tide, Pampers)

    c. Citicorp (Citibank)

    d. A firm of your choice

3. Consider the Gallo strategic decision. Describe how you would go about evaluating that decision.

4. Apply the marketing-myopia concept to print media, magazines, and newspapers. What is the implication?

5. Which criteria to pick a strategy would you consider most important? Why? How would the context affect your answer?

6. Which quote at the front of the chapter do you find the most insightful? Why? Under what circumstances would its implications not hold?

NOTES

1. Katrina Brooker, "The Un-CEO," *Fortune,* September 16, 2002, pp. 68–78.

2. Theodore Levitt, "Marketing Myopia," *Harvard Business Review,* July–August 1960, pp. 45–56.

3. Constantine von Hoffman, "Armed with Intelligence," *BrandWeek,* May 29, 2006, pp. 17–20.

PART ONE

STRATEGIC ANALYSIS

CHAPTER TWO

External and Customer Analysis

The purpose of an enterprise is to create and keep a customer.
—*Theodore Levitt*

Consumers are statistics. Customers are people.
—*Stanley Marcus*

Before you build a better mousetrap, it helps to know if there are any mice out there.
—*Mortimer B. Zuckerman*

Developing or adapting strategy in a dynamic market logically starts with external analysis, an analysis of the factors external to a business that can affect strategy. The first four chapters of Part One present concepts and methods useful in conducting an external analysis. The final chapter of Part One turns to internal analysis: the analysis of the firm's performance, strengths, weaknesses, problems, liabilities and constraints.

EXTERNAL ANALYSIS

A successful external analysis needs to be directed and purposeful. There is always the danger that it will become an endless process resulting in an excessively descriptive report. In any business there is no end to the material that appears potentially relevant. Without discipline and direction, volumes of useless descriptive material can easily be generated.

Affecting Strategic Decisions

The external analysis process should not be an end in itself. Rather, it should be motivated throughout by a desire to affect strategy. As Figure 2.1 shows, an external analysis can impact strategy directly by suggesting strategic decision alternatives or

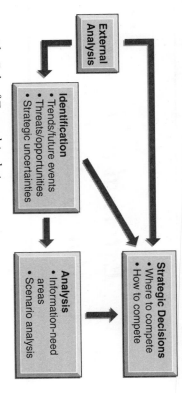

Figure 2.1 The Role of External Analysis

influencing a choice among them. More specifically, it should address questions such as:

- Should existing business areas be liquidated, milked, maintained, or a target for investment?

- Should new business areas be entered?

- What are the value propositions? What should they be?

- What assets and competencies should be created, enhanced, or maintained?

- What strategies and programs should be implemented in functional areas? What should be the positioning strategy, segmentation strategy, distribution strategy, brand-building strategy, manufacturing strategy, and so on?

Additional Analysis Objectives

Figure 2.1 also suggests that an external analysis can contribute to strategy indirectly by identifying:

- Significant trends and future events

- Threats and opportunities

- Strategic uncertainties that could affect strategy outcomes

A significant trend or event, such as concern about saturated fat or the emergence of a new competitor, can dramatically affect the evaluation of strategy options. A new technology, which can represent both a threat to an established firm and an opportunity to a prospective competitor, can signal new business arenas.

Strategic Uncertainties

Strategic uncertainty is a particularly useful concept in conducting an external analysis. If you could know the answer to one question prior to making a strategic commitment, what would that question be? If the Buick car division of General Motors were to consider whether to add a gas-electric hybrid to its line, important strategy uncertainties might include the following:

- What will the automotive sales profile of hybrids be in upcoming years? How many will be sold in what categories?
- What will be the hybrid strategies of Buick's direct competitors?
- What new technologies might emerge that will affect the performance and acceptance of hybrids?

Strategic uncertainties focus on specific unknown elements that will affect the outcome of strategic decisions. "Should Buick extend its line to hybrids?" is a strategic decision, whereas "What is the future demand for full-size hybrid sedans?" is a strategic uncertainty. Most strategic decisions will be driven by a set of these uncertainties.

Below are some examples of strategic uncertainties and the strategic decisions to which they might relate. A strategic uncertainty can often lead to additional sources of strategic uncertainty. One common strategic uncertainty, as portrayed in the figure at the bottom of this page, is what the future demand for a product (such as ultrasound diagnostic equipment) will be. Asking, "On what does that depend?" will usually generate additional strategic uncertainties. One uncertainty might address technological improvements, whereas another might consider the technological development and cost/benefit levels achieved by competitive technologies. Still another might look into the financial capacity of the healthcare industry to continue capital improvements. Each of these strategic uncertainties can, in turn, generate still another level of strategic uncertainties.

Analysis

There are three ways of handling uncertainty, as suggested by Figure 2.1. First, a strategic decision can be precipitated because the logic for a decision is compelling and/or because a delay would be costly or risky. Second, it may be worthwhile to

Strategic Uncertainties	Strategic Decisions
• Will a major firm enter? • Will a tofu-based dessert product be accepted?	• Investment in a product market • Investment in a tofu-based product
• Will a technology be replaced? • Will the dollar strengthen against an offshore currency? • Will computer-based operations be feasible with current technology? • How sensitive is the market to price?	• Investment in a technology • Commitment to offshore manufacturing • Investment in a new system • A strategy of maintaining price parity

Strategic Uncertainties	Second-Level Strategic Uncertainties
• What will be the future demand of an ultrasound test?	• Performance improvements? • Competitive technological developments? • Financial capacity of healthcare industry?

attempt to reduce the uncertainty by information acquisition and analysis of an information-need area. The effort could range from a high-priority task force to a low-key monitoring effort. The level of resources expended will depend on the potential impact on strategy and its immediacy. Third, the uncertainty could be modeled by a scenario analysis.

A scenario is an alternative view of the future environment that is usually prompted by an alternative possible answer to a strategic uncertainty or by a prospective future event or trend. Is the current popularity of fresh juice bars a fad or does it indicate a solid growth area? Such a question could be the basis for a positive and a negative scenario. Each could be associated with very different environmental profiles and strategy recommendations. In Chapter 5, information-need areas and scenario analysis will be covered in more detail.

External Analysis as a Creative Exercise

In part, external analysis is an exercise in creative thinking. In fact, there is often too little effort devoted to developing new strategic options and too much effort directed to solving operational problems of the day. The essence of creative thinking is considering different perspectives, and that is exactly what an external analysis does. The strategist is challenged to look at strategy from the perspectives of customer, competitor, market, and environment as well as from an internal perspective. Within each there are several subdimensions; in Figure 1.3, more than two dozen are identified. The hope is that by examining strategy from different viewpoints, options will be generated that would otherwise be missed.

A host of concepts and methods are introduced in this and the following three chapters. It would, of course, be unusual to employ all of them in any given context, and the strategist should resist any compulsion to do so. Rather, those that are most relevant to the situation at hand should be selected. Furthermore, some areas of analysis will be more fruitful than others and will merit more effort.

The Level of Analysis—Defining the Market

An external analysis of what? To conduct an external analysis, the market or submarket boundaries need to be specified. The scope of external analysis can involve an industry such as:

- Sporting goods
- Ski clothing and equipment
- Skis and snowboards
- Downhill skis
- High-performance skis

The level of analysis will depend on the organizational unit and strategic decisions involved. A sporting goods company, such as Wilson, will be making resource decisions across sports and thus needs to be concerned with the whole industry. A ski equipment manufacturer may only be concerned with elements of sporting goods relating to skis, boots, and clothing. The maker of high-performance skis might be interested in only a subsegment of the ski industry. One approach to defining the market is to specify the business scope. The scope can be identified in terms of the product market and in terms of the competitors. Relevant, of course, are the future product market and competitors as well as the present.

There is always a trade-off to be made. A narrow scope specification will inhibit a business from identifying trends and opportunities that could lead to some attractive options and directions. Thus, a maker of downhill skis may want to include snowboards and cross-country skis because they represent business options or because they will impact the ski equipment business. On the other hand, depth of analysis might be sacrificed when the scope is excessively broad. A more focused analysis may generate more insight.

The analysis usually needs to be conducted at several levels. The downhill ski and snowboard industry might be the major focus of the analysis. However, an analysis of sporting goods might suggest and shed light on some substitute product pressures and market trends. Also, an analysis may be needed at the segment level (e.g., high-performance skis) because entry, investment, and strategy decisions are often made at that level. Furthermore, the key success factors could differ for different product markets within a market or industry. One approach is a layered analysis, with the primary level receiving the most depth of analysis. Another approach could be multiple analyses, perhaps consecutively conducted. The first analysis might stimulate an opportunity that would justify a second analysis on a submarket.

When Should an External Analysis Be Conducted?

There is often a tendency to relegate the external analysis to an annual exercise. Each year, of course, it may not require the same depth as the initial effort. It may be more productive to focus on a part of the analysis in the years immediately following a major effort.

The annual planning cycle can provide a healthy stimulus to review and change strategies. However, a substantial risk exists in maintaining external analysis as an annual event. The need for strategic review and change is often continuous. Information sensing and analysis therefore also need to be continuous. The framework and concepts of external analysis can still play a key role in providing structure even when the analysis is continuous and addresses only a portion of the whole.

External analysis deliberately commences with customer and competitor analyses because they can help define the relevant industry or industries. An industry can be defined in terms of the needs of a specific group of customers—those buying fresh cookies on the West Coast, for instance. Such an industry definition then forms the basis for the identification of competitors and the balance of external analysis. An industry such as the cookie industry can also be defined in terms of all its competitors.

Because customers have such a direct relationship to a firm's operation, they are usually a rich source of relevant operational opportunities, threats, and uncertainties.

SEGMENTATION

- Who are the biggest customers? The most profitable? The most attractive potential customers? Do the customers fall into any logical groups based on needs, motivations, or characteristics?

- How could the market be segmented into groups that would require a unique business strategy?

CUSTOMER MOTIVATIONS

- What elements of the product/service do customers value most?

- What are the customers' objectives? What are they really buying?

- How do segments differ in their motivation priorities?

- What changes are occurring in customer motivation? In customer priorities?

UNMET NEEDS

- Why are some customers dissatisfied? Why are some changing brands or suppliers?

- What are the severity and incidence of consumer problems?

- What are unmet needs that customers can identify? Are there some of which consumers are unaware?

- Do these unmet needs represent leverage points for competitors or a new business model?

Figure 2.2   Customer Analysis

THE SCOPE OF CUSTOMER ANALYSIS

In most strategic market-planning contexts, the first logical step is to analyze the customers. Customer analysis can be usefully partitioned into an understanding of how the market segments, an analysis of customer motivations, and an exploration of unmet needs. Figure 2.2 presents a basic set of questions for each area of inquiry.

SEGMENTATION

Segmentation is often the key to developing a sustainable competitive advantage. In a strategic context, *segmentation* means the identification of customer groups that respond differently from other groups to competitive offerings. A segmentation strategy couples the identified segments with a program to deliver an offering to those segments. Thus, the development of a successful segmentation strategy requires the conceptualization, development, and evaluation of a targeted competitive offering.

A segmentation strategy should be judged on three dimensions. First, can a competitive offering be developed and implemented that will be appealing to the target segment? Second, can the appeal of the offering and the subsequent relationship with the target segment be maintained over time despite competitive responses? Third, is the resulting business from the target segment worthwhile, given the investment required to develop and market an offering tailored to it? The concept behind a successful segmentation strategy is that within a reduced market space, it is possible to create a dominant position that competitors will be unwilling or unable to attack successfully.

How Should Segments Be Defined?

The task of identifying segments is difficult, in part, because in any given context there are literally hundreds of ways to divide up the market. Typically, the analysis will consider five, ten, or more segmentation variables. To avoid missing a useful way of defining segments, it is important to consider a wide range of variables. These variables need to be evaluated on the basis of their ability to identify segments for which different strategies are (or should be) pursued.

The most useful segment-defining variables for an offering are rarely obvious. Among the variables frequently used are those shown in Figure 2.3.

The first set of variables describes segments in terms of general characteristics unrelated to the product involved. Thus, a bakery might be concerned with geographically defined segments related to communities or even neighborhoods. A consulting company may specialize in the hospitality industry. A fast food firm in the United States may target Hispanics because this segment is projected to grow to 44 million people in 2010.

CUSTOMER CHARACTERISTICS

- Geographic
- Type of organization

- Size of firm
- Lifestyle

- Sex
- Age
- Occupation

- Small Southern communities as markets for discount stores
- Computer needs of restaurants versus manufacturing firms versus banks versus retailers
- Large hospital versus medium versus small
- Jaguar buyers tend to be more adventurous, less conservative than buyers of Mercedes-Benz and BMW
- Mothers of young children
- Cereals for children versus adults
- The paper copier needs of lawyers versus bankers versus dentists

PRODUCT-RELATED APPROACHES

- User type
- Usage
- Benefits sought

- Price sensitivity

- Competitor
- Application
- Brand loyalty

- Appliance buyer—home builder, remodeler, homeowner
- Concert—season ticket holders, occasional patrons, nonusers
- Dessert eaters—those who are calorie-conscious versus those who are more concerned with convenience
- Price-sensitive Honda Civic buyer versus the luxury Mercedes-Benz buyer
- Users of competing products
- Professional users of chain saws versus homeowners
- Those committed to Heinz ketchup versus price buyers

Figure 2.3   Examples of Approaches to Defining Segments

Demographics are particularly powerful for defining segments, in part because a person's life stage affects his or her activities, interests, and brand loyalties. Another reason is that demographic trends are predictable. The U.S. population over 65 is expected to grow to 50 million in 2020, when more than 5 million people will be 85 or older. Gold Violin, recognizing this trend, has established itself as a source of products designed for the active elderly. Specialized items such as a talking watch, a bed-vibrating alarm clock, a doorknob turner, and a lighted hands-free magnifier (all with tasteful, attractive designs) are just some of the Gold Violin products that appeal to this long-ignored demographic segment.

Another demographic play is represented by the Toyota Scion, a small car with a funky design (tall, angular, and boxy) aimed at Generation Y, the so-called echo boomers. The average age of a Toyota buyer is 48, the company's inexpensive entries are considered boring, and Scion is an effort to become relevant and interesting to a key target segment. To create a buzz around Scion so that it would appeal to the next generation of drivers, Toyota targeted the 15 percent of the echo-boomer target market seen as "leaders and influencers"—those who encourage their peers to gravitate to a new style, whether it be in music, sports, or cars.[1]

The second category of segment variables includes those that are related to the product. One of the most frequently employed is usage. A bakery may follow a very different strategy in serving restaurants that rely heavily on bakery products than in serving those that use fewer such products. A manufacturer of lawn equipment may design a special line for a large customer such as Wal-Mart, but sell through distributors using another brand name for other outlets. Four other useful segment variables are benefits, price sensitivity, loyalty, and applications.

Benefits

If there is a most useful segmentation variable, it would be benefits sought from a product, because the selection of benefits can determine a total business strategy. In gourmet frozen dinners/entrées, for example, the market can be divided into buyers who are calorie-conscious, those who focus on nutrition and health, those interested in taste, and the price-conscious buyers.

The athletic shoe industry segments into serious athletes (small in number but influential), weekend warriors, and casual wearers using athletic shoes for street wear. Recognizing that the casual wearer segment is 80 percent of the market and does not really need performance, several shoe firms have employed a style-focused strategy as an alternative to the performance strategy adopted by such firms as Nike.

Price Sensitivity

The benefit dimension representing the trade-off between low price and high quality is both useful and pervasive; hence it is appropriate to consider it separately. In many product classes, there is a well-defined breakdown between those customers concerned first about price and others who are willing to pay extra for higher quality and features. General merchandise stores, for example, form a well-defined hierarchy from discounters to prestige department stores. Automobiles span the spectrum

THE MALE SHOPPER[2]

The male shopper has been long ignored. A segmentation scheme provides insight into how males differ and suggests strategies for appealing to very different segments.

The Metrosexual. An affluent urban sophisticate, aged 20 to 40, who loves to buy and looks for trendy, prestigious, and high-quality products. Into men's grooming, expensive haircuts. Think Polo Ralph Lauren, Beiersdorf, and Banana Republic.

The Retrosexual. Traditional male behavior, into football and NASCAR, rejects feminism, nostalgic for the way things were, prefers below-casual clothing, not into moisturizers for men. Think Levi's, Nike, Old Spice, Burger King, and Target.

The Modern Man. Between "metro" and "retro," this shopper shares their interests but does not go overboard. A sophisticated consumer in his twenties or thirties, he is comfortable with women but does not shop with them. Think Gap, Macy's, and fast casual restaurants.

The Dad. Good income. Involved in the family shopping. Efficient shopper. More functional clothing. Think Nordstrom's, McDonald's, and Amazon.

The Maturiteen. More savvy, responsible, and pragmatic than earlier generations of teens. A technology master adept at online research and buying. Sony, Adidas, Old Navy, Circuit City, and Internet sites of all types do well.

from the Honda Civic to the Buick Lucerne to the Lexus 460. Airline service is partitioned into first class, business class, and economy class. In each case the segment dictates the strategy.

Loyalty

Brand loyalty, an important consideration in allocating resources, can be structured using a loyalty matrix as shown in Figure 2.4. Each cell represents a very different strategic priority and can justify a very different program. Generally, it is too easy to take the loyal customer for granted. However, a perspective of total profits over the life of a customer makes the value of an increase in loyalty more vivid. A study by Bain shows that a 5 percent increase in loyalty can nearly double the lifetime profits generated by customers in several industries, including banking, insurance, automobile

	Low Loyalty	Moderate Loyalty	Loyal
Customer	Medium	High	Highest
Noncustomer	Low to Medium	High	Zero

Figure 2.4 The Brand Loyalty Matrix: Priorities

service, publishing, and credit cards.[3] The key is often to reward the loyal customer by living up to expectations consistently, providing an ongoing relationship, and offering extras that surprise and delight.

The loyalty matrix suggests that the moderate loyals, including those of competitors, should also have high priority. Using the matrix involves estimating the size of each of the six cells, identifying the customers in each group, and designing programs that will influence their brand choice and loyalty level. The loyal noncustomer would be favorable, but the cost to attract is usually prohibitive unless a competitor misstep provides an opportunity.

Applications

Some products and services, particularly industrial products, can best be segmented by use or application. A portable computer may be needed by some for use while traveling, whereas others may need a computer at the office that can be conveniently stored when not in use. One segment may use a computer for word processing and another may be more interested in data processing. Some might use a four-wheel drive for light industrial hauling and others may be buying primarily for recreation.

Christensen et al. argue that an application focus is more likely to lead to successful new products and marketing programs then other segmentation schemes.[4] They illustrate by telling the story of a milkshake seller that found that many consumers bought the product in the morning in order to help them kill time while driving to work and provide energy to tide them over to lunch. Being efficient to buy and capable of being consumed with only one hand was therefore critical. Such an insight leads to ideas like making the shake thicker (so it takes longer to consume), making the purchase even more efficient with buyer cards, and adding fruit to make it more interesting in the context of a boring commute. The basic idea is that ideas for products and marketing programs are more likely to come from a deep understanding of how the product is used than by understanding the customer. The success of Arm & Hammer in extending its business can be credited to a focus on applications involving deodorizing (carpets, kitty litter, clothes, underarms, and refrigerators).

Multiple Segments versus a Focus Strategy

Two distinct segmentation strategies are possible. The first focuses on a single segment, which can be much smaller than the market as a whole. Wal-Mart, now the largest U.S. retailer, started by concentrating on cities with populations under 25,000 in eleven south central states—a segment totally neglected by its competition, the large discount chains. This rural geographic focus strategy was directly responsible for several significant SCAs, including an efficient and responsive warehouse supply system, a low-cost, motivated workforce, relatively inexpensive retail space, and a lean and mean, hands-on management style. Union Bank, California's eighth largest bank, makes no effort to serve individuals and thus provides a service operation tailored to business accounts that is more committed and comprehensive than those of its competitors.

An alternative to a focusing strategy is to involve multiple segments. General Motors provides the classic example. In the 1920s the firm positioned the Chevrolet for price-conscious buyers, the Cadillac for the high end, and the Oldsmobile, Pontiac, and Buick for well-defined segments in between. A granulated potato company has developed different strategies for reaching fast-food chains, hospitals and nursing homes, and schools and colleges.

In many industries aggressive firms are moving toward multiple-segment strategies. Campbell Soup, for example, makes its nacho cheese soup spicier for customers in Texas and California and offers a Creole soup for southern markets and a red-bean soup for Hispanic markets. In New York, Campbell uses promotions linking Swanson frozen dinners with the New York Giants football team, and in the Sierra Nevada mountains, skiers are treated to hot soup samples. Developing multiple strategies is costly and often must be justified by an enhanced aggregate impact.

There can be important synergies between segment offerings. For example, in the alpine ski industry, the image developed by high-performance skis is important to sales at the recreational-ski end of the business. Thus, a manufacturer that is weak at the high end will have difficulty at the low end. Conversely, a successful high-end firm will want to exploit that success by having entries in the other segments. A key success factor in the general aviation industry is a broad product line, ranging from fixed-gear, single-engine piston aircraft to turboprop planes, because customers tend to trade up and will switch to a different firm if the product line has major gaps.

CUSTOMER MOTIVATIONS

After identifying customer segments, the next step is to consider their motivations: What lies behind their purchase decisions? And how does that differ by segment? It is helpful to list the segments and the motivation priorities of each, as shown in Figure 2.5 for air travelers.

Internet retailers have learned that there are distinct shopper segments, and each has a very different set of driving motivations.[5]

- *Newbie shoppers*—need a simple interface, as well as a lot of hand-holding and reassurance.
- *Reluctant shoppers*—need information, reassurance, and access to live customer support.
- *Frugal shoppers*—need to be convinced that the price is good and they don't have to search elsewhere.

Segment	Motivation
Business	Reliable service, convenient schedules, easy-to-use airports, frequent-flyer programs, and comfortable service
Vacationers	Price, feasible schedules

Figure 2.5   Customer Motivation Grid: Air Travelers

- **Strategic shoppers**—need access to the opinions of peers or experts, and choices in configuring the products they buy.

- **Enthusiastic shoppers**—need community tools to share their experiences, as well as engaging tools to view the merchandise and personalized recommendations.

- **Convenience shoppers**—(the largest group) want efficient navigation, a lot of information from customers and experts, and superior customer service.

Some motivations will help to define strategy. A truck, for example, might be designed and positioned with respect to power. Before making such a strategic commitment, it is crucial to know where power fits in the motivation set. Other motivations may not define a strategy or differentiate a business, but represent a dimension for which adequate performance must be obtained or the battle will be lost. If the prime motivation for buyers of gourmet frozen-food dinners is taste, a viable firm must be able to deliver at least acceptable taste.

Determining Motivations

As Figure 2.6 suggests, consumer motivation analysis starts with the task of identifying motivations for a given segment. Although a group of managers can identify motivations, a more valid list is usually obtained by getting customers to discuss the product or service in a systematic way. Why is it being used? What is the objective? What is associated with a good or bad use experience? For a motivation such as car safety, respondents might be asked why safety is important. Such probes might result in the identification of more basic motives, such as the desire to feel calm and secure rather than anxious.

Customers can be accessed with group or individual interviews. Griffin and Hauser of the MIT Quality Function Deployment (QFD) program compared the two approaches in a study of food-carrying devices.[6] They found that individual interviews were more cost-effective and that the group processes did not generate enough extra information to warrant the added expense. They also explored the number of interviews needed to gain a complete list of motivations and concluded that twenty to thirty will cover 90 to 95 percent of the motivations.

The number of motivations can be in the hundreds, so the next task is to cluster them into groups and subgroups. Affinity charts developed by a managerial team are commonly used. Each team member is given a set of motives on cards. One member puts a motive on the table or pins it to a wall, and the others add similar cards to the pile until there is a consensus that the piles represent reasonable groupings. An

Figure 2.6 Customer Motivation Analysis

Identify Motivations → Group and Structure Motivations → Assess Motivation Importance → Assign Strategic Roles to Motivations

BUYER HOT BUTTONS

Motivations can be categorized as important or unimportant, yet the dynamics of the market may be better captured by identifying current buyer hot buttons. Hot buttons are motivations whose salience and impact on markets are significant and growing. What are buyers talking about? What are stimulating changes in buying decisions and use patterns? In consumer retail food products, for example, hot buttons include:

- Freshness and naturalness. Grocery stores have responded with salad bars, packaged precut vegetables, and efforts to upgrade the quality and selection of their fresh produce.

- Healthy eating. Low fat, particularly saturated and trans fat, is a prime driver, but concern about sodium, sugar, and processed foods is also growing and affecting product offerings in most food categories.

- Ethnic eating. A growing interest in ethnic flavors and cooking such as Asian, Mediterranean, and Caribbean cuisines has led to an explosion of new offerings. Brands usually start in ethnic neighborhoods, move into natural-food and gourmet stores, and finally reach the mainstream markets.

- Gourmet eating. The success of Williams-Sonoma and similar retailers reflects the growth of gourmet cooking and has led to the introduction of a broader array of interesting cooking aids and devices.

- Meal solutions. The desire for meal solutions has led to groups of products being bundled together as a meal and to a host of carryout prepared foods offered by both grocery stores and restaurants.

- Low-carb foods. The influence of low-carb diets has created a demand for reduced-carb food variants in both grocery stores and restaurants.

alternative is to use customers or groups of customers to sort the motives into piles. The customers are then asked to select one card from each pile that best represents their motives. Although managers gain buy-in and learning by going through the process themselves, Griffin and Hauser report that in the twenty applications at one firm, the managers considered customer-based approaches better representations than their own.

Another task of customer motivation analysis is to determine the relative importance of the motivations. Again, the management team can address this issue. Alternatively, customers can be asked to assess the importance of the motivations directly or perhaps through trade-off questions. If an engineer had to sacrifice response time or accuracy in an oscilloscope, which would it be? Or, how would an airline passenger trade off convenient departure time with price? The trade-off question asks customers to make difficult judgments about attributes. Another approach is to see which judgments are associated with actual purchase decisions. Such an approach revealed that mothers often selected snack food based on what "the child likes" and what was "juicy" instead of qualities they had said were important (nourishing, easy to eat).

A fourth task is to identify the motivations that will play a role in defining the value proposition of the business. The selection of motivations central to strategy will depend not only on customer motivations, but on other factors as well, such as competitors' strategies that emerge in the competitor analysis. Another factor is how feasible and practical the resulting strategy is for the business. Internal analysis will be involved in making that determination, as will an analysis of the strategy's implementation.

Qualitative Research

Qualitative research is a powerful tool in understanding customer motivation. It can involve focus-group sessions, in-depth interviews, customer case studies, or ethnographic research (to be described shortly). The concept is to search for the real motivations that do not emerge from structured lists. For instance, buyers of sports utility vehicles might really be expressing their youth or a youthful attitude. The perception that a product is too expensive might really reflect a financing gap. Getting inside the customer can provide strategic insights that do not emerge any other way.

Although a representative cross-section of customers is usually sought, special attention to some is often merited. Very loyal customers are often best able to articulate the bonds that the firm is capable of establishing. Lost customers (those who have defected) are often particularly good at graphically communicating problems with the product or service. New customers or customers who have recently increased their usage may suggest new applications. Those using multiple vendors may have a good perspective of the firm relative to the competition.

Changing Customer Priorities

It is particularly critical to gain insight into changes in customers' priorities. In the high-tech area, customer priorities often evolve from needing help in selecting and installing the right equipment to wanting performance to looking for low cost. In the coffee business, customer tastes and habits have evolved from buying coffee at grocery stores to drinking coffee at gourmet cafés to buying their own whole-bean gourmet coffees. Assuming that customer priorities are not changing can be risky. It is essential to ask whether a significant and growing segment has developed priorities that are different from the basic business model.

The Customer as Active Partner

Customers are increasingly becoming active partners in the buying process, rather than passive targets of product development and advertising. The trend is illustrated by Cisco's customers helping design products, patients taking control of medical issues, the control of media shifting as audiences move from the VCR to TiVo (a device that can preprogram shows by name and even genres), and the power-enhancing access to information and fellow customers provided by the Internet. To harness this change, managers should:[7]

- *Encourage active dialogue.* Contact with customers must now be considered a dialogue of equals. The interaction of Schwab with its customers (both online and offline) shows how active dialogues can create a strong relationship.

- **Mobilize customer communities.** The Internet facilitates stronger and more widespread online customer communities. The challenge is to organize and create the context for the communities so that they become an extension of the brand experience and a source of customer input into the product and its use.

- **Manage customer diversity.** Particularly in technology products there will be a wide range of sophistication among customers, and the challenge will be to deal with multiple levels. The more sophisticated group will be the most active partners.

- **Co-creating personalized experiences.** An online florist might let customers design the type and arrangement of flowers and vases, rather than merely providing a menu of choices. Co-creating experiences go beyond customization in tailoring the offering to the needs of individuals.

UNMET NEEDS

An unmet need is a customer need that is not being met by the existing product offerings. For example, ski areas have a need for snowmaking equipment that can access steep, advanced trails. A major extension of the temporary-services industry has been created by firms responding to an unmet need for temporary lawyers, high-tech specialists, and doctors. NETJETS was formed to sell fractional interests in small jets to firms that needed their own jet transportation but could not justify buying and maintaining their own fleet.

Unmet needs are strategically important because they represent opportunities for firms to increase their market share, break into a market, or create and own new markets. They can also represent threats to established firms in that they can be a lever that enables competitors to disrupt an established position. Ariat, for example, broke into the market for equestrian footwear by providing high-performance athletic footwear to riders who were not well served by traditional riding boots. Driven by the belief that riders are athletes, Ariat developed a brand and product line that was responsive to an unmet need.

Sometimes customers may not be aware of their unmet needs because they are so accustomed to the implicit limitations of existing equipment. Who could have conceived of a need for an electric lightbulb or a tractor before technology made them possible? Unmet needs that are not obvious may be more difficult to identify, but they can also represent a greater opportunity for an aggressive business because there will be little pressure on established firms to be responsive. The key is to stretch the technology or apply new technologies in order to expose unmet needs.

Using Customers to Identify Unmet Needs

Customers are a prime source of unmet needs. The trick is to access them, to get customers to detect and communicate unmet needs. The first step is to conduct

USER-DEVELOPED PRODUCTS

For an internal application, IBM designed and built the first printed circuit card insertion machine of a particular type to be used in commercial production.[8] After building and testing the design in-house, IBM sent engineering drawings of its design to a local machine builder, along with an order for eight units. The machine builder completed this and subsequent orders and applied to IBM for permission to build essentially the same machine for sale on the open market. IBM agreed, and as a result the machine builder became a major force in the component insertion equipment business.

In the early 1970s, store owners and sales personnel in southern California began to notice that youngsters were fixing up their bicycles to look like motorcycles, complete with imitation tailpipes and chopper-type handlebars. Sporting crash helmets and Honda motorcycle T-shirts, the youngsters raced fancy 20-inchers on dirt tracks. Obviously onto a good thing, the manufacturers came out with a whole new line of motocross models. California users refined this concept into the mountain bike. Manufacturers were guided by the California customers to develop new refinements, including the 21-speed gear shift that doesn't require removing one's hands from the bars. Mountain bike firms are enjoying booming growth and are still watching their West Coast customers.

market research using group interviews or ethnographic research. The research usually starts with a discussion of an actual product-use experience. What problems have emerged? What is frustrating about it? How does it compare with other product experiences? What expectations? Are there problems with the total-use system in which the product is embedded? How can the product be improved? This kind of research helped Dow come up with Spiffits, a line of premoistened, disposable cleaning towels that addressed the need for a towel already moistened with a cleaning compound.

Customer surveys can play an important role, as can the monitoring of customer complaints. USAA, the successful Texas financial services company, mails 500,000 questionnaires to customers every year and includes some open-ended questions about problems and new product ideas. As a result, the firm has launched several mutual funds. At Hewlett-Packard each customer complaint is assigned to an employee who becomes its owner and not only makes sure that the customer receives a response but determines if a new product or service is suggested by the problem.

A structured approach, termed *problem research*, develops a list of potential problems with the product. The problems are then prioritized by asking a group of 100 to 200 respondents to rate each problem as to whether (1) the problem is important, (2) the problem occurs frequently, and (3) a solution exists. A problem score is obtained by combining these ratings. A dog-food problem research study found that buyers felt dog food smelled bad, cost too much, and was not available in different sizes for different dogs. Subsequently, products responsive to these criticisms emerged. Another study led an airline to modify its cabins to provide more leg room.

Eric von Hippel, a researcher at MIT who studies customers as sources of service innovations, suggests that lead users provide a particularly fertile ground for discovering unmet needs and new product concepts.[9] Lead users are users who:

- Face needs that will be general in the marketplace, but face them months or years before the bulk of the marketplace. A person who is very into health foods and nutrition would be a lead user with respect to health foods, if we assume that there is a trend toward health foods.

- Are positioned to benefit significantly by obtaining a solution to those needs. Lead users of office automation would be firms that today would benefit significantly from technological advancement.

Ethnographic Research

Ethnographic or anthropological research involves directly observing customers in as many contexts as possible. By accurately observing not only what is being done involving the target or service but *why* it is being done, companies can achieve a deeper level of understanding of the customer's needs and motivations and generate actionable insights. Although this research approach as been around for nearly a century, it has taken on new life in the last few years not only in packaged goods firms like Procter & Gamble but also in business-to-business firms like Intel and GE.

Ethnographic research is particularly good at identifying breakthrough innovations. Customers usually cannot verbalize such innovations, because they are used to the current offerings. Henry Ford famously observed that had he asked customers what they wanted, they would have said faster horses. By watching people buy and use in the context of their lives or their businesses, however, experienced and talented anthropologists (or executives, in the case of P&G) can generate insights that go beyond what customers could talk about.

Ethnographic research works.[10] After one study observed the difficulty people had in cleaning the bathroom, P&G developed Magic Reach, a device with a long handle and swivel head. Visits to contactors and home renovators resulted in the develop of the OXO hammer (with a fiberglass core to cut vibration and a rubber bumper on top to avoid leaving marks when removing nails) as part of a line of professional-grade tools. Sirius followed 45 people for a week, studying what music listened to, magazines read, and TV shows watched and then developed a portable satellite-radio player that can load up to 50 hours of music for later playback. Black & Decker's observation that electric drill users ran out of power led to the detachable battery pack. Intel's research in the Third World led to develop a cheap PC that could run on truck batteries in 100-degree temperatures. GE found through ethnographic research that buyers of plastic fiber for fire-retardant jackets were more concerned with performance than price. That led to a completely different business model in GE's efforts to enter the field.

Ethnographic research can also be used to improve existing products or services. Marriott had a multifunctional team of seven people (including a designer and architect) spend six weeks visiting twelve cities, hanging out with guests at hotel lobbies, cafés, and bars.[11] They learned that hotels were not doing well at service for small groups of business travelers. As a result, lobbies and adjacent area were redesigned to be more suitable for transacting business, with brighter lights and "social zones" with a mix of small tables, larger tables, and semiprivate spaces.

The Ideal Experience

The conceptualization of an ideal experience can also help to identify unmet needs. A major publisher of directories polled its customers, asking each to describe its ideal experience with the firm. The publisher found that its very large customers (the top 4 percent who were generating 45 percent of its business) wanted a single contact point to resolve problems, customized products, consultation on using the service, and help in tracking results. In contrast, smaller customers wanted a simple ordering process and to be left alone. These responses provided insights into improving service while cutting costs.[12]

Use Creative Thinking

Thinking out of the box (or just throwing away the box) is a key challenge in discovering new offerings that are responsive to unmet needs. Thinking differently can generate a new offering that creates or changes a category, making the existing competitors less relevant as the new offering becomes the frame of reference and the standard. What could be better? Some creative thinking tools are provided in Chapter 10.

For example, for years the travel-guide industry was rather mature, with little energy. Then a company called Rough Guides hit on the simple idea that a lot of 30- to 40-year-olds might be interested getting off the beaten track. So it created guides more specific not only to their interests but also to their destinations, so these travelers did not have to buy thick guide books whose material was 90 percent useless. The Rough Guides website offers guides to over 14,000 destinations and a host of related references and news items around travel, plus a travel insurance offering.[13]

FOR DISCUSSION

1. Why do a strategic analysis? What are the objectives? What, in your view, are the three keys to making a strategic analysis helpful and important? Is there a downside to conducting a full-blown strategic analysis?

2. Consider the buyer "hot buttons" described in the insert. What are the implications for Betty Crocker? What new business areas might be considered, given each hot button? Answer the same questions for a grocery store chain such as Safeway.

3. Consider the segments in the male shopper insert. Describe each further. What car would they drive? What kind of vacation would they take? What shirt brand would they buy?

4. What is a customer buying at Nordstrom? At Gap? At Old Navy?

5. Pick a company or brand/business on which to focus, such as cereals. What are the major segments? What are the customer motivations by segments? What are the unmet needs?

NOTES

1. Andrew Tilim, "Will the Kids Buy It?" *Business 2.0*, May 2003, pp. 95–99.

2. This insert was inspired by Nanette Byrnes, "Secrets of the Male Shopper," *Business Week*, September 4, 2006, pp. 45–53.

3. Patricia Sellers, "Keeping the Buyers You Already Have," *Fortune*, Autumn/Winter 1993, pp. 56–58.

4. Clayton M. Christiansen, Scott Cook, and Taddy Hall, "Marketing Malpractice: The Cause and the Cure," *Harvard Business Review*, December 2005, pp. 74–83.

5. Melinda Cuthbert, "All Buyers Not Alike," *Business 2.0*, December 26, 2000.

6. Abbie Griffin and John R. Hauser, "The Voice of the Customer," *Marketing Science*, Winter 1993, pp. 1–27.

7. C.K. Prahalad and Venkatram Ramaswamy, "Co-opting Customer Competence," *Harvard Business Review*, January–February, 2000, pp. 79–87.

8. Eric von Hippel, "Lead Users: A Source of Novel Product Concepts," *Management Science*, July 1986, p. 802.

9. Ibid.

10. Spencer E. Ante, "The Science of Desire," *Business Week*, June 5, 2006, pp. 99–106.

11. Ibid., p. 104.

12. George S. Day, "Creating a Superior Customer-Relating Capability," *Sloan Management Review*, Spring 2003, pp. 82–83.

13. Michael Lynton, Comment, *Fast Company*, January 1999, p. 78.

CHAPTER THREE

Competitor Analysis

Induce your competitors not to invest in those products, markets and services where you expect to invest the most ... that is the fundamental rule of strategy.
—*Bruce Henderson, founder of BCG*

There is nothing more exhilarating than to be shot at without result.
—*Winston Churchill*

The best and fastest way to learn a sport is to watch and imitate a champion.
—*Jean-Claude Killy, skier*

There are numerous well-documented reasons why the Japanese automobile firms were able to penetrate the U.S. market successfully, especially during the 1970s. One important reason, however, is that they were much better than U.S. firms at doing competitor analysis.[1]

David Halberstam, in his account of the automobile industry, graphically described the Japanese efforts at competitor analysis in the 1960s. "They came in groups.... They measured, they photographed, they sketched, and they tape-recorded everything they could. Their questions were precise. They were surprised how open the Americans were."[2] The Japanese similarly studied European manufacturers, especially their design approaches. In contrast, according to Halberstam, the Americans were late in even recognizing the competitive threat from Japan and never did well at analyzing Japanese firms or understanding the new strategic imperatives created by the revised competitive environment, even though the Japanese car firms were very open about their methods.

Competitor analysis is the second phase of external analysis. Again, the goal should be insights that will influence the development of successful business strategies. The analysis should focus on the identification of threats, opportunities, or strategic uncertainties created by emerging or potential competitor moves, weaknesses, or strengths.

Competitor analysis starts with identifying current and potential competitors. There are two very different ways of identifying current competitors. The first examines the perspective of the customer who must make choices among competitors. This approach groups competitors according to the degree they compete for a buyer's choice. The second approach attempts to place competitors in strategic groups on the basis of their competitive strategy.

After competitors are identified, the focus shifts to attempting to understand them and their strategies. Of particular interest is an analysis of the strengths and weaknesses of each competitor or strategic group of competitors. Figure 3.1 summarizes a set of questions that can provide a structure for competitor analysis.

IDENTIFYING COMPETITORS—CUSTOMER-BASED APPROACHES

In most instances, primary competitors are quite visible and easily identified. Coke competes with Pepsi, other cola brands, and private labels such as President's Choice. CitiBank competes with Chase, BofA, and other major banks. NBC competes with ABC, CBS, and Fox. Boeing competes with Airbus. The competitor analysis for this group should be done with depth and insight.

In many markets customer priorities are changing, and indirect competitors offering customers product alternatives are strategically relevant. Understanding these indirect competitors can be strategically and tactically important, as the following examples demonstrate.

WHO ARE THE COMPETITORS?

- Against whom do we usually compete? Who are our most intense competitors? Less intense but still serious competitors? Makers of substitute products?
- Can these competitors be grouped into strategic groups on the basis of their assets, competencies, and/or strategies?
- Who are the potential competitive entrants? What are their barriers to entry? Is there anything that can be done to discourage them?

EVALUATING THE COMPETITORS

- What are their objectives and strategies? Their level of commitment? Their exit barriers?
- What is their cost structure? Do they have a cost advantage or disadvantage?
- What is their image and positioning strategy?
- Which are the most successful/unsuccessful competitors over time? Why?
- What are the strengths and weaknesses of each competitor or strategic group?
- What leverage points (or strategic weaknesses or customer problems or unmet needs) could competitors exploit to enter the market or become more serious competitors?
- Evaluate the competitors with respect to their assets and competencies. Generate a competitor strength grid.

Figure 3.1 Questions to Structure Competitor Analysis

- Coke focused on Pepsi and ignored for many years the emerging submarkets in water, iced tea, and fruit-based drinks. The result was a missed opportunity and the eventual need to pursue an expensive and difficult catch-up strategy.

- While the major television networks struggle against each other, independent networks have emerged; strong cable networks, such as ESPN and CNN, have flourished; and home shopping, pay-per-view, and even Playstation, the Internet, and Blockbuster are competing for the leisure time of viewers.

- While banks focus on competing banks, their markets have been eroded by mutual funds, insurers, and brokers (including discount brokers, such as Charles Schwab).

- While Folgers, Maxwell House, and others compete for supermarket business using coupon promotions, other firms, such as Starbucks, succeeded in selling a very different kind of coffee in different ways.

- Steel minimills were ignored by the major steel firms until they gradually became a major player.

Of particular interest should be competitors who serve small niches through inexpensive offerings directed at low-margin customers. Again and again such firms are ignored and eventually take advantage of their foothold to become major competitors. Many Japanese firms (such as Canon in copiers and Toyota in cars) started this way.

The competitive analysis in nearly all cases will benefit from extending the perspective beyond the obvious direct competitors. By explicitly considering indirect competitors, the strategic horizon is expanded, and the analysis more realistically mirrors what the customer sees. In the real world, the customer is never restricted to a firm's direct competitors, but instead is always poised to consider other options.

The energy bar category, established in the mid-1980s by PowerBar, includes direct competitors such as Clif, Balance, and dozens of small, local niche firms. There are also a host of indirect competitors, many with very similar products: candy bars (Snickers was called "the energy bar" for many years), breakfast bars, diet bars, granola bars, and the cereal bar category. Understanding the positioning and new product strategies of these indirect competitors will be strategically important to businesses in the energy bar category.

Both direct and indirect competitors can be further categorized in terms of how relevant they are, as determined by similar positioning. Thus, candy bars will be more relevant to Balance than to PowerBar because of where the former has positioned itself (Balance Gold is even marketed as being "like a candy bar"). For the same reason, Clif will be a closer competitor to PowerBar than to Balance.

A key issue with respect to strategic analysis in general, and competitor analysis in particular, is the level at which the analysis is conducted. Is it at the level of a business unit, the firm, or some other aggregation of businesses? Because an analysis will be needed at all levels at which strategies are developed, multiple analyses might ultimately be necessary. For example, when Clif developed Luma, an energy bar designed for women, PowerBar countered with Pria. The manager of the Luma business may need a competitive analysis of energy bars for women, in which case the other energy bars might be considered indirect competitors.

Customer Choices

One approach to identifying competitor sets is to look at competitors from the perspective of customers—what choices are customers making? A Cisco buyer could be asked what brand would have been purchased had Cisco not made the required item. A buyer for a nursing home meal service could be asked what would be substituted for granulated potato buds if they increased in price. A sample of sports car buyers could be asked what other cars they considered and perhaps what other showrooms they actually visited.

Product-Use Associations

Another approach that provides insights is the association of products with specific-use contexts or applications.[3] Perhaps twenty or thirty product users could be asked to identify a list of use situations or applications. For each use context they would then name all the products that are appropriate. Then for each product they would identify appropriate use contexts so that the list of use contexts would be more complete. Another group of respondents would then be asked to make judgments about how appropriate each product is for each use context. Then products would be clustered based on the similarity of their appropriate use contexts. Thus, if Pepsi was regarded as appropriate for snack occasions, it would compete primarily with products similarly perceived. The same approach will work with an industrial product that might be used in several distinct applications.

Both the customer-choice and product-use approaches suggest a conceptual basis for identifying competitors that can be employed by managers even when marketing research is not available. The concept of alternatives from which customers choose and the concept of appropriateness to a use context can be powerful tools in helping to understand the competitive environment.

IDENTIFYING COMPETITORS—STRATEGIC GROUPS

The concept of a strategic group provides a very different approach toward understanding the competitive structure of an industry. A strategic group is a group of firms that:

- Over time pursue similar competitive strategies (for example, the use of the same distribution channel, the same type of communication strategies, or the same price/quality position)
- Have similar characteristics (e.g., size, aggressiveness)
- Have similar assets and competencies (such as brand associations, logistics capability, global presence, or research and development)

For example, there have historically been three strategic groups in the pet food industry, which is the subject of an illustrative industry analysis in the appendix to this book. One strategic group consists of very large diversified, branded consumer and food product companies. All distribute through mass merchandisers and supermarkets, have strong established brands, use advertising and promotions effectively, and enjoy economies of scale. The major players include Nestlé Ralston Petcare, Del Monte, and Mars.

A second strategic group of highly focused ultra-premium producers, such as Hill's Petfood (Science Diet and Prescription Diet) and the Iams Company, sells product through veterinary offices and specialty pet stores. They have historically used referral networks to reach pet owners concerned with health. When P&G acquired Iams and introduced it into mass merchandisers and supermarkets, the distinction between the two strategic groups blurred and new competitive dynamics were introduced. Iams became a threat to established brands in this space and the Hill's brands found their competitive context very different.

The third strategic group, private-label producers, is led by a unit of Del Monte (formerly Doanne), who supplies Wal-Mart and other major retailers.

Each strategic group has mobility barriers that inhibit or prevent businesses from moving from one strategic group to another. An ultra-premium group has the brand reputation, product, and manufacturing knowledge needed for the health segment, access to influential veterinarians and retailers, and a local customer base. Private-label manufacturers have low-cost production, low overhead, and close relationships with customers. It is possible to bypass or overcome the barriers, of course. A private-label manufacturer could create a branded entry, especially if markets are selected to minimize conflicts with existing customers. The barriers are real, however, and a firm competing across strategic groups is usually at a disadvantage.

A member of a strategic group can have exit as well as entry barriers. For example, assets such as plant investment or a specialized labor force can represent a meaningful exit barrier, as can the need to protect a brand's reputation.

The mobility barrier concept is crucial because one way to develop a sustainable competitive advantage is to pursue a strategy that is protected from competition by assets and competencies that represent barriers to competitors. Consider the PC and server market. Dell and others have marketed computers direct to consumers by telephone and the Internet. They developed a host of assets and competencies to support their direct channels, including an impressive product support system. Competitors such as HP—which has used indirect channels involving retailers and systems firms—have developed a very different set of assets and competencies. HP and Dell have both struggled to cross the channel barriers.

Using the Strategic Group Concept

The conceptualization of strategic groups can make the process of competitor analysis more manageable. Numerous industries contain many more competitors than can be analyzed individually. Often it is simply not feasible to consider thirty competitors, to say nothing of hundreds. Reducing this set to a small number of strategic groups makes the analysis compact, feasible, and more usable. For example, in the wine industry, competitor analysis by a firm like Robert Mondavi might examine three strategic groups: jug wines, premium wines ($7 to $20), and super-premium wines (over $20). Little strategic content and insight will be lost in most cases, because firms in a strategic group will be affected by and react to industry developments in similar ways. Thus, in projecting future strategies of competitors, the concept of strategic groups can be helpful.

Strategic groupings can refine the strategic investment decision. Instead of determining in which industries to invest, the decision can focus on what strategic group warrants investment. Thus, it will be necessary to determine the current profitability and future potential profitability of each strategic group. One strategic objective is to invest in attractive strategic groups in which assets and competencies can be employed to create strategic advantage.

Ultimately, the selection of a strategy and its supporting assets and competencies will often mean selecting or creating a strategic group. Thus, a knowledge of the strategic group structure and dynamics can be extremely useful.

Projecting Strategic Groups

The concept of strategic groups can also be helpful in projecting competitive strategies into the future. A classic McKinsey study of the effects of deregulation on five deregulated industries (summarized in Figure 3.2) forecasts with remarkable accuracy that successful firms will move toward one of three strategic groups.[4]

The evolution of the first group involves three phases. During the first phase, the medium and small firms attempt—usually unsuccessfully—to gain enough market share by merging to compete with the large firms. In the second phase, strong firms make acquisitions to fill in product lines or market gaps. During this phase, which occurs about three to five years following deregulation, the major firms try to develop broad product lines and distribution coverage. In the third phase, interindustry mergers occur. Strong firms merge with others outside their industry.

The second strategic group consists of low-cost producers entering the industry after deregulation by providing simple product lines with minimal service to the price-sensitive segment. The third group includes those pursuing a focus strategy, with a specialized service targeted toward a specific customer group.

Group	Industry	Examples
1. National distribution company with full line of differentiated products and emphasis on attractive service/price trade-offs	Brokerage Airlines Trucking	Merrill Lynch Delta Consolidated Freightways
2. Low-cost producer—often a new entrant following deregulation	Brokerage Airlines Trucking	Charles Schwab Southwest Airlines Overnite
3. Specialty firm with strong customer loyalty and specialized service targeted toward an attractive customer group	Brokerage Airlines Trucking	Goldman Sachs Air Wisconsin Ryder Systems

Figure 3.2   Strategic Groups Emerging from Deregulation

POTENTIAL COMPETITORS

In addition to current competitors, it is important to consider potential market entrants, such as firms that might engage in:

1. *Market expansion.* Perhaps the most obvious source of potential competitors is firms operating in other geographic regions or in other countries. A cookie company may want to keep a close eye on a competing firm in an adjacent state, for example.

2. *Product expansion.* The leading ski firm, Rossignol, has expanded into ski clothing, thus exploiting a common market, and has moved to tennis equipment, which takes advantage of technological and distribution overlap.

3. *Backward integration.* Customers are another potential source of competition. General Motors bought dozens of manufacturers of components during its formative years. Major can users, such as Campbell Soup, have integrated backward, making their own containers.

4. *Forward integration.* Suppliers attracted by margins are also potential competitors. Apple Computer, for example, opened a chain of retail stores. Suppliers, believing they have the critical ingredients to succeed in a market, may be attracted by the margins and control that come with integrating forward.

5. *The export of assets or competencies.* A current small competitor with critical strategic weaknesses can turn into a major entrant if it is purchased by a firm that can reduce or eliminate those weaknesses. Predicting such moves can be difficult, but sometimes an analysis of competitor strengths and weaknesses will suggest some possible synergistic mergers. A competitor in an above-average growth industry that does not have the financial or managerial resources for the long haul might be a particularly attractive candidate for merger.

6. *Retaliatory or defensive strategies.* Firms that are threatened by a potential or actual move into their market might retaliate. Thus, Microsoft has made several moves (including into the Internet space) in part to protect its dominant software position.

COMPETITOR ANALYSIS—UNDERSTANDING COMPETITORS

Understanding competitors and their activities can provide several benefits. First, an understanding of the current strategy strengths and weaknesses of a competitor can suggest opportunities and threats that will merit a response. Second, insights into future competitor strategies may allow the prediction of emerging threats and opportunities. Third, a decision about strategic alternatives might easily hinge on the ability to forecast the likely reaction of key competitors. Finally, competitor analysis may result in the identification of some strategic uncertainties that will be worth monitoring closely over time. A strategic uncertainty might be, for example, "Will Competitor A decide to move into the western U.S. market?"

As Figure 3.3 indicates, competitor actions are influenced by eight elements. The first of these reflects financial performance, as measured by size, growth, and profitability.

Size, Growth, and Profitability

The level and growth of sales and market share provide indicators of the vitality of a business strategy. The maintenance of a strong market position or the achievement of rapid growth usually reflects a strong competitor (or strategic group) and a successful strategy. In contrast, a deteriorating market position can signal financial or organizational strains that might affect the interest and ability of the business to pursue certain strategies. To provide a crude sales estimate for businesses that are buried in a large company, take the number of employees and multiply it by the average sales per employee in the industry. For many businesses, this method is very feasible and remarkably accurate.

After size and growth comes profitability. A profitable business will generally have access to capital for investment unless it has been designated by the parent to be milked. A business that has lost money over an extended time period or has experienced a recent sharp decrease in profitability may find it difficult to gain access to capital either externally or internally.

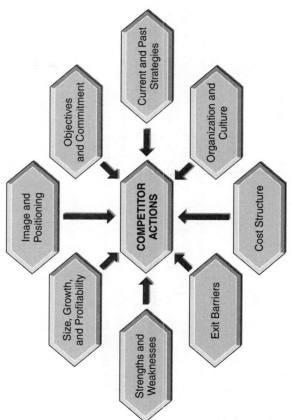

Figure 3.3   Understanding the Competitors

Image and Positioning Strategy

A cornerstone of a business strategy can be an association, such as being the strongest truck, the most durable car, the smallest consumer electronics equipment, or the most effective cleaner. More often, it is useful to move beyond class-related product attributes to intangibles that span product class, such as quality, innovation, sensitivity to the environment, or brand personality.

In order to develop positioning alternatives, it is helpful to determine the image and brand personality of the major competitors. Weaknesses of competitors on relevant attributes or personality traits can represent an opportunity to differentiate and develop advantage. Strengths of competitors on important dimensions may represent challenges to exceed them or to outflank them. In any case it is important to know the competitive profiles.

Competitor image and positioning information can be deduced in part by studying a firm's products, advertising, Web site, and actions, but often customer research is helpful to ensure that an accurate current portrayal is obtained. The conventional approach is to start with qualitative customer research to find out what a business and its brands mean to customers. What are the associations? If the business were a person, what kind of person would it be? What visual imagery, books, animals, trees, or activities are associated with the business? What is its essence?

Objectives and Commitment

A knowledge of competitor objectives provides the potential to predict whether or not a competitor's present performance is satisfactory or strategic changes are likely. The financial objectives of the business unit can indicate the competitor's willingness to invest in that business even if the payout is relatively long term. In particular, what are the competitor's objectives with respect to market share, sales growth, and profitability? Nonfinancial objectives are also helpful. Does the competitor want to be a technological leader? Or to develop a service organization? Or to expand distribution? Such objectives provide a good indication of the competitor's possible future strategy.

The objectives of the competitor's parent company (if one exists) are also relevant. What are the current performance levels and financial objectives of the parent? If the business unit is not performing as well as the parent, pressure might be exerted to improve or the investment might be withdrawn. Of critical importance is the role attached to the business unit. Is it seen as a growth area, or is it expected to supply cash to fund other areas? Does the business create synergy with other operations? Does the parent have an emotional attachment to the business unit for any reason? Deep pockets can sometimes be accompanied by short arms; just because resources exist does not mean they are available.

Current and Past Strategies

The competitor's current and past strategies should be reviewed. In particular, past strategies that have failed should be noted, because such experiences can inhibit the competitor from trying similar strategies again. Also, a knowledge of a competitor's pattern of new product or new market moves can help anticipate its future growth directions. Is the strategy based on product-line breadth, product quality, service, distribution type, or brand identification? If a low-cost strategy is employed, is it based on economies of scale, the experience curve, manufacturing facilities and equipment, or access to raw material? What is its cost structure? If a focus strategy is evident, describe the business scope.

Organization and Culture

Knowledge about the background and experience of the competitor's top management can provide insight into future actions. Are the managers drawn from marketing, engineering, or manufacturing? Are they largely from another industry or company? Clorox, for example, has a very heavy Procter & Gamble influence in its management, lingering from the years that Procter & Gamble operated Clorox before the courts ordered divestiture.

An organization's culture, supported by its structure, systems, and people, often has a pervasive influence on strategy. A cost-oriented, highly structured organization that relies on tight controls to achieve objectives and motivate employees may have difficulty innovating or shifting into an aggressive, marketing-oriented strategy. A loose, flat organization that emphasizes innovation and risk taking may similarly have difficulty pursuing a disciplined product-refinement and cost-reduction program. In general, as Chapter 15 will make clearer, organizational elements such as culture, structure, systems, and people limit the range of strategies that should be considered.

Cost Structure

Knowledge of a competitor's cost structure, especially when the competitor is relying on a low-cost strategy, can provide an indication of its likely future pricing strategy and its staying power. The following information can usually be obtained and can provide insights into cost structures:

- The number of employees and a rough breakdown of direct labor (variable labor cost) and overhead (which will be part of fixed cost)
- The relative costs of raw materials and purchased components
- The investment in inventory, plant, and equipment (also fixed cost)
- Sales levels and number of plants (on which the allocation of fixed costs is based)
- Outsourcing strategy

Exit Barriers

Exit barriers can be crucial to a firm's ability to withdraw from a business area, and thus are indicators of commitment. They include:[5]

- Specialized assets—plant, equipment, or other assets that are costly to transform from to another application and therefore have little salvage value
- Fixed costs, such as labor agreements, leases, and a need to maintain parts for existing equipment
- Relationships to other business units in the firm resulting from the firm's image or from shared facilities, distribution channels, or sales force
- Government and social barriers—for example, governments may regulate whether a railroad can exit from a passenger service responsibility, or firms may feel a sense of loyalty to workers, thereby inhibiting strategic moves
- Managerial pride or an emotional attachment to a business or its employees that affects economic decisions

Assessing Strengths and Weaknesses

Knowledge of a competitor's strengths and weaknesses provides insight that is key to a firm's ability to pursue various strategies. It also offers important input into the process of identifying and selecting strategic alternatives. One approach is to attempt to exploit a competitor's weakness in an area where the firm has an existing or developing strength. The desired pattern is to develop a strategy that will pit "our" strength against a competitor's weakness. Conversely, a knowledge of "their" strength is important so it can be bypassed or neutralized.

One firm that developed a strategy to neutralize a competitor's strength was a small software firm that lacked a retail distribution capability or the resources to engage in retail advertising. It targeted value-added software systems firms, which sell total software and sometimes hardware systems to organizations such as investment firms or hospitals. These value-added systems firms could understand and exploit the power of the product, integrate it into their systems, and use it in quantity. The competitor's superior access to a distribution channel or resources to support an advertising effort was thus neutralized.

The assessment of a competitor's strengths and weaknesses starts with an identification of relevant assets and competencies for the industry and then evaluates the competitor on the basis of those assets and competencies. We now turn to these topics.

COMPETITOR STRENGTHS AND WEAKNESSES

What Are the Relevant Assets and Competencies?

Competitor strengths and weaknesses are based on the existence or absence of assets or competencies. Thus, an asset such as a well-known name or a prime location could represent a strength, as could a competency such as the ability to develop a strong promotional program. Conversely, the absence of an asset or competency can represent a weakness.

To analyze competitor strengths and weaknesses, it is thus necessary to identify the assets and competencies that are relevant to the industry. As Figure 3.4 summarizes, four sets of questions can be helpful.

1. Why are successful businesses successful? Why are unsuccessful businesses unsuccessful?

2. What are the key customer motivations?

3. What are the industry mobility barriers?

4. Which components of the value chain can create competitive advantage?

Figure 3.4 Identifying Relevant Assets and Competencies

1. *What businesses have been successful over time? What assets or competencies have had chronically low performance? Why? What assets or competencies do they lack?*

By definition, assets and competencies that provide SCAs should affect performance over time. Thus, businesses that differ with respect to performance over time should also differ with respect to their assets and competencies. Analysis of the causes of the performance usually suggests sets of relevant competencies and assets. Typically, the superior performers have developed and maintained key assets and competencies that have been the basis for their performance. Conversely, weakness in several assets and competencies relevant to the industry and its strategy should visibly contribute to the inferior performance of the weak competitors over time.

For example, in the CT scanner industry the best performer, General Electric, has superior product technology and R&D, an established systems capability, a strong sales and service organization (owing, in part, to its X-ray product line), and an installed base.

2. *What are the key customer motivations? What is really important to the customer?*

Customer motivations usually drive buying decisions and thus can dictate what assets or competencies potentially create meaningful advantages. In the heavy-equipment industry, customers value service and parts backup. Caterpillar's promise of "24-hour parts service anywhere in the world" has been a key asset because it is important to customers. Apple has focused on the motivation of designers for user-friendly design platforms.

An analysis of customer motivations can also identify assets and competencies that a business will need to deliver unless a strategy can be devised that will make them unimportant. If the prime buying criterion for a snack is freshness, a brand will have to develop the skills to deliver that attribute. A business that lacks competence in an area important to the customer segment can experience problems even if it has other substantial SCAs.

3. *What assets and competencies represent industry mobility (entry and exit) barriers?*

Strategic groups are characterized by structural stability even when one group is much more profitable than the others. The reason is mobility barriers, which can be both entry barriers and exit barriers. Some groups have assets and competencies that will be difficult and sometimes impossible to duplicate by those seeking to enter. International deep water oil-well drilling firms, for example, have technology, equipment, and people that domestic, on-shore firms cannot duplicate. These assets also represent exit barriers because there is no other use to which they could be put.

4. ***Consider the components of the value chain. Do any provide the potential to generate competitive advantage?***

One tool to identify significant value-added components is the value chain, a conceptual model developed by Michael Porter.[6] A business's value chain (see Figure 3.5) consists of two types of value-creating activities and should be considered in assessing a competitor. The components of the value chain are defined as follows:

Primary Value Activities

- ***Inbound logistics***—material handling and warehousing
- ***Operations***—transforming inputs into the final product
- ***Outbound logistics***—order processing and distribution
- ***Marketing and sales***—communication, pricing, and channel management
- ***Service***—installation, repair, and parts

Secondary Value Activities

- ***Procurement***—procedures and information systems
- ***Technology development***—improving the product and processes/systems
- ***Human resource management***—hiring, training, and compensation

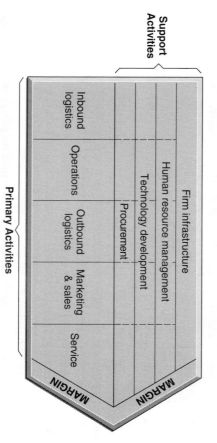

Figure 3.5   The Value Chain

- **Firm infrastructure**—general management, finance, accounting, government relations, and quality management

The linear flow suggested by the value chain may not always be the most useful representation of a competitor, especially in the Internet space. Another perspective is to simply address the question—what are the significant added-value components for a competitor, components that yield either customer benefits or reduced cost.[7] For eBay, for example, these components might be found in operations, customer support, and auction services. There will also be some network alliances that add value, such as those with AOL and iEscrow.

A Checklist of Strengths and Weaknesses

Figure 3.6 provides an overview checklist of the areas in which a competitor can have strengths and weaknesses. The first category is innovation. One of the strengths of Kao Corporation is its ability to develop innovative products in soaps, detergents, skin care, and even data storage disks. Its new products usually have a distinct technological advantage. In a highly technical industry, the percentage spent on R&D and the emphasis along the basic/applied continuum can be indicators of the cumulative ability to innovate. The outputs of the process in terms of product characteristics and performance measures of the company's ability to innovate.

The second area of competitor strengths and weaknesses is manufacturing. Perhaps the major area of strength of Texas Instruments' semiconductor and related businesses has been manufacturing. One of the key potential strength areas in manufacturing involves sources of sustainable cost advantages. Is there anything about the nature of the plant or equipment, the raw material access, the level of vertical integration, the type of workforce, or outsourcing contacts and processes that would support a sustainable cost advantage? Excess capacity can increase fixed costs, but it can also be a source of strength if the market is volatile or growing.

The third area is finance, the ability to generate or acquire funds in the short as well as the long run. Companies with deep pockets (financial resources) have a decisive advantage because they can pursue strategies not available to smaller firms. Compare General Motors with Chrysler, for example, or Miller and Budweiser with some of the smaller regional breweries. Operations provide one major source of funds. What is the nature of cash flow that is being generated and will be generated given the known uses for funds? Cash or other liquid assets provide other sources, as does a parent firm. The key is the ability of the business to justify the use of debt or equity and the will to access this source.

Management is the fourth area. Controlling and motivating a set of highly disparate business operations are strengths for GE, Sony, Disney, and other firms that have successfully diversified. The quality, depth, and loyalty (as measured by turnover) of top and middle management provide an important asset for others. Another aspect to analyze is the culture. The values and norms that permeate an organization can energize some strategies and inhibit others. In particular, some organizations, such as

INNOVATION

- Technical product or service superiority
- New product capability
- R&D
- Technologies
- Patents

MANUFACTURING

- Cost structure
- Flexible production operations
- Equipment
- Access to raw materials
- Vertical integration
- Workforce attitude and motivation
- Capacity
- Outsourcing

FINANCE—ACCESS TO CAPITAL

- From operations
- From net short-term assets
- Ability to use debt and equity financing
- Parent's willingness to finance

MANAGEMENT

- Quality of top and middle management
- Knowledge of business
- Culture
- Strategic goals and plans
- Entrepreneurial thrust
- Planning/operation system
- Loyalty—turnover
- Quality of strategic decision making

MARKETING

- Product quality reputation
- Product characteristics/differentiation
- Brand name recognition
- Breadth of the product line—systems capability
- Customer orientation
- Segmentation/focus
- Distribution
- Retailer relationship
- Advertising/promotion skills
- Sales force
- Customer service/product support

CUSTOMER BASE

- Size and loyalty
- Market share
- Growth of segments served

Figure 3.6   Analysis of Strengths and Weaknesses

3M possess both an entrepreneurial culture that allows them to initiate new directions and the organizational skill to nurture them. The ability to set strategic goals and plans can represent significant competencies. To what extent does the business have a vision and the will and competence to pursue it?

The fifth area is marketing. Often the most important marketing strength, particularly in the high-tech field, involves the product line: its quality reputation, breadth, and the features that differentiate it from other products. Brand image and distribution have been key assets for businesses as diverse as Gatorade, Dell, and Bank of America. The ability to develop a true customer orientation can be an important strength. Another strength can be based on the ability and willingness to advertise effectively. The success of Perdue chickens was due in part to Perdue's ability to generate superior advertising.

Other elements of the marketing mix, such as the sales force and service operation, can also be sources of sustainable competitive advantage. One of Caterpillar's strengths is the quality of its dealer network. Still another possible strength, particularly in the high-tech field, is a competitor's ability to stay close to its customers.

The final area of interest is the customer base. How substantial is the customer base and how loyal is it? How are the competitor's offerings evaluated by its customers? What are the costs that customers will have to absorb if they switch to another supplier? Extremely loyal and happy customers are going to be difficult to dislodge. What are the size and growth potentials of the segments served?

The Competitive Strength Grid

With the relevant assets and competencies identified, the next step is to scale your own firm and the major competitors or strategic groups of competitors on those assets and competencies. The result is termed a competitive strength grid and serves to summarize the position of the competitors with respect to assets and competencies.

A sustainable competitive advantage is almost always based on having a position superior to that of the target competitors in one or more asset or competence area that is relevant both to the industry and to the strategy employed. Thus, information about each competitor's position with respect to relevant assets and competencies is central to strategy development and evaluation.

If a superior position does not exist with respect to assets and competencies important to the strategy, it probably will have to be created or the strategy may have to be modified or abandoned. Sometimes there simply is no point of difference with respect to the firms regarded as competitors. A competency that all competitors have will not be the basis for an SCA. For example, flight safety is important among airline passengers, but if airlines are perceived to be equal with respect to pilot quality and plane maintenance, it cannot be the basis for an SCA. Of course, if some airlines can convince passengers that they are superior with respect to antiterrorist security, then an SCA could indeed emerge.

The Luxury Car Market

A competitor strength grid is illustrated in Figure 3.7 for the luxury car market. The relevant assets and competencies are listed on the left, grouped as to whether they are considered keys to success or are of secondary importance. The principal competitors are shown as column headings across the top. Each cell could be coded as to whether the brand is strong, above average, average, below average, or weak in that asset or competence category. The figure uses an above average, average, and below average scale.

The resulting figure provides a summary of the profile of the strengths and weaknesses of ten brands. Two can be compared, such as Ford and Lexus or BMW and Audi. BMW and Lexus have enviable positions.

Analyzing Submarkets

It is often desirable to conduct an analysis for submarkets or strategic groups and perhaps for different products. A firm may not compete with all other firms in the

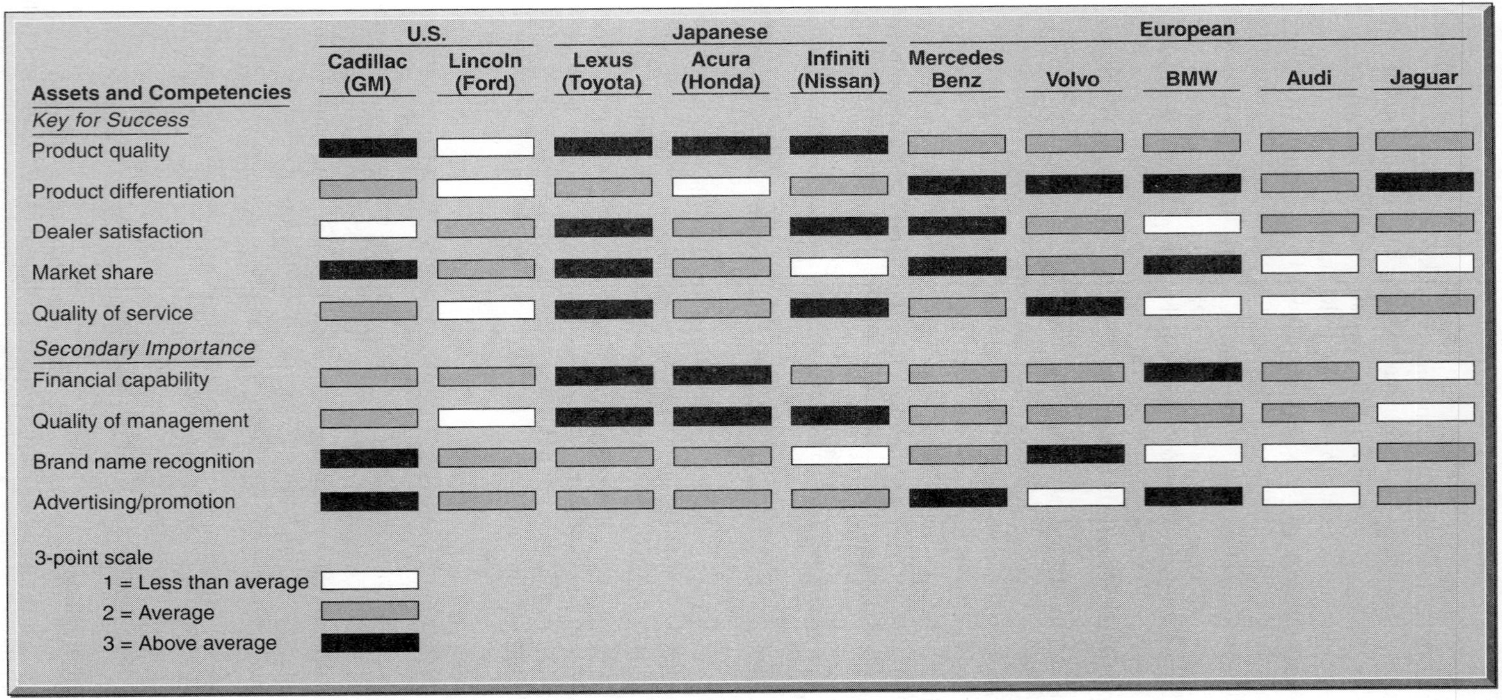

Assets and Competencies

	U.S.		Japanese			European				
	Cadillac (GM)	Lincoln (Ford)	Lexus (Toyota)	Acura (Honda)	Infiniti (Nissan)	Mercedes Benz	Volvo	BMW	Audi	Jaguar

Key for Success
Product quality
Product differentiation
Dealer satisfaction
Market share
Quality of service

Secondary Importance
Financial capability
Quality of management
Brand name recognition
Advertising/promotion

3-point scale
1 = Less than average
2 = Average
3 = Above average

Figure 3.7   Illustrative Example of a Competitive Strength Grid for the U.S. Luxury Car Market

industry but only with those engaged in similar strategies and markets. For example, a competitive strength grid may look very different for the safety submarket, with Volvo having more strength. Similarly, the handling submarket may also involve a competitive grid that will look different, with BMW having more strength.

The Analysis Process

The process of developing a competitive strength grid can be extremely informative and useful. One approach is to have several managers create their own grids independently. The differences can usually illuminate different assumptions and information bases. A reconciliation stage can disseminate relevant information and identify and structure strategic uncertainties. For example, different opinions about the quality reputation of a competitor may stimulate a strategic uncertainty that justifies marketing research. Another approach is to develop the grid in a group setting, perhaps supported by preliminary staff work. When possible, objective information based on laboratory tests or customer perception studies should be used. The need for such information becomes clear when disagreements arise about where competitors should be scaled on the various dimensions.

OBTAINING INFORMATION ON COMPETITORS

A competitor's Web site is usually a rich source of information and the first place to look. The strategic vision (along with a statement about values and culture) is often posted, and the portfolio of businesses are usually laid out. The way that the latter are organized can provide clues as to business priorities and strategies. When IBM emphasizes its e-servers, for example, that says something about their direction in the server business. The Web site also can provide information about such business assets as plants, global access, and brand symbols. Research on the competitor's site can be supplemented with search engines, access to articles and financial reports about the business. General-information sites (such as business.com) and Web sites for trade shows, trade magazines, channel members (such as retailers), and financial analysts can also provide useful information.

Detailed information on competitors is generally available from a variety of sources. Competitors usually communicate extensively with their suppliers, customers, and distributors; security analysts and stockholders; and government legislators and regulators. Contact with any of these can provide information. Monitoring of trade magazines, trade shows, advertising, speeches, annual reports, and the like can be informative. Technical meetings and journals can provide information about technical developments and activities. Thousands of databases accessible by computer now make available detailed information on most companies.

Detailed information about a competitor's standing with its customers can be obtained through market research. For example, regular telephone surveys could provide information about the successes and vulnerabilities of competitors' strategies. Respondents could be asked questions such as the following: Which store is closest to your home? Which do you shop at most often? Are you satisfied? Which has the lowest prices? Best specials? Best customer service? Cleanest stores? Best-quality meat? Best-quality produce? And so on. Those chains that were well positioned on value, on service, or on product quality could be identified, and tracking would show whether they were gaining or losing position. The loyalty of their customer base (and thus their vulnerability) could be indicated in part by satisfaction scores and the willingness of customers to patronize stores even when they were not the most convenient or the least expensive.

KEY LEARNINGS

- Competitors can be identified by customer choice (the set from which customers select) or by clustering them into strategic groups (firms that pursue similar strategies and have similar assets, competencies, and other characteristics). In either case, competitors will vary in terms of how intensely they compete.

- Competitors should be analyzed along several dimensions, including their size, growth and profitability, image, objectives, business strategies, organizational culture, cost structure, exit barriers, and strengths and weaknesses.

- Potential strengths and weaknesses can be identified by considering the characteristics of successful and unsuccessful businesses, key customer motivation, and value-added components.

- The competitive strength grid, which arrays competitors or strategic groups on each of the relevant assets and competencies, provides a compact summary of key strategic information.

FOR DISCUSSION

1. Consider the news industry. Identify the competitors to CNN and organize them in terms of their intensity of competition.

2. Evaluate Figure 3.7. What surprises are there in the figure? What are the implications for Cadillac? For Audi?

3. Pick a company or brand/business on which to focus. What business is it in? Who are its direct and indirect competitors? Which in each category are the most relevant competitors?

4. Consider the automobile industry. Identify competitors to Ford SUVs and organize them in terms of their intensity of competition. Also organize them into strategic groups. What are the key success factors for the strategic groups? Do you think that will change in the next five years?

NOTES

1. David Halberstam, *The Reckoning*, New York: William Morrow, 1986, p. 310.

2. Ibid.

3. George S. Day, Allan D. Shocker, and Rajendra K. Srivastava, "Customer-Oriented Approaches to Identifying Product Markets," *Journal of Marketing* 43, Fall 1979, pp. 8–19.

4. Donald C. Waite III, "Deregulation and the Banking Industry," *Bankers Magazine* 163, January–February 1982, pp. 76–85.

5. Michael E. Porter, *Competitive Strategy*, New York: The Free Press, 1980, pp. 20–21. The concept of exit barriers will be discussed again in Chapter 14.

6. Michael E. Porter, *Competitive Advantage*, New York: The Free Press, 1985, Chapter 2.

7. Shawn D. Cartwright and Richard W. Oliver, "Untangling the Value Web," *Journal of Business*, January–February 2000, pp. 22–27.

CHAPTER FOUR

Market/Submarket Analysis

As the economy, led by the automobile industry, rose to a new high level in the twenties, a complex of new elements came into existence to transform the market: installment selling, the used-car trade-in, the closed body, and the annual model. (I would add improved roads if I were to take into account the environment of the automobile.)
—*Alfred P. Sloan, Jr., General Motors*

Vision is the art of seeing things invisible.
—*Jonathan Swift*

To be prepared is half the victory.
—*Miguel Cervantes*

Market analysis builds on customer and competitor analyses to make some strategic judgments about a market (and submarket) and its dynamics. One of the primary objectives of a market analysis is to determine the attractiveness of a market (or submarket) to current and potential participants. Market attractiveness, the market's profit potential as measured by the long-term return on investment achieved by its participants, will provide important input into the product-market investment decision. The frame of reference is all participants. Of course, participating in an attractive market will not guarantee success for all competitors. Whether a market is appropriate for a particular firm is a related but very different question, depending not only on the market attractiveness, but also on how the firm's strengths and weaknesses match up against those of its competitors.

A second objective of market analysis is to understand the dynamics of the market. The need is to identify emerging submarkets, key success factors, trends, threats, opportunities, and strategic uncertainties that can guide information gathering and analysis. A key success factor is an asset or competency that is needed to play the game. If a firm has a strategic weakness in a key success factor that isn't neutralized by a well-conceived strategy, its ability to compete will be limited. The market trends can include those identified in customer or competitor analysis, but the perspective here is broader and others will usually emerge as well.

DIMENSIONS OF A MARKET ANALYSIS

The nature and content of an analysis of a market and its relevant product markets will depend on context, but will often include the following dimensions:

- Emerging submarkets
- Actual and potential market and submarket size
- Market and submarket growth
- Market and submarket profitability
- Cost structure
- Distribution systems
- Trends and developments
- Key success factors

Figure 4.1 provides a set of questions structured around these dimensions that can serve to stimulate a discussion identifying opportunities, threats, and strategic uncertainties. Each dimension will be addressed in turn. The chapter concludes with a discussion of the risks of growth markets.

EMERGING SUBMARKETS

The management of a firm in any dynamic market requires addressing the challenge and opportunity of relevance, as described in the boxed insert (page 61). In essence, the challenge is to detect and understand emerging submarkets, identify those that are attractive to the firm given its assets and competencies, and then adjust offerings and brand portfolios in order to increase their relevance to the chosen submarkets. The opportunity is to influence these emerging submarkets so that competitors become less relevant. A review of some of the many forces and events behind the rise or fall of submarkets will be helpful in the difficult task of detecting and understanding them.

First, the product or service can be augmented or expanded to include a new dimension. Saturn and Lexus, for example, changed the way customers interacted with car dealers and, for some, created a submarket that made some of the other brands less relevant. Banquet Homestyle Bakes successfully entered the shelf-stable meal market where Betty Crocker's Hamburger Helper resides with a meat-included meal package, thereby creating a new submarket.

Second, the market can be broken into niches. The energy bar market created by PowerBar ultimately fragmented into a variety of submarkets, including bars designed for women (Luna), high protein (Balance), low calories (Pria), and candy bar taste (Balance Gold).

SUBMARKETS

Are forces such as augmented products, the emerging of niches, a trend toward systems, new applications, repositioned product classes, customer trends, or new technologies creating worthwhile submarkets? How should they be defined?

SIZE AND GROWTH

Important submarkets? What are the size and growth characteristics of a market and submarkets? What submarkets are declining or will soon decline? How fast? What are the driving forces behind sales trends?

PROFITABILITY

For each major submarket consider the following: Is this a business area in which the average firm will make money? How intense is the competition among existing firms? Evaluate the threats from potential entrants and substitute products. What is the bargaining power of suppliers and customers? How attractive/profitable are the market and its submarkets both now and in the future?

COST STRUCTURE

What are the major cost and value-added components for various types of competitors?

DISTRIBUTION SYSTEMS

What are the alternative channels of distribution? How are they changing?

MARKET TRENDS

What are the trends in the market?

KEY SUCCESS FACTORS

What are the key success factors, assets, and competencies needed to compete successfully? How will these change in the future? How can the assets and competencies of competitors be neutralized by strategies?

Figure 4.1   Questions to Help Structure a Market Analysis

Third, the application scope can be expanded from components to systems or turnkey solutions; in essence there is an aggregation into submarkets, the inverse of breaking the category up into submarkets. In the late 1990s, Siebel took the lead in creating Internet-based customer relationship management (CRM) solutions by pulling together a host of application areas, including customer loyalty programs, customer acquisition, call centers, customer service, customer contact, and sales force automation.

Fourth, the emergence of a new and distinct application can define relevant brand options. Bayer helped define a new subcategory—taking baby aspirin regularly to ward off heart attacks—with its Bayer 81 mg. It attempted to further define the subcategory by introducing Enteric Safety Coating to reassure those who might be concerned about the effects of regular aspirin use on the stomach.

Fifth, a product class can be repositioned. In the United Kingdom, Ford Galaxy introduced itself as being roomy and comfortable, like first-class air travel, and therefore suitable for busy executives. In doing so, Ford repositioned the minivan experience

RELEVANCE

All too frequently, despite retaining high levels of awareness, attitude, and even loyalty, a brand loses market share because it is not perceived to be relevant to emerging submarkets. If a group of customers want hybrid cars, it simply does not matter how good they think your firm's SUV is. They might love it and recommend it to others, but if they are interested in an hybrid because of their changing needs and desires, then your brand is irrelevant to them. This may be true even if your firm also makes hybrids under the same brand. The hybrid submarket is different than SUVs and has a different set of relevant brands.

Relevance for a brand occurs when two conditions are met. First, there must be a perceived need or desire by customers for a submarket defined by some combination of an attribute set, an application, a user group, or other distinguishing characteristic. Second, the brand needs to be among the set considered to be relevant for that submarket by the prospective customers.

Winning among brands within a submarket, however, is not enough. There are two additional relevance challenges. One is to make sure that the submarket associated with the brand is relevant. The problem may not be that the customer picks the wrong brand, but rather that the wrong submarket (and brand set) is picked. The second challenge is to make sure that the brand is considered by customers to be an option with respect to a submarket. This implies that a brand needs to be positioned against the submarket in addition to whatever other positioning strategies may be pursued. It must also be visible and be perceived to meet minimal performance levels.

Nearly every marketplace is undergoing change—often dramatic, rapid change—that creates relevance issues. Examples appear in nearly every industry, from computers, consulting, airlines, power generators, and financial services to snack food, beverages, pet food, and toys. Hardware, paint, and flooring stores struggle with the reality of Home Depot. Xerox and Kodak face a relevance challenge as a variety of other firms (including HP, Microsoft, and Canon) are carving up the digital imaging world. Merrill Lynch faces threats to its basic value proposition from several sides. Relevance is an issue as well for brands attempting to open up new business arenas, such as Toyota's hybrid cars or TiVo's personal video recorder.

The key to managing such change is twofold. First, a business must detect and understand emerging submarkets, projecting how they are evolving. Second, it must maintain relevance in the face of these emerging submarkets. Businesses that perform these tasks successfully have organizational skills at detecting change, the organizational vitality to respond, and a well-conceived brand strategy.

There is also the option of creating or influencing the emergence of submarkets that will serve to make competitors less relevant. IBM did this with e-business. Gillette did it with the Sensor and Mach III brands. Charles Schwab did it with Schwab OneSource. Creating and owning subcategories can only occur when the right firm, armed with the right idea and offering, is ready to act at the right time. (Recall that Apple's Newton, the first PDA, was premature, while the Palm Pilot got the timing right.) But when it happens, it can be a strategic home run.[1]

(and thus a portion of the product class) as something far different than that associated with a soccer-mom or family-outing vehicle. Starbucks similarly repositioned the retail coffee market.

Sixth, a customer trend can be a driver of a submarket. The dual trends toward wellness and the use of herbs and natural supplements have supported a new category, healthy-refreshment beverages (HRBs). This arena now contains a host of subcategories, such as enhanced teas, fruit drinks, soy-based drinks, and waters. The pioneer and submarket leader is SoBe, which started in 1996 (with SoBe Black Tea 3G, containing ginseng, ginkgo, and guarana) and now has an extensive line of teas, juices, and energy drinks.

Seventh, a new technology—such as disposable razors, notebook computers, a new fabric, or hybrid cars—can drive the perception of a submarket. By creating a subcategory of dry beer, Asahi Super Dry Beer made Kirin, the leading lager beer brand, irrelevant for a significant and growing segment in Japan. A minor player with less than 10 percent of the market in 1986, Asahi grew to gain market share leadership in the late 1990s, in large part by taking share from Kirin. Kirin finally mounted a comeback by taking leadership in 2005 of a new subcategory, *happoshu* (a beer brewed with ingredients that warranted a sharply lower tax).

Finally, a whole market can simply be invented. eBay created an online auction category that has spawned many imitators, who have had difficulty matching both the operational performance and the critical mass of users established by eBay.

ACTUAL AND POTENTIAL MARKET SIZE

A basic starting point for the analysis of a market or submarket is the total sales level. If it is reasonable to believe that a successful strategy can be developed to gain a 15 percent share, it is important to know the total market size. Among the sources that can be helpful are published financial analyses of the firm, customers, government data, and trade magazines and associations. The ultimate source is often a survey of product users in which the usage levels are projected to the population.

Potential Market—The User Gap

In addition to the size of the current, relevant market, it is often useful to consider the potential market. A new use, new user group, or more frequent usage could dramatically change the size and prospects for the market.

There is unrealized potential for the cereal market in Europe and among institutional customers in the United States—restaurants and schools/day-care facilities. All these segments have room for dramatic growth. In particular, Europeans buy only about 25 percent as much cereal as their U.S. counterparts. If technology allowed cereals to be used more conveniently away from home by providing shelf-stable milk products, usage could be further expanded. Of course, the key is not only to recognize the potential, but also to have the vision and program in place to exploit it. A host of strategists have dismissed investment opportunities in industries because they lacked the insight to see the available potential and take advantage of it.

Ghost Potential

Sometimes an area becomes so topical and the need so apparent that potential growth seems assured. As a Lewis Carroll character observed, "What I tell you three times is true." However, this potential can have a ghostlike quality caused by factors inhibiting or preventing its realization. For example, the demand for computers exists in many underdeveloped countries, but a lack of funds and the absence of suitable technology inhibits buying. Many dot-com concepts were the beneficiaries of considerable hype, but failed because the growth of their application never materialized.

Small Can Be Beautiful

Some firms have investment criteria that prohibit them from investing in small markets. Chevron, Marriott, Frito-Lay, and Procter & Gamble, for example, have historically looked to new products that would generate large sales levels within a few years. Yet in an era of micromarketing, much of the action is in smaller niche segments. If a firm avoids them, it can lock itself out of much of the vitality and profitability of a business area. Furthermore, most substantial business areas were small at the outset, sometimes for many years. Avoiding the small market can thus mean that a firm must later overcome the first-mover advantage of others.

Further, there is evidence recounted in the book *The Long Tail* by Chris Anderson that many markets have changed so that the small niche business is economically viable and should not be automatically ignored.[2] The music, entertainment, and broadcasting areas illustrate the fact that the tail—the offerings that are not the large hit products—is extensive and collectively important. Netflix, for example, carries 55,000 titles, and 21 percent of its sales come from titles that do not appear in retail stores (which stock under 3,000 titles). Rhapsody, the subscription-based streaming service, offers more that 1.5 million music tracks and gets 41 percent of its sales from tracks not available in retail stores. Companies limited by retailers to a small selection can provide access to a full line from their Web sites; KitchenAid, for example, offers its products in some fifty colors. With eBay, Amazon, Google, and others, the economics of marketing small niche items has changed. The fact that some 25,000 items are introduced in the grocery stores each year and car makers offer some 250 different models indicates that niche marketing is viable outside the Internet world.

There is a downside to having too many niche offerings. First, companies can create operating and marketing costs that can be debilitating when the offerings are too extensive. Second, customers can become overwhelmed by the confusion of too many choices and rebel—looking for the equivalent of Colgate's Total, a product that simplified decision making in a cluttered environment. Thus, many firms are trimming lines that have gotten too large. Nevertheless, the analysis of niche markets needs to reflect the new reality that customers have faster and more extensive access to information than before, and products are accessible in ways not feasible too many years ago.

MARKET AND SUBMARKET GROWTH

After the size of the market and its important submarkets have been estimated, the focus turns to growth rate. What will be the size of the markets and submarkets in the future? If all else remains constant, growth means more sales and profits even without increasing market share. It can also mean less price pressure when demand increases faster than supply and firms are not engaged in experience curve pricing, anticipating future lower costs. Conversely, declining sales can mean reduced sales and often increased price pressure as firms struggle to hold their shares of a diminishing pie.

It may seem that the strategy of choice would thus be to identify and avoid or disinvest in declining situations and to identify and invest in growth contexts. Of course, the reality is not that simple. In particular, declining product markets can represent a real opportunity for a firm, in part because competitors may be exiting and disinvesting, instead of entering and investing for growth. The firm may attempt to become a profitable survivor by encouraging others to exit and by becoming dominant in the most viable segments.

The other half of the conventional wisdom, that growth contexts are always attractive, can also fail to hold true. Growth situations can involve substantial risks. Because of the importance of correctly assessing growth contexts, a discussion of these risks is presented at the end of this chapter.

Identifying Driving Forces

In many contexts, the most important strategic uncertainty involves the prediction of market sales. A key strategic decision, often an investment decision, can hinge on not only being correct but also understanding the driving forces behind market dynamics.

Addressing most key strategic uncertainties starts with asking on what the answer depends. In the case of projecting sales of a major market, the need is to determine what forces will drive those sales. For example, the sales of a new consumer electronics device may be driven by machine costs, the evolution of an industry standard, or the emergence of alternative technologies. Each of these three drivers will provide the basis for key second-level uncertainties.

In the wine market, the relationship of wine to health and the future demand for premium reds might be driving forces. One second-level strategic uncertainty might then ask on what the demand for premium red will depend.

Forecasting Growth

Historical data can provide a useful perspective and help to separate hope from reality, but they need to be used with care. Apparent trends in data such as those shown in Figure 4.2 can be caused by random fluctuations or by short-term economic conditions, and the urge to extrapolate should be resisted. Furthermore, the strategic interest is not on projections of history but rather on the prediction of turning points, times when the rate and perhaps direction of growth change.

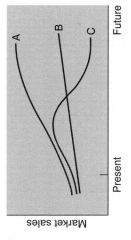

Figure 4.2   Sales Patterns

Sometimes leading indicators of market sales may help in forecasting and predicting turning points. Examples of leading indicators include:

- **Demographic data.** The number of births is a leading indicator of the demand for education, and the number of people reaching age 65 is a leading indicator of the demand for retirement facilities.

- **Sales of related equipment.** Personal computer and printer sales provide a leading indicator of the demand for supplies and service needs.

Market sales forecasts, especially of new markets, can be based on the experience of analogous industries. The trick is to identify a prior market with similar characteristics. Sales of color televisions might be expected to have a pattern similar to sales of black-and-white televisions, for example. Sales of a new type of snack might look to the history of other previously introduced snack categories or other consumer products, such as some of the energy bars or granola bars. The most value will be obtained if several analogous product classes can be examined and the differences in the product class experiences related to their characteristics.

Methods now exist to provide remarkably accurate forecasts of sales patterns for durable products such as appliances, cameras, and VCRs. They are based, in part, on decomposing sales into first purchases and replacement sales.

Detecting Maturity and Decline

One particularly important set of turning points in market sales occurs when the growth phase of the product-life cycle changes to a flat maturity phase and when the maturity phase changes into a decline phase. These transitions are important indicators of the health and nature of the market. Often they are accompanied by changes in key success factors. Historical sales and profit patterns of a market can help to identify the onset of maturity or decline, but the following often are more sensitive indicators:

- **Price pressure caused by overcapacity and the lack of product differentiation.** When growth slows or even reverses, capacity developed under a more optimistic scenario becomes excessive. Furthermore, the product evolution process often results in most competitors matching product improvements. Thus, it becomes more difficult to maintain meaningful differentiation.

- *Buyer sophistication and knowledge.* Buyers tend to become more familiar and knowledgeable as a product matures, and thus they become less willing to pay a premium price to obtain the security of an established name. Computer buyers over the years have gained confidence in their ability to select computers—as a result, the value of big names has receded.

- *Substitute products or technologies.* The sales of personal TV services like TiVo provide an indicator of the decline of VCRs.

- *Saturation.* When the number of potential first-time buyers declines, market sales should mature or decline.

- *No growth sources.* The market is fully penetrated and there are no visible sources of growth from new uses or users.

- *Customer disinterest.* The interest of customers in applications, new product announcements, and so on falls off.

MARKET AND SUBMARKET PROFITABILITY ANALYSIS

Economists have long studied why some industries or markets are profitable and others are not. Harvard economist and business strategy guru Michael Porter applied his theories and findings to the business strategy problem of evaluating the investment value of an industry or market.[3] The problem is to estimate how profitable the average firm will be. It is hoped, of course, that a firm will develop a strategy that will bring above-average profits. If the average profit level is low, however, the task of succeeding financially will be much more difficult than if the average profitability were high.

Porter's approach can be applied to any industry, but it also can be applied to a market or submarket within an industry. The basic idea is that the attractiveness of an industry or market as measured by the long-term return on investment of the average firm depends largely on five factors that influence profitability, shown in Figure 4.3:

- The intensity of competition among existing competitors
- The existence of potential competitors who will enter if profits are high
- Substitute products that will attract customers if prices become high
- The bargaining power of customers
- The bargaining power of suppliers

Each factor plays a role in explaining why some industries are historically more profitable than others. An understanding of this structure can also suggest which key success factors are necessary to cope with the competitive forces.

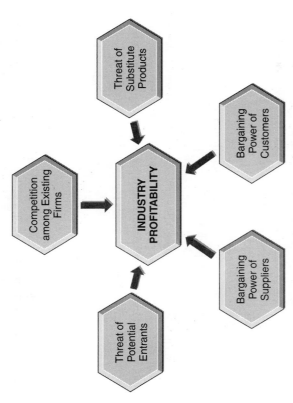

Figure 4.3   Porter's Five-Factor Model of Market Profitability

Source: The concept of five factors is due to Michael E. Porter. See his book *Competitive Advantage,* New York: The Free Press, 1985, Chapter 1.

Existing Competitors

The intensity of competition from existing competitors will depend on several factors, including:

- The number of competitors, their size, and their commitment
- Whether their product offerings and strategies are similar
- The existence of high fixed costs
- The size of exit barriers

The first question to ask is, how many competitors are already in the market or making plans to enter soon? The more competitors that exist, the more competition intensifies. Are they large firms with staying power and commitment, or small and vulnerable ones? The second consideration is the amount of differentiation. Are the competitors similar, or are some (or all) insulated by points of uniqueness valued by customers? The third factor is the level of fixed costs. A high fixed-cost industry like telecommunication or airlines experiences debilitating price pressures when overcapacity gets large. Finally, one should assess the presence of exit barriers such as specialized assets, long-term contract commitments to customers and distributors, and relationship to other parts of a firm.

One major factor in the shakeout of both e-commerce and content Internet firms was the excessive number of competitors. Because the barriers to entry were low and the offered products so similar, margins were insufficient (and often nonexistent), especially given the significant investment in infrastructure and brand building that was needed. Given the hysterical market growth and the low barriers to entry, the results should have been anticipated; at one time there were a host of pet-supply and drugstore e-commerce offerings competing for a still-embryonic market.

Potential Competitors

Chapter 3 discusses identifying potential competitors that might have an interest in entering an industry or market. Whether potential competitors, identified or not, actually do enter depends in large part on the size and nature of barriers to entry. Thus, an analysis of barriers to entry is important in projecting likely competitive intensity and profitability levels in the future.

Various barriers to entry include required capital investment (the infrastructure in cable television and telecommunication), economies of scale (the success of Internet portals like Yahoo! is largely based on scale economies), distribution channels (Frito-Lay and IBM have access to customers that is not easily duplicated), and product differentiation (Apple and Harley-Davidson have highly differentiated products that protect them from new entrants).

Substitute Products

Substitute products compete with less intensity than do the primary competitors. They are still relevant, however, as the discussion in Chapter 3 made clear. They can influence the profitability of the market and can be a major threat or problem. Thus, plastics, glass, and fiber-foil products exert pressure on the metal can market. Electronic alarm systems are substitutes for the security guard market. E-mail provides a threat to some portion of the express-delivery market of FedEx and UPS. Substitutes that show a steady improvement in relative price/performance and for which the customer's cost of switching is minimal are of particular interest.

Customer Power

When customers have relatively more power than sellers, they can force prices down or demand more services, thereby affecting profitability. A customer's power will be greater when its purchase size is a large proportion of the seller's business, when alternative suppliers are available, and when the customer can integrate backward and make all or part of the product. Thus, tire manufacturers face powerful customers in the automobile firms. Soft-drink firms sell to fast-food restaurant chains that have strong bargaining power. Wal-Mart has enormous power over its suppliers. It can dictate prices and product specifications; if companies resist, there is an Asian supplier that will comply. Wal-Mart is the leading seller of pratically all appliances. Because something like 17 percent of all Procter & Gamble sales go through Wal-Mart (a proportion that approaches 30 percent for some categories), even P&G is subject to customer power.

Supplier Power

When the supplier industry is concentrated and sells to a variety of customers in diverse markets, it will have relative power that can be used to influence prices.

Power will also be enhanced when the costs to customers of switching suppliers are high. Thus, the highly concentrated oil industry is often powerful enough to influence profits in customer industries that find it expensive to convert from oil. However, the potential for regeneration whereby industries can create their own energy supplies, perhaps by recycling waste, may have changed the balance of power in some contexts.

COST STRUCTURE

An understanding of the cost structure of a market can provide insights into present and future key success factors. The first step is to conduct an analysis of the value chain presented in Figure 4.4 to determine where value is added to the product (or service). As suggested in Figure 4.4, the proportion of value added attributed to one value chain stage can become so important that a key success factor is associated with that stage. It may be possible to develop control over a resource or technology, as did the OPEC oil cartel. More likely, competitors will aim to be the lowest-cost competitor in a high value-added stage of the value chain. Advantages in lower value-added stages will simply have less leverage. Thus, in the metal can business, transportation costs are relatively high and a competitor that can locate plants near customers will have a significant cost advantage.

It may not be possible to gain an advantage at high value-added stages. For example, a raw material, such as flour for bakery firms, may represent a high value added, but because the raw material is widely available at commodity prices, it will not be a key success factor. Nevertheless, it is often useful to look first at the highest value-added stages, especially if changes are occurring. For example, the cement market was very regional when it was restricted to rail or truck transportation. With the development of specialized ships, however, waterborne transportation costs dropped dramatically. Key success factors changed from local ground transportation to production scale and access to the specialized ships.

Production Stage	Markets That Have Key Success Factors Associated with the Production Stage
• Raw material procurement	• Gold mining, winemaking
• Raw material processing	• Steel, paper
• Production fabricating	• Integrated circuits, tires
• Assembly	• Apparel, instrumentation
• Physical distribution	• Bottled water, metal cans
• Marketing	• Branded cosmetics, liquor
• Service backup	• Software, automobiles
• Technology development	• Razors, medical systems

Figure 4.4 Value Added and Key Success Factors

DISTRIBUTION SYSTEMS

An analysis of distribution systems should include three types of questions:

- What are the alternative distribution channels?
- What are the trends? What channels are growing in importance? What new channels have emerged or are likely to emerge?
- Who has the power in the channel, and how is that likely to shift?

Sometimes the creation of a new channel of distribution can lead to a sustainable competitive advantage. A dramatic example is the success that L'eggs hosiery, with its egg-shaped package, achieved by its ability to market hosiery in supermarkets. L'eggs supported the idea of using supermarkets with a comprehensive program that addressed a host of issues. The L'eggs program involved selling on consignment, packaging the hosiery in a container that made it relatively difficult to shoplift, using a space-efficient vertical display, providing a high-quality, low-priced product supported by national advertising, and performing in-store functions, such as ordering and stocking. Thus, it is useful to consider not only existing channels but potential ones.

An analysis of likely or emerging changes within distribution channels can be important in understanding a market and its key success factors. The increased sale of wine in supermarkets made it much more important for winemakers to focus on packaging and advertising. The consolidation of department stores meant that clothing brands had fewer retailers through which to sell their products

MARKET TRENDS

Often one of the most useful elements of external analysis comes from addressing the question, what are the market trends? The question has two important attributes: it focuses on change, and it tends to identify what is important. Strategically useful insights almost always result. A discussion of market trends can serve as a useful summary of customer, competitor, and market analyses. It is thus helpful to identify trends near the end of market analysis.

While the soft-drink market stagnated in the United States, noncarbonated beverages grew sharply, and sales of herb- and vitamin-fortified beverages exploded. Not surprisingly, the major soft-drink companies sought to obtain a position in these trendy categories. Reports that dark chocolate was heart-healthy sent sales up 30 percent from 2003 to 2005. Chocolate makers scrambled to redo their lines and yet create products with authenticity.

Trends versus Fads

It is crucial to distinguish between trends that will drive growth and reward those who develop differentiated strategies, and fads that will only last long enough to attract investment (which is subsequently underemployed or lost forever). Schwinn, the classic name in bicycles, proclaimed mountain biking a fad in 1985, with disastrous results to its market position and, ultimately, its corporate health.[4] The mistaken belief that certain e-commerce markets, such as those for cosmetics and pet supplies, were solid trends caused strategists to undertake initial share-building strategies that eventually led to the ventures' demise.

One firm, the Zandl Group, suggests that three questions can help detect a real trend, as opposed to a fad.[5]

1. **What is driving it?** A trend will have a solid foundation with legs. Trends are more likely to be driven by demographics (rather than pop culture), values (rather than fashion), lifestyle (rather than a trendy crowd), or technology (rather than media).

2. **How accessible is it in the mainstream?** Will it be constrained to a niche market for the foreseeable future? Will it require a major change in ingrained habits? Is the required investment in time or resources a barrier (perhaps because the product is priced too high or is too hard to use)?

3. **Is it broadly based?** Does it find expression across categories or industries? Eastern influences, for example, are apparent in health care, food, fitness, and design—a sign of a trend.

Faith Popcorn observes that fads are about products, while trends are about what drives consumers to buy products. She also suggests that trends (which are big and broad, lasting an average of ten years) cannot be created or changed, only observed.[6]

Still another perspective on fads comes from Peter Drucker, who opined that a change is something that people do, whereas a fad is something people talk about. The implication is that a trend demands substance and action supported by data, rather than simply an idea that captures the imagination. Drucker also suggests that the leaders of today need to move beyond innovation to be change agents—the real payoff comes not from simply detecting and reacting to trends, even when they are real, but from creating and driving them.[7]

KEY SUCCESS FACTORS

An important output of market analysis is the identification of key success factors for strategic groups in the market. These are assets and competencies that provide the basis for competing successfully. There are two types. *Strategic necessities* do not necessarily provide an advantage, because others have them, but their absence will create a substantial weakness. The firm needs to achieve a point of parity with respect to strategic necessities. The second type, *strategic strengths*, are those at which a firm excels, the assets or competencies that are superior to those of competitors and provide a base of advantage. The set of assets and competencies developed in competitor analysis provides a base from which key success factors can be identified. The points to consider are which are the most critical assets and competencies now and, more important, which will be most critical in the future.

It is important not only to identify KSFs, but also to project them into the future and, in particular, to identify emerging KSFs. Many firms have faltered when KSFs changed and the competencies and assets on which they were relying became less

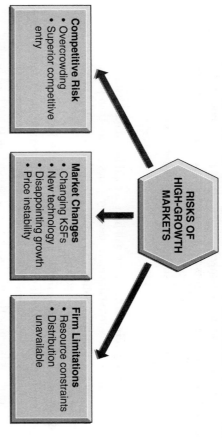

Figure 4.5   Risks of High-Growth Markets

relevant. For example, for industrial firms, technology and innovation tend to be most important during the introduction and growth phases, whereas the roles of systems capability, marketing, and service backup become more dominant as the market matures. In consumer products, marketing and distribution skills are crucial during the introduction and growth phases, but operations and manufacturing become more crucial as the product settles into the maturity and decline phases.

RISKS IN HIGH-GROWTH MARKETS

The conventional wisdom that the strategist should seek out growth areas often overlooks a substantial set of associated risks. As shown in Figure 4.5, there are the risks that:

- The number and commitment of competitors may be greater than the market can support.

- A competitor may enter with a superior product or low-cost advantage.

- Key success factors might change and the organization may be unable to adapt.

- Technology might change.

- The market growth may fail to meet expectations.

- Price instability may result from overcapacity or from retailers' practice of pricing hot products low to attract customers.

- Resources might be inadequate to maintain a high growth rate.

- Adequate distribution may not be available.

Competitive Overcrowding

Perhaps the most serious risk is that too many competitors will be attracted by a growth situation and enter with unrealistic market share expectations. The reality may be that sales volume is insufficient to support all competitors. Overcrowding has been observed in virtually all hyped markets, from railroads to airplanes, radio stations and equipment, televisions sets, and personal computers.

Overcrowding was never more vividly apparent (in retrospect, at least) than in the dot-com frenzy. At one point there were at least 150 online brokerages, 1,000 travel-related sites, and thirty health and beauty sites that were competing for attention. Dot-com business-to-business (B2B) exchanges were created for the buying and selling of goods and services, information exchanges, logistics services, sourcing industry data and forecasts, and a host of other services. The number of B2B companies grew from under 250 to over 1,500 during the year 2000, then fell to under 250 again in 2003. At the peak, there were estimated to be more than 140 such exchanges in the industrial supplies industry alone.[8]

The following conditions are found in markets in which a surplus of competitors is likely to be attracted and a subsequent shakeout is highly probable. These factors were all present in the B2B dot-com experience:

1. The market and its growth rate have high visibility. As a result, strategists in related firms are encouraged to consider the market seriously and may even fear the consequences of turning their backs on an obvious growth direction.

2. Very high forecast and actual growth in the early stages are seen as evidence confirming high market growth as a proven phenomenon.

3. Threats to the growth rate are not considered or are discounted, and little exists to dampen the enthusiasm surrounding the market. The enthusiasm may be contagious when venture capitalists and stock analysts become advocates.

4. Few initial barriers exist to prevent firms from entering the market. There may be barriers to eventual success (such as limited retail space), however, that may not be evident at the outset.

5. Some potential entrants have low visibility, and their intentions are unknown or uncertain. As a result, the quantity and commitment of the competitors are likely to be underestimated.

Superior Competitive Entry

The ultimate risk is that a position will be established in a healthy growth market and a competitor will enter late with a product that is demonstrably superior or that has an inherent cost advantage.

Thus, the Apple Newton was first to market with a handheld computing device, but it failed in part because it was priced too high, badly designed, and too complex to use. The cheaper, better, and simpler Palm Pilot won the market, even though it came later. The success of late-entry, low-cost products from the Far East has occurred in countless industries, from automobiles to TVs to VCRs.

Changing Key Success Factors

A firm may successfully establish a strong position during the early stages of market development, only to lose ground later when key success factors change. One forecast is that the surviving personal computer makers will be those able to achieve low-cost production through sourcing manufacture in low-cost countries, exploitation of the experience curve, and obtaining efficient, low-cost distribution—capabilities not necessarily critical during the early stages of market evolution. Many product markets have experienced a shift over time from a focus on product technology to a focus on process technology; operational excellence, and the customer experience. A firm that might be capable of achieving product technology-based advantages may not have the resources, competencies, and orientation/culture needed to develop the demands of the evolving market.

Changing Technology

Developing first-generation technology can involve a commitment to a product line and production facilities that may become obsolete and to a technology that may not survive. A safe strategy is to wait until it is clear which technology will dominate and then attempt to improve it with a compatible entry. When the principal competitors have committed themselves, the most promising avenues for the development of a sustainable competitive advantage become more visible. In contrast, the early entry has to navigate with a great deal of uncertainty.

Disappointing Market Growth

Many shakeouts and price wars occur when market growth falls below expectations. Sometimes the market was an illusion to begin with. Internet-based B2B exchanges did not provide value to firms that already had systems built with relationships that were, on balance, superior to the B2B exchanges. There was an absence of a compelling value proposition to overcome marketplace inertia. In other cases, the demand may be healthy, but the market is still hostile because competitors have built capacity to match overly optimistic expectations. Or the demand might simply take longer to materialize because the technology is not ready, or because customers are slow to change. Demand for electronic banking, for example, took many years longer than expected to materialize.

Forecasting demand is difficult, especially when the market is new, dynamic, and glamorized. This difficulty is graphically illustrated by an analysis of more than ninety forecasts of significant new products, markets, and technologies that appeared in *Business Week, Fortune*, and the *Wall Street Journal* from 1960 to 1979.9 Forecast growth failed to materialize in about 55 percent of the cases cited. Among the reasons were overvaluation of technologies (e.g., three-dimensional color TV and tooth-decay vaccines); consumer demand (e.g., two-way cable TV, quadraphonic stereo, and dehydrated foods), a failure to consider the cost barrier (e.g., the SST and moving sidewalks), or political problems (e.g., marine mining). The forecasts for roll-your-own cigarettes, small cigars, Scotch whiskey, and CB radios suffered from shifts in consumer needs and preferences.

Price Instability

When the creation of excess capacity results in price pressures, industry profitability may be short-lived, especially in an industry such as airlines or steel, in which fixed costs are high and economies of scale are crucial. However, it is also possible that some will use a hot product as a loss leader just to attract customer flow.

CDs, a hot growth area in the late 1980s, fueled the overexpansion of retailers who were very profitable when they sold CDs for about $15. However, when Best Buy, a home-electronics chain, decided to sell CDs for under $10 to attract customers to their off-mall locations, and when Circuit City followed suit, the result was a dramatic erosion in margins and volume and the ultimate bankruptcy of a substantial number of the major CD retailers. A hot growth area had spawned a disaster, not by a self-inflicted price cut, but by price instability from a firm that chose to treat the retailing of CDs as nothing more than a permanent loss leader.

Resource Constraints

The substantial financing requirements associated with a rapidly growing business are a major constraint for small firms. Royal Crown's Diet-Rite cola lost its leadership position to Coca-Cola's Tab and Diet Pepsi in the mid-1960s when it could not match the advertising and distribution clout of its larger rivals. Furthermore, financing requirements frequently are increased by higher than expected product development and market entry costs and by price erosion caused by aggressive or desperate competitors.

The organizational pressures and problems created by growth can be even more difficult to predict and deal with than financial strains. Many firms have failed to survive the rapid-growth phase because they were unable to obtain and train people to handle the expanded business or to adjust their systems and structures.

Distribution Constraints

Most distribution channels can support only a small number of brands. For example, few retailers are willing to provide shelf space for more than four or five brands of a housewar appliance. As a consequence, some competitors, even those with attractive products and marketing programs, will not gain adequate distribution, and their marketing programs will become less effective.

A corollary of the scarcity and selectivity of distributors as market growth begins to slow is a marked increase in distributor power. Their willingness to use this power to extract price and promotion concessions from manufacturers or to drop suppliers is often heightened by their own problems in maintaining margins in the face of extreme competition for their customers. Many of the same factors that drew in an overabundance of manufacturers also contribute to overcrowding in subsequent stages of a distribution channel. The eventual shakeout at this level can have equally serious repercussions for suppliers.

KEY LEARNINGS

- The emergence of submarkets can signal a relevance problem or opportunity.

- Market analysis should assess the attractiveness of a market or submarket, as well as its structure and dynamics.

- A usage gap can cause the market size to be understated.

- Market growth can be forecast by looking at driving forces, leading indicators, and analogous industries.

- Market profitability will depend on five factors—existing competitors, supplier power, customer power, substitute products, and potential entrants.

- Cost structure can be analyzed by looking at the value added at each production stage.

- Distribution channels and trends will often affect who wins.

- Market trends will affect both the profitability of strategies and key success factors.

- Key success factors are the skills and competencies needed to compete in a market.

- Growth-market challenges involve the threat of competitors, market changes, and firm limitations.

FOR DISCUSSION

1. What are the emerging submarkets in the fast food industry? What are the alternative responses available to McDonald's, assuming that it wants to stay relevant to customers interested in healthier eating?

2. Identify markets in which actual sales and growth was less than expected. Why was that the case? What would you say was the most important reason that the bottom fell out of the dot-com boom? Why did all the B2B sites emerge, and why did they collapse so suddenly?

3. Why were some brands (like Gatorade) able to fight off competitors in high-growth markets and others were not?

4. Pick a company or brand/business on which to focus. What are the emerging submarkets? What are the trends? What are the strategic implications of the submarkets and trends for the major players?

5. What considerations go into forecasting when dark chocolate will peak?

NOTES

1. For more details in the relevance concept see David A. Aaker, "The Brand Relevance Challenge," *Strategy & Business*, Spring 2004, and David A. Aaker, *Brand Portfolio Strategy*, New York: The Free Press, 2004, chapter 3.

2. Chris Anderson, *The Long Tail*, New York: Hyperion, 2006.

3. This section draws on Michael E. Porter, *Competitive Advantage*, New York: The Free Press, 1985, chapter 1.

4. Scott Davis of Prophet Brand Strategy suggested the Schwinn case.

5. Irma Zandl, "How to Separate Trends from Fads," *Brandweek*, October 23, 2000, pp. 30–35.

6. Faith Popcorn and Lys Marigold, *Clicking*, New York: HarperCollins, 1997, pp. 11–12.

7. James Daly, "Sage Advice—Interview with Peter Drucker," *Business 2.0*, August 22, 2000, pp. 134–144.

8. George S. Day, Adam J. Fein, Gregg Ruppersberger, "Shakeouts in Digital Markets: Lessons for GB2B Exchanges," *California Management Review*, Winter 2003, pp. 131–133.

9. Steven P. Schnaars, "Growth Market Forecasting Revisited: A Look Back at a Look Forward," *California Management Review* 28(4), Summer 1986.

CHAPTER FIVE

Environmental Analysis and Strategic Uncertainty

We are watching the dinosaurs die, but we don't know what will take their place.
—*Lester Thurow, MIT economist*

There is something in the wind.
—*William Shakespeare, The Comedy of Errors*

A poorly observed fact is more treacherous than a faulty train of reasoning.
—*Paul Valéry, French philosopher*

Thomson Corporation, in 1997, was a Toronto media company that owned some 55 daily newspapers that were doing well.[1] CEO Richard Harrington, however, observed several trends in the environment that caused him to move the firm away from newspapers. He could see that the Internet was going to undercut classified advertising and that cable television and the Internet were going to steal readers. Despite the fact that the company was profitable, he made the rather dramatic decision to divest newspapers and to move the firm into delivering information and services online to the law, education, healthcare, and finance industries. As a result of that decision, Thomson is thriving nine years later while other newspaper-based firms are struggling. The decision was based on projecting existing environmental trends and acting upon them.

In this chapter, the focus changes from the market to the environment surrounding the market. Being curious about the area outside the business is one route to generating creative ideas that could lead to products and strategies. It is also a way to anticipate threats and put a strategy in place, as Thomson did, to neutralize them. The goal is to identify and evaluate trends and events that will affect strategy either directly or indirectly.

78

The direct impact of an observed trend will be of interest, but it is important to look at indirect impact as well.[2] For example, increasing oil prices will affect costs of a firm and its suppliers. However, pursuing the indirect implications can generate additional insights. What about the rising use of oil by China and India? Will they deal with their needs by some political alliances or actions? Will that affect prices and availability? Will conservation get traction and make a difference? Will new technologies affect the supply? What about wind and solar power? Where are the oil profits going to be invested? Such questions will result in a depth of understanding and raise options that take the strategic conversation to a whole new level.

Environmental analysis is by definition very broad and involves casting a wide net. Any trend that will potentially have an impact on strategy is fair game. As a practical matter, the analysis requires some discipline to make sure that it does not become an out-of-control fishing expedition that occupies time and generates reports but provides little real insight and actionable information.

Although environmental analysis has no bounds with respect to subject matter, it is convenient to provide some structure in the form of three areas of inquiry that are often useful: technological trends, consumer trends, and government/economic

---

TECHNOLOGY TRENDS

- To what extent are existing technologies maturing?
- What technological developments or trends are affecting or could affect the industry?

CONSUMER TRENDS

- What are the current or emerging trends in lifestyles, fashions, and other components of culture? Why? What are their implications?
- What demographic trends will affect the market size of the industry or its submarkets? What demographic trends represent opportunities or threats?

GOVERNMENT/ECONOMIC TRENDS

- What changes in regulation are possible? What will their impact be?
- What tax or other incentives are being developed that might affect strategy?
- What are the political risks of operating in a governmental jurisdiction?
- What are the economic prospects and inflation outlets for the countries in which the firm operates? How will they affect strategy?

GENERAL EXTERNAL ANALYSIS QUESTIONS

- What are the significant trends and future events?
- What are threats and opportunities do you see?
- What are the key areas of uncertainty as to trends or events that have the potential to impact strategy? Evaluate these strategic uncertainties in terms of their impact.

SCENARIOS

- What strategic uncertainties are worth being the basis of a scenario analysis?

Figure 5.1   Environmental Analysis

forces. The analysis should not be restricted to these topics. Nevertheless, in the following sections each of these three will be discussed and illustrated.

After describing environmental analysis, the chapter will turn to the task of dealing with strategic uncertainty, a key output of external analysis. Impact analysis and scenario analysis are tools that help to evolve that uncertainty into strategy. Impact analysis—the assessment of the relative importance of strategic uncertainties—is addressed first. Scenario analysis—ways of creating and using future scenarios to help generate and evaluate strategies—follows.

TECHNOLOGY TRENDS

One dimension of environmental analysis is technological trends or technological events occurring outside the market or industry that have the potential to impact strategies. They can represent opportunities and threats to those in a position to capitalize. For example, the cable TV industry, with its massive investment in the wiring of homes, should be concerned with the technology related to satellite alternatives. Express delivery services such as FedEx have been affected by new forms of communication. While e-mail can replace the use of overnight delivery, Internet-based e-commerce has provided a major source of new business for FedEx.

Forecasting Technologies

It is often easy to compile a list of technologies in the wings; the hard part is sorting out the winners from the losers. The experience of the retail sector may provide some guidance. Among the big winners were the 1936 invention of the shopping cart (which allowed customers to buy more and do so more easily) and the UPC scanner (which improved checkout and provided a rich information source). Among the losers were Ted Turner's Checkout Channel (color monitors positioned by the checkout counters in grocery stores), the VideOcart (screens attached to shopping carts that could highlight specials and guide shoppers), and efforts to create home-deliver Internet supermarkets.

Ray Burke, a retail expert from Indiana University, drew upon a variety of research sources to develop a set of guidelines for separating winners from losers. Although his context is retailing, any organization exploring new technologies can benefit from considering each of the guidelines:[3]

- Use technology to create an immediate, tangible benefit for the consumer. The benefit, in short, needs to be perceived as such. The Checkout Channel was designed to help entertain, but consumers saw it as an intrusive annoyance.

- Make the technology easy to use. Consumers resist wasting time and becoming frustrated, and too often new technologies are perceived as doing exactly these things. Research shows that it takes customers an average of 20 to 30 minutes just to learn how to shop in most text-based Internet grocery-shopping systems.

- Execution matters: prototype, test, and refine. One in-store kiosk had no way to inform frustrated customers that it had run out of paper. A bank found customers more receptive to an interactive videoconferencing system when the screens were placed in inviting locations.

- Recognize that customer response to technology varies. One bank found that ATM customers rejected videoconferencing options because they actually did not want to interact with humans. Some retailers use loyalty cards to provide receipts and promotions tailored to individual customers.

Transformational, Substantial, and Incremental Innovations

Innovation can take several forms. In particular, Foster and Kaplan distinguish between incremental, substantial, and transformational innovation.[4] These differ in terms of how new they are and how much wealth they represent for the business. In general, substantial innovations have ten times the impact of incremental innovations; the impact of transformational innovations is ten times greater again.

An incremental innovation makes the offering more attractive or profitable but does not fundamentally change the value proposition or the functional strategy. Adding sails to the clipper ships of the late nineteenth century made them better, but fundamentally they remained the same mode of transport. Adding flavors and package innovations to a line of toothpaste is incremental innovation that adds energy and choice but requires little change in the business model. It is important to track incremental innovation and to recognize competitors skilled in it because it can lead to a forecast of who will be strong competitors in the future. Because firms good at incremental innovation are committed to their business model, they are unlikely to drive real change in the industry.

A transformation innovation will provide a fundamental change in the business model, likely involving a new value proposition and a new way to manufacture, distribute, and/or market the offering. It is likely to make the assets and competencies of established firms irrelevant. The advent of steam power, which ultimately spelled the end of sail-powered transport, was a transformational innovation. The automobile, Southwest Airlines, FedEx, the business model of Dell Computers, mini steel mills, and Cirque du Soleil represent innovations that have transformed markets. Transformational innovations, which sometimes take decades to emerge, are critical to analyze because they represent new competitive landscapes and often attract customers who were on the sidelines because the prior offering was too expensive or lacked some critical element.

Substantial innovations are in between in newness and impact. They often represent a new generation of products, such as the Boeing 747 or Windows XP, that make the existing products obsolete for many. Cisco introduced a videoconference technology called telepresence that uses massive amounts of bandwidth to provide a high-fidelity experience and should expand the usage of videoconferencing. In these cases, the basic value proposition and business model was enhanced but not changed. Substantial innovations are much more common than transformational innovations and involve major changes in the competitive landscape.

Innovations that are transformational or even substantial are often championed by new entrants into the industry. Incumbent firms—especially successful ones—are incented to focus on incremental innovation to protect and improve their profitable niche in the market. Their people, culture, and mix of assets and competencies are unlikely to support a transformational innovation. As a result, when transformational innovations make their appearance, the reaction of incumbent firms is denial, supported by a belief that improvements in the early offerings would not happen. So the horse-drawn buggy manufacturers never became automobile firms, telegraph companies missed out on the telephone, and 3M and others felt that the early and primitive Xerox copy technology would never replace heat-sensitive copier paper.

Impact of New Technologies

Certainly it can be important, even critical, to manage the transition to a new technology. The appearance of a new technology, however, even a successful one, does not necessarily mean that businesses based on the prior technology will suddenly become unhealthy.

A group of researchers at Purdue studied fifteen companies in five industries in which a dramatic new technology had emerged:[5]

- Diesel-electric locomotives versus steam
- Transistors versus vacuum tubes
- Ballpoint pens versus fountain pens
- Nuclear power versus boilers for fossil-fuel plants
- Electric razors versus safety razors

Two interesting conclusions emerged that should give pause to anyone attempting to predict the impact of a dramatic new technology. First, the sales of the old technology continued for a substantial period, in part because the firms involved continued to improve it. Safety-razor sales have actually increased 800 percent since the advent of the electric razor. Thus, a new technology may not signal the end of the growth phase of an existing technology. In all cases, firms involved with the old technology had a substantial amount of time to react to the new technology.

Second, it is relatively difficult to predict the outcome of a new technology. The new technologies studied tended to be expensive and crude at first. Furthermore, they started by invading submarkets. Transistors, for example, were first used in hearing aids and pocket radios. In addition, new technologies tended to create new markets instead of simply encroaching on existing ones. Throwaway ballpoint pens and many of the transistor applications opened up completely new market areas.

CONSUMER TRENDS

Consumer trends can present both threats and opportunities for a wide variety of firms. For example, a dress designer conducted a study that projected women's lifestyles. It predicted that a more varied lifestyle would prevail, that more time

INFORMATION TECHNOLOGY

In nearly every industry it is useful to ask what potential impact new information technology based on new databases will have on strategies. How will it create SCAs and key success factors? Apparel manufacturers such as Levi-Strauss, drug wholesalers such as McKesson, and retailers such as the Limited all have developed systems of inventory control, ordering, and shipping that represent substantial SCAs. FedEx has stayed ahead of competitors by investing heavily in information technology. It was the first express delivery service to have the ability to track packages throughout its systems and the first to link its systems with customers computers. Merrill Lynch's Cash Management Account provided substantial customer benefits.

In supermarket retailing, "smart cards," cards that customers present during checkout to pay for purchases, provide a record of all purchases that allow:

- Stores to build loyalty by rewarding cumulative purchase volume.
- Promotions to target individual customers based on their brand preferences and household characteristics.
- The use of cents-off coupons without the customer or store having to handle pieces of paper; the purchase of a promoted product can be discounted automatically.
- The store to identify buyers of slow-moving items and predict the impact on the store's choice of dropping an item.
- Decisions as to shelf-space allocation, special displays, and store layout to be refined based on detailed information about customer shopping,

would be spent outside the home, and that those who worked would be more career oriented. These predictions had several implications relevant to the dress designer's product line and pricing strategies. For example, a growing number and variety of activities would lead to a broader range of styles and larger wardrobes, with perhaps somewhat less spent on each garment. Furthermore, consumers' increased financial and social independence would probably reduce the number of follow-the-leader fashions and the perception that certain outfits were required for certain occasions.

Cultural Trends

Faith Popcorn has uncovered and studied cultural trends that, in her judgment, will shape the future. Her efforts provide a provocative view of the future environment of many organizations. Consider, for example, the following trends:[6]

- *Cocooning.* Consumers are retreating into safe, cozy "homelike" environments to shield themselves from the harsh realities of the outside world. This trend supports online and catalogue shopping, home security systems, gardening, and smart homes.

- **Fantasy adventure.** Consumers crave low-risk excitement and stimulation to escape from stress and boredom. Responsive firms offer theme restaurants, exotic cosmetics, adventure travel, fantasy clothes that suggest role-playing, fantasy-based entertainment, and fantasy cars.

- **Pleasure revenge.** Consumers are rebelling against rules to cut loose and savor forbidden fruits (for example, indulgent ice creams, cigars, martinis, tanning salons, and furs).

- **Small indulgences.** Busy, stressed-out people are rewarding themselves with affordable luxuries that will provide quick gratification: fresh-squeezed orange juice, chocolate-dipped Tuscan biscotti, crusty bread, and upscale fountain pens. For the financially well off, the range of possibilities might include Porsche flatware, a mahogany Cris-Craft canoe, or Range Rover night-vision binoculars.

- **Down-aging.** Consumers seek symbols of youth, renewal, and rejuvenation to counterbalance the intensity of their adult lives. The over-55 crowd going to school and participating in active sports (including iron man competitions and outdoor adventures) reflect this trend, but it really extends to a wide age group who favor products, apparel, activities, and entertainment that capture the nostalgia of youth.

- **Being alive.** Consumers focus on the quality of life and the importance of wellness, taking charge of their personal health rather than delegating it to the healthcare industry. Examples of this include the use of holistic medical approaches, vegetarian products and restaurants, organic products, water filters, and health clubs.

- **99 lives.** Consumers are forced to assume multiple roles to cope with their increasingly busy lives. Retailers serving multiple needs, ever-faster ways to get prepared food, a service that manages your second home and prepares it for visits, noise neutralizers, e-commerce, and yoga are all responsive to this trend.

There is a trend toward tribing, the affinity toward a social unit that is centered around an interest or activity and is not bound by conventional social links.[7] Harley-Davidson events such as the annual rally in Sturgis, South Dakota, can attract hundreds of thousands of participants. The Macintosh users group has been a strong part of Apple's survival in a PC world. The Internet has generated a host of communities and chat groups that play an influential role through information exchange and social networking. Tribing has significance for brand-building and communication programs, both positively and negatively.

Being Green

A trend that has been growing for decades in the United States has been the green movement (which in Europe is mature). One driver is to provide functional benefits to firms (in the form of cost savings from reduced energy consumption) and customers who benefit from energy saving products like appliances and cars and from the health benefits of organic foods. A second is to actively respond to the threat of global warming that is gaining traction. In California, for example, a 2005 poll by the Public Policy Institute found that two-thirds of the state's voters supported an aggressive attack on global warming.[8] Many firms feel a responsibility to be part of the solution. A third driver is a desire to be respected by customers and employees, both of which value a relationship with a firm that they admire. Those consumers in the generation Y age cohort are particularly sensitive to the environment and the posture firms take toward it.

A firm's response will depend on the organization and what it can do. Some companies with a legacy of concern for the environment and social responsibility will find it comfortable to dial up environmental programs. For others it will require a cultural change that is not easy. What is feasible and appropriate will depend on the nature of the business. Are cost savings associated with environmental actions? As the boxed insert describes, Wal-Mart discovered, to its surprise, that an ambitious environmental program was associated with tangible cost savings. Will customer demand provide sales and margins associated with green products and services? If there is a business rationale behind going green, it is much easier to justify and create momentum. If not, the rationale will need to be more indirect, based on the value of being an industry leader, on making employees proud, and on improving relationships—if not bonding—with those customers (and others such as government officials) that are environmentally sensitive.

Another issue is getting credit for environmental programs. Many firms have developed programs with meaningful investment and substance behind them, but their efforts are invisible. Some of these firms may not want to be visible. If, like Coke, they have a broad audience with large segments that are indifferent or even negative on being green (because they associate it with higher prices or a political agenda they oppose), credit for environmental actions may not be a net positive. Others, like The Body Shop and Ben & Jerry's, have found that being a prominent believer in the green movement raises expectations and increases the risk that they will make a visible misstep. The deforestation of South America, for example, is a complex problem, and some actions made with good intentions could have unintended consequences that would create bad publicity.

But many companies are in the more common position of wanting some image benefit of green initiatives. How can that be accomplished when one survey found that 64 percent of Americans could not name a "green" firm, a percentage that was 51 percent even among those professing to be environmentally aware?[29] One answer is branding. Consider three firms that have used a brand to help them get credit for creating programs and initiatives that are meaningful and worthwhile. BP has repositioned the corporate brand around a tagline, "Beyond Petroleum," that captures its concern for the environment and its commitment to reach out beyond petroleum (which contributes to global warming) for energy solutions. Toyota has long had substantial environmental initiatives that have been largely invisible. However, as the Prius has become the leading hybrid, it has served to make the firm's innovation in the hybrid space prominent and thus affected the Toyota brand. Finally, GE has branded a host of initiatives under the umbrella term "Ecomagination," designed to address challenges around the need for alternative energy and clean water.

WAL-MART TURNS GREEN

In 2005 Wal-Mart began to develop green programs, an amazing turnaround for a company that had prided itself on low costs and prices first and foremost.[10] The firm developed tangible energy reduction targets for its truck fleet and stores. Organic food and even clothes made from organic cotton became featured in Wal-Mart stores. Suppliers that had environmentally responsive products or packaging, from salmon fishermen in Alaska to Unilever (whose compact detergent used less space and package material) were not only favored but aided. Suppliers, some 60,000 of them around the world, were encouraged to become green. Fourteen sustainable-value networks around issues like logistics, packaging, and forest products were formed, consisting of Wal-Mart executives, suppliers, environmental groups, and regulators, with a goal to share information and ideas. Given Wal-Mart's footprint and influence around the world, these programs are likely to make a difference.

Why did Wal-Mart suddenly make such a U-turn? Three reasons. First, the CEO decided it was the right thing to do, based in part on the influence of an environmental professional who had vacationed with members of the outdoor-oriented Walton family. Second, a single-minded focus on costs and the resulting policies regarding employees, communities, and suppliers had generated press attention that was extremely negative, very visible, and affected the company's ability to grow and succeed. More communities were turning down Wal-Mart stores, and 8 percent of Americans were committed to shopping elsewhere. Wal-Mart executives felt that some positive press was needed. Finally, to the surprise of the executives, many of the green programs were helping the bottom line—a change in packaging resulted in significant savings, and the introduction of organic cotton fabrics was a customer hit.

Wal-Mart's experience raises some interesting issues. What is the responsibility for a for-profit organization to contribute to solving the problems of the nation and the world? Was Milton Friedman right when he said that the business of business is to make profits, and that other objectives should be left to the government? What are the problems worth addressing? How should they be addressed? How does an individual business determine what programs will be effective or even helpful when the problems being addressed are so complex?

Demographics

Demographic trends can be a powerful underlying force in a market and can be predictable. Among the influential demographic variables are age, income, education, geographic location, and ethnicity.

The older demographic group is of particular interest, because it is growing rapidly and is blessed with not only resources but the time to use them. The over-65 population in the United States will grow from 33 million in 2000 to 49 million in 2020. The over-85 group will grow from 3.6 million to over 6.5 million in the same time period, and its members will be much more likely to live independently (perhaps in one of roughly 50,000 assisted-living units). Women tend to outlive men, so their portion of the population increases sharply over age groups; within the 85-year-old group there are only 41 men per 100 women. Research suggests that elderly women are dissatisfied at having to choose from products generally geared to younger segments.

Ethnic populations are rising rapidly and support whole firms and industries, as well as affect the strategies of mainline companies. Hispanic populations, for example, are growing about five times faster than are non-Hispanic populations and are gaining in income as well. Hispanics will soon be the largest minority group. The Asian American population, currently numbering over 6 million in the United States, is increasing rapidly.

The nuclear family was once the model of American life. No more! The proportion of U.S. households defined as traditional families (that is, a husband, a wife, and kids under 18) was at 45 percent in 1960, 30.2 percent in 1980, and 23.5 percent in 2000.[11] One of six traditional families has the dad staying home and the mom going to work. One implication is this demographic evolution is an increased demand for handyman services, household cleaning, and meal preparation.

The movement of businesses and populations into different areas of the country has implications for many service organizations, such as brokerage houses, real estate ventures, and insurance companies. Furthermore, the revival of downtown urban areas has had considerable implications for retailers and real estate developers, just as the earlier development of suburbia had.

GOVERNMENT/ECONOMIC TRENDS

The addition or removal of legislative or regulatory constraints can pose major strategic threats and opportunities. For example, the ban of some ingredients in food products or cosmetics has dramatically affected the strategies of numerous firms. The impact of governmental efforts to reduce piracy in industries such as software (more than one-fourth of all software used is copied), CDs, DVDs, and movie videos is of crucial import to those affected. Deregulation in banking, energy, and other industries is having implications for the firms involved. The automobile industry is affected by fuel-economy standards and by the luxury tax on automobiles. The relaxation of regulatory constraints in India and China can have enormous implications for global firms.

In an increasingly global economy with interdependencies in markets and in the sourcing of products and services, possible political hot spots need to be understood and tracked. In a classic study of environmental trends and events that were forecast in *Fortune* magazine during the 1930s and 1940s, predictions were found to be remarkably good in many areas such as synthetic vitamins, genetic breakthroughs, the decline of railroads, and the advent of TVs, house-trailers, and superhighways. However, forecasting was extremely poor when international events were involved.[12] Thus, a mid-1930s article did not consider the possibility of U.S. involvement in a European war. A 1945 article incorrectly forecast a huge growth in trade with the Soviet Union, not anticipating the advent of the cold war. A Middle East scenario failed to forecast the emergence of Israel. International political developments, which can be critical to multinational firms, are still extremely difficult to forecast. A prudent strategy is one that is both diversified and flexible, so that a political surprise will not be devastating.

The evaluation of some strategies will be affected by judgments made about the economy, particularly about inflation and general economic health as measured by unemployment and economic growth. Heavy investment in a capital-intensive industry might need to be timed to coincide with a strong economy to avoid a damaging period of losses. Usually it is necessary to look beyond the general economy to the health of individual industries, such as housing, energy, and healthcare, and to sectors within industries.

A forecast of the relative valuations of currencies can be relevant for industries with multinational competitors. Thus, an analysis of the balance of payments and other factors affecting currency valuations might be needed. For example, in most developed countries, the automobile industry is extremely sensitive to changes in currency valuation.

DEALING WITH STRATEGIC UNCERTAINTY

Strategic uncertainty, uncertainty that has strategic implications, is a key construct in external analysis. A typical external analysis will emerge with dozens of strategic uncertainties. To be manageable, they need to be grouped into logical clusters or themes. It is then useful to assess the importance of each cluster in order to set priorities with respect to information gathering and analysis. Impact analysis, described in the next section, is designed to accomplish that assessment.

Sometimes the strategic uncertainty is represented by a future trend or event that has inherent unpredictability. Information gathering and additional analysis will

---

"YES, BUT..."

Some trends are real, but have obvious implications that need to be qualified. For example:

Yes, the number of women in the workforce has been increasing, *but...*

The increase is slow and long-term, with the total proportion rising from 42 percent in 1980 to 45 percent in 1990 and 47 percent in 2000. Further, only a small percentage of these women fit the image of the young MBA.

Yes, Internet access and usage are growing rapidly, *but...*

A significant proportion of the population still sees no need for the Internet and some are outright hostile toward technology.

Yes, people can and will price shop on the Internet, *but...*

Many are loyal to single sites and do not use price comparison services.

Yes, there is a strong trend to healthy eating and exercise, *but...*

Indulgent foods like upscale chocolates, super-premium ice cream, and high-fat burgers are still a substantial and sometimes growing niche.

not be able to reduce the uncertainty. In that case, scenario analysis can be employed. Scenario analysis basically accepts the uncertainty as given and uses it to drive a description of two or more future scenarios. Strategies are then developed for each. One outcome could be a decision to create organizational and strategic flexibility so that as the business context changes the strategy will adapt. Scenario analysis will be detailed in the final section of this chapter.

IMPACT ANALYSIS—ASSESSING THE IMPACT OF STRATEGIC UNCERTAINTIES

An important objective of external analysis is to rank the strategic uncertainties and decide how they are to be managed over time. Which uncertainties merit intensive investment in information gathering and in-depth analysis, and which merit only a low-key monitoring effort?

The problem is that dozens of strategic uncertainties and many second-level strategic uncertainties are often generated. These strategic uncertainties can lead to an endless process of information gathering and analysis that can absorb resources indefinitely. A publishing company may be concerned about cable TV, lifestyle patterns, educational trends, geographic population shifts, and printing technology. Any one of these issues involves a host of subfields and could easily spur limitless research. For example, cable TV might involve a variety of pay-TV concepts, suppliers, technologies, and viewer reactions. Unless distinct priorities are established, external analysis can become descriptive, ill-focused, and inefficient.

The extent to which a strategic uncertainty should be monitored and analyzed depends on its impact and immediacy.

1. The impact of a strategic uncertainty is related to:
   - The extent to which it involves trends or events that will impact existing or potential businesses
   - The importance of the involved businesses
   - The number of involved businesses

2. The immediacy of a strategic uncertainty is related to:
   - The probability that the involved trends or events will occur
   - The time frame of the trends or events
   - The reaction time likely to be available, compared with the time required to develop and implement appropriate strategy

Impact of a Strategic Uncertainty

Each strategic uncertainty involves potential trends or events that could have an impact on present, proposed, and even potential businesses. For example, a strategic uncertainty for a beer firm could be based on the future prospects of the microbrewery market. If the beer firm has both a proposed microbrewery entry and an imported beer positioned in the same area, trends in the microbrewery beer market could have a high impact on the firm. The trend toward natural foods may present opportunities for a sparkling water product line for the same firm and be the basis of a strategic uncertainty.

The impact of a strategic uncertainty will depend on the importance of the impacted business to a firm. Some businesses are more important than others. The importance of established businesses may be indicated by their associated sales, profits, or costs. However, such measures might need to be supplemented for proposed or growth businesses for which present sales, profits, or costs may not reflect the true value to a firm. Finally, because an information-need area may affect several businesses, the number of involved businesses can also be relevant to a strategic uncertainty's impact.

Immediacy of Strategic Uncertainties

Events or trends associated with strategic uncertainties may have a high impact but such a low probability of occurrence that it is not worth actively expending resources to gather or analyze information. Similarly, if occurrence is far in the future relative to the strategic-decision horizon, then it may be of little concern. Thus, the harnessing of tide energy may be so unlikely or may occur so far in the future that it is of no concern to a utility.

Finally, there is the reaction time available to a firm, compared with the reaction time likely to be needed. After a trend or event crystallizes, a firm needs to develop a reaction strategy. If the available reaction time is inadequate, it becomes important to anticipate emerging trends and events better so that future reaction strategies can be initiated sooner.

Managing Strategic Uncertainties

Figure 5.2 suggests a categorization of strategic uncertainties for a given business. If both the immediacy and impact are low, then a low level of monitoring may suffice. If the impact is thought to be low but the immediacy is high, the area may merit monitoring and analysis. If the immediacy is low and the impact high, then the area may require monitoring and analysis in more depth, and contingent strategies may be considered but not necessarily developed and implemented. When both the immediacy and potential impact of the underlying trends and events are high, then an in-depth analysis will be appropriate, as will be the development of reaction plans or strategies. An active task force may provide initiative.

SCENARIO ANALYSIS

Scenario analysis can help deal with uncertainty. It provides an alternative to investing in information to reduce uncertainty that is often an expensive and futile process. By creating a small number of marketplace or market context scenarios and assessing their likelihood and impact, scenario analysis can be a powerful way to deal with complex environments.

There are two types of scenario analyses. In the first type, strategy-developing scenarios, the object is to provide insights into future competitive contexts, then

Immediacy

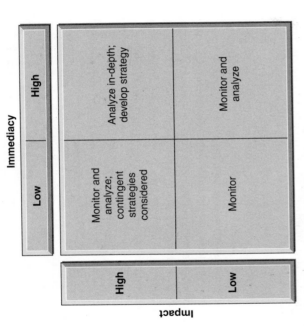

	Low	High
High	Monitor and analyze; contingent strategies considered	Analyze in-depth; develop strategy
Low	Monitor	Monitor and analyze

Impact

Figure 5.2   Strategic Uncertainty Categories

use these insights to evaluate existing business strategies and stimulate the creation of new ones. Such analyses can help create contingency plans to guard against disasters—an airline adjusting to a terror incident, for example, or a pharmaceutical company reacting to a product safety problem. They can also suggest investment strategies that enable the organization to capitalize on future opportunities caused by customer trends or technological breakthroughs.

In the second type of analyses, decision-driven scenarios, a strategy is proposed and tested against several scenarios that are developed.[13] The goal is to challenge the strategies, thereby helping to make the go/no-go decision and suggesting ways to make the strategy more robust in withstanding competitive forces. If the decision is to enter a market with a technology strategy, alternate scenarios could be built around variables such as marketplace acceptance of the technology, competitor response, and the stimulation of customer applications.

In either case, a scenario analysis will involve three general steps: the creation of scenarios, relating those scenarios to existing or potential strategies, and assessing the probability of the scenarios (see Figure 5.3).

Identify Scenarios

Strategic uncertainties can drive scenario development. The impact analysis will identify the strategic uncertainty with the highest priority for a firm. A manufacturer of a medical imagery device may want to know whether a technological advance will allow its machine to be made at a substantially lower cost. A farm equipment manufacturer or ski area operator may believe that the weather—whether a drought will continue, for example—is the most important area of uncertainty. A server firm may want to know whether a single software standard will emerge or multiple standards will coexist. The chosen uncertainty could then stimulate two or more scenarios.

A competitor scenario analysis can be driven by the uncertainly surrounding a competitor's strategy. For example, could the competitor aggressively extend its brand? Or might it divest a product line or make a major acquisition? Perhaps the competitor could change its value proposition, or become more aggressive in its pricing.[14]

When a set of scenarios is based largely on a single strategic uncertainty, the scenarios themselves can usually be enriched by related events and circumstances. Thus, an inflation-stimulated recession scenario would be expected to generate a host of conditions for the appliance industry, such as price increases and retail failures. Similarly, a competitor scenario can be comprehensive, specifying such strategy dimensions as product-market investment, acquisition or joint ventures, pricing, positioning, product, and promotions.

It is sometimes useful to generate scenarios based on probable outcomes: optimistic, pessimistic, and most likely. The consideration of a pessimistic scenario is often useful in testing existing assumptions and plans. The aura of optimism that often surrounds a strategic plan may include implicit assumptions that competitors will not aggressively respond, the market will not fade or collapse, or technological problems will not surface. Scenario analysis provides a nonthreatening way to consider the possibility of clouds or even rain on the picnic.

Often, of course, several variables are relevant to the future period of interest. The combination can define a relatively large number of scenarios. For example, a large greeting-card firm might consider three variables important: the success of small boutique card companies, the life of a certain card type, and the nature of future distribution channels. The combination can result in many possible scenarios. Experience has shown that two or three scenarios are the ideal number with which to work; any more, and the process becomes unwieldy and any value is largely lost. Thus, it is important to reduce the number of scenarios by identifying a small set that ideally includes those that are plausible/credible and those that represent departures from the present substantial enough to affect strategy development.

Relate Scenarios to Strategies

After scenarios have been identified, the next step is to relate them to strategy—both existing strategies and new options. If an existing strategy is in place, it can be tested with respect to each scenario. Which scenario will be the best one? How bad will the strategy be if the wrong scenario emerges? What will its prospects be with respect to customer acceptance, competitor reactions, and sales and profits? Could it be modified to enhance its prospects?

Figure 5.3   Scenario Analysis

Even if the scenario analysis is not motivated by a desire to generate new strategy options, it is always useful to consider what strategies would be optimal for each scenario. A scenario by its nature will provide a perspective that is different from the status quo. Any strategy that is optimal for a given scenario should become a viable option. Even if it is not considered superior or even feasible, some elements of it might be captured.

Estimate Scenario Probabilities

To evaluate alternative strategies it is useful to determine the scenario probabilities. The task is actually one of environmental forecasting, except that the total scenario may be a rich combination of several variables. Experts could be asked to assess probabilities directly. A deeper understanding will often emerge, however, if causal factors underlying each scenario can be determined. For example, the construction equipment industry might develop scenarios based on three alternative levels of construction activity. These levels would have several contributing causes. One would be the interest rate. Another could be the availability of funds to the homebuilding sector, which in turn would depend on the emerging structure of financial institutions and markets. A third cause might be the level of government spending on roads, energy, and other areas.

KEY LEARNINGS

- Environmental analysis of technology and consumer and government/economic trends can detect opportunities or threats relevant to an organization.

- The green movement provides opportunities to connect to customers and employees.

- Impact analysis involves assessing systematically the impact and immediacy of the trends and events that underlie each strategy uncertainty.

- Scenario analysis, a vehicle to explore different assumptions about the future, involves the creation of two to three plausible scenarios, the development of strategies appropriate to each, the assessment of scenario probabilities, and the evaluation of the resulting strategies across the scenarios.

FOR DISCUSSION

1. What did the fax machine replace, if anything? What will replace (or has replaced) the fax machine? When will the fax machine disappear?

2. Develop a scenario based on the proposition that hydrogen-fueled cars will continue to improve and take 15 percent of the automotive market in a few years. Analyze it from the point of view of an energy company like Shell, or a car company like Mercedes.

3. Wi-Fi, the wireless Internet access concept, which is supported by Intel's Centrino chip (which frees computers from hard-wired connections), has raised expectations throughout the computer industry. Will this change the use of computers? How? Will it change the type of computers made?

4. Pick a company or brand/business on which to focus. What are the major trends that come out of an environmental analysis? What are the major areas of uncertainty? How would a major company in the industry handle those best?

5. Focusing on the airline industry, develop a list of strategic uncertainties and possible strategic actions.

6. Address the questions posed in the Wal-Mart insert.

7. Consider Cisco's "telepresence" in videoconferencing, which upgrades the quality of the experience. Will it change the incidence of usage? What is driving usage (or lack of usage) of videoconferencing?

NOTES

1. Ram Charan, "Sharpening Your Business Acumen," *Strategy & Business*, Spring 2006, pp. 49–57.

2. Ibid., p. 50.

3. Raymond Burke, "Confronting the Challenges That Face Bricks-and-Mortar Stores," *Harvard Business Review*, July–August 1999, pp. 160–167.

4. Richard Forster and Sarah Kaplan, *Creative Destruction*, New York: Currency, 2001.

5. Arnold Cooper, Edward Demuzilo, Kenneth Hatten, Elijah Hicks, and Donald Tock, "Strategic Responses to Technological Threats," *Academy of Management Proceedings*, 1976, pp. 54–60.

6. Faith Popcorn and Lys Marigold, *Clicking*, New York: HarperCollins, 1997, pp. 11–12.

7. Sam Hill, *60 Trends in 60 Minutes*, New York: John Wiley & Sons, 2003, p. 96.

8. "California Leads on Warming," editorial, *New York Times*, August 5, 2006.

9. Wendy Melillo and Steve Miller, "Companies Find It's Not Easy Being Green," *BrandWeek*, July 24, 2006.

10. Mac Gunther, "The Green Machine," *Fortune*, August 7, 2006, pp. 42–57.

11. Sam Hill, op. cit., p. 93.

12. Richard N. Farmer, "Looking Back at Looking Forward," *Business Horizons*, February 1973, pp. 21–28.

13. Hugh Courtney, "Decision-Driven Scenarios for Assessing Four Levels of Uncertainty," *Strategy & Leadership*, Vol. 31, No. 1, 2003, pp. 14–16.

14. Liam Fahey, "Competitor Scenarios," *Strategy & Leadership*, Vol. 31, No. 1, 2003, pp. 32–44.

CHAPTER SIX

Internal Analysis

We have met the enemy and he is us.
—*Pogo*

Self-conceit may lead to self-destruction.
—*Aesop, "The Frog and the Ox"*

The fish is last to know if it swims in water.
—*Chinese proverb*

Should the existing strategy be enhanced, expanded, altered, or replaced? Are existing assets and competencies adequate to win? An internal analysis of the business will help the strategist address these questions. This exploration is similar in scope to an analysis of a competitor or strategic group, but much richer and deeper because of its importance to strategy and because much more information is available.

Just as strategy can be developed at the level of a business, a group of businesses, or the firm, internal analysis can also be conducted at each of these levels. Of course, analyses at different levels will differ from each other in emphasis and content, but their structure and thrust will be the same. The common goal is to identify organizational strengths, weaknesses, and constraints and, ultimately, to develop responsive strategies, either exploiting strengths or correcting or compensating for weaknesses.

Four aspects of internal analysis will be discussed in this chapter. The first, financial performance, provides an initial approximation as to how the business is doing. The second, an analysis of other performance dimensions such as customer satisfaction, product quality, brand association, relative cost, new products, and employee capability, can often provide a more robust link to future profitability. The third is an analysis of the strengths and weaknesses that are the basis of current and future strategies. The fourth is an identification and prioritization of the threats and opportunities facing the firm.

The final section explores the relationship between strategy and the analysis of the organization, its competitors, and the market. It suggests that successful strategy is when organization strengths are matched against market needs and competitor weaknesses.

FINANCIAL PERFORMANCE— SALES AND PROFITABILITY

Internal analysis often starts with an analysis of current financials, measures of sales and profitability. Either can signal a change in the market viability of a product line and the ability to produce competitively. Furthermore, they provide an indicator of the success of past strategies and thus can often help in evaluating whether strategic changes are needed. In addition, sales and profitability at least appear to be specific and easily measured. As a result, it is not surprising that they are so widely used as performance evaluation tools.

Sales and Market Share

A sensitive measure of how customers regard a product or service can be sales or market share. After all, if the value proposition to a customer changes, sales and share should be affected, although there may be an occasional delay caused by market and customer inertia.

Sales levels can be strategically important. Increased sales can mean that the customer base has grown. An enlarged customer base, if we assume that new customers will develop loyalty, will mean future sales and profits. Increased share can provide the potential to gain SCAs in the form of economies of scale and experience curve effects. Conversely, decreased sales can mean decreases in customer bases and a loss of scale economies.

A problem with using sales as a measure is that it can be affected by short-term actions, such as promotions by a brand and its competitors. Thus, it is necessary to separate changes in sales that are caused by tactical actions from those that represent fundamental changes in the value delivered to the customer, and it is important to couple an analysis of sales or share with an analysis of customer satisfaction and loyalty, which will be discussed shortly.

Profitability

The ultimate measure of a firm's ability to prosper and survive is its profitability. Although both growth and profitability are desirable, establishing a priority between the two can help guide strategic decision making.

A host of measures and ratios reflect profitability, includings margins, costs, and profits. Building on the assets employed leads to the return on assets (ROA) measure, which can be decomposed with a formula developed by General Motors and DuPont in the 1920s.

$$ROA = \frac{profits}{sales} \times \frac{sales}{assets}$$

Thus, return on assets can be considered as having two causal factors. The first is the profit margin, which depends on the selling price and cost structure. The second is the asset turnover, which depends on inventory control and asset utilization.

The determination of both the numerator and denominator of the ROA terms is not as straightforward as might be assumed. Substantial issues surround each, such as the distortions caused by depreciation and the fact that book assets do not reflect intangible assets, such as brand equity, or the market value of tangible assets.

Measuring Performance: Shareholder Value Analysis

The concept of shareholder value, an enormously influential concept during the past two decades, provides an answer to this question. Each business should earn an ROA (based on a flow of profits emanating from an investment) that meets or exceeds the costs of capital, which is the weighted average of the cost of equity and cost of debt. Thus, if the cost of equity is 16 percent and the cost of debt is 8 percent, the cost of capital would be 12 percent if the amount of debt was equal to the amount of equity; if there were only one-fourth as much debt as equity, then the cost of capital would be 14 percent. If the return is greater than the cost of capital, shareholder value will increase, and if it is less shareholder value will decrease.

Some of the routes to increasing shareholder value are as follows:

- Earn more profit by reducing costs or increasing revenue without using more capital.
- Invest in high-return products (this, of course, is what strategy is all about).
- Reduce the cost of capital by increasing the debt to equity ratio or by buying back stock to reduce the cost of equity.
- Use less capital. Under shareholder value analysis, the assets employed are no longer a free good, so there is an incentive to reduce it. If improved just-in-time operations can reduce the inventory, it directly affects shareholder value.

The concept of shareholder value is theoretically valid.[1] If a profit stream can be estimated accurately from a strategic move, the analysis will be sound. The problem is that short-term profits (known to affect stock return and thus shareholder wealth) are easier to estimate and manipulate than long-term profits. Investors who assume that short-term profits predict longer-term profits pay undue attention to the former, as does the top management of a company with numerical targets to meet. The discipline to invest in a strategy that will sacrifice short-term financial performance for long-term prospects is not easy to come by, especially if some of the future prospects are in the form of options. For example, the investment in Saturn by General Motors gave it an option to expand that nameplate if a gas shortage should occur and smaller cars became more popular. Similarly, when Black & Decker bought the small-appliance division of GE, it bought an option to take the business into related areas.

The impact of reducing investment is also not without risks. When, for example, Coca-Cola sold off its bottlers to reduce investment and improve shareholder value, its control of the quality of its product may have been reduced. In general, investment reduction often means outsourcing, with its balancing act between flexibility and loss of control over operations. A company that outsources its call center reduces its control over customer interaction.

One danger of shareholder value analysis is that it reduces the priority given to other stakeholders such as employees, suppliers, and customers, each of whom represents assets that can form the basis for long-term success. The radical downsizing of some firms has resulted in going beyond trimming fat to reducing future prospects. Even GE during the 1990s reduced its expenditures on R&D (as a percentage of sales) in part to enhance shareholder value. General Motors' aggressive move to reduce supplier costs damaged some relationships that were generating technological advances and cost savings. An effort to reduce costs can too easily cut into customer service and thus customer loyalty.

In fact, shareholder value management has met with very mixed results. However, one study of the experience of 125 firms found similarities among those that had applied shareholder value concepts successfully.[2] These companies:

- Gave priority to shareholder value over other goals, particularly growth goals.
- Provided intensive training throughout the organization regarding shareholder value and made it a practical tool for business managers at all levels. The philosophy was not restricted to the executive suite.
- Were disciplined in identifying the drivers of shareholder value. For example, for a call center, drivers could be the length of time to answer calls and the quality of responses.
- Reduced overhead by adapting the current accounting system and integrating shareholder value analysis with strategic planning.

These firms found a variety of benefits. First, the concept led to value-creating divestments that otherwise would not have occurred. Second, firms were able to transfer corporate planning and decision making to decentralized business units because all units tended to use the same logic, metrics, and mindset. Third, the business investment horizon tended to be longer, with projects with multi-year time frames getting approved. Fourth, the new recognition that capital had a cost tended to generate better strategic decisions.

PERFORMANCE MEASUREMENT—BEYOND PROFITABILITY

One of the difficulties in strategic market management is developing performance indicators that convincingly represent long-term prospects. The temptation is to focus on short-term profitability measures and to reduce investment in new products and brand images that have long-term payoffs.

The concept of net present value represents a long-term profit stream, but it is not always operational. It often provides neither a criterion for decision making nor

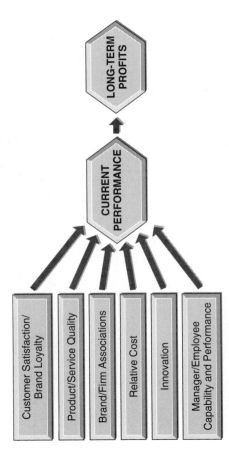

```
┌─────────────────────────┐
│  Customer Satisfaction/ │
│     Brand Loyalty       │
└─────────────────────────┘

┌─────────────────────────┐
│  Product/Service Quality│
└─────────────────────────┘

┌─────────────────────────┐
│  Brand/Firm Associations│
└─────────────────────────┘        CURRENT          ➤   LONG-TERM
                                  PERFORMANCE              PROFITS
┌─────────────────────────┐
│      Relative Cost      │
└─────────────────────────┘

┌─────────────────────────┐
│       Innovation        │
└─────────────────────────┘

┌─────────────────────────┐
│    Manager/Employee     │
│ Capability and Performance│
└─────────────────────────┘
```

Figure 6.1   Performance Measures Reflecting Long-term Profitability

a useful performance measure. It is somewhat analogous to preferring $6 million to $4 million. The real question involves determining which strategic alternative will generate $6 million and which will generate $4 million.

It is necessary to develop performance measures that will reflect long-term viability and health. The focus should be on the assets and competencies that underlie the current and future strategies and their SCAs. What are the key assets and competencies for a business during the planning horizon? What strategic dimensions are most crucial: to become more competitive with respect to product offerings, to develop new products, or to become more productive? These types of questions can help identify performance areas that a business should examine. Answers will vary depending on the situation, but, as suggested by Figure 6.1, they will often include customer satisfaction/brand loyalty, product/service quality, brand/firm associations, relative cost, new product activity, and manager/employee capability and performance.

Customer Satisfaction/Brand Loyalty

Perhaps the most important asset of many firms is the loyalty of the customer base. Measures of sales and market share are useful but potentially inaccurate indicators of how customers really feel about a firm. Such measures can reflect market inertia and are noisy, in part, because of competitor actions and market fluctuations. Measures of customer satisfaction and brand loyalty are much more sensitive and provide diagnostic value as well.

Guidelines for Measuring Satisfaction and Loyalty

First, problems and causes of dissatisfaction that may motivate customers to change brands or firms should be identified. In fact, the most sensitive and insightful information comes from those who have decided to leave a brand or firm. Thus, exit interviews for customers who have abandoned a brand can be productive. Second, there is a big difference between a brand or firm being liked and the absence of dissatisfaction. The size and intensity of the customer group that truly likes a brand or firm should be known. Third, the lifetime value of a customer based on their usage level and the time period that they are expected to be attached to the firm's offerings is often a useful concept. Estimation of lifetime value for key segments can be illuminating. Fourth, measures should be tracked over time and compared with those of competitors. Relative comparisons and changes are most important.

Product and Service Quality

A product (or service) and its components should be critically and objectively compared both with the competition and with customer expectations and needs. How good a value is it? Can it really deliver superior performance? How does it compare with competitor offerings? How will it compare with competitor offerings in the future given competitive innovations? One common failing of firms is to avoid tough comparisons with a realistic assessment of competitors' current and potential offerings. A newly appointed CEO of Frito-Lay once put all programs on hold for a year until the firm's manufacturing units around the world were able to make products that would win blind taste tests. He realized that product quality was a necessary condition for success.

Product and service quality are usually based on several critical dimensions that can be identified and measured over time. For example, an automobile manufacturer can measure defects, ability to perform to specifications, durability, reparability, and features. A bank might be concerned with waiting time, accuracy of transactions, and the quality of the customer experience. A computer manufacturer can examine relative performance specifications and product reliability as reflected by repair data. A business that requires better marketing of a good product line is very different from one that has basic product deficiencies.

Brand/Firm Associations

An often overlooked asset of a brand or firm is what customers think of it. What are its associations? What is its perceived quality? Perceived quality, which is sometimes very different from actual quality, can be based on experience with past products or services and on quality cues, such as retailer types, pricing strategies, packaging, advertising, and typical customers. Is a brand or firm regarded as expert in a product or technology area (such as designing and making sailboats)? Innovative? Expensive? For the country club set? Is it associated with a country, a user type, or an application area (such as racing)? Such associations can be key strategic assets for a brand or firm.

Associations can be monitored by regularly asking customers to describe their use experiences and to tell what a brand or firm means to them. The identification of changes in important associations will likely emerge from such efforts. Structured surveys using a representative sample of customers can provide even more precise tracking information.

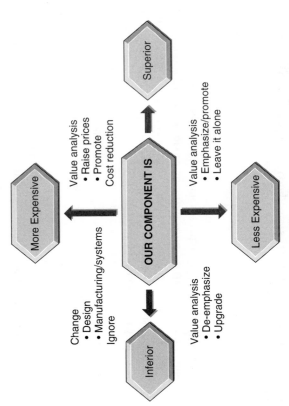

Figure 6.2 Relative Cost *vs.* Relative Performance—Strategic Implications

Relative Cost

A careful cost analysis of a product (or service) and its components, which can be critical when a strategy is dependent on achieving a cost advantage or cost parity, involves tearing down competitors' products and analyzing their systems in detail. The Japanese consultant Ohmae suggested that such an analysis, when coupled with performance analysis, can lead to one of the four situations shown in Figure 6.2.[3]

If a component such as a car's braking system or a bank's teller operation is both more expensive than and inferior to that of the competition, a strategic problem requiring change may exist. An analysis could show, however, that the component is such a small item in terms of both cost and customer impact that it should be ignored. If the component is competitively superior, however, a cost-reduction program may not be the only appropriate strategy. A value analysis, in which the component's value to the customer is quantified, may suggest that the point of superiority could support a price increase or promotion campaign. If, on the other hand, a component is less expensive than that of the competition, but inferior, a value analysis might suggest that it be de-emphasized. Thus, for a car with a cost advantage but handling disadvantage, a company might de-emphasize its driving performance and position it as an economy car. An alternative is to upgrade this component. Conversely, if a component is both less expensive and superior, a value analysis may suggest that the component be emphasized, perhaps playing a key role in positioning and promotion strategies.

Sources of Cost Advantage

The many routes to cost advantage will be discussed in Chapter 8. They include economies of scale, the experience curve, product design innovations, and the use of a no-frills product offering. Each provides a different perspective to the concept of competing on the basis of a cost advantage.

Average Costing

In average costing, some elements of fixed or semivariable costs are not carefully allocated but instead are averaged over total production. Average costing can provide an opening for competitors to enter an otherwise secure market. For example, the J. B. Kunz Company, a maker of passbooks for banks, created a situation in which large-order customers were subsidizing small-order customers because of average costing.[4] The cost system inflated the costs of processing very large orders and thus provided an opportunity for competitors to underbid Kunz on these very profitable orders. A product line that is subsidizing other lines is vulnerable, representing an opportunity to competitors and thus a potential threat to a business.

Innovation

Does the R&D operation generate a stream of new product concepts? How does the flow of patents compare to that for competitors? Is the process from product concept to new product introduction well managed? Is there a track record of successful new products that have affected the product performance profile and market position?

Are the new products arriving in the marketplace in a timely fashion? Time to market is particularly important in many industries, from cars to software.

More broadly, does the organizational culture support innovation? Is it possible to generate substantial (if not transformational) innovations in addition to incremental innovations? Are there programs to precipitate innovation?

Manager/Employee Capability and Performance

Also key to a firm's long-term prospects are the people who must implement strategies. Are the human resources in place to support current and future strategies? Do those who are added to the organization match its needs in terms of types and quality or are there gaps that are not being filled? Is there enough diversity so that the organization can identify and respond to new threats and opportunities when they are not within the existing business arena?

An organization should be evaluated not only on how well it obtains human resources but also on how well it nurtures them. A healthy organization will consist of individuals who are motivated, challenged, fulfilled, and growing in their professions. Each of these dimensions can be observed and measured by employee surveys and group discussions. Certainly the attitude of production workers was a key factor in the quality and cost advantage that Japanese automobile firms enjoyed throughout the past three decades. In service industries such as banking and fast foods, the ability to sustain positive employee performance and attitude is usually a key success factor.

STRENGTHS AND WEAKNESSES

In developing or implementing strategy, it is important to identify the assets and competencies that represent areas of strength and weakness. A successful strategy needs to be based on assets and competencies because it is generally easier for competitors to duplicate what you do rather than who you are. Further, current assets and competencies, as illustrated in Chapter 11, can be leveraged to create new businesses.

Figure 3.6 had a partial list of the types of assets and competencies that an organization might develop. There were more than three dozen, organized under the categories of innovation, manufacturing, access to capital, management, marketing, and customer base. This checklist is a good place to start when identifying the most relevant assets and competencies. Another are the motivating questions introduced in Chapter 3 that identify assets and competencies important to customers, those developed by successful competitors, and those representing large or important parts of the value added chain.

Each asset or competence relevant to the business, such as a new product development capability, access to low-cost labor, an innovative culture, brand strength, or a loyal customer base, should be evaluated as to its strength and impact.

Is it dominant in that it provides a point of advantage that has endured and is likely to remain so in the future? The manufacturing capability of Toyota, for example, is so superior that the company invites others to observe its plants, knowing that competitors cannot duplicate its culture and process. Is the organization able and willing to invest to make the asset or competence dominant into the future? Certainly, Toyota has shown this willingness over many decades. The investment commitment needs to be factored into the financial resource picture. It may mean that resources for new ventures will be limited.

Is it strong but vulnerable? Are others catching up? Should the firm attempt to invest to regain a dominant position so that it is a point of advantage? If so, what program at what cost is implied? Or should the firm retreat so that the asset or competence is simply a modest advantage over some competitors and a point of parity with respect to others?

Is the asset or competence adequate, a point of parity? Is it strong enough so that customers do not avoid the firm because of it? If so, is that a satisfactory long-term position? Can advantage be achieved on other dimensions? What investment is implied to maintain the current strength so that it does not become a point of disadvantage? Product quality is often in this situation. If Target, for example, can deliver quality adequate enough so that customers do not use a quality judgment as a reason to exclude Target for their consideration set, the battle will shift to other dimensions on which Target is likely to excel.

Is it a liability? Is it holding back the firm from gaining and retaining customers? Consider the Korean automobile firms whose quality and social acceptability deficit precluded people from buying their products. They needed to convert this liability to a point of parity.

THREATS AND OPPORTUNITIES

The other half of an internal analysis is the identification of threats and opportunities. In the external analysis, a host of potential threats and opportunities will have been identified. The internal challenge is to determine which are most relevant for the

BENCHMARKING

Comparing the performance of a business component with others is called *benchmarking*. The goal is to generate specific ideas for improvement, and also to define standards at which to aim. One target may be competitors: what cost and performance levels are they achieving, and how? Knowing your deficits with respect to the competition is the first step to developing programs to eliminate them. Best-practice companies are another target. Thus, many benchmark against Disney in terms of delivering consistent service in their theme parks, or Amazon as the standard for Internet e-commerce operations and customer support. Looking outside one's own industry is often a way to break away from the status quo and thereby create a real advantage.

firm's business and to prioritize them. The dimensions used to manage strategic uncertainly in general, immediacy and impact, are appropriate when assessing threats and opportunities.

Those threats that are imminent and have high impact should drive a strategic imperative, a program that has the highest priority. If there is a visible quality problem (such as contaminated Perrier water or defective tires on Ford Explorers, for example), fixing that problem and thus addressing the associated threat needs to be a high priority. When the threat is of low impact or is not immediate, a more measured response is possible.

The most extreme threat is one that potentially makes obsolete the business model. AOL with its "You've got mail" greeting and a route to the Internet for newbies and the intimidated, had a dominant business model with some 35 million subscribers. However, it failed to respond to the fact that its customers eventually obtained more sophistication and better equipment. AOL was in a position to be the social network Internet company, but instead watched others like myspace.com assume that role and allowed its value proposition to erode. Dialing up the threat to the business model in a timely fashion and making the organization responsive might have led to a very different outcome for AOL.

Threats can come in the form of a strategic problem or a liability. Strategic problems, events, or trends adversely affecting strategy generally need to be addressed aggressively and corrected even if the fix is difficult and expensive. Strategic liabilities—the absence of an asset (such as good location) or competence (for example, new-product introduction skills)—usually require a different response. A business often copes over time with a liability by adjusting strategies in a way that will neutralize that liability.

An opportunity similarly can be evaluated as to whether its impact will be immediate and major. If so, the organization should be set up to move quickly and decisively. One study found that most organizations only get faced with a "golden opportunity" once or twice a decade. The mark of a firm that can adapt to new conditions and still come out a market leader is recognizing and reacting to such opportunities. Opportunities that have a low impact or are in the future may justify serious investment and perhaps an experimental entry into a new business area to gain information, but the resource commitment is likely to be more modest.

In general, lost opportunities are costly and are only too common. As Drucker once said, mangers need to spend more time on opportunities and less on solving problems.

FROM ANALYSIS TO STRATEGY

In making strategic decisions, inputs from a variety of assessments are relevant, as the last several chapters have already made clear. However, the core of any strategic decision should be based on three types of assessments. The first concerns organizational strengths and weaknesses. The second evaluates competitor strengths, weaknesses, and strategies, because an organization's strength is of less value if it is neutralized by a competitor's strength or strategy. The third assesses the competitive context, the customers and their needs, the market, and the market environment in order to determine how attractive the selected market will be, given the business strategy.

The goal is to develop a strategy that exploits business strengths and competitor weaknesses and neutralizes business weaknesses and competitor strengths. The ideal is to compete in a healthy, growing industry with a strategy based on strengths that are unlikely to be acquired or neutralized by competitors. Figure 6.3 summarizes how these three assessments combine to influence strategy.

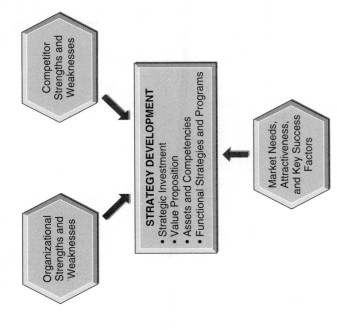

Figure 6.3   Structuring Strategic Decisions

GE's decision to sell its small-appliance division illustrates these strategic principles.[5] Small appliances were a part of GE's legacy and linked to its lamp and major-appliance product lines in the minds of retailers and customers. The small-appliance industry was not profitable, however, in part because of overcapacity and the power of the retailer. Also, cost pressures contributed to a reduction in product performance and reliability. Further, GE's strengths, such as its technological superiority and financial resources, were not leveraged in the small-appliance business, as any innovation could be copied. Thus, GE decided that a strategic fit did not exist, and it sold the small-appliance business to Black & Decker.

KEY LEARNINGS

- Sales and profitability analysis provide an evaluation of past strategies and an indication of the current market viability of a product line.

- Shareholder value holds that the flow of profits emanating from an investment should exceed the cost of capital (which is the weighted average of the cost of equity and cost of debt). Routes to achieving shareholder value—such as downsizing, reducing assets employed, and outsourcing—can be risky when they undercut assets and competencies.

- Performance assessment should go beyond financials to include such dimensions as customer satisfaction/brand loyalty, product/service quality, brand/firm associations, relative cost, new product activity, and manager/employee capability and performance.

- Assets and competencies can represent a point of advantage, a point of parity, or a liability. Threats and opportunities that are both imminent and important should trigger strategic imperatives, programs with high priority.

FOR DISCUSSION

1. Explain shareholder value analysis. Why might it help firms? Why might it result in bad decisions?

2. Look at the quotations that begin Chapters 2 through 6. Which one do you find the most insightful? Why? Under what circumstances would its implications not hold?

3. What performance measure would you consider most important for McDonald's? For Chevrolet?

4. Conduct a strengths, weakness, opportunities, and threats (SWOT) analysis for Ford.

NOTES

1. For an excellent review of the risks of shareholder value see Allan A. Kennedy, *The End of Shareholder Value*, Cambridge, MA: Perseus Publishing, 2000.

2. Philippe Haspeslagh, Tomo Noda, and Fares Boulos, "It's Not Just About the Numbers," *Harvard Business Review*, July–August 2001, pp. 65–73.

3. Kenichi Ohmae, *The Mind of the Strategist*, New York: Penguin Books, 1982, p. 26.

4. J. B. Kunz Company A, Case 9-577-115, Boston: Intercollegiate Case Clearing House, 1977.

5. Robert Slater, *The New GE*, Homewood, IL: Irwin, 1993, p. 101.

Understanding and Working with Industry Trends

TRENDS IN RETAILING

The *Wall Street Journal* in late 2005 identified trends in food and nonfood retailing. The following were among their observations.

1. *Moving away from the middle.* Retailers are offering a more upscale experience. Macy's locations are getting a face-lift and image advertising. Bath & Body Works is transforming into an affordable beauty boutique. Safeway has invested heavily in store remodeling, creating "lifestyle stores" with better produce, warmer lighting, and even classes in topics like flower arranging. Even Zales and Wal-Mart are attempting to be more similar to upscale competitors.

   At the same time, other retailers are moving down to compete with the discount stores. Albertson's has opened a limited-assortment store with low prices under the Super Saver brand. Dollar stores are doing well, and chains of grocery stores are adding dollar sections.

2. *The big get bigger.* The need to create economies of scale in merchandising, operations, and advertising has driven firms to merge. The most dramatic was Federated's purchase of May Department stores, which combined several prominent chains like Marshall Field's, Lord & Taylor, and Filene's and put them under the Macy's brand name.

3. *Toward a better shopping lifestyle.* Enclosed malls are in decline; they are being replaced by the "lifestyle center," which is a combination of stores such as Pottery Barn, Barnes & Noble, Gap, Victoria's Secret, and Williams-Sonoma, with open walkways and no department store.

4. *Installation is included.* Retailers are starting to offer services complementary to their products, in part to add to sales per square foot but also to differentiate their offerings. Circuit City, Home Depot, and Lowe's, for example, are among stores that have added installation service. Best Buy has an active repair service.

5. *Something for everyone.* Retailers are developing strategies to appeal to multiple segments. Gap, a pioneer in this vein with Gap, Baby Gap, Banana Republic, and Old Navy opened Fourth & Towne, an apparel store for women over 35. Abercrombie & Fitch has the Fitch brand for teens, Hollister for high schoolers, Ruehl for college students, and Little A for kids.

6. *Private-label strength.* Private-label goods now account for 17 percent of all global sales, up from 15 percent during the prior two years, in part because of retail consolidation, the drive for higher margins, and the increase in higher end private label brands.

7. **Making shopping fun.** Entertainment in stores is a growth area, termed *retailtainment*—climbing walls in REI, exhibitions on fishing and dog training at Bass Pro Shops, autograph sessions at Niketown stores, and fashion shows in apparel stores. The trend is even more pronounced in China.

8. **Moving into media.** Retailers are sponsoring and owning magazines, television shows, and Internet media sites. The Craft retailer introduced *Create* magazine, and Home Depot sponsors the TLC home decorating program *Trading Spaces.* Cabela compiles video clips from customers for its *Outfitter's Journal* programs.

9. **Organic offerings.** Organic food, one of the success factors of Whole Foods, is going mainstream. Sales of organic and natural foods have gone from $35 billion in 2004 to $60 billion in 2005, and the trend has spread from food to clothing. It is driven in part by a preference among young consumers for stores that carry organic products.

10. Many retailers, especially grocery stores, are tracking and rewarding customer purchases. The trend is toward rewarding the loyal customer with more information and targeted discounts. Some systems involve high-tech payment systems that allow shoppers to check out with an identification number and a touch of a finger.

FOR DISCUSSION

1. What is driving each of these trends? Which are supported by underlying consumer trends? Identify them.

2. Which three trends will be around in five years? How would you forecast the probability that the trend will persist for that long?

3. What are the trends of most significance for Macy's? For Lane Bryant? For Borders?

4. When might a retailer consider going against the trend?

5. Another potential trend is the return to a store's roots. Several retailers, such as Gap and Saks, lost core customers by attempting to appeal to younger buyers. As a result, they are now attempting to return to their roots and deliver the classic fashions that made them attractive to their now not-so-young customers. What possessed them to go trendy in the first place? Can they recapture the customers that they have alienated?

Source: Kris Hudson, "Upside Experience, Downscale Prices," *Wall Street Journal,* November 21, 2006, p. R3; Janet Adamy, "New Food, New Look," *Wall Street Journal,* November 21, 2006, p. R8.

A New, Dynamic Industry

THE ENERGY BAR INDUSTRY

In 1986, PowerBar, a firm in Berkeley, California, single-handedly created the energy bar category. Positioned as an athletic energy food, it was distributed at bike shops and events that usually involved running or biking. The target segment was the athlete who needed an efficient, effective energy source.

Six years later, seeking to provide an alternative to the sticky, dry nature of the PowerBar, a competitor, also located in Berkeley, developed an energy bar with superior taste and texture and branded it the Clif bar. About the same time, another competitor introduced the Balance bar, which offered a blend of protein, fat, and carbohydrates based on the nutrition formula associated with the "Zone diet." Faced with these challengers, PowerBar responded with Harvest (a bar with a much more accessible taste and texture) and ProteinPlus (an entry into the high-protein subcategory closely related to that defined by Balance).

The makers of the Clif bar observed that many women were athletes and many more were involved in fitness. They further observed that this half of the population had unique needs in terms of vitamins and supplements, and that the energy bar industry had yet to recognize or fill them—a classic case of unmet needs. As a result, they introduced Luna as the first nutritional (not energy) bar for women, using media and promotions targeting active females. The bar had a light crunchy texture, came in flavors like "lemon zest" and chai tea, and contained nearly two dozen vitamins, minerals, and nutrients. The target market consisted of time-strapped women who wanted both taste and nutrition and would appreciate a bar tailored to their needs.

Both in reaction to Luna's success and to expand the segments for which the category was relevant, PowerBar studied why women did not buy its products, which the firm considered to be nutritious, convenient, tasty, and able to provide a quick pick-me-up in mid-morning or mid-afternoon. One answer was that the calorie hit from any member of the PowerBar family was simply too great. In response, the firm created the almost-indulgent, PowerBar-endorsed Pria. With only 110 calories, Pria was designed to respond to Luna while attracting new users into the category.

The Balance strategy was to introduce a series of products, all of which stuck to the original bar's 40/30/30 nutritional formula but had different taste and textures. These spinoffs included Balance Plus, Balance Outdoor (with no chocolate coating to melt), Balance Gold, Balance Satisfaction, and the Balance-endorsed Oasis, a bar designed for women. The big success was Balance Gold, which was positioned close to the candy bar category (indeed, its tagline was "like a candy bar") by containing ingredients like nuts and caramel. Such a bar probably risked some of Balance's perceived authenticity as being an energy bar. However, because Balance entered the category from the diet perspective anyway and probably was never considered in the center of the energy bar world, the risk may have been acceptable.

In addition to the major brands, challengers from a variety of small and large firms advanced subcategories by positioning themselves around such factors as age (bars for seniors and kids) and health (products to fit dairy-free, diabetic, and heart-conscious diets), to say nothing of numerous textures, flavors, sizes, and coatings. Over a ten-year period, some 450 products were introduced. For example, the popularity of low-carbohydrate diets has prompted a host of entries, including Atkins Advantage, developed by the Atkins organization, which gained a substantial market share that peaked in 2003 and fell off sharply thereafter. Other participating brands include ZonePerfect, Met-Rx, GeniSoy, EAS, CarboLite, Carb Solutions, and Gatorade energy bars. Masterfoods' Snickers Marathon—a candy bar with a blend of vitamins, minerals, and protein—has blurred the division between candy and energy bars by seeking to gain share in the latter market. One concern of the energy bar industry is the skepticism among some quarters as to how qualitatively different its products are from candy bars in the first place.

The motivation for using an energy bar is primarily to provide a convenient energy boost. The original heritage of being a product to enhance the performance of top athletes engaged in demanding physical activities (like Lance Armstrong, a PowerBar endorser) created credibility and self-expressive benefits in the category's early years. Because household penetration was still under 20 percent, however, the major firms worked to generalize "performance" to be relevant to anyone who needs to perform well during the day. In fact, the industry dream is to get people to label the category "performance nutrition" and think of it as enhancing one's ability to complete any task.

New products in the category are going in several directions. A trend toward indulgent icings, coatings, and coverings has led some to morph toward candy bars. Others go the opposite way, using whole-grain ingredients for products somewhat like the original Clif bar and Quaker's Oatmeal Squares for women. The makers of the Clif bar also have introduced a Mojo line of salty snack bars to provide alternatives to sweet-tasting bars and the Clif Nectar bar, an entirely organic nut and fruit bar. Power Bar introduced Nut Naturals, a low glycemic index bar.

The energy bar category has gone mainstream, moving from the bike shops to the grocery stores and exploding from just over $100 million in revenue in 1996 to an estimated $2 billion or more a decade later, with expected future growth exceeding 10 percent per year. It is fueled both by the confluence of trends toward low-carb, portable, nutritious snacks and meal replacements (along with a general concern for health and weight control) and by the introduction of new products. Along the way, it became large enough to attract the attention of major packaged-goods firms. In 2000, Nestlé purchased PowerBar, which has remained the leading player, with the Clif bar (which has remained independent) emerging as its most formidable competitor. The Balance line of products was bought by Kraft, also in 2000.

Energy bars can be considered a part of a larger food bar category which is also growing rapidly. The market is divided fairly equally between granola bars (positioned as a snack food that is healthier than candy bars), breakfast/cereal/snack bars (used as a meal replacement), and energy bars. Energy bars have a far lower household penetration than the other food bar forms. The top marketers of food bars are Kellogg's (Nutri-grain), Quaker Oats, General Mills, and Slim-Fast.

FOR DISCUSSION

1. Conduct a thorough analysis of this category's customers, competitors, market, and environment from the perspective of PowerBar. What are the key strategic questions? What additional information would you like to obtain? How would you obtain it? What are the threats and opportunities? In particular, address the following issues:

   a. How is the market segmented? What are the key customer motivations and unmet needs? What are the similarities and differences among the segments? How might a company link customer motivations to value propositions?

   b. Identify the competitors. Who are the most direct competitors? The indirect competitors? Substitute products? What are the strategic groups?

   c. What are the market trends? The growth submarkets? The key success factors?

   d. What are the environmental trends that will affect the industry? Generate two or three viable future scenarios.

2. How would you go about evaluating emerging submarkets? What criteria would you use to enter each? Consider PowerBar's reaction to the Clif organic bar.

3. What innovation would support a new entry? How should entries be branded? Can brands such as Harvest, Luna, Balance Gold, Balance Satisfaction, and others be leveraged?

4. Will the energy bar category morph into food bars, with elements like diet, tasting like candy, and breakfast replacement dominating as the energy definition recedes? How can Nestlé's PowerBar keep that from happening and still maintain its mainstream/supermarket posture?

5. At what stage is the energy bar market relative to the product-life cycle? What strategies can be used to extend the life cycle? Do you see a consolidation on the horizon?

Source: Adapted with the permission of the Free Press, a division of Simon & Schuster Adult Publishing Group, from *Brand Portfolio Strategy: Creating Relevance, Differentiation, Energy, Leverage, and Clarity,* by David A. Aaker. Copyright © 2004 by David A. Aaker. All rights reserved.

Competing Against the Industry Giant
COMPETING AGAINST WAL-MART

Wal-Mart is the most successful retailer ever. In 2005, at $265 billion in sales, it was by far the world's largest retail company, over three times the size of the runner-up, France's Carrefour. Measures of Wal-Mart's success are mind-blowing. Its share of the U.S. grocery business was 19 percent in 2004 and could grow to 35 percent if its five-year planned growth materializes. It was the third largest pharmacy with a 16 percent share. It sold 32 percent of the disposable diapers in the United States, 30 percent of all hair care products, 26 percent of toothpaste, 20 percent of pet food, and 13 percent of home textiles. Wal-Mart regularly appears on *Fortune's* list of the most admired companies in America.

Wal-Mart was founded in Arkansas by Sam Walton in 1962. Six years later it expanded into neighboring states, and in the 1970s it ventured beyond the South. Over time it added products such as jewelry and food, as well as pharmacy and automotive departments. By 2006, there were some 1,100 Wal-Marts and over 2,140 Wal-Mart Supercenters in the United States. In 1983, Wal-Mart went into the wholesale club business under the Sam's Club brand name; this concept grew to over 500 stores within two decades. In 1991, it began its international quest by opening a store in Mexico. In 2002, Wal-Mart had nearly 1,200 stores outside the United States and was the leading retailer in both Mexico and Canada.

For its first thirty years, Sam Walton was the heart and soul of Wal-Mart. An inspirational and visionary influence, he created strategies, policies, and cultural values that fueled the firm's success. He would spend much of his time visiting stores and meeting customers and "associates" (employees). The visits would always result in customer and merchandising insights, pats on the back for workers, and suggestions for improvement. He would summon managers back to the headquarters in Bentonville, Arkansas, for Saturday morning meetings that kept the firm focused and provided a pervasive work ethic. He also enjoyed celebrating successes, once keeping a promise to do the hula on Wall Street if the company achieved an 8 percent pretax profit. For employees and customers alike, Sam Walton *was* Wal-Mart.

In 1962, Walton started his firm with three basic beliefs—respect for the individual employee, exceptional customer service, and a striving for excellence. He developed a host of rules for associates. He challenged them to engage in "aggressive hospitality," to be ready with a smile and assistance to all customers. The "ten-foot rule" decreed that whenever an associate was within ten feet of a customer, the associate was to look that customer in the eye and ask if he or she needed help. His "sun-down rule" meant that any task that could be done today would be not put off until tomorrow—especially if the task involved customer service. Exemplifying his belief in empowerment, Walton instituted the Volume Producing Item (VPI) program, in which an associate would pick an item, design a merchandising effort for it, and monitor and communicate the results.

In his 1992 book *Made in America*—a title that reflects Wal-Mart's positioning strategies in the early 1980s, as well as a comment on the founder's career—Sam

Walton listed ten key factors that he felt were key to his success. One was to appreciate your associates and their contribution; a second item was to share your profits with them. A third factor was to talk to the customer and listen to what that customer is saying. Another item was to exceed your customer's expectations ("satisfaction guaranteed" really meant something to Sam Walton). Still another factor was to control your expenses better than your competition, as Walton prided himself on having a number-one ranking in the ratio of expenses to sales.

Sam Walton offered strategies as well as charisma. One basic early strategy was to bring discount stores to cities of roughly 50,000 people. While the large discount stores of the day were fighting for prime spots in large cities, Wal-Mart had the smaller metropolitan areas to itself. Second, because of the location of its early stores and its headquarters site, Wal-Mart had an employee cost advantage from top to bottom. Third, by setting up distribution centers, Wal-Mart from the outset gained operational and logistic efficiencies. Over time Wal-Mart relentlessly innovated in warehousing, logistics, information technology, and operations to create more and more savings. In part, this innovation was done in partnership with suppliers like P&G.

Wal-Mart continued to prosper after 1992 when Sam Walton passed away. Although his strategic flair and connection with employees and customers was missed, many of his ideas had become institutionalized. Aggressive merchandising led by empowered associates and the trademark greeters, for example, remained part of the Wal-Mart profile. In addition, there was a focus on energy adding "Retailtainment," including live concert broadcasts in the home entertainment departments, exclusive promotional events around video releases, and exhibits by local organizations. Equity was built into private-label brands, such as Ol' Roy dog food (which has surpassed Purina as the world's top-selling dog food), White Cloud tissues and diapers, and the Sam's Choice and Great Value product lines.

Low prices and cost containment have continued to be the focus—some say the obsession—of Wal-Mart management. The customer promise of "Low Prices, Always" drives the culture and the strategy. Suppliers are continuously and aggressively challenged to reduce costs. Wal-Mart will set demanding cost reduction goals, on occasion showing suppliers how to achieve them. Operations are continuously made more efficient. The resulting cost savings are passed on to customers, as Wal-Mart does not support suppliers' premium-price brand policies. The firm's private-label lines are often sourced directly from foreign factories, creating significant cost advantages and disrupting price norms in many categories. Wal-Mart views itself, first and foremost, as the customer's purchasing agent, and its goal is to reduce prices. By some estimates, Wal-Mart saves consumers $20 billion a year.

Wal-Mart has significant detractors as well. One set of arguments, summarized in a *Business Week* cover story questioning whether Wal-Mart is too powerful, relate to jobs. Wal-Mart has been accused of hastening the move of jobs abroad, as its focus on costs led the company to buy over $12 billion in goods from China alone in 2002. Some even argue that suppliers, in order to meet Wal-Mart's cost targets, are forced to move jobs to China and elsewhere. In addition, it is estimated that for every supercenter that Wal-Mart opens, two supermarkets will close. When Wal-Mart went into Oklahoma

City, for example, thirty supermarkets closed. Because of the loss of local businesses, many communities have resisted Wal-Mart's entry. Even the jobs that Wal-Mart adds are said to be inferior, as the company's anti-union, low-pay policy has been hypothesized to hold down wages in retail America and throughout local regions. On average, a Wal-Mart sales clerk in 2001 made less than $14,000, which was below the poverty line for a family of three. Labor costs have been estimated to be 20 percent less than competing supermarkets with unions and because fewer employees receive benefits. Dozens of lawsuits related to overtime pay and sex discrimination have been filed against the firm. Sam Walton's values of "Made in America" and "respect for the individual" seem to some a distant memory. The Wal-Mart green initiatives, described in Chapter 6, are intended in part to counter this negative publicity.

Wal-Mart also faces some more intangible concerns. Because it controls over 15 percent of all nonsubscription magazine and video/DVD sales, some fear that the firm wields an unwelcome and arbitrary influence on culture. Wal-Mart elects to stock some magazines while banning or hiding the covers of others (a nearly naked woman on the cover of *Rolling Stone* is acceptable, but not on the front of *Glamour* and *Redbook*), and it sells only videos that meet family-friendly standards. As a result, some movie producers have felt compelled to create a "Wal-Mart version" of their films. Further, Wal-Mart's market power is so high that some people fear it has an inordinate influence on product design (for example, a particular design direction may be deemed by Wal-Mart as too costly for its customers). In a wide variety of product areas, manufacturers cannot afford to deviate from specifications set by Wal-Mart.

Wal-Mart has plans to expand dramatically as the first decade of the twenty-first century continues. The primary vehicle for this growth will be Wal-Mart supercenters, often located in malls where sites are available at distressed prices, face fewer zoning issues, and precipitate less neighborhood opposition. The obsession with low prices, costs, and efficiency will not change. In fact, suppliers have been given a deadline to attach radio-frequency identification tags to all packages and pallets in order to create a new level of efficiency. There will be a continued emphasis on the growth of private-label goods, which were estimated to represent 20 percent of Wal-Mart's sales in 2003. A program to upgrade Sam's Club by adding pharmacy, optical, one-hour photo, fuel, and other services is under way.

FOR DISCUSSION

Grocery stores and general merchandise stores must look forward to more intense challenges from Wal-Mart in the future. Such firms need to understand Wal-Mart and how it competes. What Wal-Mart strategies led to success? What was the role of Sam Walton? What is the company's likely future direction beyond its stated intentions? Would it make sense for Wal-Mart to extend its brand into stand-alone grocery stores (such as Safeway) or convenience stores (for example, 7-Eleven)?

Is Wal-Mart positive or negative for consumers? For suppliers? For employees? For communities? For the United States? Consider two competitors, Costco and Wegmans, who must design a strategy that will lead to success in the Wal-Mart environment.

Wegmans

There are sixty Wegmans Food Markets in New York, Pennsylvania, and Maryland. Wegmans has seen sales (including same-store sales) grow steadily over the years, generating healthy profits. However, thirty-nine of these stores are within twenty miles of a Wal-Mart Supercenter, and expansion plans in Baltimore and Washington, D.C., involve more competition with Wal-Mart.

1.   What are the strengths and weaknesses of Wal-Mart from the perspective of Wegmans?

2.   What strategies should Wegmans avoid?

3.   What strategies will allow Wegmans to thrive or at least survive in the face of Wal-Mart's strengths?

4.   How should Wegmans exploit the Wal-Mart resentment factor?

Costco

Costco started in 1981, just a few years before Sam's Club appeared. In 2005, it had 433 stores doing $52 billion in sales, with some 45 million individual members, 5 million business members, and more than $1 billion in net profit. Annual growth is in the 6 to 10 percent range, and per-store sales have risen from $77 million in 1996 to $120 million in 2006—performance far better than Sam's Club, the Wal-Mart entry. Unlike Sam's Club, which focuses on price, Costco offers upscale brands like Callaway golf clubs, Starbucks coffee, and expensive jewelry, and thus it attracts a different kind of shopper. Sam's Club is attempting to attack Costco by adding upscale brands and integrating more closely with Wal-Mart in order to achieve more buying power and logistical efficiencies.

1.   What are the strengths and weaknesses of Sam's Club from the perspective of Costco?

2.   How should Costco react to the Wal-Mart threat?

Sources: Wal-Mart, Costco, and Wegmans company Web sites in 2006; Wal-Mart annual report for 2005; Anthony Bianco and Wendy Zellner, "Is Wal-Mart Too Powerful?" *Business Week*, October 6, 2003, pp. 100–110.

PART TWO

CREATING, ADAPTING, AND IMPLEMENTING STRATEGY

Creating Advantage, Synergy, and Strategic Philosophies

All men can see the tactics whereby I conquer, but what none can see is the strategy out of which great victory is evolved.
—*Sun-Tzu, Chinese military strategist*

Don't manage, lead.
—*Jack Welch, GE*

Where absolute superiority is not attainable, you must produce a relative one at the decisive point by making skillful use of what you have.
—*Karl von Clausewitz, On War, 1832*

Our attention now shifts from strategic analysis to the development of a business strategy. What strategic alternatives should be considered? What assets and competencies, target segments, value propositions, and functional strategies? What investment and disinvestment decisions should be raised? These questions will be the focus of the balance of the book. One goal will be to provide a wide scope of available strategic alternatives in order to increase the likelihood that the best choices will be considered. Even a poor decision among superior alternatives is preferable to a good decision among inferior alternatives.

The nine chapters remaining in this book are portrayed in Figure 7.1. This chapter will discuss the concept and creation of a sustainable competitive advantage (SCA), the key to a successful strategy. It then turns to the challenge of creating and leveraging synergy as one basis for an SCA. Finally, four very different strategic philosophies—strategic commitment, strategic opportunism, strategy adaptability,

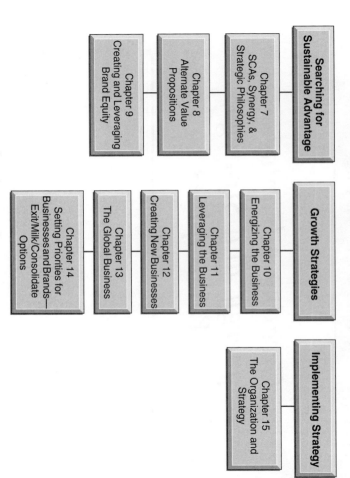

Figure 7.1   Creating and Implementing Strategy

and strategic intent—are presented that collectively offer a useful perspective on strategy and strategic choices.

Chapter 8 provides an overview of alternative value propositions. A value proposition is often an umbrella concept under which the supporting assets and competencies and functional strategies and programs can be grouped. In that sense, it represents a good overview of alternative strategies. Chapter 9 describes how to create and leverage a key asset, brand equity. The next four chapters present growth strategies: energizing the business (Chapter 10), leveraging the business (Chapter 11), creating new business models (Chapter 12), and going global (Chapter 13). Chapter 14 discusses setting priorities among business units and making disinvestment decisions. Finally, Chapter 15 introduces organizational and implementation issues.

THE SUSTAINABLE COMPETITIVE ADVANTAGE

As defined earlier in this book, a sustainable competitive advantage is an element (or combination of elements) of the business strategy that provides a meaningful advantage over both existing and future competitors (see Figure 7.2). Wal-Mart has a cost advantage because of its scale economies, market power and logistical efficiencies, value reputation, and site location assets. Southwest Airlines has a fun personality and a point-to-point model that provides for convenient, reliable, uncomplicated travel.

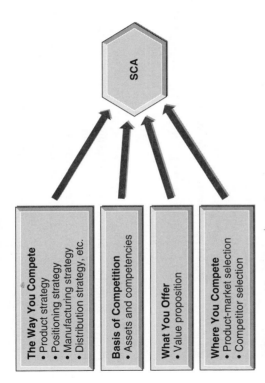

The Way You Compete
- Product strategy
- Positioning strategy
- Manufacturing strategy
- Distribution strategy, etc.

Basis of Competition
- Assets and competencies

What You Offer
- Value proposition

Where You Compete
- Product-market selection
- Competitor selection

SCA

Figure 7.2   The Sustainable Competitive Advantage

Dell Computers' efficient direct-sales model makes customized computers easy to order and service and generates personal contact with Dell people.

An SCA needs to be both meaningful and sustainable. It should be substantial enough to make a difference; a marginal superiority in quality, especially when "good" quality is good enough for most customers, will not generate an SCA. Meanwhile, sustainability (in the absence of an effective patent) means that any advantage needs to be supported and enhanced over time. There needs to be a moving target for competitors. For example, Gillette maintained its technological superiority in razors over a long time period with innovation after innovation, making copying its competitive advantage difficult.

An SCA will in part depend on the functional strategies and programs, how you compete. Wal-Mart's discount store, Southwest's point-to-point system, and the Dell direct-sales model all have SCAs based in part on their functional strategies and programs. In these cases and others, however, an effective SCA will also involve other aspects of the business strategy—assets and competencies, the value proposition, and the selection of the product market.

The Basis of Competition: Assets and Competencies

The assets and competencies of an organization represent the most sustainable element of a business strategy, because these are usually difficult to copy or counter. There is no point in pursuing a quality strategy, for example, without the design and manufacturing competencies needed to deliver quality products. Anyone can try to distribute cereal or detergent through supermarkets, but few have the competencies in logistics, shelf space management, and promotions or relationships with chain executives that make product distribution efficient and effective. Similarly, a department store's premium-service positioning strategy will not succeed unless the right people and culture are in place and are supported. Who you are, in other words, is as important as what you do.

As discussed in Chapter 3, several questions can help to identify relevant assets and competencies. What are the key motivations of the major market segments? What are the large value-added components? What are the mobility barriers? What elements of the value chain can generate an advantage? What assets and competencies are possessed by successful businesses and lacking in unsuccessful businesses?

What You Offer—The Value Proposition

An effective SCA should be visible to customers and provide or enhance a value position. The key is to link an SCA with the positioning of a business. A product's reliability may not be apparent to customers, but if it can be made visible through a brand strategy, it can support a reliability positioning strategy. Maytag is an example of a firm whose reliability positioning is supported by advertising that communicates the SCA provided by its product design and performance.

A reputation for delivering a value proposition can be a more important asset than the substance that underlies that reputation. A business with such a reputation can falter for a time, and the market will either never become aware of the weakness or will forgive the firm. Conversely, competitors often have a much easier time in matching the quality or performance of a market offering than in convincing customers that they indeed have done so. Enduring impressions are why a visible value proposition that is meaningful to customers is strategically valuable.

A solid value proposition can fail if a key ingredient is missing. Procter & Gamble's Pringles potato chips had a host of assets, such as a consistent product, long shelf life, a crushproof container, and national distribution. The problem was that these attributes were valued only if the taste was perceived to be good. As a result, Pringle's ability to penetrate the snack market was limited for decades until it made progress in terms of both actual and perceived taste. Kingsford Charcoal failed in the barbeque sauce market simply because there was no room for a third entrant in the premium segment.

Where You Compete: The Product Market Served

An important determinant for an SCA is the choice of the target product market. A well-defined strategy supported by assets and competencies can fail because it does not work in the marketplace. One way to create marketplace value is to be relevant to customers. As noted in Chapter 4, it does no good to offer the best minivan in the market if most of your target customers now want to buy SUVs.

The scope of the business also involves the identity of competitors. Sometimes an asset or competency will form an SCA only given the right set of competitors. Thus, it is vital to assess whether a competitor or strategic group is weak, adequate, or strong with respect to assets and competencies. The goal is to engage in a strategy that will match up with competitors' weak points in relevant areas.

SCAs versus Key Success Factors

What is the difference between key success factors (KSFs), introduced in Chapters 1 and 4, and SCAs? A KSF is an asset or competence needed to compete. An SCA involves an asset or competence that is the basis for a continuing advantage. For example, an automobile firm needs to have adequate distribution given its business model and objectives, so distribution is a KSF. Lexus has turned its dealer network into an SCA, however, because it is capable of delivering a superior customer experience. A KSF for value-priced economy cars is the ability to control costs in order to create profit margins. Hyundai's ability in this regard is markedly superior to its competitors, and thus it becomes an SCA.

To be a winner at poker requires skill, nerve, and money. In also requires a player to ante—to put up a certain amount of money just to see the cards and engage in betting. A KSF can be an ante in terms of the marketplace. Generating a superior quality car may have been an SCA for Lexus or Mercedes and a point of differentiation in the mid-1990s. As Jaguar, BMW, and Cadillac improve their own quality, though, the quality dimension starts to be an attribute all luxury cars are assumed to have, and thus becomes a KSF but not a basis for an SCA. Instead of winning the competitive hand, a KSF merely buys an organization a seat at the table.

Reviewing the concepts of points of parity (POPs) and points of differentiation (PODs), introduced in Chapter 1 will provide additional insight into this distinction.[1] PODs are strong, favorable, and unique brand associations based on some attribute or benefit associations. Ikea, for example, provides home furnishings at accessible prices with unique designs and by having customers handle and assemble the products. A POP, in contrast, is an association that is not necessarily unique to the brand. POPs may be necessary to present a credible offering within a certain category, as in the case of ATMs and convenient hours for a bank. A POP might also be designed to negate a competitor's point of distinction. A low-carb food brand, for example, seeks to create parity with regard to taste, thereby negating the taste POD of its competitors and leading customers to base their selection on its own POD (namely, low-carb ingredients). An SCA is analogous to a POD, whereas a KSF can be analogous to either a POP or a POD.

What Business Managers Name as Their SCAs

Managers of 248 distinct businesses in the service and high-tech industries were asked to name the SCAs of their business.[2] The objectives were to identify frequently employed SCAs, to confirm that managers could articulate them, to determine whether different managers from the same businesses would identify the same SCAs, and to find how many SCAs would be identified for each business. The responses were coded into categories. The results, summarized in Figure 7.3, provide some suggestive insights into the SCA construct.

The wide variety of SCAs mentioned, each representing distinct competitive approaches, is shown in the figure. Of course, the list did differ by industry. For high-tech firms, for example, name recognition was less important than technical superiority, product innovation, and installed customer base. The next two chapters discuss several SCAs in more detail.

	High-Tech	Service	Other	Total
1. Reputation for quality	26	50	29	105
2. Customer service/product support	23	40	15	78
3. Name recognition/high profile	8	42	21	71
4. Retain good management and engineering staff	17	43	5	65
5. Low-cost production	17	15	21	53
6. Financial resources	11	26	14	51
7. Customer orientation/feedback/market research	13	26	9	48
8. Product-line breadth	11	23	13	47
9. Technical superiority	30	7	9	46
10. Installed base of satisfied customers	19	22	4	45
11. Segmentation/focus	7	22	16	45
12. Product characteristics/differentiation	12	15	10	37
13. Continuing product innovation	12	17	6	35
14. Market share	12	14	9	35
15. Size/location of distribution	10	11	13	34
16. Low price/high-value offering	6	20	6	32
17. Knowledge of business	2	25	4	31
18. Pioneer/early entrant in industry	11	11	6	28
19. Efficient, flexible production/operations adaptable to customers	4	17	4	25
20. Effective sales force	10	9	4	23
21. Overall marketing skills	7	9	7	23
22. Shared vision/culture	5	13	4	22
23. Strategic goals	6	7	9	22
24. Powerful well-known parent	7	7	6	20
25. Location	0	10	10	20
26. Effective advertising/image	5	6	6	17
27. Enterprising/entrepreneurial	3	3	5	11
28. Good coordination	3	2	5	10
29. Engineering research and development	8	2	0	10
30. Short-term planning	2	1	5	8
31. Good distributor relations	2	4	1	7
32. Other	6	20	5	31
Total	315	539	281	1,135
Number of businesses	68	113	67	248
Average number of SCAs	4.63	4.77	4.19	4.58

Figure 7.3 Sustainable Competitive Advantages of 248 Businesses

Most of the SCAs in Figure 7.3 reflect assets or competencies. Customer base, quality reputation, and good management and engineering staff, for example, are business assets, whereas customer service and technical superiority usually involve sets of competencies.

For a subset of ninety-five of the businesses involved, a second business manager was independently interviewed. The result suggests that managers can identify SCAs with a high degree of reliability. Of the ninety-five businesses, seventy-six of the manager pairs gave answers that were coded the same and most of the others had only a single difference in the SCA list.

Another finding is instructive—the average number of SCAs per business was 4.58, suggesting that it is usually not sufficient to base a strategy on a single SCA. Sometimes a business is described in terms of a single competency or asset, implying that being a quality-oriented business or a service-focused business explains success. This study indicates, however, that it may be necessary to have several assets and competencies.

THE ROLE OF SYNERGY

Synergy between business units can provide an SCA that is truly sustainable because it is based on the characteristics of a firm that are unique. A competitor might have to duplicate the organization in order to capture the assets or competencies involved.

A core element in the GE strategic vision has always been to achieve synergy across many businesses. The concept was that a GE business can call on the resources of the firm and of other GE businesses to create advantage. The turbine technology that GE pioneered as it established the infrastructure for electricity helped in the jet engine business. The SCAs of General Electric in the CT scanner (an X-ray-based diagnostic system) business were in part based on its leadership in the X-ray business, in which it had a huge installed base and a large service network, and in part based on the fact that it operated other businesses involving technologies used in CT scanners. Tecnologies in one business can become innovations in another.

A cornerstone of the IBM strategy under Lou Gerstner was to create synergy by pushing core technologies across more product lines.[3] The intent was to leverage the IBM size, scale, and technologies. This vision was a far cry from that of Gerstner's predecessors, who planned to break IBM up into autonomous business units.

Sony exploits the synergy of its many product groups by showcasing them together in stores (such as one on Chicago's Michigan Avenue) and even on several Celebrity Cruise ships. The ships are outfitted with Sony entertainment products, including television sets, movie theaters, and sound equipment. The result is an integrated package that has the cumulative impact of reinforcing Sony's role of providing high quality and technologically advanced entertainment.

Synergy means that the whole is more than the sum of its parts. In this context, it means that two businesses (or two product-market strategies) operating together will be superior to the same two businesses operating independently. In terms of products, positive synergy means that offering a set of products will generate a higher return over time than would be possible if each of the products were offered separately. Similarly, in terms of markets, operating a set of markets within a business will be superior to operating them autonomously.

As a result of synergy, the combined businesses will have one or more of the following:

1. Increased customer value and thus increased sales.
2. Lower operating costs.
3. Reduced investment.

Generally the synergy will be caused by exploiting some commonality in the two operations, such as:

- Customers and sometimes customer applications (potentially creating a systems solution).
- A sales force or channel of distribution.
- A brand name and its image.
- Facilities used for manufacturing, offices, or warehousing.
- R&D efforts.
- Staff and operating systems.
- Marketing and marketing research.

Synergy is not difficult to understand conceptually, but it is slippery in practice, in part because it can be difficult to predict whether synergy will actually emerge. Often two businesses seem related, and sizable potential synergy seems to exist but is never realized. Sometimes the perceived synergy is merely a mirage or wishful thinking, perhaps created in the haste to put together a merger. At other times, the potential synergy is real, but implementation problems prevent its realization. Perhaps there is a cultural mismatch between two organizations, or the incentives are inadequate. In Chapter 11, the difficulties of realizing potential synergy will be revisited.

Alliances

Obtaining instant synergy is a goal of alliances. Pairing McDonald's with an oil company, for example, provides traffic and added value for the oil company and valuable locations for McDonald's. Dentsu, the largest Japanese advertising agency, has more than a hundred alliances—many based on partial ownership—that allow it to offer a broader communication solution to clients.

Alliances are often the key to a successful Internet strategy. Yahoo! and Amazon have hundreds of major alliances and thousands of smaller ones that combine to help them reach their goals of driving Internet traffic and offering differentiated value to their visitors. Chapter 13, Global Strategies, covers the difficult process of putting together alliances and joint ventures and making them work.

Core Assets and Competencies

A firm's asset or competency that is capable of being the competitive basis of many of its businesses is termed a core asset or competency and can be a synergistic advantage.

Prahalad and Hamel suggest a tree metaphor, in which the root system is the core asset or competency, the trunk and major limbs are core products, the smaller branches are business units, and the leaves and flowers are end products.[4] You may not recognize the strength of a competitor if you simply look at its end products and fail to examine the strength of its root system. Core competence represents the consolidation of firm-wide technologies and skills into a coherent thrust. A core asset, such as a brand name or a distribution channel, merits investment and management that span business units.

Consider, for example, the core competencies of Sony in miniaturization, 3M in sticky-tape technology, Black & Decker in small motors, Honda in vehicle motors and power trains, Samsung in semiconductors (which underlies its product innovation in consumer electronics and cell phones), and Canon in precision mechanics, fine optics, and microelectronics. Each of these competencies underlies a large set of businesses and has the potential to create more. Each of these firms invests in competence in a variety of different ways and contexts. Each would insist on keeping its primary work related to the core competency in-house. Outsourcing would risk weakening the asset, and each firm would rightfully insist that there is no other firm that could match its state-of-the-art advances.

Highly effective business processes often represent a core competence that can be applied across businesses leading to a sustainable advantage. One such process is the new product development and introduction process. Japanese automobile firms that have reduced the process from five years to three years while making it more responsive to the needs of the market have achieved a huge advantage. Another is the management of international operations, considered an SCA by IDV, the spirits subsidiary of Grand Metropolitan. Still another is the order and logistics process in retailing. By developing dramatic improvements in its order and logistics process through distribution center innovations, a dedicated trucking system, and computerized ordering, Wal-Mart developed huge cost and inventory handling advantages over its competition.

Developing superior capabilities in key processes involves strategic investments in people and infrastructure, the use of cross-functional teams, and clear performance targets. True process improvement does not occur without control and ownership of the parts of the process. Thus, the virtual corporation, which draws pieces from many sources in response to the organizational task at hand, is not a good model for capabilities-based competition.

STRATEGIC PHILOSOPHIES

There are three very different philosophies or approaches to the development of successful strategies and sustainable competitive advantages that can be labeled strategy commitment, strategy opportunism, and strategic adaptability. Descriptions of each, summarized in Figure 7.4, provide a good perspective on choices as to management style, processes, and philosophy of business. There is no right way; given the right context, people, culture, and strategy, each can work. Further, most firms in fact use some combination of the three. In addition, the concept of strategic intent provides a fourth perspective on strategy.

Organizational Characteristics	Strategic Commitment	Strategic Opportunism	Strategic Adaptability
Perspective	Continuous improvement	Opportunistic	Adapt to changing marketplace
Orientation	Commitment	Fast response	Being relevant
Leadership	Charismatic	Tactical	Visionary
Structure	Centralized	Decentralized	Flat
Future perspective	Long term	Short term	Medium term
People	Eye-on-ball	Entrepreneurial	Diverse
Risk	Lose relevance	Also ran	Misread trends

Figure 7.4 Three Strategic Philosophies

Strategic Commitment

Strategic commitment involves a passionate, disciplined loyalty to a clearly defined business strategy that can result in an ever stronger and more profitable business over time. This "stick to your knitting" focus avoids being distracted by enticing opportunities or competitive threats that involve expending resources which do not advance the core strategy. Wal-Mart with its single-minded focus on costs and value has excelled with a strategic commitment philosophy.

Strategic commitment is based on an assumption that the future will be enough like the past that today's effective business model will also be successful in the future. There is a long-term perspective, the focus is on the future in investment decisions and strategy development. The planning horizon may extend into the future two, five, or more than ten years, depending on the business involved.

There should be an understanding and buy-in throughout the organization as to what the strategy is and why it is persuasive, achievable, and worthwhile. In particular, people should know and believe in the value proposition, the target market, the functional strategies, and the role of assets and competencies. The business rationale should be more than achieving financial objectives; there should be a purpose that is valued, if not inspirational.

Execution and improving the strategy are the keys to success. The emphasis is on continually improving (rather than changing) the existing implementations of the strategy, reducing the cost, improving efficiency, enhancing the value proposition, improving customer satisfaction, and strengthening the assets and competencies. Each year the operations and its output should be better than the last. Japanese firms such as Toyota or Canon call this continuous improvement *kaizen* and have built successful companies around it. In pursuing continuous improvement, what is needed is incremental rather than transformational or even substantial innovation. The goal is improvement of the existing strategy rather than the creation of a new strategy. In that regard, the information needs are on technology developments and consumer attitudes within the framework of the existing competitive context.

Strategic commitment places demands on the organization and its people, culture, structure, and systems. In general, a centralized organization that can be disciplined in resource allocation and keep it "on strategy" will be helpful, as will the

Strategic Approach	Strategic Risk
Strategic commitment	Strategic stubbornness
Strategic opportunism	Strategic drift
Strategic adaptability	Strategic blunders; misread trends

Figure 7.5   Vision versus Opportunism

presence of a strong, charismatic leader who can sell the vision to relevant constituencies inside and outside the organization. The people should be specialized, each with skills that will advance the strategy and its underlying assets and competencies. The culture should revolve around the strategic vision that is supporting the strategy. It should go beyond financial goals to include those that will inspire those implementing the strategy.

Strategic Stubbornness

The risk of the strategic commitment route, as suggested by Figure 7.5, is that the vision may become obsolete or faulty and its pursuit may be a wasteful exercise in strategic stubbornness. Of the host of pitfalls that could prevent a vision from being realized, three stand out.

Implementation barriers. The picture of the future may be substantially accurate, but the firm may not be able to implement the strategy required. That was, in part, the problem with the efforts of GE and others to crack the computer market in the 1960s and with the attempt of Sony to promote its beta VCR format as the industry standard.

Faulty assumptions of the future. The vision might be misguided because it is based on faulty assumptions about the future. For example, the concept of a one-stop financial services firm that drove the vision of American Express, Sears, Merrill Lynch, and others was based, in part, on the erroneous assumption that customers would see value in a one-stop financial service. It turned out that consumers preferred to deal with specialists. GE's concept of factory automation was similarly faulty, as it discovered after some big losses. Customers wanted hardware and software components, not a factory system.

A paradigm shift. A third problem occurs when there is a paradigm shift, perhaps brought about by a transformational innovation. For example, computers changed from mainframes to minicomputers to workstations to servers. In the semiconductor industry, the vacuum-tube business first gave way to transistors and then, in sequence, to semiconductors, integrated circuits, and microprocessors. In both cases, each new paradigm brought with it a remarkable change in the cast of characters. It was extremely rare for a leader in one paradigm to be a leader in the next, often because of strategic stubbornness.

New operating models can also change the paradigm. Starbucks and others have changed the way coffee is purchased and consumed, leaving those selling canned coffee in supermarkets to fight in a declining, unprofitable segment. Dell has changed the way both individuals and organizations buy their computers, leaving those selling through retail channels at a disadvantage. Nucor changed the steel industry by creating dispersed minimills that used scrap steel as raw material, leaving the big steel companies to compete on price and watch their sales decline and profits disappear. In each case, it is no coincidence that the new paradigm has been dominated by new entries or by entries that had been considered insignificant niche players by the leading companies.

Strategic Opportunism

Strategic opportunism is driven by a focus on the present. The premise is that the environment is so dynamic and uncertain that it is at least risky, and more likely futile, to predict the future and invest behind those predictions. The more prudent and profitable route is to detect and capture opportunities when they present themselves, with a goal of achieving immediate profits. When short-term successes flow, the long term will take care of itself as at least some of these short-term winners will grow to major businesses and the rest, in the aggregate, will not be a burden.

One key to success in strategic opportunism is an entrepreneurial culture and the willingness to respond quickly to opportunities as they emerge. The people should be entrepreneurial, sensitive to new opportunities and threats, and fast to react. The organization needs to be decentralized, with people empowered to experiment and invest behind emerging opportunities. The culture needs to support empowered managers, new ventures, and change. The strategy will be dynamic, and change the norm. New products will be continuously explored or introduced and others de-emphasized or dropped. New markets will be entered and disinvestment in existing ones will always be an option. The organization will be on the lookout for new synergies and assets and competencies to be developed.

Another key is to be close to the market. The management team needs to be talking to customers and others about the changing customer tastes, attitudes, and needs. Information systems must monitor customers, competitors, and the trade to learn of trends, opportunities, problems, and threats as they appear. Information gathering and analysis should be both sensitive and online. Frequent, regular meetings to analyze the most recent developments and news may be helpful. The organization should be quick to understand and act on changing fundamentals.

Strategic opportunism provides several advantages. One is that the risk of missing emerging business opportunities is reduced. Firms such as General Mills in cereals,

Purina in pet foods, and Ziff Davis Communications in special interest computer publishing all seek emerging niche segments and develop brands tailored to specialty markets. Thus, Purina brands such as Deli-Cat, Kitt'N Kaboodle, and Purina One and General Mills brands such as Berry Burst Cheerios and Cinnamon Toast Crunch are designed to appeal to a current taste or trend. Ziff Davis is continuously introducing niche magazines such as *CIO Insight*. The risk of strategic stubbornness is also reduced.

Strategic opportunism tends to generate a vitality and energy that can be healthy, especially when a business has decentralized R&D and marketing units that generate a stream of new products. Within 3M, for example, new businesses are continually created and evaluated with respect to their prospects. HP is another firm that believes in decentralized entrepreneurial management. These decentralized firms are often close to the market and technology and are willing to pursue opportunities.

Strategic opportunism results in economies of scope, with assets and competencies supported by multiple product lines. Nike, which applies its brand assets and competencies in product design and customer sensing to a wide variety of product markets, is a good example. A key part of the Nike strategy is to develop strong emotional ties and relationships with focused segments through its product design and brand name strengths. The organization is extremely sensitive to emerging segments (such as outdoor basketball) and the need for product refinements and product innovation. Nike has strategic flexibility, which characterizes successful strategically opportunistic firms.

Strategic Drift

The problem with the strategic opportunism model is that, as suggested by Figure 7.5, it can turn into strategic drift. Investment decisions are made incrementally in response to opportunities rather than directed by a vision. As a result, a firm can wake up one morning and find that it is in a set of businesses for which it lacks the needed assets and competencies and that provide few synergies.

At least three phenomena can turn strategic opportunism into strategic drift. First, a short-lived, transitory force may be mistaken for one with enough staying power to make a strategic move worthwhile. If the force is so short-lived that a strategy does not pay off or does not even have a chance to get into place, the result will be a strategy that is not suitable for the business or the environment.

Second, opportunities to create immediate profits may be rationalized as strategic when, in fact, they are not. For example, an instrumentation firm might receive many requests from some of its customers for special-purpose instruments that could conceivably be used by other customers but that have little strategic value for the company. Such opportunities might result in a sizable initial order, but could divert R&D resources from more strategic activities.

Third, expected synergies across existing and new business areas may fail to materialize owing to implementation problems, perhaps because of culture clashes or because the synergies were only illusions in the first place. A drive to exploit core assets or competencies might not work. As a result, new business areas would be in place without the expected sustainable advantages.

Strategic drift not only creates businesses without needed assets and competencies, but it can also result in a failure to support a core business that does have a good vision. Without a vision and supporting commitment, it is tempting to divert investment into seemingly sure things that are immediate strategic opportunities. Thus, strategic opportunism can be an excuse to delay investment or divert resources from a core vision.

One example of strategic drift is a firm that designed, installed, and serviced custom equipment for steel firms. Over time, steel firms became more knowledgeable and began buying standardized equipment mainly on the basis of price. Gradually, the firm edged into this commodity business to retain its market share. The company finally realized it was pursuing a dual strategy for which it was ill suited. It had too much overhead to compete with the real commodity firms, and its ability to provide upscale service had eroded to the point that it was now inferior to some niche players. Had there been a strategic vision, the firm would not have fallen into such a trap.

Another example is a discounter that did well when operating a limited product line in a local market with a low-cost message. The customer value was clear, and the hands-on management style was effective. However, when the firm expanded its geographic and product scope (even going into groceries), the management systems were no longer adequate and the value proposition become fuzzy as well. It had drifted into a business requiring assets and competencies it did not have.

Strategic Adaptability

Strategic adaptability, like strategic opportunism, is based on the assumption that the market is dynamic, the future will not necessary mimic the past, and an existing business model, however successful, may not be optimal in tomorrow's marketplace. Unlike in strategic opportunism, however, there is also an assumption that it is possible to understand, predict, and manage responses to market dynamics that emerge and even create or influence them.

Strategic adaptability is about managing relevance, a topic introduced in Chapter 4. As the market dynamics evolve and the niches and submarkets emerge, one goal is to adapt the offering so that it maintains its relevance. The firm wants to avoid investing behind SUVs when the market is shifting to hybrids. Another is to seize opportunities to influence the creation of markets and submarkets. One study determined that such an opportunity occurs about once or twice a decade on average, and that the window of opportunity is often short. A strategically adaptable firm does not want to miss such an opportunity. In that respect, it is more likely to go beyond incremental innovation to substantial and even transformational innovation if that is what it takes to create new markets.

Identifying and evaluating trends. The strategically adaptable firm needs to have a good external sensing mechanism to detect underlying customers trends and market dynamics involving drivers such as technology and distribution. In addition,

A firm that aspires to be strategically adaptable needs to have competence in identifying and evaluating trends, a culture that supports aggressive response, and organizational flexibility so that business creation and modification can occur quickly.

the organization will need to be able to distinguish fads from trends and to evaluate the substance, dynamics, and implications of those trends. This is not an easy assignment. Being close to the customer, through direct contact and through research, will be important.

Adaptation-supporting culture. When trends are detected, the strategically adaptable firm needs to have a culture that supports aggressive response to opportunities represented by the trend analysis. That means that innovation, entrepreneurship, and experimentation should be valued and that it is okay to fail. Innovation is a mindset, but it also involves an R&D capability, in house or with alliance firms, to provide the potential to broaden the firm's offerings. The entrepreneurial style should be supported by organizational structures and reward systems that encourage managers to exploit opportunities with action-oriented strategies. There has to be some ability to tolerate a "ready, fire, aim" mentality and to allow pilot tests to thrive. Unlike strategic opportunism, the short-term product will be less important than the priority of getting the offering right and establishing a value position in the emerging market.

Strategic flexibility. Strategic adaptability usually requires flexibility so that the firm will be ready when a window of opportunity arises. Strategic flexibility—the ability to adjust or develop strategies to respond to external or internal changes—can be achieved in a variety of ways, including participating in multiple product markets and technologies, having resource slack, and creating a flexible brand portfolio.

Participation in multiple product markets or technologies means that the organization is already "on the ground" in different arenas and has purchased strategic options. Thus, if it appears that demand will shift to a new product market or that a newer technology will emerge, the organization can just expand its current product market rather than start from zero with all the risks and time required. An organization may also participate in business areas with weak returns in order to gain the strategic flexibility to deal with possible market changes. For example, GM's investment in Saturn resulted in a very modest return. However, having Saturn could allow GM some very nice competitive options if gas supplies were curtailed by OPEC or by a war.

Investing in underused assets provides strategic flexibility. An obvious example is maintaining liquidity (as with Toyota's $20 billion cash hoard) so that investment can be funneled swiftly to opportunity or problem areas. Maintaining excess capacity in distribution, organizational staffing, or R&D can also enhance a firm's ability to react quickly.

A flexible brand portfolio may be needed so that brand assets will be in place to support a move in a new direction. Such flexibility can be based in a strong umbrella brand; GE not only has the GE brand but other brands, like NBC and Universal, that can be the basis of a growth platform. It can also be based on a system of endorsed brands, subbrands, and branded features such as Marriott's portfolio that includes Fairfield Inn, Courtyard, and others. The idea is to have a portfolio robust enough so that a new offering does not have to create a brand asset in order to compete.

Two firms that have shown strategic adaptability are Nucor and Charles Schwab.

In the 1970s, facing price pressures from fully integrated steel firms plus efficient Japanese brands, Nucor developed a strategy of producing joists (higher-value products used in construction) in rural minimills that employed nonunionized labor and used scrap steel as raw material. For a decade, this model made Nucor a strategic and financial success. By the mid-1980s, however, others had started to copy the strategy, scrap steel was no longer as plentiful, and aluminum had made serious inroads into traditional steel markets. In response to these changes, Nucor again reinvented the paradigm by focusing on flat-rolled, upmarket products using a scrap steel substitute, and drawing on iron ore in Brazil and a processing plant in Trinidad.

Charles Schwab shifted from being a discount broker for individual investors to being an innovative supplier of no-load, no-transaction-fee mutual funds under the Schwab OneSource brand. It has now enlisted an army of fee-only financial advisers called Schwab Institutional to guide investors who are attracted to the Schwab investment options. Microsoft's focus progressed from operating systems to applications to the Internet. Both Schwab and Microsoft chose not to abandon the old vision, but rather to augment it with a new direction.

Strategy Blunders—Misreading Trends

Investing behind trends and emerging submarkets is inherently risky because of the uncertainty and judgment involved and because the execution of the strategy is often difficult.

An error in interpreting a trend or emerging submarket can result in a substantial blunder that can damage or even cripple the firm. Not only will resources be wasted that could have been productively used elsewhere, it can also have a deleterious impact on the brand assets and on the internal culture. A visible failure can inhibit future strategy choices. Consider, for example, Nabisco's Snackwells, which responded to a low-fat eating trend that turned out to be less of a long-term phenomenon than expected. The loss of equity for both the Snackwell and Nabisco brands was significant to the firm.

In addition to a trend being misinterpreted, there is an execution issue. The most astute and insightful analysis can lead to a strategy that simply cannot be implemented. Consider the merger of AOL with Time Warner. Time Warner hoped to provide content to the then-leading Internet portal and in the process become relevant in the Internet world. The failure of this concept was at least in part due to the inability to execute behind the strategy. The two organizations, with very different cultures and incentives, were unable to work together to execute the vision. Even had the vision been on target, the execution difficulties doomed the effort.

Strategic Intent

Hamel and Prahalad have suggested that some firms have strategic intent, which couples a clear strategic vision a sustained obsession with winning at all levels of the organization.[5] They note that this model explains the successful rise to global leadership of companies such as Canon, Komatsu, Samsung (see box), and Honda. Canon was out to "beat Xerox," Komatsu to "encircle Caterpillar," and Honda to become a "second Ford."

SAMSUNG AND MICROWAVE OVENS

In 1977, Samsung decided to make microwave ovens, even though major established competitors with seemingly unbeatable SCAs were making millions of ovens per year.[6] During the next four years, it saw its first two prototypes melt down, redesigned its product again and again, bought the last magnetron factory from the United States, and received its first order for 240 ovens from Panama. In 1980, a J. C. Penney order requiring Samsung to build a unit 25 percent less expensive than existing ones necessitated still another redesign. In 1983, GE, under pressure from Japanese firms, turned to Samsung to source some of its products, Samsung's labor costs of $1.47 contrasted sharply with GE's $52.00. By the late 1980s, Samsung was building more than 4 million units per year and had cornered more than one-third of the U.S. market.

It is clear that Samsung had a strategic intent to enter the microwave oven market. Its goals during the first decade were production and meeting whatever customer needs were required to gain sales. Financial return was of no consequence. An enormous investment was made in design, manufacturing, and engineering. To make it happen, a large, competent staff carefully analyzed how competitors had solved problems and what customers expected. The firm was very responsive to customer needs, even despite sizable losses. It capitalized on its cost advantage and the willingness of production and engineering personnel to work 68-hour weeks. Samsung virtually willed its own remarkable success.

A strategic intent to achieve a successful strategy has several characteristics in addition to strategic commitment and an obsession with success. First, it should recognize the essence of winning. Coca-Cola's strategic intent has included the objective of putting a Coke within "arm's reach" of every consumer in the world, because distribution and accompanied visibility are the keys to winning. NEC decided it needed to acquire the technologies that would allow it to exploit the convergence of computing and telecommunications. That became its guiding theme.

Second, strategic intent involves stretching an organization with a continuing effort to identify and develop new SCAs or to improve those that exist. Thus, it has a dynamic, forward-looking perspective: What will our advantage be next year, and two years after that? Consider Matsushita, Toshiba, and the other Japanese television manufacturers. They first relied on the advantage of low labor cost. By servicing private-label needs, they added economies of scale. The next step was to build advantages in quality, reliability, features, brand name, and distribution. An analysis of their strengths and weaknesses might have led to the conclusion that they should focus on a low-cost niche. But they extended their capabilities, which in turn made their strategic options broader.

Third, strategic intent often requires real innovation, a willingness to do things very differently. Savin entered the U.S. copier market with a product that could be sold through dealers instead of leased and was simple, low priced, and reliable. As a result, Xerox's huge advantage in sales and service and its ability to finance leased equipment were neutralized. Honda made real advances in motor design in order to attack the large motorcycle market.

Strategic intent provides a long-term drive for advantage that can be essential to success. It provides a model that helps break the mold, moving a firm away from simply doing the same things a bit better and working a bit harder than the year before. It has the capability to elevate and extend an organization, helping it reach levels it would not otherwise attain.

KEY LEARNINGS

- To create an SCA, a strategy needs to be valued by the market and supported by assets and competencies that are not easily copied or neutralized by competitors. The most common SCAs are quality reputation, customer support, and brand name.

- Synergy is often sustainable because it is based on the unique characteristics of an organization.

- Strategic commitment, involving a stick-to-your-knitting focus on a clearly articulated strategy, is based on an assumption that the business model needs to be refined and improved and not changed.

- Strategic opportunism assumes that the environment is so dynamic and uncertain that it is futile to predict the future and invest behind those predictions. The more prudent and profitable route is to detect and capture opportunities when they present themselves, with a goal of achieving immediate profits.

- Strategic adaptability, based on the assumption that it is possible to understand, predict, and manage responses to market dynamics that emerge and even create or influence them, is about managing relevance.

- Strategic intent couples a clear strategic vision with a sustained obsession with winning at all levels of the organization.

FOR DISCUSSION

1. What is a sustainable competitive advantage? Identify SCAs for Dell, P&G, Tide, and Citibank.

2. Pick a product class and several major brands. What are each brand's points of parity and point of difference? Relate POPs to KSFs, and the POD to SCAs.

3. What is synergy? What are the sources of synergy? Give examples. Why is it so elusive?

4. What is strategic commitment? Can you name examples that fit besides those mentioned in the book? What examples of strategic stubbornness

come to mind? Why are good strategists so blind to this problem? How does strategic commitment differ from strategic intent? Illustrate with examples.

5. What is the difference between strategic opportunism and strategic adaptability? Can you give examples of each? What is the difference between the risks of both? Can you give examples of firms that have experienced drift or misread trends?

NOTES

1. Keller introduced points of parity in the branding context in Kevin Lane Keller, *Strategic Brand Management*, 2nd edition, Upper Saddle River, New Jersey: Prentice Hall, 2003, pp. 131–136.

2. David A. Aaker, "Managing Assets and Skills: The Key to a Sustainable Competitive Advantage," *California Management Review*, Winter 1989, pp. 91–106.

3. Louis V. Gertner, Jr, *Who Says Elephants Can't Dance?*, New York: Harper Business, 2002.

4. C. K. Prahalad and Gary Hamel, "The Core Competence of the Corporation," *Harvard Business Review*, May–June 1990, pp. 79–91. This book uses the phrase "core assets and competencies," which is an extension of the term "core competencies" used in Prahalad and Hamel's article.

5. Gary Hamel and C. K. Prahalad, "Strategic Intent," *Harvard Business Review*, May–June 1989, pp. 63–76.

6. Ira C. Magaziner and Mark Patinkin, "Fast Heat: How Korea Won the Microwave War," *Harvard Business Review*, January–February 1989, pp. 83–92.

CHAPTER EIGHT

Alternative Value Propositions

Ever since Morton's put a little girl in a yellow slicker and declared, "When it rains, it pours," no advertising person worth his or her salt has had any excuse to think of a product as having parity with anything.
—*Malcolm MacDougal, Jordan Case McGrath & Taylor*

If you don't have a competitive advantage, don't compete.
—*Jack Welch, GE*

You can't depend on your eyes when your imagination is out of focus.
—*Mark Twain*

A business strategy, as defined in Chapter 1, involves four components—the product-market investment decision, the customer value proposition, the organization's assets and competencies, and functional strategies and programs. For a given industry and organizational context, a strategist will have uncountable ways to compete. Alternative markets, submarkets, product extensions, and new product arenas can always be considered. A bewildering variety of customer value propositions, each with its own nuances and spins, will represent strategy variants. Hundreds of conceivable assets and competencies can be developed, nurtured, exploited, and combined, and there are potentially thousands of viable functional strategies and programs.

Usually, however, business strategies cluster around a limited number of value propositions for a product market, supported by assets and competencies and functional strategies and programs. These value propositions include a superior attribute or benefit (BMW's drivability), appealing design (Apple's iPod), offering a complete systems solution (UPS Supply Chain Solutions), social responsibility (Avon Breast Cancer Crusade), a familiar brand (Intel Inside), a superior customer relationship

(Nordstrom's), a specialist niche (Victoria's Secret), superior quality (Lexus), and superior value (Wal-Mart). Each of these value propositions needs to be adapted to a given context, but all should potentially affect customer-firm relationships.

Looking at business strategies through the lens of value propositions provides a way to consider of broad set of strategies. As a summary indicator of complex strategies, value propositions provide a shorthand way to visualize a business strategy. Reflecting on a value proposition and its implied target markets, assets, competencies, and functional strategies is easier than dealing with complete detailed business strategy. As a result, more strategies can be considered, and creating multiple alternatives is a way to make sure that superior ones are allowed to surface.

Considering strategies at the level of a value proposition also allows a firm to make preliminary evaluative judgments as to the problems that will have to be overcome, the investments required, the appeal in the marketplace, and the fit with the organization. Thus, some strategies can be rejected or put on hold before a lot of resources have been invested.

A business may select more than one value proposition—choosing to walk and chew gum at the same time, so to speak. It is not an either/or situation. In fact, most successful strategies will represent an integration of several value propositions. A solid understanding of each, however, can guide you not only in making the decision which to include but also in specifying their respective roles and priorities in the overall strategy. Which should be dialed up? How should various propositions interact?

Although multiple value propositions can be supported and employed, there is a limit as to how many can be addressed—it is not credible or feasible to create or communicate too many value propositions simultaneously. More than two or three will generally stretch resources too thin, and the customer will become confused and skeptical.

BUSINESS STRATEGY CHALLENGES

Which value proposition or propositions—with their supporting target market, assets, competencies, and functional strategies—should form the basis for a business strategy? To answer this question, each value proposition should be challenged with respect to whether it contains a real and perceived value proposition and whether it is feasible, relevant, and sustainable. The goal of this analysis is to identify not only the potential impact of the strategic option, but also its limitations and feasibility.

Is There a Real Customer Value Proposition?

A successful business strategy needs to add value for the customer, and this value needs to be real rather than merely assumed. The one-stop financial service vision, for example, had much less value to customers than was hoped when it was first tried in the early 1980s. Customers wanted excellence and competence from investment managers, and all-in-one convenience was relatively unimportant. Similarly, Bayer tried to apply its familiar brand name on nonaspirin products, only to find that the value of the Bayer name diminished greatly outside of the aspirin category.

Value is more likely to be real if it is driven from the customer's perspective rather than from that of the business operation. How does the point of differentiation affect the customer's experience of buying and using the product? Does it serve to reduce cost, add performance, or increase satisfaction? The concepts of unmet needs and customer problems, outlined in Chapter 2, are relevant. Does market research confirm that value is added from the customer's perspective?

Is There a Perceived Customer Value Proposition?

Further, the value proposition must be recognized and perceived as worthwhile by the customers. Delivering a value proposition is pointless unless customers know about it and believe it. For example, a customer may be unaware that Burger King has a convenient ordering process, that Buick is delivering quality equal to Toyota, or that Subaru has a superior braking system. This may occur because customers have not have been exposed to the information, because the information was not packaged in a memorable and believable way, or because the attribute or service was not considered to be relevant or of value.

The perceived value problem is particularly acute when the customer is not capable of judging the added value easily. Customers, for example, cannot evaluate airline safety or the skill of a dentist without investing significant time and effort. Instead the customer will look for signals, such as the appearance of the aircraft or the professionalism of the dentist's front office. The firm's task, then, is to manage the signals or cues that imply added value.

Is the Strategy Feasible?

If the value proposition is aspirational, is it feasible. It is one thing to create the perfect strategy with respect to customers, competitors, and the marketplace. It is another to execute that strategy effectively. The strategy may require assets and capabilities that are currently inadequate or do not exist, and programs to develop or upgrade them may turn out to be unrealistic. Alliance partners to fill the gap may be difficult to find or to work with. Further, an objective analysis of the customer trends, competitor strengths, or market dynamics may reveal that any strategic success will be short-lived.

Is the Value Proposition Relevant to Customers?

A business has to make what customers want to buy. The product or service has to be considered relevant to the markets in which the business chooses to compete. It does no good, for example, to make the best SUV if customers are interested in hybrid cars. If a business has a value proposition that is of secondary interest to customers, the latter may look elsewhere even if the business is executing its value proposition effectively. If the products are considered passé or inferior, the business will lack relevance.

Is the Value Proposition a Point of Difference That Is Sustainable?

Does the value proposition represent a point of superiority over the competition? Or is it simply a point of parity, with customer believing that the offerings are acceptable but not superior with respect to the value proposition? And if there is a point of difference, is it sustainable? Sustainability is often a tough challenge, because most points of differentiation are easily copied. One route to a sustainable advantage is to own an important product dimension, perhaps with the aid of a branded differentiator (such as the Cadillac Northstar engine or the GM OnStar guidance systems), as described in Chapter 10. A second route would be creating a program of continuous investment and improvement that enables the strategy to remain a moving target, always ahead of competitors or poised to leapfrog them. Third, a business could create points of differentiation that are based on unique assets and competencies of the organization, which are inherently difficult to copy.

Overinvestment in a value-added activity may pay off in the long run by discouraging competitors from duplicating a strategy. For example, competitors might be deterred from developing a service backup system that is more extensive than current customers expect. The same logic can apply to a broad product line. Some elements of that line might be unprofitable, but still might be worth retaining if they plug holes that competitors could use to provide customer value.

ALTERNATIVE VALUE PROPOSITIONS

While there are an infinite number of business strategy variants in any context, certain value propositions with supporting strategy elements tend to be used most often. In this chapter a snapshot of a handful of value propositions will be described, as noted in Figure 8.1. They are among the most commonly used, and their description provides a glimpse of the scope of choices available to the business strategist.

Two of the value propositions—quality and value—will be discussed in some detail. Each is frequently employed, has led to performance successes, and is associated with a body of knowledge and experience. Two more, brand familiarity and delivering emotional/self-expressive benefits, will be covered in the next chapter and another, being global, is the subject of Chapter 13.

A Superior Attribute or Benefit

If a product or service attribute or benefit is central to the purchase and use of an offering, one strategic option is to dominate or even own that attribute. Volvo has long owned safety by designing its cars and positioning its brand so that it has extremely strong credibility on that dimension. Pringles offers both a product form and package that allow convenient, compact storage of the product. Heinz has catsup that pours slowly because it is so thick and rich but easily because of innovative "Top Down" package designs. British Airlines offers business-class passengers more comfortable sleeping space. In each case, the attribute is relevant to customers, and the brands are clearly positioned on that attribute.

If such an option is to be viable over time, it needs to be protected against competitors. Having patent protection is one route. Dolby Laboratories has created a position based on an ever-expanding set of patents to support its sound offerings. Another route is to have a programmatic investment strategy in order to maintain the

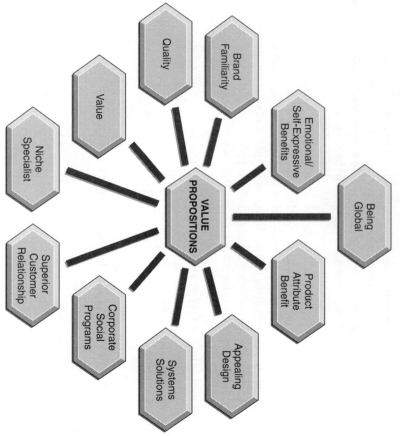

Figure 8.1   Strategic Options

real and perceived edge. Thus, Volvo has an investment program and clear design philosophy to ensure that it can deliver on its safety promise.

Another route to owning an attribute over time is to brand it and then actively manage that brand and its promise. For example, OnStar provides a visible, branded point of differentiation for GM cars. Again, this concept will be elaborated in Chapter 10.

Appealing Design

An offering can appeal to a person's aesthetics, providing substantial self-expressive as well as functional benefits. Jaguar has long pursued this strategy and is somewhat unique among competitors that look all too similar, as if they all use the same wind tunnel. W Hotels have a unique look and feel (which extends to their rooms) that appeals to fashion-forward travelers. The translucent Apple iMac showed that even computers could have design flair. (Steve Jobs has been quoted as saying, "Design is the soul of a manmade creation.") The Volkswagen Beetle came back with a new design that retained the original Beetle look and its authentic personality.

Pursuing a design option requires the firm to really have a passion for design and to support a home for a creative design team. Creating such a culture and infrastructure is a key to success for firms like Jaguar, W Hotels, and Apple, as well as other design-driven firms such as Disney and Ralph Lauren. Because achieving a home for design can be difficult, another route is to create an alliance with a design firm, which allows access to best-of-breed designers when needed. Outsourcing can succeed if the firm manages the alliance properly and establishes exclusive ownership of the output.

Making the design credible and visible is another challenge. The used of branded personality designers allowed Target to break through its utilitarian image. The well-known designer Isaac Mizrahi in 2004 launched an affordable Target line of sweaters, blouses, pants, skirts, dresses, shoes, and purses that was well received. The renowned architect Michael Graves developed for Target a collection of cookware and other dining products.

Systems Solutions

A compelling value proposition can be based on moving from selling products to selling systems solutions, based on packaging products that work together to create a total system. Competitors selling ad hoc products, even thought they might be superior, will be at a disadvantage. Sears offers a one-stop place to deliver home improvement projects. Sony, because it makes a complete line of home entertainment products, offers customers total system design and a single source for upgrades and service.

Especially in the business-to-business space, many firms are trying to move from being component suppliers to being systems solution players. One reason is that a systems-based organization will be more likely to control the customer relationship. Another is a need to capture greater margins in a context where components are becoming commodities. Simply bundling products, though, is rarely enough. To deliver value to the customer, a firm must offer not only product breadth but a systems orientation and expertise, and it must be willing and able to deliver a high level of customer service.

Corporate Social Programs

BP is serious about its motto of "Beyond Petroleum," aggressively promoting conservation and investing in cleaner energy sources. The Body Shop built up a following through its visible endorsement of Third World ecology and other causes. Ben & Jerry's has supported environmental causes in a colorful way that has enhanced the company's image. The Ronald McDonald House and the Avon Breast Cancer Crusade provide unmistakable expressions of organizational values. The "HP way" involved a commitment to employees, customers, suppliers, and the community to which people could relate.

CEOs believe that corporate social responsibility (CSR) can pay off. In one survey, more than 90 percent thought that socially responsible management creates shareholder value.[1] In another study, 300 firms judged to have high commitment to CSR had a slightly higher stock return during a two-year period beginning in October 2000.[2] Providing a more direct measurement, a U.K. study compared the marketplace performance of three energy companies. Two of these, BP and Shell, were perceived as environmentally friendly; while the third, Esso, had visibly taken the position that renewable energy was not a viable solution and that the Kyoto international accords on the environment were flawed. Greenpeace subsequently attacked Esso with a high-profile "StopEsso" campaign. A subsequent Greenpeace poll found that the proportion of British gasoline buyers who said they regularly used Esso stations dropped by 7 percent during the year of the campaign.[3]

There are good reasons why CSR could influence profitability. Many people fundamentally want to have a relationship with good people who can be trusted, and they perceive that CSR programs reflect a firm's values. A strong and visible CSR program can deliver to customers self-expressive benefits, particularly for the core group of customers who have strong feelings about environmental issues. Certainly, many drivers of Toyota's Prius, the leading gas-electric hybrid car, achieve significant self-expressive benefits. In fact, the glamorous CEO of The Body Shop Japan drives a Prius as a statement about both herself and her firm. With Prius as the flagship of dozens of environmental programs, Toyota has taken the leadership position with respect to CSR, at least in North America. A CSR program can also be defensive, in that it can help a firm deal with an accident or criticism by activists based on social responsibility issues.

Ad hoc programs, though, are not the way to pursue CSR. Rather, the programs need to be focused, meaningful, consistent over time, and hopefully branded. All firms will give lip service and some resources toward CSR. The firms that stand out, such as Toyota and BP, however, have a real commitment—even a passion—and find ways to make it visible.

There are challenges in pursuing a CSR strategy. One, perhaps the most serious, involves creating unreasonable expectations. If a firm is visible and active with regard to CSR, people will expect it to be flawless. Given the complexity of the issues, however, a firm can be making strides and still be criticized. BP can make significant investments in renewable energy relative to its competitors, for example, but some may correctly point out that the investment is still small relative to BP's size. Nike can make progress in addressing the labor practices of its offshore suppliers, but still draw fire because problems remain. Another challenge is to make CSR programs visible and relevant to customers, many of whom will find a firm's CSR activities too far removed from its offering's attributes and benefits.

Superior Customer Relationship

All firms place an emphasis on the customer. A few, however, create an experience that connects the offering to the customer on a more involving and passionate level. For these firms, customer intimacy is a strategic option. Starbucks' vision of a "third place" (after home and office) where people feel comfortable and secure represents an experience that many customers view as a high point in their day. Some local hardware stores create offerings, specialized services like hot popcorn, and personal customer relationships that allow them to prosper while competing with "big boxes" such as Home Depot or Wal-Mart. Nordstrom's has generated a customer link by offering personalized service and a shopping experience that often delights rather than merely satisfies. Apple and 3M have similarly connected by providing products that generate a "Wow!" response.

Firms that create intimacy understand customers at a deep level. They deliver an experience that is satisfying on several levels, going beyond functional benefits to provide emotional, social, and self-expressive benefits. The open-road experience associated with Harley-Davidson, for example, has important social and self-expressive elements. The result is an intensely loyal customer base that will talk about the brand and the experience, not just to others in the "club" but also to those who should be.

The key to really turning on customers and achieving intimacy might be resolving unmet needs in the marketplace—finding answers to annoyances that customers have tolerated because there was no option. For example, the automobile buying experience was distasteful before Saturn and Lexus introduced a very different buying experience that became a basis for a new customer relationship. Lexus also earns loyalty with a dozen clever design features in its cars. Intimacy can also come from delight at an unexpected experience, such as the massages that come with Virgin's first-class seats, the piano in a Nordstrom's store, or Harley-Davidson's biking parties. Or it could develop from an over-the-top product, such as In-N-Out hamburgers or Apple's iPod.

The highly loyal, even fanatical customer base sometimes created through an intimacy strategy needs active programs to nurture and support it. Harley-Davidson, for example, supports its Harley Owners' Groups (HOGs) with local and national events, clothing and accessories, and a Web site with a host of supporting services, including a trip planner and online photo center. Virgin continually adds new features and services designed to support its image of being creative and willing to ignore convention in pursuit of enjoyable customer experiences.

Niche Specialist

Being a niche specialist means that the firm concentrates on one part of the market or product line and can emerge in virtually any arena. Portman Hotels, who use a Rolls-Royce to transport guests, focus on the upscale segment. An industrial distributor may focus on large-volume users or even a single user. A clothing store might offer hot fashions for plus-sized teen girls. Armstrong Rubber has performed well over the years by focusing on replacement tires. Castrol Motor Oil focuses on male car owners who buy and change their own oil. Lets-go-fly-a-kite features kites. An online business with focus is Gold Violin, which provides products and services for the retired generation (whom it conceptualizes as modern-day heroes). Another is myspace, an online brand that is differentiated in large part by its relentless reliance on community.

Because a niche specialist by its nature tends to avoid strategy dilution or distraction, it is more likely to pursue a strategic commitment strategy leading to a sustainable advantage. When internal investments, programs, and culture have all been directed toward a single end and there is buy-in on the part of everyone in the organization, the result will be assets, competencies, and functional strategies that match market needs. There are no compromises or diluted investments. It is no accident that specialized retailers such as Williams-Sonoma and Victoria's Secret have

SHOULDICE HOSPITAL

Shouldice Hospital near Toronto only does hernia operations. Since its founding in 1945, over 300,000 operations have been conducted, with a 99 percent success rate. Measured by how often repeat treatment is needed, Shouldice is ten times more effective than are other hospitals. The surgical procedure used is branded as the Shouldice Technique.

The experience of the doctors and staff are appealing, but so are the Shouldice setting and its recovery program. Located on a country estate, the hospital has a calming ambience and facilities tailored to needs of recovering hernia patients. Patients walk to watch TV, to eat, and even to and from the operating room, because walking is good therapy for hernias. There is thus no need to deliver food to rooms, or to have wheelchair facilities. The length of a hospital visit at Shouldice is around half the norm elsewhere. No general anesthesia is administered, because local anesthesia is safer and cheaper for hernia operations.

By concentrating on one narrow segment of the medical market, Shouldice has developed a hospital that is proficient, inexpensive, and capable of delivering an extraordinary level of patient satisfaction. Patients are so pleased that the Shouldice Hospital annual reunion attracts some 1,500 "alumni."

been much more successful than department stores and others that are spread thin. One reason is the strategic and operational advantages of focusing.

A product focus can result in technical superiority because the people are developing and bringing to the market products that they are passionate about. When the products of a firm capture the imagination of its key people, they tend to be exciting, innovative, and of high quality.

A niche specialist strategy can translate into a value proposition for customers. First, a focused firm will have more credibility than a firm that makes a wide array of products, as demonstrated by Shouldice Hospital in hernia surgeries, Williams-Sonoma in cooking, Raymond Corporation in lift trucks, and the In-N-Out chain in making hamburgers. If you are really interested in the best, you will go to a firm that specializes in and has a passion for the business. Second, the bond between the loyal user and the brand will tend to be greater when the brand is focused and the people are seen to have passion for their product. The reunions of Shouldice Hospital patients and the passion of Harley-Davidson customers would not happen without a focus strategy.

This list of strategic options could be extended in any given context. For now, we will explore two options, quality and value, in more detail.

SUPERIOR QUALITY

A quality strategy means that the brand—whether it be hotels, cars, or computers—will be perceived as superior to other brands in its reference set. The point of superiority

LEXUS—A PASSION FOR EXCELLENCE

For more than a decade, Lexus has been among the leaders on a variety of objective quality indicators. Among the many reasons behind the Lexus achievement, several stand out. First, the Lexus concept was based on quality from its inception. Toyota launched Lexus in the early 1980s as a brand that would take automobile design, manufacturing, and retailing to a new level. Second, the brand delivered on the concept, as Lexus drew on assets and competencies developed by Toyota to make cars that were more reliable and had fewer defects. Third, a new dealer network offered the potential to break from industry norms and provide a pleasant buying experience. Fourth, the positioning of the Lexus brand (with the classic "relentless pursuit of perfection" tagline) delivered the quality message consistently over the years.

The challenge facing Lexus now is that despite its success with a quality mission and message, it has failed to develop much personality in comparison to BMW, Mercedes, Jaguar, and Cadillac. When the latter brands gradually closed the quality gap over the years, the Lexus message became less compelling. In response, Lexus belatedly has tried to inject some emotional and self-expressive benefits, as demonstrated by its modified tagline, "The passionate pursuit of perfection." It has not been an easy task.

---

spans the brand offerings, delivering exceptional quality across products and individual attributes. Usually, such superiority will be associated with a price premium. As the Lexus insert illustrates, perceived quality can be the driver of a business strategy.

Superiority can also be demonstrated with respect to value offerings. Thus, Target may be regarded as higher in quality than other discount retailers, although no one would confuse it with Bloomingdale's or Nordstrom's. It will simply be judged on a different set of criteria, including ease of parking, waiting time at checkout, courtesy of the checkout person, and whether desired items are in stock. In much the same manner, Gillette's Good News is the quality option among disposable blades.

Superiority will be defined by customers. In nearly all contexts, a single overall indicator of quality exists, is relevant to customers, and in fact drives other, more specific dimensions of performance. To understand what drives perceived quality and to actively manage it, however, the underlying dimensions in any given context need to be determined.

Figure 8.2 lists several dimensions of quality that are often relevant. Of course, each of these dimensions has multiple components (for example, performance for a printer will involve attributes such as speed, resolution, and capacity). Further, the list itself will depend on the context. The dimensions of quality in a service or software context will differ from those in a product context.

In a service context—such as a bank, restaurant, or theme park—research has shown that quality is based in large part on the perceived competence, responsiveness, and empathy of the people with whom customers interact.[4] A successful organization therefore must deliver consistently on those dimensions. Delivering service

1. **Performance.** What are the specifications? How well is the task performed? Does the lawn mower cut grass well? Does the bank handle transactions with speed and accuracy?

2. **Conformance to specifications.** Does the product or service perform reliably and provide customer satisfaction?

3. **Features.** Does the product offer the latest features? Are there any "Wow" attributes?

4. **Customer support.** Does the firm support the customer with caring, competent people and efficient systems?

5. **Process quality.** Is the process of buying and using the product or service pleasant, rather than frustrating and disappointing?

6. **Aesthetic design.** Does the design add pleasure to the experience of buying and using the product or service?

Figure 8.2   Product Quality Dimensions

quality, however, also means managing expectations. If expectations are too high, the service experience might be unsatisfactory even if it is at a high level. Generating clarity about the service promise, whenever possible, will thus be helpful.

Understanding what drives quality in a given segment is a critical step in creating a quality program and monitoring its effectiveness. One risk in focusing on specific dimensions, however, is that the resulting measures can be counterproductive. For example, a company sought to improve the quality of its phone service by measuring the percentage of calls answered after the first ring. Unfortunately, the pressure to answer promptly caused agents to become abrupt and impatient with callers, and thus customer satisfaction suffered. The saying "Be careful what you wish for" is especially true in performance measurement.

Total Quality Management

To pursue a quality strategic option successfully, a business must distinguish itself with respect to delivering quality to customers. To accomplish this goal, it needs a quality-focused management system that is comprehensive, integrative, and supported throughout the organization. Such a total quality management (TQM) system[5] should incorporate a host of tools and precepts, including the following:

- The commitment of senior management to quality.

- Cross-functional teams empowered to make changes by initiating and implementing quality improvement projects.

- A process (rather than results) orientation. The goal is not a one-time quality enhancement, but to develop processes and cross-functional teams that will lead to quality improvements on an ongoing basis.

- A set of systems, such as suggestion systems, measurement systems, and recognition systems.

- A focus on the underlying causes of customer complaints and areas of dissatisfaction. One approach used in TQM is to explore a problem in depth by repeatedly asking, "Why?" This process has been dubbed the five whys.

- The tracking of key quality measures—including customer satisfaction, the ultimate quality measure.

- The involvement of suppliers in the system through supplier audits, ratings, and recognition, as well as joint team efforts.

Signals of High Quality

Most quality dimensions, such as performance, durability, reliability, and serviceability, are difficult if not impossible for buyers to evaluate. As a result, consumers tend to look for attributes that they believe indicate quality. The fit-and-finish dimension can be such a quality signal. Buyers assume that if a firm's products do not have good fit and finish, they probably will not have other, more important attributes. In pursuing a quality strategy, it is usually critical to focus on a visible dimension pivotal in affecting perceptions about more important dimensions that are very difficult to judge. Some examples:

- **Cable suppliers.** A professional attitude on the part of the installation team means quality.

- **Tomato juice.** Thickness means high quality.

- **Cleaners.** A lemon scent can signal cleaning power.

- **Supermarkets.** Produce freshness means overall quality.

- **Cars.** A solid door-closure sound implies good workmanship and a safe body.

- **Clothes.** Higher price means higher quality.

- **Airlines.** A stain on a seat can reflect on perceived maintenance standards.

One somewhat ironic problem of achieving high actual and perceived quality is that expectations are raised and thus the potential of disappointing is higher. The Schlitz story shown in the insert illustrates how a failure to deliver can be disastrous. Because negative experiences are more salient than positive ones, a quality strategy needs to focus on avoiding them. The challenge is to seek points of annoyance and attempt to reduce their incidence and intensity. For example, in order to make even waiting in line at their respective locations bearable, Disney provides entertainment with its delightful characters, and Schwab provides stock news.

Perceived Quality and Financial Performance

Perceived quality is powerful usually associated with a wide variety of attribute dimensions. Further, it has been shown by Aaker and Jacobson to drive stock return, a measure that truly reflects long-term performance.[6] They analyzed annual measures of perceived quality obtained from the Total Research EquiTrend database for 35 brands (including IBM, Hershey, Pepsi, and Sears) for which brand sales were a substantial part of firm sales. The impact on stock return of perceived quality on stock return, they found, was nearly as strong as the impact of ROI. Given that ROI is an established and accepted influence on stock return, the performance of perceived

SCHLITZ: WHEN PERCEIVED QUALITY FALTERS

The story of Schlitz beer dramatically illustrates the strategic power of perceived quality and how fragile it is. From a strong number two position in 1974 (selling 17.8 million barrels of beer annually) supported by a series of well-regarded "go for the gusto" ad campaigns, Schlitz fell steadily until the mid-1980s, when it had all but disappeared (with sales of only 1.8 million barrels). The stock market value of the brand fell more than a billion dollars.

The collapse can be traced to a decision to reduce costs by converting to a fermentation process that took four days instead of twelve, substituting corn syrup for barley malt, and using a different foam stabilizer. Word of these changes got into the marketplace. In early 1976, when bottles of flaky, cloudy-looking Schlitz beer appeared on the shelves, the condition was eventually traced to the new foam stabilizer. Worse still, in early summer of that same year, an attempted fix caused the beer to go flat after a few months on the shelf. In the fall of 1976, 10 million bottles and cans of Schlitz were "secretly" recalled and destroyed. Despite a return to its original process and aggressive advertising, Schlitz never recovered.

quality is noteworthy. It means that investors are able to detect and respond to programs that affect intangible assets such as perceived quality. Figure 8.3 shows the dramatic relationship between perceived quality and stock return.

VALUE

In nearly every market, from appliances to economy sedans to toothpaste to booksellers to brokerage services, there will be a segment that is motivated by price. Even in high-end markets such as luxury sports sedans, some brands (Acura, for example) will stake out a value position. Whether it comprises 10 or 80 percent of the market, the value segment will usually be a significant one.

Ignoring the value segment can be risky because even healthy markets can evolve into situations where price grows in importance. In consumer electronics,

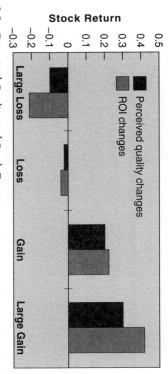

Figure 8.3   Perceived Quality and Stock Return

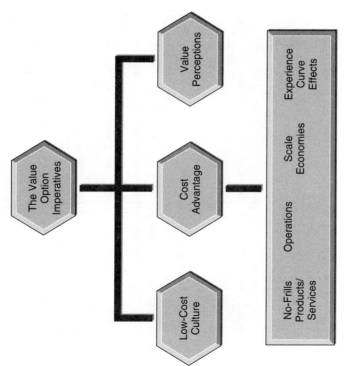

Figure 8.4   The Value Option

appliances, and other product arenas, competitors have created overcapacity, causing a need to create or maintain a critical mass in the market. Power retailers with their own brands as competitive tools are another potential contributing force. Thus, ignoring the value segment may not be an option. It may be necessary to participate, perhaps with a value brand or as a private label supplier, in order to maintain scale economies.

As Figure 8.4 suggests, to compete successfully in the value arena it is necessary to:

- Have a cost advantage (or at least avoid a cost disadvantage)
- Make sure the quality perception does not erode to the point that the offering is considered unacceptable
- Create a cost culture in the organization

Each of these imperatives is explored further below.

Creating a Cost Advantage (or Avoiding a Cost Disadvantage)

Although there is a tendency to think of low cost as a single approach, there actually are many dimensions to cost control and thus many routes to a cost reduction. The successful low-cost firms are those that can harness multiple approaches, including the use of no-frills products/services, operational efficiency, scale economies, and the experience curve.

SOUTHWEST AIRLINES

Southwest Airlines was founded in 1971, with three planes serving three Texas cities, as a low-fare airline whose goal was to make air travel efficient and pleasant. Its airfares were so aggressively low from the start that Southwest often competed as much with automobile travel as with other airlines. Even as it has grown, Southwest's point-to-point, no-frills approach has made it the consistent price leader in the markets it serves. The brand personality allows the staff to crack jokes and host games, injecting fun into what could be a boring time and further distinguishing Southwest from its competitors. The relationship of the staff to customers and its outstanding on-time record has helped Southwest win numerous customer satisfaction honors over the years.

The low-fare position often came under attack by aggressive and sometimes desperate competitors, who failed because Southwest had established a sustainable cost advantage supported by its no-frills operation. Southwest has no assigned seats, peanuts as meal service, and wages that are below the industry average. The company also shuns fancy hubs, reservation systems, and global schedules. Because of its service model, Southwest could turn around planes more quickly, which resulted in more trips and scale economies. The business model and brand personality were supported by a culture that valued cost containment and customer service.

No-Frills Product/Service

One direct approach to low cost is simply removing all frills and extras from a product or service and using materials and components that are functionally adequate. Membership warehouses, no-frills airlines, legal services clinics, and discount brokers all provide settings with limited amenities and personal service. Value furniture lines that use pressed wood create significant sustainable cost advantages.

A major risk, especially in the service sector, is that competitors will position themselves against a no-frills offering by adding just a few features. Motel 6 pioneered the concept of economy lodging in the early 1960s by giving the world a $6 hotel room with no phone or TV set. The industry has attracted a host of competitors since that time, many promising just a bit more in terms of creature comforts. The result of such strategies can be a feature war.

Operations

Enduring cost advantages can also be created through efficiencies in operations based on government subsidies, process innovation, distribution efficiency (as in Dell's direct sales model), access to target markets (USAA insurance is available only to military personnel), outsourcing competencies, and the management of overhead.

To obtain significant operational economies, it is useful to examine the value chain and look for inherently high-cost components that could be eliminated or reduced by changing the way that the business operates. The best example is the disintermediation of channel members. By selling direct, Dell and Amazon strip large components out of the value chain. For instance, in the conventional bookstore model, about 30 percent of sold books are returned, representing a huge deadweight on costs. In the Amazon model, that proportion is reduced to 3 percent—an enormous potential savings.[7]

Another place to find operations-based cost savings is in the interface with a supplier or customer. Uniqlo (a Japanese Gap-like retailer) links its store sales and inventory to its factories in China to create breathtaking efficiencies. Similarly, Procter & Gamble created an ongoing partnership with Wal-Mart, resulting in a continuous replenishment system for reordering, shipping, and restocking that minimizes shipping and warehouse costs, inventory, and out-of-stock conditions. Ten years after the partnership program began, stockkeeping units were down 25 percent, sales staffing was down 30 percent, inventory was down 15 percent, and the program was expanded to all major P&G customers.[8]

Scale Economies

The scale effect reflects the natural efficiencies associated with size. Fixed costs such as advertising, sales force overhead, R&D, staff work, and facility upkeep can be spread over more units. Furthermore, a larger operation can support specialized assets and activities (such as market research, legal staff, and manufacturing-engineering operations) dedicated to a firm's needs. Amazon has long based its business model on creating scale economies by driving sales higher.

When a business is too small to support needed assets or operations, the result can be a severe competitive disadvantage. The solution might be to prune or consolidate business units. Scale economy effects are particularly relevant in brand building, where each brand may seek a share of limited resources. Nestlé, Unilever, P&G, HP, UBS, and other firms are deleting, consolidating, and prioritizing brands in their portfolios in order to make sure that the important brands are fully funded.

In retailing, scale can be obtained by combining business units. Yum! has introduced dual-branded stores from its stable of KFC, Pizza Hut, Taco Bell, Long John Silver's, and A&W. Such dual-brand outlets can compete with McDonald's and Burger King for expensive sites that require a large annual sales volume.

The Experience Curve

The experience curve, empirically verified in hundreds of studies, suggests that as a firm accumulates experience in building a product, its costs in real dollars will decline at a predictable rate. When the experience curve applies, the first market entry attaining a large market share will have a continuing cost advantage. The experience curve effect is based on the fact that over time people will learn to do tasks faster and more efficiently, that technological process improvements will occur, and that products will be redesigned to be simpler to build.

The classic experience curve is represented by the Ford Model T, introduced in 1908 as a reliable, easy to drive, and remarkably inexpensive car. The Model T, which sold over 15 million units, began its life priced at $850 (around $18,000 in modern dollars), but the price fell continuously until in 1922 it cost less than $300, a price that served to expand the market dramatically. Because of the production-friendly and unchanging design, vertical integration, and the building of the huge River Rouge

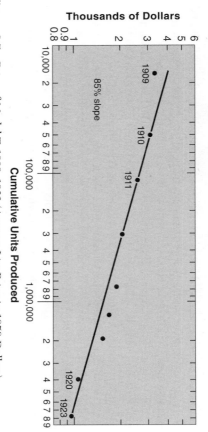

Figure 8.5   Price of Model T, 1909–1923 (Average List Price in 1958 Dollars)

plant, production cost declined according to an 85 percent experience curve (that is, costs fell roughly 15 percent every time cumulative production doubled). Figure 8.5 presents the pattern.

Several issues need to be understood in working with the experience curve concept. First, the experience curve is not automatic. It must be proactively managed with efficiency-improvement goals, quality circles, product design targets, and equipment upgrading. Further, a late entry can often gain the same advantage as the more experienced vendors simply by accessing the most recent design. Second, if the technology or market changes, the experience curve may become obsolete. The auto market in the early 1920s turned away from the Model T, and Ford had to close down for a year to retool to make what GM was offering and the market wanted. Third, the experience curve model implies that cost improvements, whatever their source, should be translated into low prices and higher share so that the business can stay ahead on the experience curve. Lower prices can trigger price wars, however, leading to reduced margins, as has occurred in consumer electronics numerous times.

Perceived Value

Creating a credible value story—the perception that there is real value in the offering—requires substance. The core is a perceived price point that will deliver value. In this respect, the way that customers process price information is important. What price element is most visible? Grocery stores have long learned that customers tend to be knowledgeable about a few categories and brands. Similarly, the major book chains pay close attention to best-selling books, because those are the ones most likely to receive a price comparison. Car manufacturers are concerned most with base prices and much less about accessories and options, because prices for the latter will be harder to compare.

Managing prices is tricky, because price is often a quality cue and customers may perceive low price as a signal for inferior quality. If the quality is perceived to be unacceptably low, the offering will be deemed irrelevant to the customer's needs. This is particularly troublesome for offerings in categories where it is difficult to judge actual quality (perfume or motor oil, for example).

One responsive approach is to make cost (and thus price) differences as visible and understandable as possible. Dell's direct sales model, Southwest's point-to-point travel and no-frills service, Ford's mass production, the scale economies of Amazon and Wal-Mart, and the warehouse feel of Ikea, Home Depot, and Costco are all transparent to customers and thus reduce the risk of a perceived quality problem. Another approach is to manage the relevance issue by positioning the offering with respect to the appropriate product category and set of competitors. Acura, which aspires to be considered alongside BMW and Lexus, needs to manage its product category associations so it is not perceived as a sub-luxury car.

A Low-Cost Culture

A successful low-cost strategy is usually multifaceted and supported by a cost-oriented culture. Performance measurement, rewards, systems, structure, top management values, and culture are all fronts where cost reduction should be stressed. The single-minded focus needed is comparable to that required for total quality management. Such a commitment is evident at Dell, Southwest, Wal-Mart, and other firms that have succeeded with a value strategy.

There are many examples of firms that decided to go into the low-cost world and failed because their cultures never could adapt. One large supermarket chain decided to create a discount beverage chain. When the chain failed to deliver on the promise and still be profitable, an analysis determined that the people and processes were not compatible with the cost structure needed to succeed in that market. A successful discount operation almost always requires a new organization with different culture, processes, and people.

KEY LEARNINGS

- Business strategies usually cluster around a limited number of value propositions, such as a superior attribute, appealing design, systems solutions, social responsibility, a superior customer relationship, a niche specialist, superior quality, and superior value. The value proposition should be real, believed, feasible, relevant, and sustainable.

- A value position needs to be communicated effectively and supported by a cost advantage, which can be based on a no-frills offering, operations, scale economies, and/or the experience curve.

- Superior quality, which has been shown to drive stock return, has to be continuously addressed through processes and programs and transferred into quality perceptions.

FOR DISCUSSION

1. Consider three industries, such as hotels or appliances or automobiles. For several of the firms in the industry, identify what value propositions

are representing their strategy. Were there multiple propositions? Evaluate. Are they successful or likely to be successful?

2. Consider three of the following value propositions: systems solutions, corporate social responsibility, superior customer relationship, quality, and value. For each of these, think of two firms not mentioned in the book that have pursued them. Which of the two firms has done better with respect to the five business strategy challenges? Discuss why and how that firm was able to do better.

3. Evaluate the quality strategy of Lexus with respect to the business strategy challenges. How might Lexus add more personality and emotion to its brand? Think of role models that have achieved a quality reputation and a strong personality.

4. Pick a product or service offering. How would you develop a set of customer survey questions that would measure its quality on an ongoing basis? How would you administer the survey?

NOTES

1. Stan L. Friedman, "Corporate America's Social Conscience," *Fortune*, June 23, 2003, p. S6.

2. Ibid., p. S4.

3. "Esso—Should the Tiger Change Its Stripes?" Reputation Impact, October 2002, p. 16.

4. Valarie A. Zeithaml, *Service Quality*, Boston: Marketing Science Institute, 2004.

5. For a summary of total quality management in the United States, see the special issue on this subject in *California Management Review*, Spring 1993.

6. David A. Aaker and Robert Jacobson, "The Financial Information Content of Perceived Quality," *Journal of Marketing Research*, May 1994.

7. Timothy M. Saseter, Patrick W. Houston, Joshua L. Wright, and Juliana U. Park, "Amazon: Extracting Value from the Value Chain," *Strategy and Business*, First Quarter 2000, pp. 94–105.

8. Material is drawn in part from Lawrence D. Milligan, "Keeping It Simple, The Evolution of Customer-Business Development at Procter & Gamble," remarks made at the American Marketing Association Doctoral Symposium, Cincinnati, July 1997.

CHAPTER NINE

Building and Managing Brand Equity

You do not merely want to be considered just the best of the best. You want to be considered the only ones who do what you do.
—*Jerry Garcia, The Grateful Dead*

You cannot make a business case that you should be who you're not.
—*Jeff Bezos, Amazon*

The secret of success is constancy of purpose.
—*Benjamin Disraeli*

A business strategy is enabled by brand assets. A brand gives a firm permission to compete in product markets and services, and it represents the value proposition of the business strategy. Thus, it is strategically crucial to develop, refine, and leverage brand assets.

Anecdotes abound about the power of a brand to improve financial performance, but solid research also shows that, on average, building brands generates a payoff in terms of stock return. In fact, as noted in Chapter 8, the brand effect on stock return is nearly as large as that of accounting ROI in such diverse settings as large-cap, Internet, and high-tech firms. Further, efforts to estimate the value of brand assets as compared to other intangible assets—like people and IT technology—and tangible assets reveal that the brand assets represent from 15 percent or so (Toyota and GE) to more than 75 percent (BMW and Nike) of the value of the firm. Even the lower number is significant strategically.

Brand equity is the set of assets and liabilities linked to the brand. The conceptualization of brand equity, which occurred in the late 1980s, was pivotal because it changed the way that marketing was perceived. Where brand image could be delegated to an advertising manager, brand equity—as a key asset of the firm—needed to

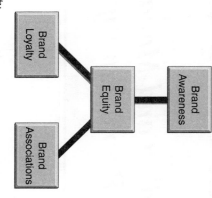

Figure 9.1   Brand Equity

be elevated to part of the business strategy; the purview of the CEO. Its management was strategic and visionary instead of tactical and reactive, long term in orientation rather than short term, and involved a different set of metrics. It truly changed the role of marketing and the CMO.

There are three types of brand assets—brand awareness, brand loyalty, and brand associations (see Figure 9.1). Each creates formidable competitive advantages, and each needs to be actively managed.

BRAND AWARENESS

Brand awareness is often taken for granted, but it can be a key strategic asset. In some industries that have product parity, awareness, the third most mentioned SCA (see Figure 7.3), provides a sustainable competitive difference. It serves to differentiate the brands along a recall/familiarity dimension.

Brand awareness can provide a host of competitive advantages. First, awareness provides the brand with a sense of familiarity, and people like the familiar. For low-involvement products, such as soap or chewing gum, familiarity can drive the buying decision. Taste tests of such products as colas and peanut butter show that a recognized name can affect evaluations even if the brand has never been purchased or used.

Second, name awareness can be a signal of presence, commitment, and substance, attributes that can be very important even to industrial buyers of big-ticket items and consumer buyers of durables. The logic is that if a name is recognized, there must be a reason. The "Intel Inside" program was remarkably successful at creating a perception of advanced technology and earned a significant price premium for Intel for well over a decade even though it did not communicate anything about the company or the product. Pure awareness power was at work.

Third, the salience of a brand will determine if it is recalled at a key time in the purchasing process. The initial step in selecting an advertising agency, a car to test drive, or a computer system is to decide on which brands to consider. The extreme case is name dominance, where the brand is the only one recalled when a product class is cued. Consider Kleenex tissue, Clorox bleach, Band-Aid adhesive bandages, Jell-O gelatin, Crayola crayons, Morton salt, Lionel trains, Philadelphia cream cheese, V-8 vegetable juice, and A-1 steak sauce. In each case, how many other brands can you name? How would you like to compete against the dominant brand?

Brand awareness is an asset that can be extremely durable and thus sustainable. It can be very difficult to dislodge a brand that has achieved a dominant awareness level. Customers' awareness of the Datsun brand, for example, was as strong as that of its successor, Nissan, four years after the firm changed its name.[1] An awareness study on blenders more than two decades after GE stopped making the product found that the GE brand was still the second most-preferred brand.[2] Another study of familiarity asked homemakers to name as many brands of any type as they could; they averaged 28 names each. The ages of the brands named were surprising: more than 85 percent were over 25 years old, and 36 percent were more than 75 years old.[3]

There is a great deal of difference between recognition (have you ever heard of Brand X) and unaided recall (what brands of SUVs can you name). Sometimes recognition for a mature brand is not even desirable when unaided recall is low. In fact, brands with high recognition and low recall are termed graveyard brands. Without recall, they are not in the game; their high recognition means they are considered yesterday's news, and thus it is difficult for them to gain visibility and energy.

Because consumers are bombarded every day by more and more marketing messages, the challenge of building awareness and presence—and doing so economically and efficiently—is formidable, especially considering the fragmentation and clutter that exist in mass media. One route to visibility is to extend the brand over product categories. For that reason, firms such as 3M, Sony, Toshiba, and GE have an advantage because wide product scope provides brand exposure. Another route is to go beyond the normal media channels by using event promotions, publicity, sampling, and other attention-grabbing approaches. For example, consider the impact of Samsung's Olympic sponsorship, the Niketown showcase stores, Swatch hanging a 165-yard-long watch from skyscrapers in Frankfurt and Tokyo, and the Buitoni Club program. All of these firms were able to increase their awareness levels much more effectively than if they had relied only on mass media advertising.

BRAND LOYALTY

A enduring asset for some businesses is the loyalty of the installed customer base (listed as item 10 in Figure 7.3). Competitors may duplicate or surpass a product or service, but they still face the task of making customers switch brands. Brand loyalty, or resistance to switching, can be based on simple habit (there is no motivation to change from the familiar gas station or supermarket), preference (people genuinely like the brand of cake mix or its symbol, perhaps based on use experience over a long time period), or switching costs. Switching costs would be a consideration for a software user, for example, when a substantial investment has already been made in training employees to learn a particular software system.

An existing base of loyal customers provides enormous sustainable competitive advantages. First, it reduces the marketing costs of doing business, since existing customers usually are relatively easy to hold—the familiar is comfortable and reassuring. Keeping existing customers happy and reducing their motivation to change is usually considerably less expensive than trying to reach new customers and persuading them to try another brand. Of course, the higher the loyalty, the easier it is to keep customers happy.

Second, the loyalty of existing customers represents a substantial entry barrier to competitors. Significant resources are required when entering a market in which existing customers must be enticed away from an established brand that they are loyal to or even merely satisfied with. The profit potential for the entrant is thus reduced. For the barrier to be effective, however, potential competitors must know about it; they cannot be allowed to entertain the delusion that customers are vulnerable. Therefore signals of strong customer loyalty, such as customer interest groups, can be useful.

Third, a relatively large, satisfied customer base provides an image of a brand as an accepted, successful, enduring product that will include service backup and product improvements. A set of loyal customers also provides reassurance to others. Customers find comfort in the fact that others have selected the brand.

Finally, brand loyalty provides the time to respond to competitive moves—it gives a firm some breathing room. If a competitor develops a superior product, a loyal following will allow the firm the time needed to respond by matching or neutralizing the offering. With a high level of brand loyalty, a firm can allow itself the luxury of pursuing a less-risky follower strategy.

The management of brand loyalty is a key to achieving strategic success. Firms that manage brand loyalty well are likely to:

- Measure the loyalty of existing customers. Measurement should include not only sensitive indicators of satisfaction but also measures of the relationship between the customer and the brand. Is the brand respected? Liked? Trusted? The ultimate measure is, will the customer recommend the brand to others?

- Conduct exit interviews with those who leave the brand to locate points of vulnerability.

- Have a customer culture, whereby people throughout the organization are empowered and motivated to keep the customer happy.

- Measure the lifetime value of a customer so expected future purchases are valued.

- Reward loyal customers with frequent-buyer programs or special unexpected benefits or premiums.

- Make customers feel that they are part of the organization, perhaps through customer clubs.

- Have continuing communication with customers, using direct mail, the Internet, toll-free numbers, and a solid customer backup organization.

- Manage customer touchpoints to ensure that the brand does not falter in key contexts.

BRAND ASSOCIATIONS

The associations attached to a firm and its brands can be key enduring business assets, as they reflect the strategic position of the brand. A brand association is anything that is directly or indirectly linked in the consumer's memory to a brand (see Figure 9.2). Thus, McDonald's could be linked to Ronald McDonald, kids, the Golden Arches, Ronald McDonald House, Newman's Own Salad Dressing, having fun, fast service, family outings, or Big Macs. All these associations potentially serve to make McDonald's interesting, memorable, and appealing to its customers.

Product attributes and customer benefits are the associations that have obvious relevance because they provide a reason to buy and thus a basis for brand loyalty. Heinz is the slowest-pouring (thickest) ketchup, Bayer is faster acting, Texas Instruments has a faster chip, Jaguar is stylish, Volvo is durable and safe, and Wal-Mart delivers value. Companies love to make product claims, for good reason. They often engage in shouting matches to convince customers that their offering is superior in some key dimension—Brand One is a high-fiber cereal, or a Boeing plane has more range.

There are several problems with such specmanship. First, a position based on some attribute is vulnerable to an innovation that gives your competitor more speed, more fiber, or a greater range. In the works of Regis McKenna, the Silicon Valley marketing guru, "You can always get outspeced."

Second, when firms start a specification shouting match, they all eventually lose credibility. After a while, customers start to doubt whether any aspirin is more effective or faster acting than another. There have been so many conflicting claims that all of them are discounted.

Associations	Brands
Attributes/Benefits	Volvo, Crest
Design	Jaguar, Calvin Klein
Systems Solution	Siebel, IBM
Social Programs	Avon, McDonald's
Customer Relationships	Nordstrom's, Ritz Carlton
Niche Specialists	Ferrari, Gold Violin
Quality	Lexus, Hertz
Value	Wal-Mart, Hyundai
Product Category	TiVo, Toyota's Prius
Breadth of Product Line	Amazon, Marriott
Organizational Intangibles	3M, Accenture
Emotional & Self-Expressive Benefits	BMW, Jaguar, Tiffany's
The Experience	Nike, Heineken
Being Global	Visa, Ford
Being Contemporary	MySpace, Apple
Brand Personality	MetLife, Singapore Airlines

Figure 9.2 Brand Associations

Third, people do not always make decisions based upon a particular specification. They may feel that small differences in some attribute are not important, or they simply lack the motivation or ability to process information at such a detailed level.

Strong brands go beyond product attributes to develop associations on other dimensions that can be more credible and harder to copy. It is useful to understand some of these other dimensions and learn how they have been used by firms to create customer relationships and points of differentiation.

The value propositions described in the last chapter in addition to attributes or benefits—design, systems solutions, social programs, customer relationships, niche specialist, quality, and value—are all prominent candidates for actual or aspirational associations. Several additional ones, all with a proven ability to drive successful firms, will be described to provide a feel for the scope of potential associations.

Product Category

The choice of a product category or subcategory to which a business will associate itself can have enormous strategic and tactical implications. Schweppes positioned its tonic in Europe as an adult soft drink, and the popularity of new-age adult drinks carried it to a dominant position. In the United States, however, Schweppes (perhaps wanting to avoid the Coke/Pepsi juggernaut) positioned its entry as a mixer for alcoholic drinks, which relegated it to being a minor player when the market changed. Energy bars became a big business by creating a category distinct from candy. Wasa Crispbread, in contrast, expanded its market by positioning itself as an alternative to bread rather than sharing a category with rice cakes and Ry-Krisp. Siebel created the customer relationship management (CRM) category and benefited from an association with it.

Maintaining Relevance

As suggested in Chapter 4, the relevance concept can help with the difficult task of managing an evolving category with emerging and receding subcategories. Relevance is, in essence, being perceived as associated with the product category in which the customer is interested. In the Brand Asset Valuator, the product of Young & Rubicam's mammoth study of global brands, relevance was one of four key dimensions identified (along with differentiation, esteem, and knowledge). And although differentiation got top billing in the study's results, relevance may be as powerful in dynamic markets. If a business loses relevance, differentiation may not matter.

The ability of a firm to maintain relevance varies along a spectrum, as shown in Figure 9.3. At one extreme are trend neglectors—firms that miss or misinterpret trends, perhaps because they are too focused on a predetermined business model. Such firms are often characterized as having inadequate strategic analysis capability,

Figure 9.3 Staying Relevant

Trend Neglectors ←→ Trend Responders ←→ Trend Drivers

organizational inflexibility, and/or a weak brand portfolio strategy; they eventually wake up in surprise to find their products are no longer relevant. At the other end of the spectrum are trend drivers, those firms which actually propel the trends that define the category (or subcategory). In the middle are trend followers, firms that track closely the trends and the evolution of categories and subcategories, making sure that their products stay current.

Virgin Atlantic Airlines, IBM, and Schwab all have been trend drivers. Virgin created a new subcategory by introducing and owning new services such as massage services in first class. IBM defined a new category with its e-business label, supported by enormous brand-building resources. Schwab's OneSource defined a new subcategory of brokerage firm services.

Trend responders—those firms who can recognize and evaluate trends, then create and implement a response—can sustain success in dynamic markets. Some fashion brands such as Tommy Hilfiger have been nimble in staying abreast of fashion trends. Barbie has changed with the times, from being an astronaut in 1965, a surgeon in 1973, and a presidential candidate in 1992, to appearing in the video *Barbie in the Nutcracker* in 2001 and launching Barbie couture in 2004. L. L. Bean has evolved its position from hunting, fishing, and camping to a broader outdoors theme that is relevant to hikers, mountain bikers, cross-country skiers, and water-sports enthusiasts, the heart of its marketplace. Fuji Film was quick to adapt to the digital age and became a leader with its Super CCD high-quality image sensor for digital cameras, plus several other products such as digital photo printers.

Being a successful trend responder, however, is not easy. As suggested by Chapter 4, it can be difficult to identify and evaluate trends, separating the trends from the fads. It is also difficult to respond to emerging subcategories, especially if they start small and if the existing business and brand are established. Consider the difficulty that McDonald's, Burger King, KFC, and the other fast food giants have had in responding to the healthy eating trend. They are simply not good at product development and delivery in that arena because it is not in their DNA—they lack the people and culture to be successful. Even worse, their brand becomes a liability as they attempt to change perceptions ingrained by decades of doing what they do.

Breadth of Product Line

A broad product offering signals substance, acceptance, leadership, and often the convenience of one-stop shopping. For example, the strategic position that drove Amazon's operations and marketing was never about selling books, even at the beginning when it was simply a book store (Amazon had the vision to avoid calling itself books.com). Rather, the firm positioned itself as delivering a superior shopping/buying experience based on the "Earth's Biggest Selection"—an array of choices so wide that customers would have no reason to look anywhere else. This position allows Amazon to enter a variety of product markets, although it also puts pressure on the company to deliver in each venue.

Breadth also works well as a dimension for other firms, such as Chevrolet, Wal-Mart, and Black & Decker. Even under a strong brand, however, expanding the product offering involves risks. The firm may venture into business areas in which it lacks skills and competencies, the brand might be eroded, and resources needed elsewhere may be absorbed.

Organizational Intangibles

As already noted, attribute and benefit associations can often be easily copied. In contrast, it is difficult to copy an organization, which will be uniquely defined by its values, culture, people, strategy, and programs. Organizational attributes such as being global (Visa), innovative (3M), quality driven (Cadillac), customer driven (Nordstrom), involved in community or social issues (Avon), or concerned about the environment (Toyota) are usually more resistant to competitive claims than product-attribute associations.

A laboratory study of cameras demonstrated the power of an intangible attribute. Customers were shown two camera brands, one of which was positioned as being more technically sophisticated, and the other as easier to use. Detailed specifications of each brand, which were also provided, clearly showed that the easier-to-use brand in fact had superior technology as well. When subjects were shown both brands together, the easy-to-use brand was rated superior on technology by 94 percent of the subjects. However, when this brand was shown two days after exposure to the supposedly (but not actually) more sophisticated brand, only 36 percent felt that it had the best technology. Using technology as an abstract attribute dominated the actual specifications.

Emotional and Self-Expressive Benefits

Another way to move beyond attribute/functional claims is to create a position based on emotional or self-expressive benefits.

Emotional benefits relate to the ability of the offering to make the customer feel something during the purchase or use experience. The strongest brands often offer emotional benefits. Thus, a buyer or user can feel

- safe in a Volvo
- exhilarated in a BMW
- energized while watching MTV
- important when at Nordstrom's
- healthy when drinking Evian
- warm when buying or reading a Hallmark card
- strong and rugged when driving a Ford Explorer

Emotional benefits are all about the "I feel…" statement: I feel energized, I feel warm, I feel elegant. To see if an emotional benefit can play a role in differentiating a brand, try the "I feel" question with customers. If the hard-core loyalists consistently come up with a particular emotional benefit associated with using the branch, then it should be considered as part of the strategic position of the brand.

Self-expressive benefits reflect the ability of the purchase and use of an offering to provide a vehicle by which a person can express him- or herself. To illustrate, a person might express a self-concept of being

- adventurous or daring by owning Rossignol powder skis
- hip by buying fashions from the Gap
- sophisticated by using Ralph Lauren
- successful, in control, and a leader by driving a Lincoln
- frugal and unpretentious by shopping at Kmart
- competent by using Microsoft Office
- nurturing by preparing Quaker Oats hot cereal for one's children in the morning

Self-expressive benefits are all about the "I am . . ." statement: I am successful, I am young, I am a great athlete. To see if a self-expressive benefit can play a role in differentiating a brand, try the "I am" question with loyal customers and see if any consistent self-expressive benefits are associated with using the brand.

The Experience

The experience of using the brand could include emotional or self-expressive benefits without any functional advantage, but when an experience combines two or even all three, it is usually broader and more rewarding. The experience at Nordstrom's includes a host of factors (such as the merchandise, the piano, the ambience, and the service) that combine to provide a pleasant, satisfying time and make a statement about shopping and buying at the store. The experience of using Nike combines functional, emotional, and self-expressive benefits to provide a depth of connection that competitor brands lack.

In addition to the breadth of its offering, Amazon is also positioned with respect to the experience it delivers. Its promise is to create a world-class shopping experience that is both efficient and enjoyable. The fast and easy selection, one-click ordering, special-occasion reminders, safe-shopping guarantee, and reliable delivery lie behind the experience Amazon creates. The Amazon experience also provides emotional benefits by offering the excitement of discovering a book, CD, or other gift that is just right (as enhanced by its "personalize item" recommendation). The Amazon river, representing the ultimate in discovery and adventure, provides an aspirational metaphor. One of the challenges for the Amazon brand is to make sure this emotional aspect is not submerged by the functional benefits the site provides.

Being Global

CitiGroup is a global financial institution. Visa is a global credit card. Toyota is a global car company. Being global provides functional benefits in that you can access the services of CitiGroup or Visa anywhere. It also provides the prestige and assurance that comes from knowing that the firm has the capability of competing successfully throughout the world. Knowing that Toyota is strong in the United States helps it in Europe, where customers might otherwise look at it as a modest player. More information on global associations and strategy is provided in Chapter 13.

Being Contemporary

Most established businesses face the problem of remaining or becoming contemporary. A business with a long heritage is given credit for being reliable, safe, a friend, and even innovative if that is part of its tradition. However, it also can be perceived as "your father's (or even grandfather's) brand." The challenge is to have energy, vitality, and relevance in today's marketplace—to be part of the contemporary scene. The answer usually entails breaking out of the functional-benefit trap. Approaches to add energy will be explored in Chapter 10.

Lane Bryant, a retailer to plus-sized women, developed a dowdy, apologetic image that was holding it back. To break out, it developed a new, contemporary strategic position. It spread the message with new, even sexy fashions; a Lane Bryant fashion show in New York; revitalized stores; and a new spokesperson, rapper/actress Queen Latifah, in ads, on its Web site, and in a voter-registration program. Ironically, Lane Bryant's sister company, Victoria's Secret, had to reposition itself previously from an edgy (Frederick's of Hollywood) brand to a more mainstream one, albeit at the edge of the mainstream market.

Brand Personality

As with human beings, a business with a personality tends to be more memorable and better liked than one that is bland, nothing more than the sum of its attributes. And like people, brands can have a variety of personalities, such as being professional and competent (CNN and McKinsey), upscale and sophisticated (Jaguar and Tiffany's), trustworthy and genuine (Hallmark and John Deere), exciting and daring (Porsche and Benneton), or active and tough (Levi's and Nike). Certainly, Virgin is a brand whose strategic position includes a strong personality.

Harley-Davidson has a strong personality reflecting a macho, America-loving, freedom-seeking person who is willing to break out of confining social norms. The experience of riding a Harley (or even the association that comes from wearing Harley-Davidson clothing) helps some people to express a part of their personality, which results in intense loyalty. More than 250,000 of these people belong to one of the eight hundred chapters of the Harley Owners Group (HOG). Twice a year, believers from all over the country gather for a bonding experience. Harley is much more than a motorcycle; it is an experience, an attitude, a lifestyle, a vehicle to express "who I am."

Joie de Vivre is a San Francisco firm whose boutique hotels are each inspired by a theme that reflects a personality. The "Rolling Stone" Phoenix hotel attracts rock-and-roll and other entertainment personalities with its irreverent sense of cool and funky, adventurous decor. The "New Yorker" Rex hotel is clever and sophisticated, with a literary sensibility. The "1920s luxury liner" Commodore Hotel, with its Titanic Café, looks and feels like a party straight out of *The Great Gatsby*. The "movie palace" Hotel Bijou has a miniature movie theater in the lobby, accompanied by dramatic Hollywood portraits.

VIRGIN ATLANTIC AIRLINES

In 1970, Richard Branson and a few friends founded Virgin as a small mail-order record company in London, England. By the mid-1980s, this modest beginning had led to a chain of record shops and the largest independent music label in the United Kingdom, with artists as diverse and important as Phil Collins, the Sex Pistols, Boy George, and the Rolling Stones. By the 1990s, there were more than a hundred Virgin "megastores," many making a significant brand statement with their signage, size, and interior design.

In February 1984, Branson decided to start Virgin Atlantic Airlines to make flying fun and enjoyable for all classes, not just first-class passengers. Defying the odds, Virgin became the number two airline in most of its markets by the end of the 1990s. Not only that, it enjoyed the same consumer awareness and reputation as much larger international carriers, including service-oriented airlines such as Singapore Airlines. Virgin Atlantic's success is due in part to its image of service quality, value for money, being the underdog, and having an edgy personality.

Extraordinary Service Quality

Virgin has delivered a high quality of service and, more important to perceptions, has often dazzled customers with original, "wow" experiences. Virgin pioneered sleeper seats in 1986 (British Airways followed nine years later with the cradle seat), limo services at each end of the flight (or motorcycle service for those flying light), in-flight massages, child safety seats, individual TVs for business class passengers, drive-through check-in at the airport, and new classes of service. First-class passengers are offered a new tailor-made suit to be ready at their destination, masseurs or beauty therapists, and a facility to shower or nap.

Value for Money

Virgin Atlantic's Upper Class is priced at the business-class level, but not much different from many other airlines' first-class service. Mid Class is offered at full-fare economy prices, and most Virgin Economy tickets are available at a discount. While this lower price point offers a clear consumer advantage, Virgin does not emphasize the price position in its promotion. Cheapness per se is not the message at Virgin.

The Underdog

Virgin's business model is straightforward. The company typically enters markets and industries with large, established players (such as British Airways, Coca-Cola, Levi-Strauss, British Rail, and Smirnoff) that can be portrayed as being somewhat complacent, bureaucratic, and unresponsive to customer needs. In contrast, Virgin presents itself as the underdog who cares, innovates, and delivers an attractive, viable alternative to customers. When British Airways attempted to prevent Virgin from gaining routes, Virgin painted British Airways as a bully standing in the way of an earnest youngster who offered better value and service.

The Virgin Personality

The Virgin brand has a strong, perhaps edgy personality, largely reflecting its flamboyant service innovations and the values and actions of Richard Branson. Virgin as a person would be perceived as someone who:

(continued)

- Flaunts the rules
- Has a sense of humor that can be outrageous at times
- Is an underdog, willing to attack the establishment
- Is competent, always does a good job, and has high standards

Interestingly, this personality spans some extremes, from competent to a feisty, fun-loving, rule-breaker—an accomplishment envied by other businesses. The key is not only the personality of Branson himself but also the fact that Virgin has delivered on each facet of this personality.

Virgin is a remarkable example of how the right set of brand associations can allow a business to stretch far beyond what would be considered its acceptable scope of operations. Rather than restrict itself to records and entertainment, Virgin has used its associations to extend from record stores to airlines, colas (Virgin Cola), vodka (Virgin Vodka), a rail service (Virgin Rail), jeans (Virgin Jeans), and dozens of other categories. In each business, the Virgin associations work to provide differentiation and advantage.

In fact, the decision to extend Virgin, a business then associated with rock music and youth, to an airline could have become a legendary blunder if it had failed. However, because the airline was successful and was able to deliver value with quality, flair, and innovation, the master Virgin brand developed associations that were not restricted to a single type of product. The elements of the Virgin strategic position—extraordinary service quality, value for money, the underdog position, and a quirky personality—work over a large set of products and services. It has become a lifestyle brand with an attitude whose powerful relationship with customers is not solely based on functional benefits within a particular product category.

Virgin's success has been driven in part by pure visibility, largely based on publicity personally generated by Richard Branson. For the launching of Virgin Bride, a company that arranges weddings, he showed up in a wedding dress. At the 1996 opening of Virgin's first U.S. megastore in New York's Times Square, Branson (a balloonist holding several world records) was lowered on a huge silver ball from 100 feet above the store. These and other stunts have turned into windfalls of free publicity for Virgin, helping the brand in all contexts.

Branson has fully mastered his role. By employing British humor and the popular love of flouting the system, he has endeared himself to consumers. By never deviating from the core brand values, he has gained their loyalty and confidence. When BBC Radio asked 1,200 people who they thought would be most qualified to rewrite the Ten Commandments, Branson came in fourth, after Mother Teresa, the pope, and the arch-bishop of Canterbury. When a British daily newspaper took a poll on who would be most qualified to become the next mayor of London, Branson won in a landslide.

THE BRAND IDENTITY

Creating and managing a brand requires a brand strategy, the heart of which is the *brand identity*, which provides direction, purpose, and meaning for the brand. A brand identity is a set of brand associations that the firm aspires to create or maintain, an aspirational external brand image. These associations represent what the brand aspires to stands for and imply a promise to customers from the organization. It differs from brand image in that it could include elements that are not present in

Value creation	In-depth understanding of customers
Flexible	Close to customers
Resourceful	Team oriented
Dynamic	Partner with customers
Broad capability	Collaborator
Committed to excellence	Open communication
Best-of-breed	Multi-cultural
World class	Risk-sharing partner
Gets job done	Diversified workforce
Experienced	Technology that works
Confident	Global
Competent	Bold (without arrogance)
Straightforward	World health

Figure 9.4 Partial List of Aspirational Associations for Ajax

the current image (you now make trucks as well as cars) or even conflict with it (you aspire to have a quality reputation that is superior to the current perceptions).

The brand identity can best be explained in terms of three steps. These steps assume that a comprehensive strategic analysis has been done. Customer, competitor, and internal analyses are particularly critical to the development of a brand identity.

1. What the Brand Stands For

The first step is to create a set of from six to twelve distinct associations that are desired for the brand. The process starts by putting down all the associations that are desired given what is known about the customers, competitors, and the business strategy going forward. A list of more than two dozen is shown in Figure 9.4 for a business-to-business service company here termed Ajax. In actuality, the list is more often from 50 to 100. During this process there is no effort to zero in on categories of associations, although there is an effort to make sure that organizational intangibles and personality dimensions are at least considered.

These items are then grouped, and each group is given a label. Ajax was created with a set of a half-dozen acquisitions, each of which continued to operate somewhat autonomously. It was becoming clear, though, that customers preferred a single-solution firm with broad capabilities. The new Ajax strategy was to orient its service to broad customer solutions and to get its operating units to work together seamlessly. The strategy represented a significant change in culture and operations. With respect to the brand identity, the elements "partner with customers," "customized solutions," "collaborative," and "close to customers" were clustered and given the name Team Solutions, which became one of eight identity elements. The brand goal was to provide a face to customers that matched this new strategy.

2. The Core Identity

The second step is to prioritize the brand identity elements. The most important and potentially the most impactful are classified as *core identity* elements. The core identity will be the primary drivers of the brand-building programs. They will be the focus of the brand investments, as they are the most critical to the success for the businesses that they are supporting. The balance of the elements are termed the *extended identity*. They serve to help define the brand, make decisions as to what actions and programs are compatible with the brand, and drive minor programs that will have lesser impact and take modest resources.

In developing the core and extended identity, four criteria should guide the process. Identity elements are sought that:

- **Resonate with the target market.** Ultimately, the market dictates success, and thus the identity should resonate with customers. It is useful to think in terms of how customers relate to the brand over time rather than simply what drives purchase decisions. Also, consider emotional and self-expressive benefits in addition to functional ones.

- **Differentiate from competitors.** Differentiation is the often the key to winning. There should be some points of differentiation throughout the brand identity so that there is always an answer to the question as to how our brand is different.

- **Provide parity where competitors have an advantage that is compelling to customers.** It is not always necessary to be different or better on all dimensions. There may be some dimensions where the goal is simply to be close enough so that this dimension is no longer a reason to not buy the brand. Hyundai need not, for example, be equal to Toyota in quality; it just needs to be close enough so that its quality image does not prevent purchase.

- **Reflect the strategy and culture of the business.** Ultimately, the brand needs to enable and support the strategy of the business. Particularly when the strategy represents a change from the status quo, and requires a change in brand image, the brand identity needs to reflect the new strategy. The brand identity should also support and reflect the culture and values of the firm, because it is the organization that has to deliver on the aspirational brand promise.

3. The Brand Essence

The core identity compactly summarizes the brand vision. However, it is often useful to provide even more focus by creating a *brand essence*, a single thought that captures the heart of the brand. The purpose of an essence is to communicate the brand internally. Thus, while there are times when an external tagline, designed to communicate the message of the day externally, can and does represent the essence, that is often not the case. Figure 9.5 shows the final brand identity for Ajax, including the brand essence.

A good brand essence will capture much of the brand identity from a different perspective, will provide a tool to communicate the identity, and will inform and inspire those inside the organization. Consider "transforming futures," the brand essence of the London School of Business. It provides an umbrella over what the

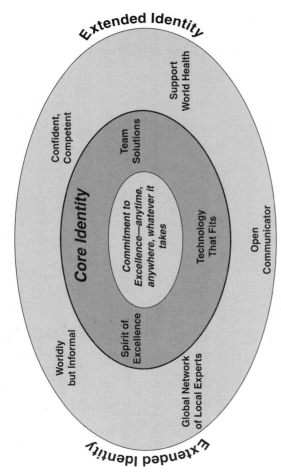

Figure 9.5 The Ajax Brand Identity

LBS is and what it does in a way that is uplifting and inspiring to students, alumni, and donors, as well as faculty and staff. Another business school, the Haas School of Business at UC Berkeley, has as its essence "leadership through innovation," which also packages a set of programs and values in a way that inspires.

A key essence choice is whether to focus on what the brand is, or on what it does for customers. The former, such as Banana Republic's "casual luxury," or the Lexus essence reflected in the "passionate pursuit of perfection," would tend to involve functional benefits; the latter, such as American Express' "do more" or BMW's "ultimate driving machine," tend to look to emotional and self-expressive benefits.

Proof Points and Strategic Initiatives

A brand identity should not simply reflect something that appeals to customers. Rather, the firm needs to be willing to invest behind it and create products and programs that will deliver on the promise. Toward that end, each identity element should have proof points and/or strategic initiatives associated with it.

Proof points are programs, initiatives, and assets already in place that provide substance to the strategy position and help communicate what it means. L.L. Bean has a position around outdoor enthusiasts. Proof points include the brand's heritage of outdoor activities, a flagship store geared to the outdoors, and the expertise and professionalism of the customer contact staff. Nordstrom's has a customer service position supported by the following proof points:

- A current reputation for customer service
- A policy that attaches a service person to a customer rather than a product area
- A current return policy that is well known and has credibility

- A compensation program that makes the customer experience a priority
- The quality of the staff and the hiring program
- An empowerment policy permitting innovative responses to customer concerns

A gap between what the brand now delivers (even given the proof points) and the promise implied by the strategic position should lead to strategic imperatives. A *strategic imperative* is an investment in an asset or program that is essential if the promise to customers is to be delivered. What organizational assets and competencies are implied by the strategic position? What investments are needed in order to deliver the promise to customers?

If a regional bank aspires to deliver a relationship with customers, two strategic imperatives might be needed. First, a customer database might need to be created so that each customer contact person would have access to all of the customer's accounts. Second, a program might be needed to improve the interpersonal skills of customer contact people, including both training and measurement.

The Role of the Brand Identity

The need to articulate a brand identity and position introduces discipline and clarity into the strategy formulation process. The ultimate strategy is usually more precise and elaborated as a result. However, the brand identity and position have other, more explicit roles to play.

One role is to drive and guide strategic initiatives throughout the organization, from operations to product offering to R&D project selection. The overall strategic thrust captured by the identity and position should imply certain initiatives and programs. For example, given that we want to be an e-business firm, what tools and programs will customers expect from us? Initiatives and programs that do not advance the identity and position should be dialed down or killed.

A second role is to drive the communication program. A strategic identity and position that truly differentiates the product and resonates with customers will provide not only punch and effectiveness to external communication, but consistency over time because of its long-term perspective.

A third role is to support the expression of the organization's values and culture to employees and business partners. Such internal communication is as vital to success as reaching out to customers. Lynn Upshaw, a San Francisco communication consultant, suggests asking employees and business partners two questions:

- Do you know what the business stands for?
- Do you care?

Unless the answers to these questions are yes—that is, employees and business partners understand and believe in the business strategy—the strategy is unlikely to fulfill its potential. Too many businesses drift aimlessly without direction, appearing to stand for nothing in particular. Lacking an organizational sense of soul and a sound strategic position, they always seem to be shouting "on sale," attached to some deal, or engaging in promiscuous channel expansion.

Multiple Brand Identities

Arbitrarily insisting that a brand identity should apply to all products or market segments can be self-defeating. Rather, consideration should be given to adapting it to each context. One approach is to augment the brand identity to make it appropriate to a specific context. For example, Honda is associated with youth and racing in Japan while being more family oriented in the United States, but both positions share a focus on quality and motor expertise. Another is to define one of the brand identity elements differently in disparate contexts. Quality for GE Capital might be different than quality at GE Appliances, but high standards apply to both.

The Brand Position

The brand position represents the communication objectives—what parts of the identity are to be actively communicated to the target audience. The conceptualization of a brand position independent of a brand identity frees the latter to become a rich, textured picture of the aspirational brand. The brand identity does not have to be a compact view appropriate to guide communication.

The brand position will be inherently more dynamic than the brand identity. As the strategy and market context evolve and communication objectives are met, new ones become appropriate. A series of four or five positions over many years may be required to achieve the brand identity.

One fundamental choice often in front of strategists is whether to create a position that is credible or aspirational. In the case of Ajax, the firm's energy and over-the-top quality was legendary and created a value proposition with both functional and emotional components. An associated brand position would be credible, compelling, and relative easy to implement. However, it would not move the needle as far as supporting the new strategy. A position around collaboration and team solutions, on the other hand, would be on-strategy but would also not be credible for a firm noted as being arrogant and silo-driven and would be expensive and maybe even infeasible. The choice depends on the answers to two questions. Does the firm have programs in place to deliver on the new promise? Is the market ready to accept the changed firm? The answer to either question is no, it might be prudent to delay the aspirational position.

Another positioning choice is whether to emphasize points of differentiation or points of parity. The answer will depend on which direction will affect the target market. If the brand has a well-established image on a point of differentiation (such as value for Kmart, safety for Volvo), it may be more effective to attempt to create a point of parity on another dimension that is holding it back (quality for Kmart or styling for Volvo).

KEY LEARNINGS

- Brand equity, a key asset for any business, consists of brand awareness, brand loyalty, and brand associations.

- Awareness provides a sense of familiarity, credibility, and relevance in that customers are more likely to consider brands that are top-of-mind.

- A core loyal customer base reduces the cost of marketing, provides a barrier to competitors, supports a positive image, and provides time to respond to competitor moves.

- Brand associations can and should go beyond attributes and benefits to include such associations as brand personality, organizational intangibles, and product category associations.

- The brand identity represents aspirational associations. The most important of these, the core identity, should be supported by proof points and/or strategic imperatives and should be the driver of strategic programs, including product development.

- While the identity represents long-term aspirational associations and is multidimensional, the position represents the short-term communication objectives and is more focused.

FOR DISCUSSION

1. Explain how each of the three brand equity dimensions provide value to the firm. Explain how they provide value to customers.

2. What is the difference between identity and position? Develop alternative positioning statements for Ajax. Include a tagline and the rationale for that tagline.

3. Create a brand identity for Virgin Atlantic Airlines. Are there potential dimensions, such as high quality and superior service, that are inconsistent with the brand's personality? If so, how is that handled? How has the identity been brought to life? What are the proof points? Why don't more brands emulate Virgin's brand-building programs?

4. Pick out three brands from a particular industry. How are they positioned? Which is the best in your view? Does that brand's positioning provide any emotional or self-expressive benefits? How would you evaluate each brand's positioning strategy? Hypothesize proof points and strategic imperatives for each brand.

5. Consider the Joie de Vivre hotel concept described on page 166. Think of themes stimulated by magazines or movies, and discuss how you would design a hotel around each concept. For each theme, choose five words that reflect that theme.

NOTES

1. David A. Aaker, *Managing Brand Equity*, New York: Free Press, 1991, p. 57.

2. "Shoppers Like Wide Variety of Houseware Brands," *Discount Store News*, October 24, 1988, p. 40.

3. Leo Bogart and Charles Lehman, "What Makes a Brand Name Familiar?" *Journal of Marketing Research*, February 1973, pp. 17–22.

CHAPTER TEN

Energizing the Business

Many of the failures are people who did not realize how close to success they were before they gave in.
—*Thomas Edison*

One never notices what has been done, one can only see what remains to be done.
—*Marie Curie*

Where there is no wind, row.
—*Portuguese proverb*

Businesses need growth and not only for financial reasons. Certainly shareholders, employees, and partners look to enhance sales and profits. However, growth also introduces vitality to an organization by providing challenges and rewards. An organization that cannot improve and grow may not even be viable.

Firms can improve performance by downsizing, restructuring, redeploying assets, and reducing costs. While efficiency should be a goal, most firms eventually come to the point of diminishing returns; there is a limit to how much you can improve profits with efficiency programs. Only so many people and offices can be eliminated. Further, downsizing can eventually be debilitating to the organization. Muscle needed to create and support growth opportunities is often lost along with the fat. Employees and partners will lose motivation when they see that productivity innovations will cost them roles and jobs. There is thus an increasing realization that the road to improved performance must involve a renewed emphasis on growth.

There are four ways to grow a business, as suggested by Figure 10.1. The first, energizing the current business, is covered in this chapter. The focus is on the existing product markets with the current assets and competencies. The second, covered in Chapter 11, leverages the current business. That can mean taking the existing products into new markets, or finding new products or services for the existing customer base, or leveraging assets such as brand equity or competencies such as introducing products into a channel. The third, introduced in Chapter 12, involves

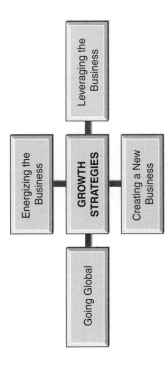

```
        Going Global

Energizing the      GROWTH        Leveraging the
Business          STRATEGIES       Business

        Creating a New
        Business
```

Figure 10.1 Growth Strategies

creating a new business based on finding a white space in the market or by transformational innovation, a business for which a substantial competitive advantage will exist and persist. The fourth, going global, is covered in Chapter 13. Globalization can mean leveraging the business into new countries to create a broader market. However, it can also mean creating new or improved assets and competencies that will lead to sustainable advantage in a global marketplace.

ENERGIZING THE BUSINESS

The existing business can be an attractive growth avenue because an established firm has market and operating experience, assets, competencies, and a customer base on which to build. Developing new products or entering new markets is inherently risky and can stretch the firm in ways that may dilute the existing strategy and culture.

There are many ways to stimulate the basic business. In particular, the business could:

- **Improve the customer experience.** Look at all the touchpoints, value each in terms of customer impact and performance, and create programs to turn problem areas into points of superiority and make them more visible. Exceeding expectations with respect to the value proposition may generate momentum. Engage in incremental innovation improving the product. During a one-year period, Kimberly Clark Huggies Supreme introduced a cottony Gentle Care lineup for newborns and a Natural Fit lineup for older babies that was better shaped, thinner, and more flexible, while P&G's Pampers introduced a Caterpillar Flex diaper and Feel 'n Learn training pants. Such activity shows a lot of vitality for the category and the two leading brands.

- **Remove or reduce the reasons not to buy by creating points of parity.** A business often reaches a ceiling because there are potential buyers who have a reason not to buy. Kmart clothes might be considered unfashionable, so the firm's challenge is to create enough credibility with respect to fashion so that its gap on this dimension is no longer enough to prevent buying.

- **Expand the loyal customer base.** A loyal customer base usually provides the bulk of the profits. In general, the need is to enhance the value proposition and the bases of relationship of loyal buyers. Loyalty programs provide a direct path to growth, especially if they are focused on the loyal segment as opposed to rewarding all buyers.

- **Expand the buyer base.** Although new buyers are often expensive targets, expanding the buyer base will directly affect the top line. When awareness is low for a well-received offering, investments to attract new buyers are most worthwhile.

- **Develop home-run marketing programs.** Programs that will move the needle often mean moving beyond media advertising to other vehicles such as sponsorships, the Internet, the digital world, and even "buzz marketing" whereby word-of-mouth is stimulated. It also means focusing on and connecting to the activities and interests of consumers. Look for role models such as Samsung's Olympic sponsorships, the Virgin publicity stunts, and the Apple stores for inspiration.

- **Introduce line extensions.** New flavors, packaging, or sizes can add energy, interest, and the creation of new segments. However, line extensions need to balance their value with the risk that customers might rebel over the added confusion and complexity. Colgate made significant gains when it introduced Total, which simplified a purchase decision for consumers faced with a bewildering array of choices for toothpaste.

- **Introduce or enhance a lively, humorous personality.** Most competitors are serious about their offerings, and a business that takes itself lightly will often stand out. This is especially true in the insurance industry. Aflac made great strides on the awareness front by developing the Aflac duck, and MetLife has benefited from associations with the Peanuts characters.

Three particularly important concepts for energizing a brand—increasing usage among existing customers, creating differentiation through branded differentiators, and creating energy through branded energizers—are discussed in the sections that follow.

INCREASING PRODUCT USAGE

Attempts to increase market share will very likely affect competitors directly and therefore precipitate competitor responses. An alternative, attempting to increase usage among current customers, is usually less threatening to competitors.

When developing programs to increase usage, it is useful to begin by asking some fundamental questions about the user and the consumption system in which the product is embedded. Why isn't the product or service used more? What are the barriers to increased use? Who are the light users, and can they be influenced to use more? What about the heavy users?

Greater usage can be precipitated in two ways, by increasing either the frequency of use or the quantity used. In either case, there are several approaches that can be effective. All are based on becoming obsessed with what stimulates use and the use experience itself.

Motivate Heavy Users to Use More

Heavy users are usually the most fruitful target. It is often easier to get a holder of two football season tickets to buy four or six than it is to get an occasional attendee of games to buy two. It is helpful to look at the extra-heavy user subsegment—special treatment might solidify and expand usage by a substantial amount. Examples include Schwab's Gold Signature Services, the special dinner parties and courier service offered by Chase Manhattan to its biggest accounts, or the first-class treatment provided to high rollers by Las Vegas casinos.

Make the Use Easier

Asking why customers do not use a product or service more often can lead to approaches that make the product easier to use. For example, a Dixie cup or paper-towel dispenser encourages use by reducing the usage effort. Packages that can be

CREATIVE THINKING METHODS

Not all growth strategies are obvious. In fact, the obvious ones are likely to be marginal in terms of likely success and impact, so it is useful to look for breakthrough ideas. Methods and concepts of creative thinking can help in this process. Among the guidelines suggested most often are the following:

- Pursue creative thinking in groups, as multiple perspectives and backgrounds can stimulate unexpected results.

- Begin with warm-up exercises that break down inhibitions. To make whimsy acceptable, for example, ask individuals to identify what animal expresses their personality and to imitate the sound made by that animal. To stretch minds, ask someone to start a story based on two random words (e.g., *blue* and *sail*), then ask the group to create a position for a brand based on that story.

- Focus on a particular task, such as how to exploit an asset (a brand name, for example) or a competence (such as the ability to design colorful plastic items).

- Develop options without judging them. Discipline in avoiding evaluation while generating alternatives is a key to creative thinking.

- Engage in lateral thinking to change the perspective of the problem. Challenge an obvious assumption ("What if we had two telephones in a booth?"), or simply pick a random word or object (such as *tiger*, or the Rockefeller Center) to stimulate a new line of thought.

- Evaluate the options based on potential impact without regard to how feasible they are.

- Engage in a second stage of creative thinking aimed at improving the success chances of an attractive option—possibly one with high potential impact that seems too expensive or too difficult to implement.[1]

- Evaluate the final choices not just rationally ("What do the facts say?") but emotionally ("What does your gut say?").

- Create an action plan to go forward.

placed directly in a microwave make usage more convenient. A reservation service can help those who must select a hotel or similar service. The classic but long-dormant Crock-Pot slow cookers were in 80 percent of homes, but used by only 20 percent. A hot product in the early 1970s, it fell victim to out-of-home eating but is making a sharp comeback in part due to a desire to have home-cooked meals with minimal preparation. A catalyst is the Banquet line of frozen entrees called Banquet Crock-Pot Classics, which have made the process of cooking with the Crock-Pot much easier.

Provide Incentives

Incentives can be provided to increase consumption frequency. Promotions such as double mileage trips offered by airlines with frequent-flyer plans can increase usage. A fast-food restaurant might offer a large drink at a discounted price if it is purchased with a meal. A challenge is to structure the incentive so that usage is increased without creating a vehicle for debilitating price competition. Price incentives, such as two for the price of one, can be effective, but they also may stimulate price retaliation.

Reduce Undesirable Consequences of Frequent Use

Sometimes there are good reasons why a customer is inhibited from using a product more frequently. If such reasons can be addressed, usage may increase. For example, some people might believe that frequent hair washing may not be healthy. A product that is designed to be gentle enough for daily use might alleviate this worry and thereby stimulate increased usage. A low-calorie, low-sodium, or low-fat version of a food product may sharply increase the market. The brand that becomes associated with a product change will be in the best position to capitalize on the increased market.

Provide Reminder Communications

For some use contexts, awareness or recall of a brand is the driving force. People who know about a brand and its use may not think to use it on particular occasions without reminders.

Reminder communication may be necessary. An e-mail program to remind Red Envelope customers about an upcoming birthday may ensure that they buy a present. Several brands, including Jell-O, have conducted advertising campaigns aimed at getting their product out of the cupboard and onto the table. It is not enough for people to have recipes if they never get around to using them.

Routine maintenance functions such as dental checkups or car lubrication are easily forgotten, and reminders can make a difference. An Arm & Hammer consumer survey revealed that people who use baking soda as a deodorizer in refrigerators thought that they changed the box every 4 months when actually they did so only every 14 months. An advertising campaign geared to seasonal reminders about replacing the box resulted.

Strategy	Examples
Motivate heavy users to use more	Perks with more season tickets
Make the use easier	Microwaveable containers
Provide incentives	Frequent flyer miles
Reduce undesirable consequences	Gentle shampoo for frequent use
Provide reminder communication	E-mail birthday reminder
Position for regular use	Floss after meals
Find new uses	Snowmobiles for delivery

Figure 10.2 Increasing Usage in Existing Product Markets

Position for Regular or Frequent Use

Provide a reason for more frequent use. On Web sites, what works is to have information that is frequently updated. People go to My Yahoo to see the latest headlines or learn how their stocks are doing, as often as every few minutes when important things are happening. Other incentives might include a new cartoon each day at a teen Web site, or a best-practices bulletin board at a brand consulting site.

The image of a product can change from that of occasional to frequent usage through a repositioning campaign. For example, the advertising campaigns for Clinique's "twice-a-day" moisturizer and "three glasses of milk per day" both represent efforts to change the perception of the products involved. The use of programs such as the Book-of-the-Month Club, CD clubs, DVD clubs, and flower-of-the-month or fruit-of-the-month delivery can turn infrequent purchasers into regular ones.

Find New Uses

The detection and exploitation of a new functional use for a brand can rejuvenate a business that has been considered a has-been for years. Jell-O, for example, began strictly as a dessert product but found major sources of new sales in applications such as Jell-O salads. Another classic story is that of Arm & Hammer baking soda, which saw annual sales grow tenfold by persuading people to use its product as a refrigerator deodorizer. An initial 14-month advertising campaign boosted the use as a deodorizer from 1 to 57 percent. The brand subsequently was extended into other deodorizer products, dentifrices, and laundry detergent. A chemical process used in oil fields to separate waste from oil found a new application when it was applied to water plants to eliminate unwanted oil.

New uses can best be identified by conducting market research to determine exactly how customers use a brand. From the set of uses that emerge, several can be selected to pursue. For example, users of external analgesics were asked to keep a diary of their uses.[2] A surprising finding was that about one-third of BenGay's usage and more than one-half of its volume was for arthritis relief instead of muscle aches. A separate marketing strategy was developed for this use, and the brand caught a wave of growth. Another tactic is to look at the applications of competing products. The widespread use of raisins prompted Ocean Spray to create dried cranberries, which can be found in cookies and in cereal such as Müeslix with a "made with real

Ocean Spray cranberries" seal on the package. They are also being sold as a snack food called Ocean Spray Craisins.

Sometimes a large payoff will result for a firm that can provide applications not currently in general use. Thus, surveys of current applications may be inadequate. Firms such as General Mills have sponsored recipe contests, one objective of which has been to create new uses for a product by discovering a new "recipe classic." For a product that can be used in many ways, such as stick-on labels, it might be worthwhile to conduct formal brainstorming sessions or other creative exercises.

If some application area is uncovered that could create substantial sales, it needs to be evaluated. Consideration needs to be given to the possibility that a competitor will take over an application area, whether through product improvement, heavy advertising, or engaging in price warfare. Can the brand achieve a sustainable advantage in its new application to justify building the business? Ocean Spray is associated with cranberries, which might protect its entry into a cranberry snack, but the firm's name will be less helpful in a processed application such as cookies or cereals.

BRANDED DIFFERENTIATORS

Differentiation is a key to winning in any marketplace because it is the basis for customer choice and loyalty. Stuart Agris, the father of the mammoth Young & Rubicam brand database covering over 35 countries and 13,000 brands, has noted that "differentiation is the engine of the brand train.... if the engine stops, so will the train." Product areas without differentiated brands are usually boring and lack energy.

The problem is that differentiation is increasingly difficult to create and maintain as competitors proliferate products and quickly copy any advances. How can a firm own an innovation? One approach toward that end is the use of a branded differentiator.[3]

A *branded differentiator* is an actively managed, branded feature, ingredient or technology, service, or program that creates a meaningful, impactful point of differentiation for a branded offering over an extended time period.

For example, the Westin Hotel Chain created in 1999 the "Heavenly Bed," a custom-designed mattress set (by Simmons) with 900 coils, a cozy down blanket adapted for climate, a comforter with a crisp duvet, high-quality sheets, and five goosedown pillows. The Heavenly Bed became a branded differentiator in a crowded category in which differentiation is a challenge.

A branded differentiator does not occur simply by slapping a name on a feature. The definition suggests rather demanding criteria that need to be satisfied. In particular, a branded differentiator needs to be meaningful (that is, it matters to customers) and impactful (that is, not a trivial difference). The Heavenly Bed was meaningful in that it was truly a better bed and addressed the heart of a hotel's promise—to provide a good night's sleep. It was also impactful. During the first year of its life, those hotels sites that featured the Heavenly Bed had a 5 percent increase in customer satisfaction, a noticeable increase in perceptions of cleanliness, room decor, and maintenance, and increased occupancy.

A branded differentiator also needs to warrant active management over time and justify brand-building efforts. It should be a moving target. The Heavenly Bed has received that treatment with an active and growing set of brand-building programs. The reception to the bed was so strong that Westin starting selling it; in 2004, some 3,500 beds were sold. Imagine, selling a hotel bed. Think of the buzz. The concept has been extended to the Heavenly Bath, with dual shower heads plus soap and towels. The Heavenly Online Catalog is a place to connect and order all the branded products.

The Heavenly Bed was developed and owned by Westin. It is not always feasible to develop such products and brands, in part because the time and resources may not be available and in part because it is simply difficult. An alternative is to explore alliances in order to create branded differentiators with instant credibility. The Ford Explorer Eddie Bauer Edition, for example, was an offering that sold more than one million vehicles over two decades. It was successful from the outset because the Eddie Bauer brand was established with associations of style, comfort, and the outdoors. Ford never could have achieved that success with its own brand (the Ford Explorer LeatherRide, for example). It would be difficult to imbue such a brand with the self-expressive benefits offered by the Eddie Bauer brand even if the necessary brand-building resources and time been available.

An effective differentiator needs to augment or buttress the product with something that is meaningful to the customer and capable of influencing choice and loyalty. The KC Masterpiece brand when applied to snacks clearly added a flavor perceived to be tasty and unique. In contrast, Pizza Hut Doritos and Taco Bell Doritos failed because they offered nothing; there was no flavor or customer connection leveraged to the co-brand.

A branded differentiator, as suggested by Figure 10.3 and the definition, will be either a feature, ingredient or technology, service, or program affecting the offering. A branded feature such as General Motor's OnStar often provides a graphic way to signal superior performance. The OnStar system provides automatic notification of air bag deployment to roadside assistance agencies, stolen vehicle location, emergency services, remote door unlocking, remote diagnostics, and concierge services.

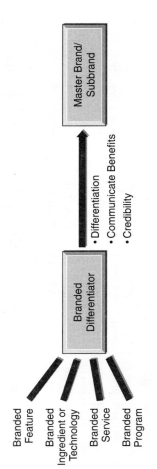

Figure 10.3   Branded Differentiators

A branded ingredient (or component or technology) such as Chevron's Techron or Intel Inside can add credibility even if customers do not understand how the ingredient works, just because someone believed it was worth branding. A branded service such as the Tide Stain Detective, which provides stain removal information on the Tide Web site, provides product reinforcement and credibility to Tide. A branded program such as the Harley-Davidson Ride Planner can provide a way to deepen customer relationships.

A valued feature, ingredient or technology, service, or program will serve to differentiate a product whether or not it is branded. Why brand it? For one reason, a brand can add credibility and legitimacy to a claim. The brand specifically says that the benefit was worth branding, that it is not only meaningful but impactful. The ability of a brand to add credibility was rather dramatically shown in a remarkable study of branded attributes. Carpenter, Glazer, and Nakamoto, three prominent academic researchers, found that the inclusion of a branded attribute (such as "Alpine Class" fill for a down jacket, "Authentic Milanese" for pasta, and "Studio Designed" for compact disc players) dramatically affected customer preference toward premium-priced brands. Respondents were able to justify the higher price because of the branded attributes even though they had no idea why the attributes were superior.[4]

A second reason is that a brand name makes communication easier. A branded feature such as Oral B's Action Cup provides a way to crystallize feature details, making the feature easier to both understand and remember. Communication is particularly difficult with a service or program such as Best Buy's Geek Squad, a service team that will fix or set up your computer or laptop. For the intimidated or the frustrated, the service is very welcome. The Geek Squad brand not only communicates what they do but also their energy and personality, who they are. In general, a branded service can help capture the essence and scope of a concept that otherwise could be multidimensional and complex and directed to an audience that simply does not care enough to make any effort.

Finally, brand equity around the point of differentiation creates a basis for a sustainable competitive advantage. A competitor may be able to replicate the feature, ingredient or technology, service, or program, but if it is branded, they will need to overcome the power of the brand. Other hotels can create great beds and even brand them, but only one hotel will ever have the Heavenly Bed and the authenticity that goes with it. Only one retailer has the Geek Squad. It helps to make the branded differentiation a moving target, continually improving and enhancing it so that copying will be more difficult and the danger of being stale will be reduced.

Amazon developed a powerful feature, the ability to recommend books or whatever based on a customer's interests as reflected by his or her purchase history and the purchase history of those that bought similar offerings. But they never branded it. How tragic is that? As a result, the feature became basically a commodity that is an expected feature of many e-commerce sites. If Amazon had branded it and then actively managed that brand, improving the feature over time, it would have become a lasting point of differentiation that today would be invaluable. They missed a golden opportunity. They did not make that same mistake with One-Click, a branded service that plays a key role in defining Amazon in what has become a messy marketplace.

BRANDED ENERGIZERS

How do you energize a brand especially when there is little interest not only in the brand but in the product category as well? One solution is to use a *branded energizer*—**a branded product, promotion, sponsorship, symbol, program, or other entity that by association significantly enhances and energizes a target brand. The branded energizer and its association with the target brand are actively managed over an extended time period.**

As Figure 10.4 and the definition suggest, a branded energizer can be a wide variety of branded entities and should have several characteristics. First, a branded energizer should itself have energy and vitality as opposed to being lethargic. An effective branded energizer should do well when asked whether it would be described as being:

- Interesting vs. stale
- Youthful vs. mature
- Interesting vs. boring
- Dynamic vs. unchanging
- Contemporary vs. traditional
- Assertive vs. passive
- Involving vs. separated

Second, the branded energizer needs to be connected to the master brand even if, unlike a branded differentiator, it is not part of the master brand offering and does not promise any functional benefits. This connection task can be difficult and expensive. Even the Energizer bunny, one of the top icons among U.S. brands, is associated by some with Duracell rather than Energizer despite the exposure over a long time period.

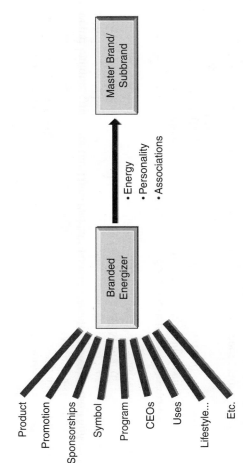

Figure 10.4   Branded Energizers

One connection route is to use a subbrand such as Ronald McDonald House, where the master brand has a connection in the name. A second is to select a program or activity that is so "on-brand" that it makes the link easier to establish. A baby-oriented program would require little effort to connect to Gerber. A third is to simply forge the link by consistently building it over time with significant link-building resources, as MetLife has done with the Peanuts characters.

Third, a branded energizer should significantly enhance as well as energize the target brand and should not detract or damage the brand by being "off-brand" or making customers uncomfortable. Offbeat, underdog brands such as Virgin, Apple, or Mountain Dew, which are perceived as unpredictable to begin with, have more leeway. "Senior" brands, in contrast, can develop branded energizers edgier than the parent brand but have a lot of options foreclosed.

Fourth, the problems of finding and managing internal branded energizers leads firms to look outside the organization. The challenge is to find an external energizer brand that is linked into the lifestyle of customers, that will have the needed associations to energize and enhance, that is not tied to competitors, that can be linked to the target brand, and that represents a manageable alliance. The task takes discipline and creativity.

Fifth, branded energizers (like branded differentiators) represent a long-term commitment; the brands involved should be expected to have a long life and merit brand-building investments. If the energizers are internally developed, the cost of brand building will have to be amortized over a long enough period to make it worthwhile. If they are externally sourced, the cost and effort of linking them to the parent brand will take time as well. And they need to be actively managed over time so that they can continue to be successful in their roles. The concepts of branded energizers and differentiators do *not* provide a rationale to add brands indiscriminately.

There are many types of branded energizers. Some of the most useful include products, sponsorships, symbols, endorsers, promotions, programs, and even CEOs.

New Branded Products

The gold standard for creating on-brand energy is a flow of new products that are worth branding because they are sufficiently different and promise to support sales over time. The introduction of the ThinkPad brand moved the image of the IBM brand, even though in sales it was a negligible part of the IBM business. As a result, brand-building efforts for the ThinkPad had a double benefit. Now that the ThinkPad brand is owned by Lenovo, its potential for being a branded energizer is even greater because the Lenovo name could use more help than the IBM brand.

Some new products with strong subbrands that energized their master brand include:

- Bose Wave Radio, which sells for over $300 but delivers performance far superior to other radios, provides energy and brand reinforcement to Bose.
- Apple iPod, the portable digital music player, expanded and energized the Apple brand.
- The Sky Roadster created a sense of excitement and energy for Saturn by adding an European design flavor to a brand that was respected and admired but was a bit boring.

- Nike's Presto shoe is versatile and comfortable, with a unique design that permits S-M-L sizing and still fits. Available in 13 colors, the brand provided a fashion uplift to Nike and was a huge hit among the target teen audience.

Branded products can be externally sourced. Target has used a branded designer and architect, Michael Graves, to create a host of products from bedding to games to houseware items. They also got the trendy southern California designer Mossimo Giannulli to design an extensive line of clothing and shoes. Dreyer's Ice Cream Limited Edition flavors are offered for a limited time around themes like Scooby Doo, a professional football team like the Oakland Raiders, and the Girl Scout Cookies to attract attention and create bursts of energy and sales.

Branded Sponsorships

The right sponsorship, handled well, can energize a brand and create strong relationships with customers. Consider a rather utilitarian product like motor oil and a venerable brand like Valvoline. Such a brand would normally have trouble generating interest and energy, to say nothing of becoming an important part of a person's life. Few would be motivated to read ads about motor oil, which is perceived by many to be an undifferentiated product. However, through sponsorship activities Valvoline becomes part of the NASCAR scene, and everything changes.

The Valvoline racing program is multidimensional. Valvoline is not just a sponsor of NASCAR but has a NASCAR racing team as well. At the Valvoline Web site, a destination site for those involved with racing, a visitor can access the schedule for NASCAR and other racing circuits and learn the results of the most recent races, complete with pictures and interviews. A "Behind Closed Garage Doors" section provides inside information and analyses. The visitor can adopt the Valvoline NASCAR racing team and learn about their current activities and recent finishes. In addition, it is possible to send Valvoline racing greeting cards, buy Valvoline racing gear, download a Valvoline racing screensaver, and sign up for a weekly newsletter (TrackTalk) that provides updates on the racing circuits. Valvoline thus becomes closely associated with the racing experience, much more than simply being a logo on a car.

The core segment for Valvoline are buyers who change their own oil, are very involved in cars, and live for NASCAR races. The Valvoline racing program has the potential to influence this group in several ways. At a most basic level, it provides credibility and associations of being a leader in motor oil technology. Top teams would not use Valvoline if it was not superior—there is too much riding on the engine's performance. But there are more subtle possibilities. A customer by choosing Valvoline can receive self-expressive benefits, as it is a way to tangentially associate oneself with the top drivers and teams. And research shows that it has tangible benefits. One study found that 47 percent of the U.S. public had an interest in watching NASCAR racing. In another, 60 percent of NASCAR fans said they trusted sponsors' products (as compared to 30 percent of NFL fans), and more than 40 percent switch brands when a company becomes a sponsor.[5]

A sponsorship can provide the ultimate in relevance, the movement of a brand upward into the acceptable if not leadership position. A software firm trying unsuccessfully to make a dent into the European market became a perceived leader in a few months when it sponsored one of the top three bicycle racing teams. Part of Samsung's breakthrough from being just another Korean price brand to becoming a real player in the U.S. market was its sponsorship of the Olympics. It says so much about the brand, so much more than product advertising could ever say. Tracking data confirms that well-conceived and well-managed sponsorships can make a difference. The Visa lead in perceived credit card superiority went from 15 percentage points prior to the Olympics to 30 points during to 20 points one month after—huge movements in what are normally very stable attitudes.[6]

A significant problem with sponsorship—indeed, with any external branded energizer—is linking it to the brand. DDB Needham's Sponsor-Watch, which measures such linkage, has shown that sponsorship confusion is common.[7] Of the 102 official Olympic sponsors tracked since 1984, only about half have built a link (defined as having sponsor awareness of at least 15 percent and at least 10 percent higher than that of a competitor who was not a sponsor, hardly demanding criteria). Those successful at creating links, such as Visa and Samsung, surround the sponsorship with a host of brand-driven activities including promotions, publicity events, Web site content, newsletters, and advertising over an extended time period.

Although most sponsorships are external to the firm, there are cases of internally controlled sponsorships. The Adidas Streetball Challenge is a branded weekend event centered around local three-person basketball tournaments and featuring free-throw competitions, a street dance, graffiti events, and extreme sports demonstrations, all accompanied by live music from bands from the hip-hop and rap scenes. The Challenge was right in the sweet spot of target customers, a party. And it was connected to Adidas by its brand and supporting signage and Adidas-supplied caps and jackets. It revitalized Adidas at a critical time in its history.

Endorsers

A brand may lack energy, but there are plenty of personalities who are contemporary, on-brand, energetic, and interesting. Buick struggled to maintain relevance as its owner base became the oldest among all car brands, older than Cadillac and Lincoln.[8] It needed to become acceptable if not cool to those who would turn to Japanese or European options and who consider successful, young professionals as being a reference group. Turning a brand like Buick around, especially among the target market of younger buyers, is just about impossible with products or advertising. Enter Tiger Woods, who began a long-term Buick relationship in 1999, using a Buick golf bag, appearing in commercials, supporting Buick promotional events, and playing in Buick tournaments. The association with Tiger Woods made it more acceptable to drive Buicks, made new Buick products like the Rendezvous truck more credible, and served to start a substanial decline in the age of the user base.

The connection to the brand and the resulting leverage for any celebrity endorser will be more effective if it is part of a larger program. The association of Buick with Tiger Woods is embedded in Buick's extensive involvement with golf that dates back to 1958, when the Buick Open was inaugurated. There are now four Buick-sponsored PGA tour events. In addition, there is the amateur Buick Scramble (formerly the Oldsmobile Scramble), an amateur event started in the mid-1980s that attracts over 100,000 participants and holds a highly visible finals in Orlando; Tiger Woods is the honorary chairman. The Web site has links to a Buick Pro Shop that sells Buick golf bags, Buick-labeled sportswear, and Tiger Nike balls. So Tiger Woods is the centerpiece of a brand portfolio involving golf tournaments and supporting activities, Web sites, and programs.

Selecting and engaging an endorser is a critical first stop in creating a strategic brand energizer. There are a host of considerations. An endorser target should have:

- An appealing image
  - o Visible among the target audience (low visibility will limit the impact)
  - o Attractive, liked (simple liking can and does get transferred to the endorsed brand)
  - o Sincere (will there be a feeling that the endorser is doing it for money and lacks a sincere belief in the product?)
  - o Fresh, not overexposed (an endorser's impact can be diluted by over-exposure as an endorser)
- On-brand associations
  - o Matching the brand identity goals
  - o A natural match to the brand (does the link make sense?)
  - o Confidence that the positive associations can be leveraged and that the negative ones can be managed
- Potential for a long-term relationship (How long will the endorser have the desired associations and how likely will it be that a compatible relationship will endure? A hot personality may not always be the one that will wear well. Tiger Woods is on his second five-year contract with Buick.)
- Potential to create programs surrounding the endorser
- Cost effectiveness and availability (Tiger Woods cost Buick $25 million over five years, but the real cost will be the programs surrounding the endorser.)

Branded Promotional Activities

Kraft's Oscar Mayer Wienermobiles provide energy to a very boring category. There are eight vehicles shaped like a huge Oscar Mayer Weiner touring the United States, with license plates with appropriate wording like "HOT DOG." They turn up at events and parties and support the annual contest to find a child to sing the signature Oscar Mayer jingle. The Wienermobile, which has been shown to bump the product sales, also lives on the Web where visitors can be taken on a tour of Oscartown featuring the Oscar Museum, the OscarMart, and Town Hall. The brand Weinermobile, by its linkage to the product category, also links it to Oscar Mayer.

Memorable Branded Symbols

Brands that are blessed with strong relevant symbols such as the Pillsbury Doughboy, the Maytag repairman, P&G's Mr. Clean, or the Michelin Man can actively manage and use the symbols to become energizer brands. Such symbols can give a personality to even the blandest of brands. They can also suggest attributes. The Doughboy is upbeat, with a sense of humor, and means freshness and superb quality. The Maytag repairman is relaxed, confident, and symbolizes the reliability of Maytag. The Michelin Man is strong and positive and means safety. Mr. Clean is strong and reliable.

Symbols can be leased as well as developed. MetLife adopted the Peanuts characters in 1985. Their goal was to provide a warm, light, nonthreatening approach to insurance—a tough sell in the context of an industry perceived by many to be boring, greedy, and bureaucratic. The familiar, funny characters provide a vehicle toward those objectives while also providing interest and energy. Snoopy's appearance on the Web site, on a blimp (which costs $2.5 million each per year), in ads, and even on the logo also serves to inhibit what psychologists call counterarguing. The natural tendency to be cynical toward an insurance company's ad or claim is reduced for MetLife in the presence of the likable Snoopy; in part because it would make no sense to argue with a cartoon character.

It is important to understand the role of the symbol. Is it to create a personality? To suggest or reinforce associations? To be a vehicle to interject humor and likability into an otherwise bland and uninteresting message? To create interest and visibility, like the duck has done for Aflac? With the role in mind, it is possible to proactively look for or develop the right one.

Branded Programs

A branded program, such as one in the corporate citizenship arena, can be an effective energizer. Consider the Avon Breast Cancer Crusade, which covers a wide-ranging set of branded programs involving research, early detection, clinical care, support services, and education. With its signature activity, the Avon Walk for Breast Cancer, the program has substance and significance—one measure of which is the fact that it raised $400 million over a thirteen year period. It gives "The Company for Women" a higher purpose and a heart. Or consider Ronald McDonald House, the program by McDonald's to provide housing for families with seriously ill children. It not only contributes something of real substance to the larger good, it contributes to the McDonald's relationship to kids and families.

Branded CEOs

Some firms have branded CEOs who can serve to capture and magnify the energy in the brand, or even create energy that can be transferred to the brand. Lee Iacocca helped save Chrysler by exuding confidence and competence when customers and investors had assumed the firm would collapse. Richard Branson's outlandish stunts (some involving hot-air balloons) have been a large part of the energy and personality of the Virgin brand. Herb Kelleher personified the Southwest Airlines brand with his visible and colorful expression of its culture. Steve Jobs and Bill Gates have driven much of the energy of Apple and Microsoft with their visible thought leadership.

The right CEO with the right message can often create news with credibility and has the advantage of being able to access media. To be an energizer, however, the CEO should have energy with respect to ideas, a distinctive personality, and be around for a long enough time period to become a recognized representative of the brand.

Brand It

Energizers, like differentiators, need to be branded, but creating or having a brand is only half the story. The brands must justify investments in brand building and active management, otherwise the brand will at best be a waste of money.

KEY LEARNINGS

- Increasing product usage can be based on motivating heavy users to use more, making the use easier with reduced undesirable consequences, providing usage incentives, reminder communications, positioning for frequent use, and finding new use.

- A branded differentiator is an actively managed, branded feature, ingredient or technology, service, or program that creates a meaningful, impactful point of differentiation for a branded offering over an extended time period.

- A branded energizer is a branded product, promotion, sponsorship, symbol, program, or other entity that by association significantly enhances and energizes a target brand—the branded energizer and its association with the target brand is actively managed over an extended time period.

FOR DISCUSSION

1. Using the creative thinking guidelines, think about how would you increase the usage of products if you were the managers of:

   a. Doritos

   b. Charles Schwab

   c. Gap

2. Think of some highly differentiated brands. Do they have branded differentiators? If not how did they achieved differentiation? Will it be lasting?

3. Think of some branded differentiators. How differentiated are they? Do the customers care? Are they impactful? Have they been managed well over time? Do they have legs? Evaluate Best Buy's Geek Squad.

4. Think of some brands that have high energy. What gives them that energy? Will that continue into the future?

5. Think of some brands that have branded energizers that made a difference. Evaluate them in terms of whether they are "on-brand," energetic, and linked to the master brand.

NOTES

1. This suggestion is due to Alex Biel, an active and successful creative-thinking innovator and facilitator.

2. Linden A. Davis, Jr. "Market Positioning Considerations," *Product-Line Strategies*, New York: The Conference Board, 1991, pp. 37–39.

3. Branded differentiators and branded energizers are introduced and discussed in more detail in David Aaker, *Brand Portfolio Strategy*, New York: The Free Press, 2005.

4. Gregory S. Carpenter, Rashi Glazer, and Kent Nakamoto, "Meaningful Brands from Meaningless Differentiation: The Dependence on Irrelevant Attributes," *Journal of Marketing Research*, August 1994, pp. 339–350.

5. Kevin Lane Keller, *Strategic Brand Management*, 2nd ed. Saddle River, NJ: Prentice Hall, 2003, p. 317.

6. James Crimmins and Martin Horn, "Sponsorship: From Management Ego Trip to Marketing Success," *Journal of Advertising Reaserch*, July–August 1996, pp. 11–21.

7. Ibid.

8. Ed Garsten, "Youthful Buyers Wanting Rendezvous with Buick," Associated Press, July 23, 2002.

CHAPTER ELEVEN

Leveraging the Business

Results are gained by exploiting opportunities, not by solving problems.
—*Peter Drucker*

The more opportunities I seize, the more opportunities multiply before me.
—*Sun Tzu*

The most dangerous moment comes with victory.
—*Napoleon*

*U*ltimately, growth avenues outside the existing business need to be explored. While it is risky to leave the comfort of the familiar and the tested, it also removes the ceiling on the firm's growth potential. There is virtually unlimited potential when you agree to extend the business.

The goal discussed in this chapter is to leverage the existing business into new product markets. The assets and competencies of the business, in particular, are potential sources of advantage in a new marketplace. The capabilities around developing and manufacturing products, service systems, marketing skills, distribution clout, customer relationships, sourcing networks, and brand equities are among the potential bases for advantage for a new growth business. The idea is to build on the core business to create a synergy. The challenge, though, is to achieve real synergy with real impact on the customer value proposition, costs, or investments. Too often, apparent synergy is not realized.

The spectrum of available choices can be categorized generally as to how removed they are from the core business. Those that are close will represent less risk and have the greatest chance of leveraging business assets and competencies to achieve a real advantage. As more distance is allowed from the current business, opportunities become more plentiful but the risk goes up as well. It can be difficult to gain the necessary knowledge and operational competence to run a business successfully that is far removed from one's core abilities. Enron fell in part because it attempted growth options such as broadband futures, consulting, and water treatment that were far from its core. Of course, creating a new core business can have a huge upside, and taking the risk of moving far from the core business may pay off. But the risk should be visible and part of the analysis.

There are many ways to generate growth options that leverage the core business. Creative thinking processes, introduced in Chapter 10, can help. Good outcomes more often come from having good options on the table rather than making optimal decisions among mediocre ones. The creative-thinking exercises can best be engaged around the following series of questions, which have proved to be a good source of options.

After these questions have been discussed, some option evaluation issues will be addressed and, finally, the critical concept of synergy will be analyzed.

- Which assets and competencies can be leveraged?
- What brand extensions are possible?
- Can the scope of the offering be expanded?
- Do viable new markets exist?

WHICH ASSETS AND COMPETENCIES CAN BE LEVERAGED?

A focus on assets and competencies starts by creating an inventory in order to identify the real strengths of the business. In doing so, the discussion in Chapter 3 around identifying and evaluating assets and competencies can be helpful. What are the key assets and competencies that are supporting the core business? What are their characteristics? How strong is each?

The second step is to find a business area where the assets and competencies can be applied to generate an advantage. A line of greeting cards sold through drugstores might have an artistic capability and a distribution asset that could be leveraged. What other items are in drugstores that might employ artistic talents? Are there items in the drugstore that the retailers have difficulty sourcing, for whatever reason? A retailer problem might suggest an opportunity.

One fruitful exercise is to examine each asset for excess capacity. Are some assets underutilized? A legal firm that considered this question took advantage of excess office space to offer tax services. A supermarket chain with obsolete sites went into the discount liquor business. A cookie plant began making muffins. If a growth initiative can use excess capacity, a substantial, sustainable cost advantage could result.

The final step is to address implementation problems. Assets and competencies may require adaptations when applied to a different business. Further, new capabilities may have to be found or developed. Existing core business are sometimes best leveraged by making an acquisition, because developing the business internally may be not be economic or even feasible. When acquisitions are involved, two organizations with different systems, people, and cultures will have to be merged. Many efforts at achieving synergy falter because of implementation difficulties.

As the partial list profiled in Chapter 3 suggests, there are a wide range of exportable assets and competencies. To give a flavor of the opportunities, consider the following: marketing skills, sales and distribution capacity, manufacturing skills, and R&D capabilities.

Marketing Skills

A firm will often either possess or lack strong marketing skills for a particular market. Thus, a frequent motive for expanding into new product markets is to export or import marketing skills. Black & Decker had developed and exploited an aggressive new-products program (e.g., cordless screwdrivers and HandyChopper), effective consumer marketing (for brands such as Spacemaker, Dustbuster, and ThunderVolt cordless tools), and intensive customer service and dealer relations. The acquisition of Emhart, with its branded door locks, decorative faucets, outdoor lighting, and racks, provided Black & Decker with an opportunity to apply its marketing skills and distribution clout to a firm that lacked a marketing culture.

Applying marketing skills is not always as easy as it appears. Philip Morris, a successful marketer of Miller Lite and other brands, failed with 7-Up, which it attempted to position as a caffeine-free soft drink in response to health interests of consumers. After a seven-year battle, Philip Morris gave up and sold the line. The problems that beset Philip Morris included the reaction of competitors who rushed caffeine-free drinks to the market, the power of existing distributors, and the limited appeal of lemon-lime drinks. Coca-Cola made a similar misjudgment when it created Wine Spectrum and failed in its efforts to overcome Gallo, in part because of Gallo's control over distribution.

Capacity in Sales or Distribution

A firm with a strong distribution capability may add products or services that could exploit that capability. Thus, Black & Decker's distribution strength helped provide a boost to the Emhart lines. A joint venture between Nestlé and Coca-Cola in the canned tea business combined Coke's distribution strength with the product knowledge and name of Nestlé.

E-commerce firms usually have operations that can add capacity just by adding a button to access another product group. The result can be additional sales and margins to offset the fixed costs of the operation.

Manufacturing Skills

Manufacturing or processing ability can be the basis for entry into a new business area. The ability to design and make small motors helped Honda succeed in the motorcycle business and led to its entry into lawn-care equipment, outboard motors, and a host of other products. The ability to make small products has been a key for Sony as it has moved from product to product in consumer electronics.

R&D Skills

Expertise in a certain technology can lead to a new business based on that technology. GE's early research has spawned very successful businesses. For example, its research on turbines for electricity generation provided the basis for its aircraft engine business, and its light bulb research provided the foundation for what became the medical instrumentation business. P&G has actively applied technology from one business area to another to create both incremental and game-changing innovation. In general, breakthroughs in a business area tend to come from technologies owned by other industries. Creativity, often in short supply, is needed to provide opportunities for basic technology and the R&D capability that supports it.

Achieving Economies of Scale

Product-market expansion can sometimes provide economies of scale. Two smaller consumer-products firms, for example, may not each be able to afford an effective sales force, new product development or testing programs, or warehousing and logistics systems. However, the combination of these firms may be able to operate at an efficient level. Similarly, two firms, when combined, may be able to justify an expensive piece of automated production equipment.

Sometimes a critical mass is needed in order to be effective. For example, a specialized electronics firm may need an R&D effort, but R&D productivity may be low if it is not feasible to have several researchers who can interact.

BRAND EXTENSIONS

One common exportable asset is a strong, established brand name—a name with visibility, associations, and loyalty among a customer group. The challenge is to take this brand asset and use it to enter new product markets. The name can make the task of establishing a new product more feasible and efficient, because it makes developing awareness, trust, interest, and action all easier.

Lenox, a maker of fine china, exploited its traditional, high-quality image and its distribution system by expanding into the areas of jewelry and giftware. H&R Block added legal services to its chain of income tax services, hoping to gain synergy by exploiting (and enhancing) its brand. A ski boot manufacturer leveraged its brand into skis and then ski clothing.

Many firms have built large, diverse businesses around a strong brand, including Sony, HP, IBM, Mitsubishi, Siemens, GE, Schwab, Virgin, and Disney. More than 300 businesses carry the Virgin name, and all gain from the public-relations flair of Richard Branson, its owner. Mitsubishi has its name on thousands of products, each of which benefits from the name exposure and from the cumulative new-product vitality.

Disney, founded in 1923 as a cartoon company with Mickey Mouse (made famous in the cartoon "Steamboat Willie") as its initial asset, might be the most successful firm ever at leveraging its brand. In the 1950s, the company built Disneyland and launched a TV show (the *Mickey Mouse Club*), dramatically changing the brand by making it

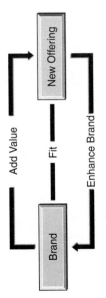

Figure 11.1   Brand Extension Logic

much richer and deeper than before. Particularly after extending the theme parks to Florida, Paris, and Japan and establishing its own retail stores, resorts, and a cruise line, Disney can deliver an experience that goes far beyond watching cartoons. As a result of this brand power, the Disney Channel has become a strong, differentiated TV network, an incredible achievement if you consider what others have put into that space.

It is instructive to see why Disney has done so well with an aggressive brand extension strategy. First, from the beginning the company has known what it stands for—magical family entertainment, executed with consistent excellence. Everything Disney does reinforces that brand identity; when it went into adult films, it did so under the name Touchstone rather than Disney. Second, Disney has a relentless, uncompromising drive for operational excellence that started with Walt Disney's fanatical concern for detail in the earliest cartoons and theme parks. The parks are run so well that Disney holds schools for other firms seeking to learn how to maintain energy and consistency. The cruise line was delayed, despite ballooning costs, until everything was judged perfect. Third, the organization actively manages a host of subbrands that have their own identities, including Mickey Mouse, Donald Duck, a mountain (the Matterhorn), a song ("It's a Small World"), film characters like Mary Poppins or the Lion King, and on and on. Fourth, Disney understands synergy across products. *The Lion King* is not only a film but supports a video, the Disney store, and an exhaustive set of promotions at fast-food chains and elsewhere.

Brand extension options can be created by determining the current brand image and what products and services would fit these associations (see Figure 11.1). In what arenas would the brand be considered relevant? McDonald's has associations with fun and kids, fast delivery of consistent food, Big Macs, and fries. The fun and kids might suggest a theme park, a line of toys, or a day-care center. The brand, of course, will evolve over time in part by the brand extensions. So the addition of a healthy submenu to McDonald's may allow the firm to venture into areas that would have not made sense before. Virgin was a record company, and an airline under that brand name made no sense. But after the organization became not only successful but known for an over-the-top attitude, customer service and innovation, and an ability to face up to large, established competitors, its new associations provided the basis to go into a host of business areas.

The evaluation of each extension alternative is based on three questions. Each must be answered in the affirmative for the extension to be viable.

1. *Does the brand fit the new product context?* If the customer is uncomfortable and senses a lack of fit, acceptance will not come easily. The brand may not be seen as having the needed credibility or expertise, or it may have the wrong associations for the context. In general, a brand that has strong ties to a product class and attributes (for example, Boeing, Books.com, or Kleenex) will have a more difficult time stretching than a brand that is associated with intangibles such as fashion, German engineering, or active lifestyles. Certainly, all of the Disney extensions fit because they were supporting or part of the "magical family entertainment" brand identity. The Disney store, for example, fits because it is full of Disney characters, videos, and spirit.

2. *Does the brand add value to the offering in the new product class?* A customer should be able to express why the brand would be preferred in its new context. Despite the fact that cruise ships are difficult to tell apart, nearly anyone could verbalize rather clearly how a Disney cruise ship would be different from others—it would have Disney characters aboard, contain more kids and families, and provide magical family entertainment.

If the brand name does not add value in the eyes of the customer, the extension will be vulnerable to competition. For example, Pillsbury Microwave Popcorn initially benefited from the Pillsbury name but was vulnerable to the entry of an established popcorn name. Thus, although Orville Redenbacher entered the microwave category late, it still won with a name that meant quality and authenticity in popcorn. Rice-a-Roni's Savory Classics did not fit the consumer's notion of the role of Rice-a-Roni in the kitchen. The Arm & Hammer name also spawned two failures—a spray underarm deodorant, for which the Arm & Hammer name may have had the wrong connotations, and a spray disinfectant.

A concept test can help determine what value is added by the brand. Prospective customers can be given only the brand name, then asked whether they would be attracted to the product and why. If they cannot articulate a specific reason why the offering would be attractive to them, it is unlikely that the brand name will add significant value.

3. *Will the extension enhance the brand name and image?* The ideal is to have extensions that will provide visibility, energy, and associations that support the brand. Coach was a successful but a bit stodgy maker of leather bags until it hired a new designer and extended the brand to hats, shoes, sunglasses, coats, watches, and even straw beach hats, all with the signature "C" in leather. The extensions provided energy to the brand and helped attract younger customers, who are vital to the firm's long-term future. Sunkist's associations with oranges, health, and vitality are reinforced by the promotion of Sunkist juice bases and vitamin C tablets, while Sunkist fruit rolls may be a risk. The Disney extensions have reinforced the brand.

If an extension will damage the brand but represents a viable business opportunity, another brand option needs to be found. When Gap introduced a value chain and called it Gap Warehouse, the Gap brand was in danger of being confused and tarnished. Gap quickly reconsidered and protected its namesake brand by changing the name of the new chain to Old Navy. The use of subbrands and endorsed brands provide alternatives to a creating a new brand with all its costs and risks.

Subbrands and Endorsed Brands

Subbrands and endorsed brands become options when two unfortunate realities exist. First, the existing brands are judged to have the wrong associations or to have a risk of being damaged by the extension. Second, the organization does not have the size or resources to build a new brand, perhaps because the task is too difficult in a cluttered context or because the business does not justify the needed investment.

In such a situation, the answer may lie in the use of subbrands or endorsed brands. The GE Profile subbrand allowed General Electric to stretch into a premium segment in order to participant in the energy and high margins afforded by that subbrand market. Similarly, the Pentium Zeon subbrand allowed Intel to offer a high-end server microprocessor. A subbrand lets the offering separate itself somewhat from the parent brand, and it offers the parent brand some degree of insulation.

An endorsed brand offers even more separation. The Schwinn brand name in bicycles has given its Johnny G. Spinner bike an edge with its endorsement. And Marriott needed to enter the business hotel arena, because it was huge and growing. Because it would have been extremely expensive to create a stand-alone brand in that area and the existing brands were all too messy to buy, the company created Courtyard by Marriott. The endorsement indicated that Marriott as an organization stood behind the Courtyard brand, so visitors could be confident that the chain would deliver a reliable experience. Leveraging a brand by using it to endorse other brands provides a trust umbrella.

EXPANDING THE SCOPE OF THE OFFERING

The existing customer might be served by considering a broader use context. Thus, instead of being in the orange juice business, be in the breakfast business. Instead of selling only basketballs, consider making baskets and courts. GE's Jack Welch was quoted as saying that dominant companies in slow-growing businesses should redefine their markets, looking at broader scope that will have more opportunities.

The manager and originator of Microsoft's Office, Jeffrey Raikes, was inspired by Welch's concept and decided to develop products not just for office workers but to anyone who uses information.[1] As a result, the goal became to develop products for a variety of information users such as pilots, nurses, factory workers, and truck drivers. Toward that end he researched customers needs, developed new products and extended existing ones, and tested innovations in prototypical workplaces of the future.

Slywotsky and Wise make a similar suggestion in their book *How to Grow When Markets Don't*.[2] They recommend identifying and serving the customer needs that emanate from the use of existing products. Cardinal Health, for example, moved beyond distributing drugs to pharmacies to managing drug dispensing and related record-keeping with hospitals and creating medical-supply kits for surgeons. Clarke American Checks went from check printing for banks to managing their customer relations, including running call centers and helping them come up with incentives to increase customer retention. John Deere, the equipment manufacturer, decided to offer a one-stop shop for landscaping.

An analysis of the total set of tasks surrounding the customer use experience is a good way to begin determining whether there is a viable growth option in expanding the view of the offering. This task set could include buying, paying, transporting, storing, preparing for use, using, restoring, and disposal. It can be determined by walking through exactly what the customer needs to do in order to use the product or service. P&G, for example, has worked with Wal-Mart to provide a seamless integration of the two firms to determine what product is needed where and arrange the shipping so that administrative expenses, store outages, and inventory costs are all reduced. The net result is that P&G has an expanded scope beyond its products and a strong link to a customer.

The analysis of a consumption system may not result in an end-to-end solution. But even if two parts can be combined, replaced by an alternative, or made to work better, the result may have added value or a point of differentiation for the customer. Annie Chun created a meal kit whereby the sauce and noodles are combined into an easily microwaved dinner dish. In doing so, several steps for the cook were eliminated or combined, and the easy cook/serve features were appealing.

NEW MARKETS

A logical avenue of growth is to move existing products into new markets by duplicating the business operation, moving into another region, perhaps with minor adaptive changes. With market expansion, the same expertise and technology and sometimes even the same plant and operations facility can be used. Thus, there is potential for synergy and resulting reductions in investment and operating costs. Of course, market development is based on the premise that the business is operating successfully; there is no point in exporting failure or mediocrity.

Expanding Geographically

Geographic expansion may involve changing from a regional operation to a national operation, moving into another region, or expanding to another country. KFC, McDonald's, GE, IBM, and Visa have successfully exported their operations to other countries. Most of these companies and many others are counting on countries such as China, India, and Russia to fuel much of their growth for the coming decades. They realize that success will involve significant investment in logistics, distribution infrastructures, and organization building and adaptation. (Chapter 13 will elaborate.)

Moving from local to regional to national is another option. Samuel Adams and other microbreweries have generated growth by geographic expansion. Often, however, this expansion is best implemented by connecting, through an alliance or merger, to a partner that already has the capability to market more broadly.

Expanding into New Market Segments

A firm can also grow by reaching into new market segments. If the target segments are well defined, there are always a host of other segments to consider that would provide growth directions. Consider, for example:

- **Distribution channel.** A firm can reach new segments by opening up a second or third channel of distribution. A retail sporting goods store could market to schools via a direct sales force. A direct marketer such as Avon could introduce its products into department stores, perhaps under another brand name.

- **Age.** Johnson & Johnson's baby shampoo was languishing until the company looked toward adults who wash their hair frequently.
- **Home vs. office.** A supplier of office equipment to business might look to the home office market.

A key to detecting new markets is to consider a wide variety of segmentation variables. Sometimes looking at markets in a different way will uncover a useful segment. It is especially helpful to identify segments that are not being served well, such as the women's computer market or the fashion needs of older people. In general, segments should be sought for which the brand can provide value. Entering a new market without providing any incremental customer value is very risky.

EVALUATING BUSINESS LEVERAGING OPTIONS

There will be no shortage of ways to leverage the existing business. Ultimately these need to be evaluated to see whether one or more should be pursued either immediately or within a planning horizon. This section proposes several questions that represent important criteria to consider.

These criteria are all supported by a series of studies of initiatives that leverage existing businesses conducted by Chris Zook of Bain and Company (as reported in two books, *Profit from the Core* with James Allen and *Beyond the Core*).[3] In the first study, case studies were created of twenty-five companies that had achieved sustainable growth performance over the decade from 1992 to 2002 far in excess of their peers. In the second study, twelve pairs of firms were examined each within the same industry and with a similar starting point but with very different financial trajectories over a ten-year period—the resulting database contained 150 attempts to leverage a business. The third study focused on 180 attempts to leverage a core business sourced from the United States and United Kingdom. The focus of these studies was to attempt to determine what was associated with successful initiatives to leverage core businesses.

Is the Product Market Attractive?

Successful initiatives involve a foray into a market that has a robust profit pool going forward. Recall the five-factor Porter model introduced in Chapter 4. The most logical expansion will fail if there simply are no profits to be had because competitors control them or because the margins have been squeezed by overcapacity or the nature of the customer demand. The stampede of utility companies into telecommunications turned out to be a disaster because the profit pool was shrinking to the point that their ventures were uneconomic. In contrast, the controlled product expansion of EAS, the vitamin supplement firm, was always into areas in which the margins were healthy. Projecting a market forward, particularly a new one with potential new entrants, is difficult, but the risk of entering a hostile market can be significant. Recall the discussion of the risks of growth markets in Chapter 4.

Is the Core Business Successful?

There is no point in extending mediocrity. A weak business will seldom have either resources or assets and competencies to spin out to a growth initiative. The chances of success of leveraging a business has been estimated by the Zook studies to be around 25 percent.[4] And this falls to well under 8 percent when the core business is weak.[5] Budget Rent A Car, for example, attempted to a host of strategies without success to improve on their also-ran status, including efforts to enter the travel arena and the truck rental business.

Can the Core Business Be Transferred to the New Product Market? How Much of a Stretch Is It?

The ability of the business to adapt to a new product-market and the chances for success increase the closer the leveraged business is to the core business. Tesco, the United Kingdom grocery chain, refined its retail offering by improving the checkout experience, parking, and the fresh produce. They grew in part by expanding into in-store pharmacies, optical product stations, auto fuel, kitchen products, and coffee shops. Each of these leverage efforts enhanced their core business. Such synergy is healthy not only because the core business benefits but because the new business is more likely to draw on the strengths of the core as well. In contrast to this disciplined expansion, their competitor Sainsbury, whose performance lagged Tesco, strayed farther from its core, investing in a grocery chain in Egypt and two do-it-yourself chains in the United Kingdom.

This effect has been quantified by the Zook studies in which the new business initiative was separated from the core in terms of whether the involved customers, competitors, channels of distribution, cost structure, and asset and competencies were the same or different. The sum of differences could range from zero to five (there could be a partial match on some dimensions). The success probability sinks from over 25 percent to under 10 percent if the sum of differences was two or more.[6]

The task of adapting a business into a new market is easy to underestimate as the experience of FedEx when it attempted to duplicate its concept in Europe illustrates. Setting up a hub-and-spoke system in Europe was inhibited by regulatory roadblocks at every turn. Attempts to short-circuit regulations by acquiring firms with related abilities resulted in something of a hodgepodge—FedEx at one point owned a barge company, for example. The firm also lacked a first-mover advantage in Europe because DHL and others had employed the FedEx concept years earlier. A reliance on the English language and a decision to impose a pickup deadline of five o'clock in Spain (where people work until eight o'clock) caused additional implementation problems.

Will the New Business Be Successful, Become a Market Leader?

The first question, which is not trivial, is whether the new business can avoid failure because it simply lacks market acceptance for whatever reason. The acceptance of new products is low. Even for firms with high levels of competence in a market and with real synergy to buttress the new entry, failure rates are extremely high. And we know the primary reason. Dozens of studies in very different contexts and in different markets have concluded that the main reason for failure is that the new products lacked a point of difference, a reason to succeed. Too often they were "me-too" products, at least as perceived by customers. There was in essence no reason to succeed, so they didn't. There should be evidence that customers will value the product or service and that the offering can withstand the response of existing and potential competitors.

Even real advances may not be so perceived by customers. They may even read an advance as a reason not to buy. Clairol failed with Small Miracle hair conditioner, which could be used through several shampoos, in part because customers could not be convinced that the product would not build up on their hair if it were not washed off with each use. Even the use of an established brand cannot guarantee success. The concept of a colorless cola, Crystal Pepsi, did not achieve acceptance, and the appearance had a negative flavor connotation.

The goal, of course, should not be simply to survive but to become a market leader at least with an attractive submarket. Simply becoming the fourth or fifth or even third player creates the danger that it will be impossible to keep up with the ongoing investment needed. Without substantial market and financial success, needed resources from the firm may be hard to justify. There is always a competition for resources even in "wealthy" organizations.

Is the Leverage Strategy Repeatable?

There is great value in creating initiatives that are repeatable. Repeatability leads to learning curve effects, speed of execution, organizational simplicity, strategic clarity, and the ability to get the details right. In the Zook database, around two-thirds of the most successful, sustained growth companies had one or two repeatable formulas.[7] Nike, for example, has done much better over time than Reebok. While Reebok was buying a boat company, Nike was duplicating its success in basketball with a move into tennis, baseball, football, volleyball, hiking, soccer, and golf. In all these efforts the strategy was very similar, starting with a prominent credible endorser from Michael Jordan to Tiger Woods and systematically moving from shoes, to clothing, to equipment.

THE MIRAGE OF SYNERGY

Synergy, as suggested in Chapter 7, is an important source of competitive advantage. However, synergy is often more mirage than real. Synergy is often assumed when in fact it does not exist, is unattainable, or is vastly overvalued.

Potential Synergy Does Not Exist

Strategists often manipulate semantics to delude themselves that a synergistic justification exists. But when a packaged-goods manufacturer bought Burger Chef, a chain of 700 fast-food restaurants, the fact that both entities were technically in the food business was of little consequence. Because the packaged-goods firm never could master the skills needed to run restaurants, there was considerable negative organizational synergy. The dream of Sony and others to combine digital entertainment with content in the form of movies and TV shows seems misguided, at least for the foreseeable future, and has resulted in billions of questionable investments.

Potential Synergy Exists But Is Unattainable

Sometimes there is real potential synergy, but implementation difficulties—usually far greater than expected—inhibit or block this synergy from being realized. When two organizations (perhaps within the same firm) have different cultures, strategies, and processes, there are significant issues to overcome. The effort to combine United Airlines, Westin Hotel and Resorts, and Hertz into one organization was a classic case in which the operational problems coupled with a confused brand face to customers doomed the idea. The efforts to create multi-service telecommunication companies and fully integrated entertainment companies in order to achieve synergies have struggled.

Even when progress occurs, the patience and resources may not last long enough to see success. And it can take a long time. The ultimate integration challenge is when a group of entities are integrated to provide a comprehensive customer solution. Lou Gerstner indicated that integrating the country, product, and service silos at IBM in part in order to provide integrated customer solutions, was his most significant task and legacy.[8] He noted that it took five years to make this progress. The synergies expected from the merger of Daimler-Benz and Chrysler, which seemed to have a host of paper synergies, have also been very slow to materialize.

Potential Synergy Is Overvalued

One risk of buying a business in another area, even a related one, is that the potential synergy may seem more enticing than it really is. Perhaps carried away by its success with Gatorade, Quaker Oats purchased the Snapple business in 1994 for $1.6 billion, only to sell it two years later for a mere $300 million. Quaker had difficulties in distribution and was inept at taking a quirky personality brand into the mainstream beverage market (its program was based on pedestrian advertising and a giant sampling giveaway). Moreover, the fact that Quaker paid several times more than Snapple was worth was a fatal handicap.

The acquisition of The Learning Company—a popular children's software publisher with titles like *Reader Rabbit*, *Learn to Speak*, and *Oregon Trail*—seemed like a logical move by Mattel, the powerful toy company with Barbie among its properties. Yet less than a year and a half after paying $3.5 billion for it, Mattel basically gave The Learning Company away to get out from under mounting losses.

One study of 75 people from 40 companies that were experienced at acquisition led to several conclusions. First, few companies do a rigorous risk analysis looking at the least and most favorable outcome. With optimistic vibes abounding, it is particularly wise to look at the downside: What can go wrong? Second, it is useful to set a price over which you will not pay. Avoid getting so exuberant about the synergistic potential that you ultimately pay more than you will ever be able to recoup.[9]

One-Stop Shopping for Financial Services

During the 1980s, conglomerate financial services firms were created to provide one-stop financial services to customers and to take advantage of operational synergies. One of these was formed when Sears brought the real estate company Coldwell Banker and the brokerage house Dean Witter into a firm that already had Allstate Insurance, Allstate S&L, and 25 million active Sears charge-card users. To exploit the synergy represented by this array of financial services, Sears opened more than 300 financial boutiques in its larger stores where various combinations of Allstate salespeople, Dean Witter brokers, and Coldwell Banker agents were located. In addition, it introduced the Discover credit card.

The hoped-for synergy did not happen. The Sears name and culture, which meant value and trust in tires and tools, was not an asset in securities and contributed to departure of key Dean Witter mortgage banking people. Nor was the Sears customer base a source of profitable brokerage customers. The basic assumption that customers would value one-stop shopping in financial services was simply wrong. They wanted the lowest cost mortgages, the best brokerage advice, the most convenient banking, and so on. Having these were under one roof did not add value. In addition, the implementation of cross-selling was disappointing because it was difficult to motivate the financial

THE ELUSIVE SEARCH FOR SYNERGY

The concept of a total integrated communications firm that comprises advertising, direct marketing, marketing research, public relations, design, sales promotions, and now Internet communications has been a dream of many organizations for two decades. The concept has been that synergy will be created by providing clients with more consistent, coordinated communication efforts and by cross-selling services. Thus, Young & Rubicam had the "whole egg" and Ogilvy & Mather talked about "Ogilvy orchestrations."

Despite the compelling logic and considerable efforts, though, such synergy has been elusive. Because each communication discipline involved different people, paradigms, cultures, standards, and processes, the disparate groups had difficulty not only working together but even doing simple things like sharing strategies and visuals. A related problem was a reluctance to refer clients to sister units who were suspected to deliver inferior results, which created client-relationship ownership issues.

Young & Rubicam has been perhaps the most successful, in large part because it merged its direct marketing, public relations, Internet communications, and advertising firms into one organization, with shared locations and client-relations leadership. Each major account has a director and dedicated space. With these four units together already, it became easier to include a sister design firm such as Landor in client engagements.

DDB Needham has had success with virtual client teams drawn from its family of communication companies. These cross-discipline teams create their own culture and processes that allow them to provide the coordinated communication that clients need.

The lesson here is that synergy does not just happen, despite logic and motivation. It can require real innovation in implementation—not just trying harder.

service units to recommend each other. Sears ultimately gave up on the concept, and the financial units were spun off to again operate independently.

More recently, one-stop financial shopping has reemerged with better prospects of achieving synergy, although the verdict is still in doubt. One enabler is the maturity of Internet sites as devices to expose customers to services and to provide a reporting device that potentially spans products. Another is the more forceful and effective use of cross-selling by Wells Fargo and others using targeted marketing efforts, customer incentives, and the use of cross-selling performance measures. Still another is the realization of cost savings by combining organizations. One lesson is that capturing synergy can require real effort, substance, the right brand portfolio strategy, and timing.

KEY LEARNINGS

- Leveraging assets and competencies involves identifying them and creatively determining in what business areas they might be able to contribute.

- Brand extensions should both help and be enhanced by the new offering, in addition to being perceived to have a fit with it.

- The business can be leveraged by introducing new products to the market or expanding the market for the existing products.

- Entering a new product market is risky, as the new offering might lack market acceptance or needed resources. Success likelihood goes up if the core business is healthy, if the new product market is attractive (competitors will be profitable), if the business model is repeatable, if market leadership is possible, and if the stretch from the core is small.

- Synergy can be a mirage. Too often, it does not exist, or it exists but is unattainable or overvalued.

FOR DISCUSSION

1. Pick an industry and a product or service. Engage in a creative-thinking process, as outlined on page 179 in Chapter 10, to generate an improved offering. Do the same to create an entirely new offering that uses one or more of the assets and competencies of the firm.

2. Evaluate the following extension proposals.

   Dell selling TV sets

   Bank of America going into home safes

   Crest into a chain of dentist offices

   Caterpillar into automobiles

   Snackwells into exercise clubs

3. Pick a branded offering such as Southwest Airlines. Come up with 20 products or services that are alternative extension options. Include some that would be a stretch. Then evaluate each using the three criteria provided in the chapter.

4. Consider the following mergers or acquisitions. What synergy was or would be logically possible? What would inhibit synergy? Consider operations, culture, and brand equities.

   a. Citicorp acquired Providian, a credit card firm serving low-income segments

   b. Pepsi (the owners of Frito-Lay) acquires Quaker Oats.

   c. Chrysler and Daimler-Benz.

5. Evaluate Starbucks' extension decisions: To put Starbucks on United Airlines, to open Starbucks in Barnes & Noble bookstores, to open Starbucks outlets in grocery chains such as Safeway, to license Starbucks ice cream to Dreyer's.

6. Financial institutions are merging to again move toward one-stop financial shopping. Do you think that this movement will be any more successful than the one in the early 1980s that failed? Why or why not?

7. Identify and evaluate a combination of businesses that have achieved synergy and another that has failed to do so.

NOTES

1. Jay Greene, "Beyond the Office," *Business Week*, September 16, 2002, pp. 54–56.
2. Adrian Slywotsky and Richard Wise, *How to Grow When Markets Don't*, New York: Warner Business Books, 2003.
3. Chris Zook with James Allen, *Profit from the Core*, Boston: Harvard Business School Press, 2001; Chris Zook, *Beyond the Core*, Boston: Harvard Business School Press, 2004.
4. Zook, *Beyond the Core*, p. 22.
5. Ibid, p. 112.
6. Ibid, pp. 87–88.
7. Ibid, p. 36.
8. Louis V. Gerstner, Jr, *Who Says Elephants Can't Dance*, New York: Harper Business, 2002, pp. 251–252.
9. Robert G. Eccles, Kirsten L. Lanes, and Thomas C. Wilson, "Are You Paying Too Much for That Acquisition?" *Harvard Business Review*, July–August 1999, pp. 136–143.

CHAPTER TWELVE

Creating New Businesses

The most effective way to cope with change is to help create it.
—*I. W. Lynett*

Only the paranoid survive.
—*Andrew Grove, Former CEO, Intel*

The unexpected is the best source of inspiration.
—*Peter Drucker*

Enterprise Rent-A-Car, which passed Hertz in sales during the 1990s, was estimated to have sales of $9 billion in 2005 with profits of $700 million—nearly twice that of Hertz, which was having its best year. Enterprise, formed in 1957 in St. Louis, focused on the off-airport market, catering to leisure travelers and (more importantly) to insurance companies who needed to supply a car to customers whose car was being repaired, a market that Enterprise created and nurtured. With a signature "We'll pick you up" offer, its inexpensive off-airport sites were run by entrepreneur managers motivated in part by a bonus system tied to customer satisfaction. Not until the late 1980s when it was already nipping at the heels of Hertz did Enterprise begin national advertising and get on the radar screen of its competitors, who were all after the prime market of business travelers who wanted a car at the airport.

Cirque du Soleil started in 1984 with a few street performers. A traditional circus with animals, trapeze artists, clowns, three-ring entertainment, and tents was oriented to families with children. Competitors were always tweaking the acts and setting. Cirque du Soleil ("We reinvented the circus") was qualitatively different, appealing to a different customer group—adults and corporate clients, who would pay a significantly higher price. The performers were talented acrobats, the clowns were more sophisticated, and there was a motivating story line somewhat like a theater. Further, much of the expense was eliminated: There was only one "ring," no animals, no star performers, and no aisle concessions. It was so different that it made the traditional circus irrelevant and changed what the customer was buying.

Yamaha revitalized a declining piano market by developing the Disklavier, which functioned and played like other pianos except that it also included an electronic control system, thus creating a modern version of the old player piano. The system allowed a performance to be recorded and stored in memory. It provided a professional piano experience (with an artist that did not charge or get tired) for the home, hotel lobby, restaurant, or wherever entertainment would be welcome.

During the last century, the automobile industry experienced a dozen or more innovations that have created new businesses arenas—the Model T, the enclosed car, the GM spectrum of cars from the Chevrolet to Cadillac, installment selling, the automatic transmission, the original Ford Thunderbird, the VW bug, the inexpensive and reliable Japanese cars of the 1970s, minivans, SUVs, and hybrids. In each case the innovators achieved above-average profits that extended for years. In particular, the Chrysler minivan, introduced in 1983 with first year sales over 200,000, maintained leadership in the category for at least a decade, and was a critical contributor to the very survival of the firm.

THE NEW BUSINESS

It is natural to look for growth by energizing the current business or by leveraging that business into new products or markets using the approaches described in the last two chapters. The organization understands the existing business and probably has programs in place to improve margins, beat competition, enhance the customer experience, upgrade the products, and leverage their considerable assets and competencies.

There is another strategic route, though, that needs to be understood if not employed—to bypass established business arenas with their fixed boundaries and create a new business in which by definition there will be no direct competitors, at least initially. That route, as illustrated by Enterprise, Cirque du Soleil, Yamaha, and the major innovations within the automobile industry, involves changing what the customer is buying by creating a new market or submarket. It is usually based on a transformational innovation that transforms the market by introducing a qualitatively different business strategy from what came before.

Consider the new industries that have emerged through time, such as mutual funds, cell phones, servers, coffee houses, snowboards, video rentals, 24-hour news networks, multiplex theaters, express package delivery, discount retail in various categories, SUVs, low-carb foods, organic foods, and so on. Each of these innovations has supported high returns, sometimes for a lengthy period of time, for its participants. If a firm can develop or participate in such an emerging arena and do it successfully, growth and profits will follow.

Kim and Mauborgne suggest that such new businesses enter "blue oceans," a space that contains all business arenas not in existence, an unknown market space.[1] In contrast, "red oceans" are established markets where boundaries and operating parameters are established and accepted. When competing in a blue ocean, the challenge is to create demand where it did not exist and to make competition irrelevant. In red oceans the goal is to beat competition, to improve market share. As the red ocean space gets crowded, overcapacity, commoditization, and low margins are often seen.

Successful blue-ocean businesses usually are based on significant innovations that create a new business model. The innovation is more often conceptual rather than technological, although a technological advance such as the mini-steel mills can be a driver. It can be based on an innovative idea such as mutual funds, a new product form such as the iPod, a new concept such as Southwest Airline's city-to-city no-frills service, or a new channel such as Amazon's online store.

The innovation often involves a qualitative leap in value. Innovations that may be dramatic but do not lead to a value jump are seldom drivers of a new business arena. The value achieved can have a cost component as well as delivering customer benefits. In fact, while in red-ocean strategies there is usually a trade-off between differentiation and cost, in blue-ocean strategy firms such as Enterprise and Cirque du Soleil, it is often possible to achieve both low cost and differentiation.

The concept of "newness" is not black and white (or blue or red). There is a spectrum, from the creation to a new category to something less dramatic. A key indicator is the competitive climate—the length of time in which there is little or no competition, and the ability of competitors to become a factor when they do enter. A business that truly establishes a new category could have no competitors at all, perhaps for a decade or more as was the case for Enterprise, Cirque du Soleil, and CNN, the first 24/7 news channel. Another indicator is how different is the business strategy from that seen before—the market served, the products or services offered, the value proposition, the assets and competencies employed, and the functional strategies. Many of the businesses discussed in the last chapter represented some degree of newness because some elements of the strategy were new and different, and the subcategories established had reduced or little competition.

In the energy bar category, for example, the introduction of Luna created an energy bar for women. It changed what women bought and affected what brands were relevant and what were not. However, the business could draw upon the same manufacturing, distribution, and marketing assets as the original energy bar business and had the same competitors.

Asahi Dry Beer changed what was bought for large chunks of the Japanese market and required a different technology to make. Even though it did involve the same brand name and distribution channel, it had more strategy differences, which would put it further out on the "newness" scale. That also could be said of Yoplait's Go-Gurt, the yogurt in a tube that kids slurp up, which created a new business with a different target market, value proposition, and competitors although it did rely on the same distribution channel and manufacturing capacity as the core yogurt products.

In the case of Enterprise and Cirque du Soleil, the business could be described as radically different because it differed on so many dimensions of strategy from what came before and because the competition was subdued. In particular, new assets and competencies had to be developed.

There is evidence suggesting that blue-ocean businesses have attractive financial returns. In a study by Kim and Mauborgne of 150 strategic moves spanning a century, the 14 percent that were categorized as being blue ocean contributed 38 percent of the revenues and 61 percent of the profits of the group.[2]

Studies of the dynamics of companies provide supporting evidence. Of the S&P 500 in 1957, only 74 firms remained in 1997, and these firms performed 20 percent under the S&P average during that period—meaning that the newer firms performed at a higher level.[3] McKinsey has collected a database of over 1,000 firms (all with sales of over 50 percent in one industry) from fifteen industries over forty years. One finding was that new entrants into the database (84 percent of the firms were new entrants at one point) achieved a higher shareholder return than their industry average for the first ten years after entry.[4] That return premium was 13 percent the first year, falling to 3 percent in the fifth and never rising above that level for the second five years. Further, there was an extremely high correlation between industry newness (defined as the number of new firms entering, less the number of firms leaving during a seven-year period) and industry profitability. Thus, since new firms are more likely to bring new business models than existing businesses, the implication is that blue-ocean businesses will earn superior profits.

The fact is that firms with established businesses struggle to grow and thrive no matter how excellent their management is. An analysis of a database of some 1,850 companies in seven countries followed for ten years revealed that only 13 percent of companies were able to achieve modest growth (5.5 percent real growth) and profitability targets (exceeding the cost of capital) over a ten-year period.[5] It a firm has performed well for several years, the chances are high that it will falter soon.

There are several barriers to long-term success in existing product markets. First, competitors respond faster and more vigorously than ever. It is hard to turn a product advantage into a sustainable market position or point of differentiation. Second, incremental innovations are difficult to hide because of the "flat world" phenomenon and information technology. A firm's strategy in established product markets is transparent. Third, the markets are so dynamic that it is easy to get behind and become less relevant. Fourth, overcapacity, which seems to emerge in all established industries as firms make capacity decision based on their growth objectives that collectively are unrealistic, results in price and margin pressures. Thus, despite their risk, new business models in the aggregate offer the best hope for sustainable growth and financial success.

THE INNOVATOR'S ADVANTAGE

A prime reason that new business innovators earn more than the average firm is the innovator's advantage. Innovation can create what is often termed a first-mover advantage based on several factors. First, competitors will often be inhibited from responding in a timely matter. They may believe that the new business will cannibalize their existing business. Thus, competitors to Chrysler held back in responding to the minivan because they wanted to protect their station wagon business. Chrysler was "blessed" with a weak position in station wagons and thus had less to lose. Further, they could be worried about the impact on their brand; Xerox did not want to be associated with the low-end desktop copiers that were being offered by Canon even though Xerox had access to one from its Japanese affiliate Fuji-Xerox. Because of these two concerns, firms are tempted to minimize the long-term impact of the innovation and make themselves believe that it is a passing fad.

Second, competitors often are simply not able to respond. They may be playing catch-up technologically, especially if the technology is evolving or if patents are involved. Sometimes there might be natural monopolies (an area might be able to support only one multiplex cinema, for example). More common are organizational constraints. Responding to an innovation might require changes in organizational culture, people, and systems, which can be all but impossible. Many retailers attempted to duplicate Nordstrom's customer service but were unsuccessful because, although they could copy what Nordstrom's did, they could not duplicate what Nordstrom's was as an organization.

Third, the innovator can create customer loyalty based on the exposure and experience with its product or service. If the concept and experience are satisfactory, there may be no incentive for a customer to risk trying something that is different. The innovator can also earn the valuable "authentic" label. This was a factor facing competitors such as Kirin when they tried to duplicate Asahi Dry Beer's success in Japan. Customer-switching costs, perhaps involving long-term commitments, can create a distinct disadvantage for a follower. Or there could be network externalities. If a large community begins to use a service such as eBay, it may be difficult for a competitor to create a competing community.

To capture a first-mover advantage, it is important to hit the market first and invest to build position. While high initial prices may be an attractive way to capture margin and recover development costs, a low-price strategy may serve to build share and thus increase the barrier to followers. Followers will have the benefit of seeing the innovation, but will often need to be significantly better to have a chance of dislodging the first mover among the user base. So it is helpful to make that user base as large as possible.

It turns out that true market pioneers often do not survive, perhaps because they entered before the technology was in place or because they got blown away by larger competitors.[6] Pioneers such as Dreft in laundry detergent, daguerreotypes in photography, Star in safety razors, and Harvard Graphics in presentation software did not or could not capitalize on their first-mover status. In contrast, Golder and Tellis found that early market leaders, firms which assume market leadership during the early product growth phase, had a minimal failure rate and an average market share almost three times that of market pioneers, and a high rate of market leadership.[7] They noted that successful early market leaders tended to share certain traits:

- *Envisioning the Mass Market.* While pioneers such as Ampex in video recorders or Chux in disposable diapers charged high prices, the early market leaders (such as Sony and Matsushita in video recorders or P&G in diapers) priced the product at a mass market level. Timex in watches, Kodak in film, Gillette in safety razors, Ford in automobiles, and L'eggs in women's hosiery all used a vision of a mass market to fuel their success.

- *Managerial Persistence.* The technological advances of early market leaders often took years of investment. It took ten years of research for P&G to create the successful Pampers entry and two decades for the Japanese firms to develop the video recorder.

- **Financial Commitment.** The willingness and ability to invest are nontrivial when the payoff is in the future. For example, when Rheingold Brewery introduced Gablinger's light beer, it had a promising start, but financial downturns in other sectors caused it to withdraw resources from the brand. In contrast, Philip Morris invested substantially in Miller Lite for five years in order to achieve and retain a dominant position.

- **Relentless Innovation.** It is clear that long-term leadership requires continuous innovation. Gillette learned its lesson in the early 1960s when the U.K. firm Wilkinson Sword introduced a stainless steel razor blade that lasted three times longer than Gillette's carbon steel blade. After experiencing a sharp share drop, Gillette returned to its innovative heritage and developed a new series of products, from the Trac II to the Mach 3.

- **Asset Leverage.** Early market leaders often also hold dominant positions in a related category, allowing them to exploit distribution clout and a powerful brand name to achieve shared economies. Diet Pepsi and Coke's Tab, for example, were able to use their distribution power and brand names to take over the diet cola market from the pioneer, Royal Crown Cola.

MANAGING CATEGORY PERCEPTIONS

When a new product category or subcategory such as iPods, Pringles, or hybrid cars emerges, the innovators need to be aware that their challenge is not only to create an offering and a brand, but also to manage the perception of the new category or subcategory. A new business will change what people are buying. Instead of buying a car, some customers will be looking for a hybrid. As new entrants come in, there will be different types of hybrids. So Toyota, the early hybrid leader, has an opportunity to manage the perceptions of the category while simultaneously linking itself to the category as the leading brand, one with authenticity and ability to deliver. For a business

PETER DRUCKER'S DO'S AND DON'TS OF INNOVATION[8]

Do:

- Analyze the opportunities
- Go out and look, ask, and listen
- Keep it simple, keep it focused
- Start small—try to do one specific thing
- Aim at market leadership

Don't:

- Try to be clever
- Diversify, splinter, or do too many things at once
- Try to innovate for the future

innovator, the focus is no longer just on what brand to buy (the preference question,), but rather what product category or subcategory to buy (the relevance question).

In managing perceptions of a category, there are some guidelines. Incidentally, these guidelines apply whenever the category is new to the market, even if it is established elsewhere. For example, many categories of products (like vans) are new to markets like China long after they have been established in the Western world. First, there may be a need to focus on attributes and functional benefits at the outset to make sure that the category and its value proposition are communicated. The emotional and self-expressive benefits can have secondary status at the outset. Second, labels help. TiVo struggled with defining a product class in part because it never could gain acceptance for a label for its offering such as minivan or SUV.

CREATING NEW BUSINESS ARENAS

The first step to innovation is to get ideas on the table and refine the best ones to obtain potential business concepts. Good ideas are more likely to happen if they are valued by the organization and if there is a process to stimulate them. GE has set a goal that each business should generate technology breakthrough ideas, concepts that could lead to a $50 million to $100 million idea in the foreseeable future. As a result, time and resources are given to idea generation.

In the last chapter, the starting point was the assets and competencies of the firm and how they could be leveraged. Here, the starting point is the customer in relation to offerings. In what way are the offerings disappointing? What are the unmet needs? What activities are the existing product or service a part of, and what are the goals?

New business ideas can come from anywhere. However, the history of blue-ocean ventures contains patterns and can suggest possibilities. In the sections that follow, six will be described: creating a dramatically lower price point, analyzing alternative industries, going from components to systems, customer insights, harnessing trends, and collaborative processes.

Creating a Dramatically Lower Price Point

Many blue-ocean businesses occur when an offering appears that is simpler and cheaper than that of established firms. Clayton Christensen, a noted Harvard strategy researcher, has studied a wide variety of industries with a series of colleagues and developed two theories about disruptive innovations. His research is reported in three books: *The Innovator's Dilemma*, *The Innovator's Solution* (with Michael Raynor), and *Seeing What's Next* (with Scott Anthony and Erik Roth).[9]

The first theory is termed *low-end disruptive innovation*, where industries are altered by emerging products whose price appears dramatically low. In these industries, established firms target the best customers and attempt to sell them better products for more money. More features, services, and reliability are all aimed to capture a higher level of loyalty and margin. The firms that are successful develop structures, staffs, incentives, and skills designed to generate and implement a continuous flow of "sustaining innovations"—the pursuit of which is considered a reliable route to profitable growth, and the absence of which risks loss of position. Incumbent organizations are not always the first to market with a sustaining innovation, but they usually win because of their resources and motivation. Financial institutions, for example, put a lot of investment into the wealthy clients. Packaged goods firms offer line extensions to provide variety and interest to loyal customers. Retailers and others invest in loyalty programs.

This drive to service the most profitable customers provides an opening in the form of the low-end customer. These customers, often ignored or considered a nuisance by the established firms, are typically "overserved" and would be happy with a simpler, cheaper product that delivered satisfactory performance. Capitalizing on this opportunity, firms (often new to the industry) engage in "low-end disruptive innovation." They introduce an entry that is easier to use and much less expensive. Typically, the entrant's product is so inferior that its appeal is to a limited number of applications and customers, which incumbent firms consider marginal anyway. But often these firms then improve their offering over time and become competitors in a broad section of the market.

The steel minimills in the 1960s initially made low-quality steel, serving a market for rebar (reinforcing concrete) that did not require high quality and was a low-margin, unattractive business. Over the decades they improved their technology and products, however, and began to challenge the incumbents on a broad front. There are many similar examples. The Japanese car companies entered the market in the late 1960s and provided an option for buyers who did not need the features and self-expressive benefits of the large American firms. The copier market in the 1970s was changed by Canon's low-end disruptive innovation strategy, which met the needs of small businesses that did not need the power of Xerox products.

The Christensen team also advance a second theory, that of *new-market disruptive innovations* aimed at noncustomers. In many markets, large groups of noncustomers either do not buy because the products or services are considered too expensive or complex, or buy much less than they would like because the process is inconvenient. A more accessible offering that is priced right can open up the market. Apple's Macintosh attracted new users into the computer market, and online retail stockbrokers enabled day traders to thrive. The single-use camera provided a new market just as the Kodak Brownie did a century earlier. Vanguard's low-cost index funds attracted new buyers into the industry. The noncustomers have typically been ignored by the established firms who, again, tend to focus their efforts on the current "heavy users," the most profitable customers.

An attractively priced option can appeal to both the low-end and noncustomer segments simultaneously. Southwest Airlines targeted not only customers looking for a value airline but also people who could be lured from their automobiles, a segment that was ignored by the established airlines of the day. Dell Computer also succeeded both serving the low end and attracting new users.

Analyze Alternative Industries

Kim and Mauborgne suggest that one source of potential blue-ocean business concepts is the analysis of alternative industries or strategic groups within the same industry.[10] It is a way to break out of the conventional boundaries that fence in thinking. The concept is to evaluate the appeal and the disadvantages of each to see if a new option can be developed that would maximize the appeals and reduce the disadvantages. A mutual fund, for example, competes with bank CDs, stocks, bonds, gold, and holding cash. Understanding this broader framework has helped Schwab and others illuminate new investment vehicles.

Consider executive air travel. One option is first-class travel, which is relatively inexpensive but involves the hassles of the airport and is confined to a schedule that may be inconvenient, resulting in lost hours (particularly if the travel involves one of the lesser airports). An alternative is to own aircraft, which would result in the most efficient travel but would be extremely expensive. NetJets, which has grown larger than many airlines in around twenty years, found a niche in between those options by selling fractional ownership in planes. The buyer gets the use of a plane when needed; NetJets will even lease a plane if its fleet is tied up. Thus, the end result is the convenience and efficiency of one's own aircraft at a fraction of the cost. In fact, for some trips, the cost can be less than a first-class ticket, especially if the time saved is factored in.

Curves, a Texas women's fitness firm, has grown dramatically since it began franchising in 1995 a concept that joins many appealing features of health clubs and home fitness equipment for its target audience. Women desired the discipline, guidance, and equipment of a health club. However, they did not care for the high cost, the complicated machinery, the inconvenient locations, and the presence of men. Curves provides simple machines, set in a circle that can provide an efficient workout, at a convenient location (in some cities they are everywhere).

From Components to Systems

A classic way to change the market is to move from components to systems. The idea is to look at the system in which the product or service is embedded, to expand perceptions horizontally. Siebel, for example, changed what people bought by creating customer relationship management (CRM). CRM combined a host of software programs (such as call center management, loyalty programs, direct mail, customer acquisition, customer service, sales force automation, and much more) into a single umbrella package. It no longer was enough to prove the best direct mail program, because firms were now buying something much broader and were simply not interested in stand-alone programs that would require idiosyncratic training and would not be linked to other complementary programs.

KLM Cargo's offering was providing space on its airplanes, a commodity that was becoming a low-margin business. [11] After studying the total system needs for customers who were shipping perishables, KLM determined that significant value could be added by providing not just cargo space but a transportation solution that would include end-to-end responsibility for the product. These customers, importers and retailers, were experiencing spoilage, and it was never clear who in the logistics chain was responsible. Under its Fresh Partners initiative, **KLM** provided an umbrella "cool chain" from the producer to the point of delivery, with three levels of service—fresh regular, fresh cool, and fresh supercool (where products are guaranteed to have a specific temperature from truck to warehouse to plane to warehouse to truck to the retailer). Firms importing orchids from Thailand and salmon from Norway were among those using the service. This initiative allowed KLM to move from a commodity business to one that could capture attractive margins based on the value delivered to customers.

Customer Insights

Breakthrough business ideas often are driven by an in-depth understanding of the consumer. Ethnographic (or anthropological) research and the study of unmet needs, two approaches introduced in Chapter 2, are particularly helpful.

Unmet needs provide insight that when translated into products or services will be highly likely to be relevant to the customer. When Saturn and Lexus, for example, changed the way customers interacted with car dealers, they were addressing a significant unmet need. The result made some other brands less relevant for an important segment. Betty Crocker's Hamburger Helper addressed the need to have a shelf-stable meal preparation tool.

Cemex, a concrete company, realized that its customers had a lot of money riding on predictable delivery because concrete was highly perishable.[12] As a result, Cemex created capabilities of using digital systems that allowed drivers to adjust in real time to traffic patterns and changing customer timetables. It can now deliver product within minutes and process change orders on the fly. It addressed an unmet need, and the totally new business model that resulted has led to Cemex going from a regional player to being the third largest concrete company in the world, serving thirty countries.

Customers are not always a good source for some kinds of unmet needs, especially those involving emotional and self-expressive benefits, and so insight from creative and knowledgeable people might be required. The attractiveness of an SUV, for example, did not really result from its functional benefits. Further, customers have a difficult time getting around the boundaries of the current offering and may not have been much help in going from a horse to a car to an airplane. So in analyzing the customer, it is important for the analysis to have both breadth and depth, and that is where ethnographic research excels.

Ethnographic research involves simply observing customer in their "native habitat." The goal is to have a depth of understanding that will be the basis for a fresh way of looking at the problems customers are facing. As noted in Chapter 2, P&G is such a believer that it has executives regularly spend a day observing and interacting with customers.

Market Trends

Market dynamics are in part driven by trends, some very powerful and macro in nature. Chapter 4 discusses trend detection and evaluation. Within a trend, particularly one that is just emerging, will always be a potential blue-ocean business arena. The challenge is to understand if the trend is real and substantial and then attempt to find a niche market that is ownable in that context. The expression "Find a parade and get in front of it" has some applicability. That was part of the strategy of Whole Foods with organic foods and Apple's iPod with music sharing.

The dual trends of wellness and the use of herbs and natural supplements have supported a new category, healthy-refreshment beverages (HRB). It now contains a host of subcategories such as enhanced teas, fruit drinks, soy-based drinks, and waters. The pioneer and submarket leader is SoBe, which started in 1996 with SoBe Black Tea 3G (with ginseng, ginkgo, and guarana) and now has an extensive line of teas, juices, and energy drinks. The large beverage companies ignored this trend for too long and have been playing a frustrating and expensive game of catch-up.

Collaborative Processes

Customers are not the only source of unmet needs and potential response offerings. Experts in the field can be used, particularly experts outside the firm. The concept of collaborative thinking with people and organizations external to the firm is becoming a key to enhancing creativity and innovation. It can be employed to get ideas for new business arenas. In the toy industry, the Big Idea Group (BIG) is a company that sources ideas for toys which have the potential to impact the market.[13] It created a panel of experts that listen to toy ideas from people around the country. This process ensures a wide variety of ideas, and there is no question that when the number and variety of options is high, the chances of a good idea being in the mix is enhanced. BIG then licenses the best ideas from the inventors, refines them, and ultimately licenses them to toy manufacturers.

Procter & Gamble basically doubled the size of the its R&D capability by creating a network of people and organization around the world that are available to participate in dealing with technical problems and in offering innovation options. This network can provide firsthand exposure to innovations and help adapt them to different cultures and contexts. Other firms are sourcing ideas around the world. Virgin got a proposal from some Indian comic book distributors to create a new global comics and animation firm.[14] A few months later the venture began; the willingness to collaborate across continents and firms made it happen.

Related to collaboration is the concept of monitoring the environment for the products that are promising but are being marketed by innovators who lack the resources to fully exploit the potential—and particularly to scale it to a large market. P&G bought the Spinbrush, a battery-driven toothbrush, and used the Crest brand and its own distribution clout to turn it into a growth platform, creating a new business arena.

FROM IDEAS TO MARKET

The payoff for creating a successful new business is huge. Historically, most financially successful firms are based on the creation of a new business. Yet few firms can have a history of creating multiple new businesses. It turns out that it is not easy for an organization to be successful with an established business and still provide an environment that will foster new business ideas and allow them to flourish. That is exactly what is required, though, when markets get dynamic. The challenge is to create an organization that can excel in existing businesses and still allow a new business, especially a transformational business, to survive if not thrive. In the terms of Chapter 8, strategic adaptability needs to play a more prominent role, either in addition to or perhaps in place of strategic commitment or strategy opportunism.

Some organizational options to make the firm more open to new business ventures will be discussed. First, however, it is helpful to consider why organizations have historically failed to innovate new business areas.

Fatal Biases Inhibiting New Business Creation

Understanding the several biases that inhibit firms from innovating new business areas is a first step to dealing with them. These biases can be expressed in terms of five related "curses" —short-term pressures, success, incumbency, commitment, and size.

The short-term financial pressure curse. When the organization is doing well, there is pressure to create short-term growth and margins, in part driven by the desire for stock return and in part driven by managers with short job tenures. Short-term results can best be obtained by diverting R&D funds to sustaining innovation and focusing effort on improving the business model, enhancing the value proposition, and improving efficiency and productivity. Creating a new business platform is risky and expensive and likely to result in short-term financial pain. A new firm, perhaps funded by venture capitalists, will have a time horizon to start making profits.

The curse of success. When times are good and the business is doing well, resources should be available to take risks and create new business areas. Curiously, however, complacency usually wins the day. Why change if the current business is generating growth and profits? Why not instead invest in a sure thing, to make the costs even lower and the profits even higher? It is much easier to change when there is a crisis than when things are going well, although in a crisis both resources and time may be in short supply.

The incumbent curse. When a transformational innovation is aimed at the marginal customer or the noncustomer, there is a tendency to ignore the threat to the basic business. The natural strategy is to focus on the good, high-margin customers. If the new concepts steal marginal customers, so what? Those customers were more of a nuisance anyway. Further, it does not seem wise to invest in an offering that will kill the golden goose. Why invest in an offering that may cannibalize your business?

The commitment curse. Successful incumbent firms often have a tunnel focus on their strategic vision. In the terms of Chapter 7, they engage in strategic commitment. They invest vigorously in incremental innovation to reduce costs, improve the offering, and satisfy their loyal customers. The people hired, the culture created, the systems developed, and the organizational structure employed all are tailored to the task of making the existing business better. In that context, it is difficult for any new business concepts to get resources or serious traction within the firm.

The size curse. A new business by definition will start small. If a firm has been successful and grown to a meaningful size, it will look to business concepts that can make a difference to shareholders. McDonald's, for example, is inhibited from trying new restaurant concepts because even a successful concept aggressively expanded will have no impact on its financials; the core business is simply too huge. As a result, it became stuck in a model that was not supported by customer trends. Coke resisted marketing waters and other beverages in part because it was so unlikely for such business ventures to materially affect its shareholder value. A related problem is that a huge business like McDonald's or GE has built assets, processes, and organizations that are not adapted to run smaller businesses. One snack company once proclaimed that it was not capable of handling a business that was under $250 million. That inhibited it from participating in potential growth areas.

Making New Business Viable in Established Organizations

The basic problem is that a new business, particularly a transformational one, will require an organization that is very different from that of the core business. It will require people, a systems, a culture, and a structure that must adapt quickly to an emerging market area, one that is almost by definition going to be very different from the core business.

One approach is to create a separate organization, either by acquiring the industry innovator and retaining its autonomy or by creating a stand-alone entity within the corporate framework. In either case, the separate organization will be free—indeed, encouraged—to create its own people, systems, culture, and structure. Of course, it can borrow elements of the core business, such as its accounting systems or perhaps marketing skills, but it needs to be committed to the strategic vision of the new organization while still being entrepreneurial and flexible. As the business matures, the link with the core business can become greater.

The other approach is to create a dual organization within the same firm. People who excel at "start-up" adaptability and change, as well as those who have proven to be good at incremental innovation, will need to be developed side by side. A more diverse set of people will likely be the result. Entrepreneurial cultural values will need to be tolerated within the organization. Experimentation, trial and error, will need to be accepted if not encouraged. Different cost control systems and performance metrics will be needed. The new ventures will probably require a flatter organization.

Developing a dual organization is difficult and requires active management. However, it is possible and can result in providing new ventures with access to significant assets and competencies while also breathing energy into the core businesses.

In any case, an innovative new business cannot be starved for resources. The reason that most new businesses succeed as start-ups is because they have access to money from the stock market and from venture capitalists. Internally funded ventures are often at a disadvantage in obtaining needed resources. Too often, executives in large firms are said to have deep pockets but short arms.

To overcome resource shortfalls, top management has to make a commitment to grow through internal innovation and allocate resources toward that goal. Then a new venture will be able to compete for these resources with other new ventures and not from the existing business units. GE, with its program of encouraging and supporting breakthrough initiatives, does just that. Another key to resource availability is the disciplined process to disinvest in businesses that are not going to be the future of the firm, so that they do not exert their priority over future resources. Chapter 14 discusses the disinvestment decision process.

KEY LEARNINGS

- In general, above-average earnings come from new business arenas, and those attempting to excel in existing business arenas on average do less well financially.

- A business can vary in its "newness" depending on how much it departs from existing businesses in terms of value proposition, target market, assets and competencies employed, how it defines what customer is buying, and the intensity of competitors.

- An innovator has an advantage because it can build up a core loyal customer segment and because competitors, committed to their own business, may lack the motivation and capability to respond.

- Successful early market leaders envision a mass market, are persistent, make a commitment, continue to innovate, leverage firm assets, and manage category perception.

- Transformational new business arenas can be based on offering a dramatically lower price point, analyzing alternative industries to find white space, offering systems rather than components, building on customer insights or market trends, and by collaborating with other people and firms.

- Established firms tend to be focused on their own business and regard new ventures as a distraction that is unlikely to help their financials and may make them worse. To overcome these biases they need to create a space for entrepreneurial initiatives and a mechanism that ensures new ventures will get the resources they need.

QUESTIONS FOR DISCUSSION

1. Why didn't Hertz or Avis start an off-airport business directed at insurance companies and vacationers? What advantages would they have had over Enterprise? Why didn't Steinway come up with the electronic organ? Why didn't Barnum and Bailey create the Cirque du Soleil?

2. Think of some transformational new businesses.

   a. How was each different from what came before? What was similar? Scale them in terms of "newness" from truly transformational to substantial (some elements common to what came before, but enough new to create a new subcategory).

   b. Was there an innovator advantage? How long did it last and why?

   c. Did the business originate from an established business? If not, why not?

d. Where did the idea for the business come from? If you don't know, try to speculate.

3. Consider some new businesses that have managed category perceptions well. Consider others that have not.

4. What firms have changed from components to offering systems? Have they obtained an innovator's advantage?

NOTES

1. W. Chan Kim and Renee Mauborgne, *Blue Ocean Strategy*, Boston: HBS Press, 2005.

2. Ibid., p. 7.

3. Richard Foster and Sarah Kaplan, *Creative Destruction*, New York: Doubleday, 2001, p. 8.

4. Ibid., p. 47.

5. Chris Zook and James Allen, *Profit from the Core*, Boston: HBS Press, 2001, p. 11.

6. Peter N. Golder and Gerard J. Tellis, "Pioneer Advantage: Marketing Logic or Marketing Legend?" *Journal of Marketing Research*, May 1993, pp. 158–170.

7. Gerard J. Tellis and Peter N. Golder, "First to Market, First to Fail? Real Causes of Enduring Market Leadership," *Sloan Management Review*, Winter 1996, pp. 65–75.

8. James Daly interview with Peter Drucker, "Sage Advice," *Business 2.0*, August 22, 2000, p. 139.

9. Clayton M. Christensen, *The Innovator's Dilemma: When New Technologies Cause Great Firms to Fail*, Boston: Harvard Business School Press, 1997; Clayton M. Christensen and Michael E. Raynor, *The Innovator's Solution: Creating and Sustaining Successful Growth*, Boston: Harvard Business School Press, 2003; Clayton M. Christensen, Scott D. Anthony, and Erik A. Roth, *Seeing What's Next: Using the Theories of Innovation to Predict Industry Change*, Boston: Harvard Business School Press, 2004.

10. Kim and Mauborgne, op. cit., Chapter 3.

11. The example is recounted in James C. Anderson and James A. Narus, "Selectively Pursuing More of Your Customer's Business," *MIT Sloan Management Review*, Spring 2003, pp. 43–49.

12. Rita Gunther McGrath and Ian C. MacMillan, "Market Busting," *Harvard Business Review*, March 2005, pp. 81–89.

13. Christiansen and Rayner, op. cit., p. 19.

14. Steve Hamm, "How Smart Companies Are Creating New Products—And Whole New Businesses—Almost Overnight," *BusinessWeek*, March 27, 2006, pp. 69–74.

CHAPTER THIRTEEN

Global Strategies

Most managers are nearsighted. Even though today's competitive landscape often stretches to a global horizon, they see best what they know best: the customers geographically closest to home.
—*Kenichi Ohmae*

A powerful force drives the world toward a converging commonality, and that force is technology. … The result is a new commercial reality—the emergence of global markets for standardized consumer products on a previously unimagined scale of magnitude.
—*Theodore Levitt*

My ventures are not in one bottom trusted, nor to one place.
—*William Shakespeare, The Merchant of Venice*

Many firms find it necessary to develop global strategies in order to compete effectively. A global strategy is different from a multidomestic or multinational strategy, in which separate strategies are developed for different countries and implemented autonomously. Thus, a retailer might develop different store groups, in several countries, that are not linked and that operate autonomously. A multidomestic operation is usually best managed as a portfolio of independent businesses, with separate investment decisions made for each country.

A global strategy, in contrast, represents a worldwide perspective in which the interrelationships between country markets are drawn on to create synergies, economies of scale, strategic flexibility, and opportunities to leverage insights, programs, and production economies.

A global strategy can result in strategic advantage or neutralization of a competitor's advantage. For example, products or marketing programs developed in one market might be used in another. Or a cost advantage may result from scale economies generated by the global market or from access to low-cost labor or materials. Operating in various countries can lead to enhanced flexibility as well as meaningful sustainable competitive advantages (SCAs). Investment and operations can be shifted to respond to trends and developments emerging throughout the world or to counter competitors that are similarly structured. Plants can be located to gain access to markets by bypassing trade barriers.

Even if a global strategy is not appropriate for a business, making the external analysis global may still be useful. A knowledge of competitors, markets, and trends from other countries may help a business identify important opportunities, threats, and strategic uncertainties. A global external analysis is more difficult, of course, because of the different cultures, political risks, and economic systems involved. A global strategy requires addressing a set of issues that include the following:

1. What are the motivations (objectives) for a global strategy?

2. How can the global footprint be expanded successfully?

3. To what extent should products and service offerings be standardized across countries?

4. To what extent should the brand name and marketing activities (such as brand position, advertising, and pricing) be standardized across countries?

5. How should the brand be managed globally?

6. To what extent should strategic alliances be used to enter new countries?

Each of these issues will be explored in turn. The next section, in which the motivations for global strategies are presented, will be followed by discussions of how to select which countries to enter, standardization versus customization, global brand management, and the use of alliances in developing global strategies.

MOTIVATIONS UNDERLYING GLOBAL STRATEGIES

A global strategy can result from several motivations in addition to simply wanting to invest in attractive foreign markets. The diagram of these motivations shown in Figure 13.1 provides a summary of the scope and character of global strategies.

Obtaining Scale Economies

Scale economies can occur from product standardization. The GM global footprint, for example, allows product design, tooling, parts production, and product testing to be spread over a much larger sales base. Standardization of the development and execution of a marketing program can also be an important source of scale economies. Consider Coca-Cola, which since the 1950s has employed a marketing strategy—the brand name, concentrate formula, positioning, and advertising theme—that has been virtually the same throughout the world. Only the artificial sweetener and packaging differ across countries.

Scale economies can also occur from standardization of marketing, operations, and manufacturing programs. Brands that share advertising (even when it is adjusted for local markets) spread the production and creative effort over multiple countries and thus a larger sales base. A firm similarly benefits when fixed costs involving IT and production technologies can be distributed over countries.

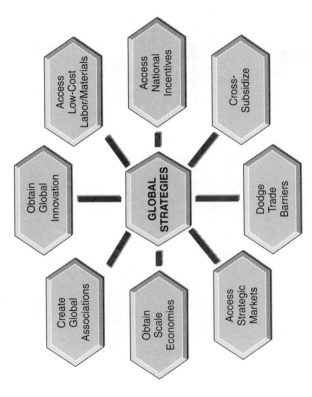

Figure 13.1   Global Strategy Motivations

Global Brand Associations

Being global generates the image of being global, which turns out to be a significant advantage. A study of associations made of global brands involved qualitative interviews with 1,500 consumers over 41 countries, followed up with a quantitative study that included a preference scale of three leading brands in six product categories.[1] The result showed that associations with being global impacted preference. In fact, 44 percent of the variance in preference is caused by the fact that consumers believe that global brands have higher quality in part because they tend to have the latest innovations. Two other associations, the prestige of being global and social responsibility, also influence preference but much less so (12 percent and 8 percent, respectively) than the quality dimensions.

Global Innovation

Being global means that innovation around brand building, new product, and product improvements can be sourced anywhere. At P&G for example, the successful Pantene positioning ("For hair that shines") came from P&G Taiwan, and the midtier priced feminine protection brand featuring the herbal ingredient chamomile, Naturella, came from P&G Mexico. And collaboration from other firms is becoming important for most global companies. P&G has people all over the world coordinating the development efforts of firms that have a collaborative relationship with P&G. As a result, their R&D budget and capability is highly levered. IBM and others are creating major R&D centers in India to access talent, but also to participate in the intellectual vitality of the region.

INDICATORS THAT STRATEGIES SHOULD BE GLOBAL

- Major competitors in important markets are not domestic and have a presence in several countries.
- Standardization of some elements of the product or marketing strategy provides opportunities for scale economies.
- Costs can be reduced and effectiveness increased by locating value-added activities in different countries.
- There is a potential to use the volume and profits from one market to subsidize gaining a position in another.
- Trade barriers inhibit access to worthwhile markets.
- A global name can be an advantage and the name is available worldwide.
- A brand position and its supporting advertising will work across countries and has not been preempted.
- Local markets do not require products or service for which a local operation would have an advantage.

Access to Low-Cost Labor or Materials

Another motivation for a global strategy is the cost reduction that results from access to the resources of many countries. Substantial cost differences can arise with respect to raw materials, R&D talent, assembly labor, and component supply. Thus, a computer manufacturer may purchase components from South Korea and China, obtain raw materials from South America, and assemble in Mexico and five other countries throughout the world in order to reduce labor and transportation costs. Access to low-cost labor and materials can be an SCA, especially when it is accompanied by the skill and flexibility to change when one supply is threatened or a more attractive alternative emerges.

Access to National Investment Incentives

Another way to obtain a cost advantage is to access national investment incentives that countries use to achieve economic objectives for target industries or depressed areas. Unlike other means to achieve changes in trade, such as tariffs and quotas, incentives are much less visible and objectionable to trading partners. Thus, the British government has offered Japanese car manufacturers a cash bonus to locate a plant in the United Kingdom. The governments of Ireland, Brazil, and a host of other countries offer cash, tax breaks, land, and buildings to entice companies to locate factories there.

Cross-Subsidization

A global presence allows a firm to cross-subsidize, to use the resources accumulated in one part of the world to fight a competitive battle in another.[2] Consider the following: One firm uses the cash flow generated in its home market to attack a domestically oriented competitor. For example, in the early 1970s, Michelin used its European home profit base to attack Goodyear's U.S. market. The defensive competitor (i.e., Goodyear) can reduce prices or increase advertising in the United States to counter; but by doing so, it will sacrifice margins in its largest markets. An alternative is to attack the aggressor in its home market, where it has the most to lose. Thus, Goodyear carried the fight to Europe to put a dent in Michelin's profit base.

The cross-subsidization concept implies that it is useful to maintain a presence in the country of a competitor. The presence should be large enough to make the threat of retaliation meaningful. If the share is only 2 percent or so, the competitor may be willing to ignore it.

Dodge Trade Barriers

Strategic location of component and assembly plants can help gain access to markets by penetrating trade barriers and fostering goodwill. Peugeot, for example, has plants in twenty-six countries from Argentina to Zimbabwe. Locating final-assembly plants in a host country is a good way to achieve favorable trade treatment and goodwill, because it provides a visible presence and generates savings in transportation and storage of the final product. Thus, Caterpillar operates assembly plants in each of its major markets, including Europe, Japan, Brazil, and Australia, in part to bypass trade barriers. An important element of the Toyota strategy is to source a significant portion of its car cost in the United States and Europe to deflect sentiment against foreign domination.

Access to Strategically Important Markets

Some markets are strategically important because of their market size or potential or because of their raw material supply, labor cost structure, or technology. It can be important to have a presence in these markets even if such a presence is not profitable. Because of its size, the U.S. market is critical to those industries in which scale economies are important, such as automobiles or consumer electronics.

Sometimes a country is important because it is the locus of new trends and developments in an industry. A firm in the fashion industry may benefit from a presence in countries that have historically led the way in fashion. Or a high-tech firm may want to have operations in a country that is in the forefront of the relevant field. For example, an electronics firm without a Silicon Valley presence will find it difficult to keep abreast of technology developments and competitor strategies. Sometimes adequate information can be obtained by observers, but those with design and manufacturing groups on location will tend to have a more intimate knowledge of trends and events.

EXPANDING THE GLOBAL FOOTPRINT

Motivation to be global naturally leads to global initiatives to expand a firm's market footprint, a task that can be messy and difficult. Strategy development gets much harder when the context is a different language, an unfamiliar culture, new competitors and channels, and very different set of market trends and forces. There are many routes to failure. A study of some 150 international expansion initiatives during a five-year period ending in 2000 showed that less than half avoided failure. However, the examination of those that survived suggested that success was usually accompanied by four conditions:[3]

- **A strong core.** A strong home market provides resources and experience that can be leveraged in geographic expansion. It is a rare firm that finds success abroad without a successful home market.

- **A repeatable formula for expansion.** When the same model works in country after country, the risk of entry is reduced. Avon, for example, uses its direct model everywhere and has refined the execution to a science.

- **Customer differentiation that travels.** When the same segments are targeted and the same product and position works across countries, there is no need to research the market and reinvent the offering every time a new country is entered. Nike, Pampers, and Heineken, for example, have been able to differentiate their respective brands the same way everywhere.

- **Industry economics.** It is important to recognize whether global share or local share will drive success. Some industries like razors or computers, for example, provide cost advantages for global scale. Others, like beer, cement, and software, reward high local share.

To the extent that any of these conditions are missing, the task will be more difficult, but strategic considerations may still make it imperative to find a way to succeed.

What Country to Enter?

Once a firm has decided to become global, deciding what country or countries to enter—and in what sequence—is a key challenge. Entering any new market can be risky and take away resources that could be used to make strategic investments elsewhere. A frequently unforeseen consequence of global expansion is that healthy markets, especially the home market, are put at risk by this diversion of resources. It is thus important to select markets for which the likelihood of success will be high and the resource drain minimized.

Market selection starts with several basic dimensions:

- Is the market attractive in terms of size and growth? Are there favorable market trends? For many companies, China and India often appear attractive because of their sheer size and growth potential.

- Can the firm add value to the market? Will the products and business model provide a point of differentiation that represents a relevant customer benefit? Tesco has developed an Internet-based home delivery system for grocery retailers that adds value in many markets.[4]

- How intense is the competition? Are other firms well entrenched with a loyal following, and are they committed to defending their position? Tesco, a major retailer in the United Kingdom, found that expansion to France was unattractive because of the established competition, whereas eastern European countries had much less formidable competition. As a result, Hungary was the first country in continental Europe that Tesco entered.[5]

- Can the firm implement its business model in the country, or do operational or cultural barriers exist? How feasible is any adaptation that is required? Marks & Spencer, a U.K. retailer spanning food, clothing, and general merchandise, attempted to export its products and the look and feel of its stores to the Continent, only to find that these offerings had little appeal to Europeans.

- Are there political uncertainties that will add risk? In addition to the obvious risks of political instability, there are more subtle issues. Coke and Pepsi got blindsided in India when a nongovernmental entity claimed to have found residue of pesticides in their products. Despite the firms' protestations and evidence that the claims were unfounded, their business took a 12 percent dive and their image suffered. A false claim of contamination similarly hurt P&G's cosmetics effort in China.

- Can a critical mass be achieved? It is usually fatal to enter countries lacking the sales potential needed to support the marketing and distribution effort needed for success.

Wal-Mart's surprising failure in Germany shows the power of the last three dimensions.[6] In 2006, the firm gave up a ten-year effort to get a successful presence in Germany in the wake of several mistakes and misjudgments. For example, the first CEO spoke only English and insisted that his managers do the same. The next CEO tried to manage from the United Kingdom. The short shopping hours in Germany and the fact that Germans did not want assistance in the store were just a few of the conditions to which Wal-Mart had trouble adjusting. Wal-Mart also seemed to underestimate the major German competitors, which did not provide much of an opening for a value offering. Finally, Wal-Mart failed to achieve the economies of scale needed to justify its infrastructure. Wal-Mart's failure in Germany and the fact that it is weak elsewhere in the world makes visible the difficulty of exporting even successful business models, especially those based on scale.

A strategy of entering countries sequentially has several advantages. It reduces the initial commitment, allows the product and marketing program to be improved based on experience in preceding countries, and provides for the gradual creation of a regional presence. Other factors, however, argue that global expansion should be done on as wide a front as possible. First, economies of scale, a key element of successful global strategies, will be more quickly realized and will be a more significant factor. Second, the ability of competitors to copy products and brand positions—a very real threat in most industries—will be inhibited because a first-mover advantage will occur in more markets. Third, standardization, a topic to which we now turn, is more feasible.

STANDARDIZATION VS. CUSTOMIZATION⁷

Standardized products and brands gained widespread credence as a strategy because of Ted Levitt's classic 1983 *Harvard Business Review* article, "The Globalization of Markets," which gave three reasons why they would succeed.⁸ First, the forces of communication, transport, and travel were breaking down the insulation of markets, leading to a homogeneity of consumer tastes and wants. Second, the economics of simplicity and standardization—especially with respect to products and communication—represented compelling competitive advantages against those who held on to localized strategies. Third, customers would sacrifice preferences in order to obtain high quality at lower prices. The article provided an academic underpinning to the logical premise that standardization should be the goal of a global business.

Pringles, Visa, MTV, Sony, Dove, Vodafone, BP, DeBeers, Nike, McDonald's, Pantene, Disney, and IBM are the envy of many because they seem to have generated global businesses with a high degree of similarity in terms of product, brand, position, advertising strategy, personality, packaging, and look and feel. Pringles, for example, stands for "fun," a social setting, freshness, less greasiness, resealability, and the whole-chip product everywhere in the world. Further, the Pringles package, symbols, and advertising are almost the same globally. Disney's brand of magical family entertainment is implemented by theme parks, movies, and characters that are remarkably consistent across countries.

These "standardized" products and brands are often not as identical worldwide as one might assume. McDonald's has disparate menus, advertising, and retail architectures in various countries. Pringles uses different flavors in different countries, and advertising executions are tailored to local culture. Heineken is the premium beer to enjoy with friends everywhere—except at home in the Netherlands, where it is more of a mainstream beer. Visa even has had different logos in some countries (such as Argentina), and Coke has a sweeter product in areas like southern Europe. Regardless of these variations, however, brands that have moved toward the global end of the local-global spectrum demonstrate some real advantages.

A standardized offering can achieve significant economies of scale. For example, when IBM decided to exchange some three dozen advertising agencies for one in order to create a single global campaign (even if it needed some adapting from market to market), one motivation was to achieve efficiencies. The task of developing packaging, a Web site, a promotion, or a sponsorship will also be more cost-effective when spread over multiple countries. Economies of scale across countries can be critical for sponsorships with global relevance, such as the World Cup or the Olympics.

Perhaps more important though, is the enhanced effectiveness that results from better resources. When IBM replaced its roster of agencies with Ogilvy & Mather, it immediately became the proverbial elephant that can sit wherever it wants. As the most important O&M client, it gets the best agency talent from top to bottom. As a result, the chances of a well-executed breakout campaign are markedly improved.

Cross-market exposure produces further efficiencies. Media spillover, where it exists, allows the standardized brand to buy advertising more efficiently. Customers who travel can get exposed to the brand in different countries, again making the campaign work harder. Such exposure is particularly important for travel-related products such as credit cards, airlines, and hotels.

A standardized brand is also inherently easier to manage. The fundamental challenge of brand management is to develop a clear, well-articulated brand identity (what you want your brand to stand for) and to find ways to make that identity a driver of all brand-building activities. The absence of multiple strategies makes this task less formidable with a global brand. In addition, simpler organizational systems and structures can be employed. Visa's "worldwide acceptance" position is much easier to manage than dozens of country-specific strategies.

The key to a standardized brand is to find a position that will work in all markets. Sprite, for example, has the same position globally—honest, no hype, refreshing taste. It is based on the observation that kids everywhere are fed up with hype and empty promises and ready to trust their own instincts. The Sprite advertising tagline ("Image is nothing. Thirst is everything. Obey your thirst.") resonates around the world. In one scene from a Sprite ad, kids are discussing why their basketball hero would drink Sprite.

Several generic positions seem to travel well. One is being the "best," the upscale choice. High-end premium brands such as Mercedes, Montblanc, Heineken, and Tiffany's can cross geographic boundaries because the self-expressive benefits involved apply in most cultures. Another is the country position. For example, the "American" position of brands such as Coke, Levi's, Baskin-Robbins, KFC, and Harley-Davidson will work everywhere (with the possible exception of the United States). A purely functional benefit such as Pampers' dry, happy baby can also be used in multiple markets. Not all brands that are high-end or American or have a strong functional benefit, however, can be global.

Standardization can come from a centralized decision to create a global product. Canon, for example, developed a copier that had a common design throughout the world in order to maximize production economies. Unfortunately, the copier could not use the standard paper size in Japan, resulting in substantial customer inconvenience. The risk inherent in a truly global standardization objective is that the result will be a compromise. A product and marketing program that almost fits most markets may not be exactly right anywhere; such a result is a recipe for failure or mediocrity.

Another strategy is to identify a lead country, a country whose market is attractive because it is large or growing or because the brand has a natural advantage there. A product is tailored to maximize its chances of success in that country, then exported to other markets (perhaps with minor modification or refinements). A firm may have several lead countries, each with its own product. The result is a stable of global brands, with each brand based in its own home country. Nissan has long taken this approach, developing a corporate fleet car for the United Kingdom, for example, and then offering it to other countries. Lycra, a 35-year-old ingredient brand from DuPont, has lead countries for each of the product's several applications all under the global tagline "Nothing moves like Lycra." Thus, the Brazilian brand manager is also the global lead for swimsuits, the French brand manager does the same for fashion, and so on.

Global Leadership, Not Standardized Brands

The fact is that a standardized global brand is not always optimal or even feasible. Yet, attracted by the apparent success of other brands, many firms are tempted to global-ize their own brand. Too often the underlying reason is really executive ego and a per-ception that a standardized brand is the choice of successful business leaders.

Such decisions are often implemented by a simple edict—that only standardized global programs are to be used. The consolidation of all advertising into one agency and the development of a global advertising theme are typically cornerstones of the effort. Even when having a standardized brand is desirable, though, a blind stampede toward that goal can be the wrong course and even result in significant brand dam-age. There are three reasons.

First, economies of scale and scope may not actually exist. The promise of media spillover has long been exaggerated, and creating localized communication can some-times be less costly and more effective than adapting "imported" executions. Further, even an excellent global agency or other communication partner may not be able to execute exceptionally well in all countries.

Second, the brand team may not be able to find a strategy to support a global brand, even assuming one exists. It might lack the people, the information, the creativ-ity, or the executional skills and therefore end up settling for a mediocre approach. Finding a superior strategy in one country is challenging enough without imposing a constraint that the strategy be used throughout the world.

Third, a standardized brand simply may not be optimal or feasible when there are fundamental differences across markets. Consider the following contexts where a standardized global brand would make little sense:

- *Different market share positions.* Ford's European introduction of a new van, the Galaxy, into the United Kingdom and Germany was affected by its market share position in each country. As the number-one car brand in the United Kingdom with a superior quality image, Ford sought to expand the Galaxy's appeal beyond soccer moms to the corporate market. So the U.K. Galaxy became the "nonvan," and its roominess was compared to first-class airline travel. In Germany, however, where Volkswagen held the dominant position, the Galaxy became the "clever alternative."

- *Different brand images.* Honda means quality and reliability in the United States, where it has a legacy of achievement based on the J.D. Powers ratings. In Japan, however, where quality is much less of a differentiator, Honda is a car-race participant with a youthful, energetic personality.

- *Preempted positions.* A superior position for a chocolate bar is to own associations with milk and the image of a glass of milk being poured into a bar. The problem is that different brands have preempted this position in different markets (for example, Cadbury in the United Kingdom, and Milka in Germany).

- *Different customer motivations.* In Finland, after finding that users were apprehensive about perceived machine complexity, Canon became the copier that empowered the user, making him or her the boss. In Germany and Italy, however, more traditional attribute-oriented messages did better. The key to Toyota's 50 percent share in Thailand is its superior service capability, an attribute valued much less in other countries.

- *Names and symbols may not be available or appropriate everywhere.* The Ford truck name Fiera means "ugly old woman" in some Spanish-speaking countries. Procter & Gamble's Pert Plus needed to be sold as Rejoice in Japan, Rejoice in much of the Far East, and Vidal Sassoon in the United Kingdom because the Pert Plus name had been preempted.

A global business strategy is often misdirected. The priority should not be to develop standardized brands (although such brands might result) but global brand *leadership*, strong brands in all markets. Effective, proactive global brand management should be directed at enhancing brands everywhere by allocating brand-building resources globally, creating global synergies, and coordinating and leveraging the strategies in individual countries.

GLOBAL BRAND MANAGEMENT

A study of some fifty global firms, conducted by David Aaker and Erich Joachimsthaler and extended by the Dentsu advertising agency, concluded that an effective global brand management system needs to address four challenges—developing an internal communication system to facilitate the sharing of insights and experiences, creating a global brand planning system, forming an organizational structure to foster cross-country synergy, and finding ways to achieve brilliance in brand-building (see Figure 13.2).[9]

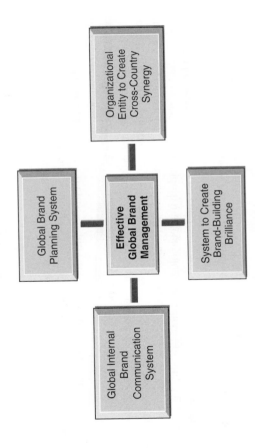

Figure 13.2 Effective Global Brand Management

Global Internal Brand Communication System

A cross-country communication system that shares insights, methods, and best practices is the most basic and nonthreatening element of global brand management. A customer insight that may be obvious in one country might be more subtle and difficult to access in another. For most companies, a cross-country system includes a person or small team that identifies and disseminates experiences, supplemented by global meetings where involved managers can exchange experiences (both formally and informally). Intranets often play an active role in the process, with the principal challenges being how to encourage people to express their experiences and preventing information overload. One firm addressed these challenges by having each intranet sponsored by a senior manager and directed by a leader/facilitator who provides the necessary energy, ideas, and continuity.

Global Brand Planning System

Every country manager needs to use the same vocabulary and planning template when developing strategies. Without this commonality, there is little chance of creating synergy across countries. The planning template (such as the one developed in this book, in Appendix A) should include some basic elements of strategic analysis, self-analysis, a business strategy, tactical plans, and goals and measurement.

Creating Cross-Country Synergy—The Global Brand Manager

The goal of achieving significant global synergies is usually inhibited by local biases when developing strategies. Without this commonality, there is little chance of creating synergy across countries. The planning template (such as the one developed in this book, in Appendix A) should include some basic elements of strategic analysis, self-analysis, a business strategy, tactical plans, and goals and measurement.

To have any hope of creating synergy and leveraging programs to achieve market success in the face of such biases, someone or some group needs to be in charge of the global brand. A global brand manager serves this role in some firms. There might also be a global brand team, with cross-country representation that can play either a leadership or supporting role.

Whether the global brand is represented by a person or a team, the people involved need three key ingredients for success, or at least access to these ingredients. The first is an in-depth knowledge of the local markets, including trends, competitor dynamics, segmentation, and customer motivations. The second is an understanding of the product or service, its underlying technology, and how the offering might be extended. The third is real authority and resources, as well as the ability to participate in the development of country-specific business strategies.

The global brand manager or team can influence country strategies in a variety of ways. The best approach in a particular case will depend on the maturity of the global operation and the extent to which the decentralized culture is ingrained. At one extreme is the centralized command-and-control model, where external analysis and strategy are

DYSFUNCTIONAL GLOBAL BRAND MANAGEMENT STYLES

When the centralized brand group lacks brand expertise, product/market knowledge, or resources/authority, brand management risks becoming one of the following models:

- *Uninformed dictator model.* In this model, a person with organizational power (sometimes the CEO) becomes a convert to brand power and standardization. This reborn brand champion, however, lacks market and/or product knowledge and, most importantly, patience. As a result, he or she is prone to make arbitrary decisions without research or analysis. Perhaps, for example, a hasty decision is made to change a brand name or position after an acquisition, or whenever a brand appears inconsistent across markets. If such a decision damages the brand (or even if it is not supported within the organization), the ability and willingness of employees to support the brand going forward can be affected as well.

- *Brand bureaucracy model.* The brand group in this model lacks adequate market knowledge and is seriously deficient in authority and/or resources. The team becomes little more than a logo cop charged with making sure that the visual presentation is correct and perhaps sending out forms to be filled in by the business units. This model can work for a while, especially when the visual presentation is clearly confused across markets. But over time, the team is often ignored as others recognize its lack of influence.

- *All hat, no cattle model.* This expression comes from the old West popularized by cowboy movies where people with no resources (cattle) talk big (and wear "big" hats) while others with thousands of head of cattle talk softly. In much the same way, management sometimes decides that brands are important, but fails to provide the brand team with enough authority and/or resources. As a result, regardless of how capable the people are or how much market and product knowledge they have, the brand team cannot influence autonomous business units, hire outside brand experts, or really do anything of significance. As a result, the organization gets frustrated or suspects that top management is only giving lip service to the brands. This model is all too common in Japanese firms.

- *Anarchy model.* In the anarchy model, the organization has an extremely decentralized structure, with little guidance or cross-country communication. Market understanding, product knowledge, and strategic talent are sprinkled unevenly throughout the organization. Some business units will do well, but the organization as a whole will be underleveraged, and most countries will be vulnerable to underperformance.

centralized and the country mangers are simply implementers. At the other is the anarchy model, one of five dysfunctional models described in the insert. In between are some combination of the service provider, facilitator, and consultant models.

Service provider model. The central brand group will be a service provider developing a staff and knowledge base around topics such as marketing research, segmentation, sponsorship, and advertising that country managers can access. It can also coordinate the advertising effort, especially if there is a single agency, and any firm-wide sponsorship.

Facilitator model. The central group becomes a facilitator in helping the business units work within a defined brand management process to develop sound strategies and would have less responsibility for knowing the markets and making strategy suggestions. This model is usually a good choice when introducing global brand management into an organization because it does not appear threatening.

Consultative model. The central brand group learns about the markets, competitors, and customers and develops insights and brand options. It would then meet with the business units, provide insights, and make suggestions as to what brand strategy should be considered and what brand-building programs are likely to be effective.

Delivering Brilliance in Brand Strategy Implementation

Global brand leadership, especially in these days of media clutter, requires implementation brilliance—"good enough" is *not* good enough. The dilemma is how to achieve brilliance in local markets while still gaining synergy and leverage as a global organization. Here are some guidelines:

- Consider what brand-building paths to follow (for example, advertising versus sponsorship, retail presence, or promotions). The genius may not be in execution per se but in the selection of the vehicles.

- Get the best and most motivated people to work on the brand. Some agency-client tension can be helpful in this regard; Audi, for instance, uses multiple agencies.

- Develop multiple options. In general, the more attempts you make at brilliance, the higher the probability that it will be reached. Procter & Gamble finds exceptional ideas by empowering its country brand teams to develop breakthrough brand-building programs. When one is found (such as Pantene Pro-V's "Hair so healthy it shines"), it is rolled out country by country.

- Measure the results. Measurement drives excellence, and a global brand measurement system is fundamental to excellence.

STRATEGIC ALLIANCES

Strategic alliances play an important role in global strategies because it is common for a firm to lack a key success factor for a market. It may be distribution, a brand name, a sales organization, technology, R&D capability, or manufacturing capability. To remedy this deficiency internally might require excessive time and money. When the uncertainties of operating in other countries are considered, a strategic alliance is a natural alternative for reducing investment and the accompanying inflexibility and risk.

A strategic alliance is a collaboration leveraging the strengths of two or more organizations to achieve strategic goals. There is a long-term commitment involved. It is not simply a tactical device to provide a short-term fix for a problem—to outsource a component for which a temporary manufacturing problem has surfaced, for example. Furthermore, it implies that the participating organizations will contribute and adapt needed assets or competencies to the collaboration and that these assets or competencies will be maintained over time. The results of the collaboration should have strategic value and contribute to a viable venture that can withstand competitive attack and environmental change.

A strategic alliance provides the potential for accomplishing a strategic objective or task—such as obtaining distribution in Italy—quickly, inexpensively, and with a relatively high prospect for success. This is possible because the involved firms can combine existing assets and competencies instead of having to create new assets and competencies internally.

A strategic alliance can take many forms, from a loose informal agreement to a formal joint venture. The most informal arrangement might be simply trying to work together (selling our products through your channel, for example) and allowing systems and organizational forms to emerge as the alliance develops. The more informal the arrangement, the faster it can be implemented and the more flexible it will be. As conditions and people change, the alliance can be adjusted. The problem is usually commitment. With low exit barriers and commitment, there may be a low level of strategic importance and a temptation to back away or to disengage when difficulties arise.

Motivations for Strategic Alliances

Strategic alliances can be motivated by a desire to achieve some of the benefits of a global strategy, as outlined in Figure 13.1. For example, a strategic alliance can:

- ***Generate scale economies.*** The fixed investment that Toyota made in designing a car and its production systems was spread over more units because of a joint venture with GM in California.

- ***Gain access to strategic markets.*** The Japanese firm JVC provided VCR design and manufacturing capability but needed a relationship with Thompson to obtain help in accessing the fragmented European market.

- ***Overcome trade barriers.*** Inland Steel and Nippon Steel jointly built an advanced cold-steel mill in Indiana. Nippon supplied the technology, capital, and access to Japanese auto plants in the United States. In return, it gained local knowledge and, more important, the ability to get around import quotas.

Perhaps more commonly, a strategic alliance may be needed to compensate for the absence of or weakness in a needed asset or competency. Thus, a strategic alliance can:

- ***Fill out a product line to serve market niches.*** Ford, General Motors, and Chrysler have, for example, relied on alliances to provide key components of its product line. Ford's longtime relationship with Mazda has resulted in many Ford models, as well as access to some Far East markets. When Mazda decided not to build a minivan, Ford turned to

Nissan for help. One firm simply cannot provide the breadth of models needed in a major market such as the United States.

- *Gain access to a needed technology.* While JVC gained access to the European market, its European partner accessed a competitive VCR source.

- *Use excess capacity.* The GM/Toyota joint venture used an idle GM plant in California.

- *Gain access to low-cost manufacturing capabilities.* A host of companies from Wal-Mart to Dell have alliances in China to source products.

- *Access a name or customer relationship.* NGK bought an interest in a GE subsidiary whose product line had become obsolete in order to access the GE name and reputation in the U.S. electrical equipment market. A U.S. injection molder joined with Mitsui in order to help access Japanese manufacturing operations in the United States that preferred to do business with Japanese suppliers.

- *Reduce the investment required.* In some cases, a firm's contribution to a joint venture can be technology, with no financial resources required.

The Key: Maintaining Strategic Value for Collaborators

A major problem with strategic alliances occurs when the relative contribution of the partners becomes unbalanced over time and one partner no longer has any proprietary assets and competencies to contribute. This has happened in many of the early partnerships involving U.S. and Japanese firms in consumer electronics, heavy machinery, power-generation equipment, factory equipment, and office equipment.

The result, when the U.S. company has become de-skilled or hollowed out and no longer participates fully in the venture, can be traced in part to the motivation of the partners. Offshore firms are motivated to learn skills; they find it embarrassing to lack a technology and they work to correct deficiencies. U.S. firms are motivated to make money by outsourcing elements of the value chain in order to reduce costs. They start by outsourcing assembly and move on to components, to value-added components, to product design, and finally to core technologies. The U.S. partner is then left with just the distribution function, whereas the offshore firm retains the key business elements, such as product refinement, design, and production.

One approach to protecting assets and competencies is to structure the situation so that operating management is shared. Compare, for example, the joint Toyota/GM manufacturing facility, where GM is involved in the manufacturing process and its refinements, to Chrysler's effort to sell a Mitsubishi car designed and manufactured in Japan. In the latter case, Mitsubishi eventually developed its own name and dealer network and now sells its car directly. When the motivation for an alliance is to avoid investment and achieve attractive short-term returns instead of to develop assets and competencies, the alliance will break down.

Another approach is to protect assets from a partner by controlling access. Many Japanese firms have a coordinated information transfer. Such a position avoids uncoordinated, inappropriate information flow. Other firms put clear conditions on access to a part of the product line or a part of the design. Motorola, for example, releases its microchip technology to its partner, Toshiba, only as Toshiba delivers on its promise to increase Motorola's penetration in the Japanese market. Still others keep improving the assets involved so that the partner's dependence continues. Of course, the problem of protecting assets is most difficult when the asset can be communicated by a drawing. It is somewhat easier when a complex system is involved—when, for example, the asset is manufacturing excellence.

A second set of problems involves execution of the alliance. With strategic alliances, at least two sets of business systems, people, cultures, and structures need to be reconciled. In addition, the culture and environment of each country must be considered. The Japanese, for example, tend to use a consensus-building decision process that relies on small group activity for much of its energy; this approach is very different from that of managers in the United States and Europe. Furthermore, the interests of each partner may not always seem to be in step. Many otherwise well-conceived alliances have failed because the partners simply had styles and objectives that were fundamentally incompatible.

When a joint venture is established as a separate organization, research has shown that the chances of success will be enhanced if:

- The joint venture is allowed to evolve with its own culture and values—the existing cultures of the partners will probably not work even if they are compatible with each other.

- The management and power structure from the two partners is balanced.

- Venture champions are on board to carry the ball during difficult times. Without people committed to making the venture happen, it will not happen.

- Methods are developed to resolve problems and to allow change over time. It is unrealistic to expect any strategy, organization, or implementation to exist without evolving and changing. Partners and the organization thus need to be flexible enough to allow change to occur.

Alliances are a widespread part of business strategy (the top 500 global businesses have an average of sixty major alliances each) but need to be actively managed. One study of some 200 corporations found that the most successful at adding value through alliances employed staff who coordinated all alliance-related activity within the organization.[10] This function would draw on prior experiences to provide guidance to those creating and managing new alliances. One firm, for example, has "thirty-five rules of thumb" to manage alliances from creation to termination. The dedicated alliance staff would also increase external visibility (an alliance announcement has been found to influence stock price), coordinate internal staffing and management of alliances, and help identify the need to change or terminate an alliance.

KEY LEARNINGS

- A global strategy considers and exploits interdependencies between operations in different countries.

- Among the motivations driving globalization are obtaining scale economies, accessing low-cost labor or materials, taking advantage of national incentives to cross-subsidize, dodging trade barriers, accessing strategic markets, enhancing firm innovation, and creating global associations.

- Companies successful at expanding their global footprint usually had a strong core market, a repeatable expansion formula, customer differentiation that travels, and an understanding of local vs. global scale. The selection of a country to enter should involve an analysis of the attractiveness of the market and the ability of the firm to succeed in that market.

- A standardized brand is not always optimal. Economies of scale may not exist, the discovery of a global strategy (even assuming it exists) may be difficult, or the context (for example, different market share positions or brand images) may make such a brand impractical.

- Global brand management needs to include a global brand communication system, a global brand planning system, a global management structure, and a system to encourage excellence in brand building. The brand group can operate under a command-and-control system or a less ambitious service provider, consultative, or facilitator style.

- Strategic alliances (long-term collaboration leveraging the strengths of two or more organizations to achieve strategic goals) can enable an organization to overcome a lack of a key success factor, such as distribution or manufacturing expertise. A key to the long-term success of strategic alliances is that each partner contributes assets and competencies over time and obtains strategic advantages.

FOR DISCUSSION

1. Pick a product or service that is offered in a limited number of countries. Assess the advantages of expanding to a more global presence.

2. For a particular product or service, how would you evaluate the countries that would represent the best prospects? Be specific. What information would you need, and how would to obtain it? Prioritize the criteria that would be useful in deciding which countries to enter.

3. What is the advantage of a global brand team? What are the problems of using a team to devise and run the global strategy? When should a team lead, and when should it take on a supporting role? Would your answer differ for BP versus P&G? Why?

4. For a firm such as Bank of America, P&G, or Ford, how would you go about creating blockbuster global brand-building programs—for example, sponsorships, promotions, or advertising? How would you leverage those programs?

5. Select a company. How would you advise it to find an alliance partner to gain distribution into China? What advice would you give regarding the management of that alliance?

NOTES

1. Douglas B. Holt, John A. Quelch, and Earl L. Taylor, "How Global Brands Compete," *Harvard Business Review*, September 2004, pp. 68–75.

2. Gary Hamel and C. K. Prahalad, "Do You Really Have a Global Strategy?" *Harvard Business Review*, July–August 1985, pp. 139–148.

3. James Root and Josef Ming, "Keys to Foreign Growth: Four Requisites for Expanding Across Borders," *Strategy & Leadership*, Vol. 34, No. 3 (2006), pp. 59–61.

4. Victoria Griffith, "Welcome to Your Glocal Superstore," *Strategy+Business*, Vol. 26, 2002, p. 95.

5. Ibid.

6. "Heading for the Exit," *Economist*, August 5, 2006, p. 54.

7. The material in this section draws from Chapter 10 of the book *Brand Leadership* by David A. Aaker and Erich Joachimsthaler, New York: Free Press.

8. Theodore Levitt, "The Globalization of Markets," *Harvard Business Review*, May–June 1983, pp. 92–102.

9. David A. Aaker, "The Lure of Global Branding," (with Erich Joachimsthaler), *Harvard Business Review*, November–December 1999.

10. Jeffrey H. Dyer, Prashant Kale, and Harbir Singh, "How to Make Strategic Alliances Work," *MIT Sloan Management Review*, Summer 2001, pp. 37–43.

CHAPTER FOURTEEN

Setting Priorities for Businesses and Brands—The Exit, Milk, and Consolidate Options

There is nothing so useless as doing efficiently that which should not be done at all.
—*Peter Drucker*

If you want to succeed, double your failure rate.
—*Thomas Watson, founder, IBM*

Anyone can hold the helm when the sea is calm.
—*Publilius Syrus*

All firms, from GM to GE to P&G to Marriott to Intel, should view their business units as a portfolio. Some should receive investment because they are cash-generating stars in the present and will be into the future. The investment is needed to keep them healthy and to exploit growth opportunities. Others need investment because they are the future stars of the company, even though they now have more potential than sales and profits. Identifying the priority business units, the ones that merit financial and managerial resources, is a key to a successful strategy.

Equally important is to identify those business units that are not priorities. Some of them should assume the role of generating cash through a milking or harvesting strategy. These units, termed *cash cows*, should no longer absorb investments aimed at growing the business. Still other units should be divested or closed or merged because they lack the potential to become either stars or cash cows—their profit prospects may be unsatisfactory, or they may lack a fit with the strategic thrust going forward. These decisions, which are strategically and organizationally difficult, often are crucial to organizational success and even survival.

A related issue is dealing with too many brands by eliminating or merging them. Brand strategy and business strategy are closely related because a brand will often represent a business. As a result, brand strategy is often a good vehicle to develop and clarify the business strategy. Too many brands, like too many business units, result in confusion and inefficiency. The firm can support only so many brands, and brand proliferation has often grown to the point of paralyzing the organization. In the automobile field there are now over 300 brands, and GM and several other firms are strategically handicapped by the resulting confusion, overlap, and inefficiency.

We start with an overview of portfolio strategy and then discuss the divest and milk strategy options. We then turn to the problem from the perspective of brand strategy and explore how brand portfolios can be reduced so that more brand focus becomes possible and clarity can be enhanced in both the brand strategy and the accompanying business strategy.

THE BUSINESS PORTFOLIO

Portfolio analysis of business units dates from the mid-1960s with the growth-share matrix, which was pioneered and used extensively by the BCG consulting group. The concept was to position each business within a firm on the two-dimensional matrix shown in Figure 14.1. The market-share dimension (actually the ratio of share to that of the largest competitor) was a summary measure of firm strength and cost advantages resulting from scale economies and manufacturing experience. The growth dimension was defended as the best single indicator of market attractiveness.

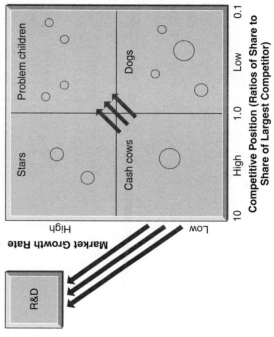

Figure 14.1 The Growth-Share Matrix

The BCG growth-share matrix is associated with a colorful cast of characters representing strategy recommendations. According to the BCG logic, the stars, important to the business and deserving of any needed investment, resided in the high-share, high-growth quadrant while the cash cows, the source of cash, occupied the high-share, low-growth quadrant. In addition, we have the dogs, potential cash traps and candidates for liquidation, in the low-growth, low-share quadrant and problem children, who have heavy cash needs but will eventually convert into stars, in the low-share, high-growth quadrant.

The BCG growth-share model, although naive and simplistic in its analysis and recommendations, was very influential in its day. Its lasting contribution was to make visible the issue of allocation across business units, that some businesses should generate cash that supports others. It also introduced the experience curve (discussed in Chapter 10) into strategy and showed that, under some conditions, market share could lead to experience-curve–based advantage.

A more realistic, richer portfolio model associated with GE and McKinsey also evaluates the business on two dimensions—market attractiveness and the business position. Each of these dimensions, as suggested by Figure 14.2, are richer and more

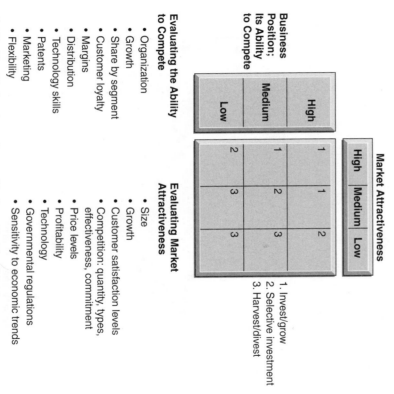

Market Attractiveness

	High	Medium	Low
High	1	1	2
Medium	1	2	3
Low	2	3	3

1. Invest/grow
2. Selective investment
3. Harvest/divest

Business Position; Its Ability to Compete

Evaluating Market Attractiveness

- Size
- Growth
- Customer satisfaction levels
- Competition: quantity, types, effectiveness, commitment
- Price levels
- Profitability
- Technology
- Governmental regulations
- Sensitivity to economic trends

Evaluating the Ability to Compete

- Organization
- Growth
- Share by segment
- Customer loyalty
- Margins
- Distribution
- Technology skills
- Patents
- Marketing
- Flexibility

Figure 14.2 The Market Attractiveness/Business Position Matrix

robust those used in the BCG model. The investment decision is again suggested by the position on a matrix. A business that is favorable on both dimensions should usually be a candidate to grow using the tools of the last four chapters.

When both market attractiveness and business position evaluations are unfavorable, the harvest or divest options should be raised. Of course, even in a hostile environment, routes to profitability can be found. Perhaps the business can turn to new markets, growth submarkets, superpremium offerings, new products, new applications, new technologies, or revitalized marketing. When the matrix position is neither unambiguously positive or negative, the investment decision will require more detailed study.

DIVESTMENT OR LIQUIDATION

One motivation to consider an exit strategy is to avoid a drain on profits caused by a business with projected losses or unsatisfactory profits given the investment required. The market may be unfavorable because of aggressive or desperate competitors creating margin squeezes. If the market condition is acceptable, the competitive business position might still be so weak (perhaps because of inadequate assets and competencies) that it would be hard to justify further investment. To make such decisions, difficult judgments and projections will be involved. Consider the analysis required to address the decision by GM to drop Buick, or for Ford to let go of Jaguar. The most difficult aspect may be assessing the competitive posture going forward given strategies now being implemented.

Another motivation is to exit businesses that no longer fit the strategic thrust of the firm. In fact, the business may be not only a resource drain but a distraction to the internal culture and the external brand image. When there are many business units, it is likely that focusing attention on a few strategic platforms based on a small set of assets and competencies will be helpful and will require pruning the business portfolio. Assessing strategic fit means that a well-developed strategy needs to be in place, with an assessment of what will and what will not be the growth platforms. If Ford were to sell Jaguar, a statement would be made about the strategic viability of the prestige platform for the future growth of the firm.

Being able to make and implement an exit decision can be healthy and invigorating. The opportunity cost of overinvesting in a business, and of hanging on to business ventures that are not performing and never will perform, can be damaging and even disastrous. Further, this cost is often hidden from view because it is shielded by a nondecision. When a business that is not contributing to future profitability and growth absorbs resources in the firm—not only financial capital but also talent, the firm's most important currency—those businesses that do represent the future of the firm will suffer. Perhaps worse, some businesses with the potential to be important platforms for growth will be left on the sidelines or starved, victims of false hopes and stubborn, misplaced loyalty.

Jack Welch, the legendary GE CEO, believed that identifying the talent of the future was his most important job and equally important was identifying those who did not fit the future plans and letting them seek careers elsewhere. He believed the firm would be stronger, and the people involved would benefit in the long run as well. He felt the same about business units. Welch, during his first four years as GE's CEO, divested 117 business units accounting for 20 percent of the corporation's assets. Such an active divestiture program can generate cash at a fair (as opposed to a forced-sale) price, liberate management talent, help reposition the firm to match its strategic vision, and add vitality. The divested businesses often benefit as well, as many will move into environments that are more supportive in terms of not only assets and competencies but also the commitment to succeed. It is healthy all around to trim businesses. And there will always be businesses units to trim; one study by Bain & Company estimated that of the major growth initiatives, only 20 percent are successful.[1] Many of the rest are ill-advised investments in businesses that should have been milked or divested.

As noted in Chapter 12, achieving sustained growth is rare, and when it appears it is often fueled by new businesses. One theory advanced by James Brian Quin, a strategy theorist, and others on how to find and develop successful new businesses is to "let a thousand flowers bloom," tend those that thrive, and let the rest wither. The venture capital industry lives by the mantra that if you fund ten ventures, two will be home runs, and they will represent overall success. Getting home runs requires funding many ventures. The key to the prescription that it takes many tries to find success is to have a process and the will to terminate business units that are not going to fuel growth in the future. Without that process, a thousand flowers will result in an overgrown garden where none are healthy.

Many firms avoid divestiture decisions until they become obvious or are forced by external forces. In addition to wasted resources, delayed divestiture decisions result in lower prices being obtained for the business. One study showed that the total return to shareholders from a divestiture declines as the decision is delayed.[2] Another found that organizations who actively manage these decisions by systematically evaluating the strategic fit and future prospects of each business, then regularly making divestiture decisions or placing business units on a probationary status, are more profitable.[3]

When any of the following are present, an exit strategy should be considered:

Business Position

- The business position is weak—the assets and competencies are inadequate, the value proposition is losing relevance, or the market share is in third or fourth place and declining in the face of strong competition.
- The business is now losing money, and future prospects are dim.

Market Attractiveness

- Demand within the category is declining at an accelerating rate, and no pockets of enduring demand are accessible to the business. It is unlikely that a resurgence of the category or a subcategory will occur.
- The price pressures are expected to be extreme, caused by determined competitors with high exit barriers and by a lack of brand loyalty and product differentiation.

Strategic Fit

- The firm's strategic direction has changed, and the role of the business has become superfluous or even unwanted.

- Firms' financial and management resources are being absorbed when they could be employed more effectively elsewhere.

Exit Barriers

Even when the decision seems clear, there may be exit barriers that need to be considered. Some involve termination costs. A business may support other businesses within the firm by providing part of a system, by supporting a distribution channel, or by using excess plant capacity. Long-term contracts with suppliers and with labor groups may be expensive to break. The business may have commitments to provide spare parts and service backup to retailers and customers, and it may be difficult to arrange alternative acceptable suppliers.

An exit decision may affect the reputation and operation of other company businesses, especially if that business is visibly tied to the firm. Thus, GE was concerned about the impact its decision to discontinue small appliances would have on its lamp and large-appliance business retailers and consumers. At the extreme, closing a business could affect access to financial markets and influence the opinion of dealers, suppliers, and customers about the firm's other operations.

If there is any reason to believe the market may change, making the business more attractive, the exit decision could be delayed or changed to a milk or hold decision. Remaining in the business may be a contingency play. For example, the Saturn line has been a costly drain on General Motors for two decades. However, if an oil crisis hits and the auto industry turns to small cars in a major way, the Saturn operation could be the salvation of GM. Thus, the decision to keep the division alive could turn out to be smarter than it seemed, given an analysis of the market attractiveness and business position.

Biases Inhibiting the Exit Decision

There are well-documented psychological biases in analyzing a business. One such bias is reluctance to give up. There may be an emotional attachment to a business that has been in the "family" for many years, or that may even be the original business on which the rest of the firm was based. It is difficult to turn your back on such a valued friend, especially if it means laying off good people. Managerial pride also enters in. Professional managers often view themselves as problem solvers and are reluctant to admit defeat. Several anecdotes describe firms that have had to send a series of executives to close down a subsidiary. Too frequently, the executive would become convinced that a turnaround was possible, only to subsequently fail at the effort.

Another obstacle is called confirmation bias.[4] People naturally seek out information that supports their position and discount disconfirming information, whatever the context. The audiences for Rush Limbaugh or Al Franken, partisan political observers, do not represent a cross-section but involved people who seek out those who support their beliefs. Confirmation bias can be rampant in evaluating a business to which some have emotional and professional ties. Information that confirms that the business can be saved is more likely to be uncovered and valued than disconfirming information. Questions asked in market research may be slanted, perhaps inadvertently, toward providing an optimistic future for the business. When there is uncertainty, the bias can get large. When predicting future sales or projecting costs, for example, extreme numbers may be put forth as plausible. Such a tendency is seen in major governmental decisions, such as funding a fighter plane or building a bridge, as well as forecasting sales.

Another bias to deal with is the escalation of commitment. Instead of regarding prior investments as sunk costs, there is a bias toward linking them to the future decisions. Thus, a decision to invest $10 million more is framed as salvaging the prior $100 million investment.

Injecting Objectivity into Disinvest Decisions

To deal with these biases, the decision needs to be more objective in terms of both process and people. The process should be transparent and persuasive, thereby encouraging the discussion to be professional, centered on key issues and discouraging emotional gut reactions. It helps if it is applied to a spectrum of business units instead of just the marginal ones. It is well known that the only way to close down a defense plant is to evaluate all of them and let the process identify which ones are no longer needed. When politicians are faced with such objective evidence and required to make an up or down vote, it becomes harder to fight for "their base."

It is also helpful to have people interjected into the analysis without a history that prevents them from being objective. Such people can be from within the firm, but sometimes an outside party from a consulting company or a new hire can be more objective. This can be done vicariously as well. There is the often-repeated story of how Intel made the painful decision to turn its back on the memory business, which represented not only its heritage but the bulk of its sales. Intel's president Andy Grove at one point looked at CEO Gordon Moore and asked what a new outside CEO would do. The answer was clear—get out of memory. So the two men symbolically walked out the door and walked back in, then made the fateful decision to exit a business that had been destroyed by Asian competitors. Even after making the decision, it was difficult to cut out all R&D and close it down. Two people sent to close the business dragged their heels and continued to invest; finally, Grove himself had to step in. It turns out that the implementation of an exit decision is also difficult.

Peter Drucker recounted a story about a leader firm in a specialized industry that organized a group of people every three months to look critically at one segment of the company's offerings. This group was a cross-section of young managers and changed every quarter. They addressed the Andy Grove question—if we were not in this business now, would we go into it? If the answer was no, an exit strategy would be considered. If the answer was yes, then the next question was whether the existing business strategy would be used. A negative judgment would lead to proposed changes. One key to the firm's success was that this process led to the exit or modification of every single one of its businesses over a five-year period.

THE MILK STRATEGY

A milk or harvest strategy aims to generate cash flow by reducing investment and operating expenses to a minimum, even if that causes a reduction in sales and market share. The underlying assumptions are that the firm has better uses for the funds, that the involved business is not crucial to the firm either financially or synergistically, and that milking is feasible because sales will stabilize or decline in an orderly way without supporting investment. The milking strategy creates and supports a cash cow business.

There are variants of milking strategies. A fast milking strategy would be disciplined about minimizing the expenditures toward the brand and maximizing the short-term cash flow, accepting the risk of a fast exit. A slow milking strategy would sharply reduce long-term investment but continue to support operating areas such as marketing and service. A hold strategy would provide enough product development investment to hold a market position, as opposed to investing to grow or strengthen the position.

Conditions Favoring a Milking Strategy

A milking strategy would be selected over a growth strategy when the current market conditions make investments unlikely to improve a rather negative environment caused by competitor aggressiveness, consumer tastes, or whatever. Sometimes it is precipitated by a new entrant that turns a market hostile. Chase & Sanborn was once a leading coffee; the "Chase & Sanborn Hour," starring Edgar Bergen, was one of the most popular radio shows of its time. After World War II, though, Chase & Sanborn decided to retreat to a milking strategy rather than fight an expensive market retention battle against the rising popularity of instant coffee and the appearance of General Foods' heavily advertised Maxwell House brand.

Several conditions support a milking strategy rather than an exit strategy:

- The business position is weak but there is enough customer loyalty, perhaps in a limited part of the market, to generate sales and profits in a milking mode. The risk of losing relative position with a milking strategy is low.
- The business is not central to the current strategic direction of the firm, but has relevance to it and leverages assets and competencies.
- The demand is stable and the decline rate is not excessively steep, and pockets of enduring demand ensure that the decline rate will not suddenly become precipitous.
- The price structure is stable at a level that is profitable for efficient firms.
- A milking strategy can be successfully managed.

One advantage of milking rather than divesting is that a milking strategy can often be reversed if it turns out to be based on incorrect premises regarding market prospects, competitor moves, cost projections, or other relevant factors. A resurgence in product classes that were seemingly dead or in terminal decline gives pause. Oatmeal, for example, has experienced a sharp increase in sales because of its low cost and associations with nutrition and health. In men's apparel, suspenders have shown signs of growth. Fountain pens, invented in 1884, were virtually killed by the appearance in 1939 of the ballpoint. However, the combination of nostalgia and a desire for prestige has provided a major comeback for the luxury fountain pen. As a result, the industry has seen years in which sales doubled.

Implementation Problems

It can be organizationally difficult to assign business units to a cash cow role, because in a decentralized organization (and most firms pride themselves on their decentralized structure), it is natural for the managers of cash-generating businesses to control the available cash that funds investment opportunities. The culture is for each business to be required or encouraged to find its own growth, and of course all business units have investment options with accompanying rationales. It requires a sometimes-disruptive centralized decision to assign a large business unit a cash cow role. As a result, a fast-growing business with enormous potential but relatively low sales volume will often be starved of needed cash. The irony is that the largest businesses involving mature products may have inferior investment alternatives, but because cash flow is plentiful, their investments will still be funded. The net effect is that available cash is channeled to areas of low potential and withheld from the most attractive areas. A business portfolio analysis helps force the issue of which businesses should receive the available cash.

Another serious problem is the difficulty of placing and motivating a manager in a milking situation. Most SBU managers do not have the orientation, background, or skills to engage in a successful milking strategy. Adjusting performance measures and rewards appropriately can be difficult for both the organization and the managers involved. It might seem reasonable to use a manager who specializes in milking strategies, but that is often not feasible simply because such specialization is rare. Most firms rotate managers through different types of situations, and career paths simply are not geared to creating milking specialists.

There are also market risks associated with a milking strategy. If employees and customers suspect that a milking strategy is being employed, the resulting lack of trust may upset the whole strategy. As the line between a milking strategy and abandonment is sometimes very thin, customers may lose confidence in the firm's product and employee morale may suffer. Competitors may attack more vigorously. All these possibilities can create a sharper-than-anticipated decline. To minimize such effects, it is helpful to keep a milking strategy as inconspicuous as possible.

The Hold Strategy

A variant of the milking strategy is the hold strategy, in which growth-motivated investment is avoided, but an adequate level of investment is employed to maintain product quality, production facilities, and customer loyalty. A hold strategy will be superior to a milk strategy when the market prospects and/or the business position is not as grim. There may be more substantial and protected pockets of demand, better margins, a superior market position, a closer link to other business units in the firm, or the possibility of improved market prospects. A hold strategy would be preferable to an invest strategy when an industry lacks growth opportunities and a strategy of increasing share would risk triggering competitive retaliation. The hold strategy can be a long-term strategy to manage a cash cow, or an interim strategy employed until the uncertainties of an industry are resolved.

Sometimes a hold strategy can result in a profitable "last survivor" of a market that is declining slower than most assume. A strong survivor may be profitable, in part because there may be little competition and in part because the investment to maintain a leadership position might be relatively low. The cornerstone of this strategy is to encourage competitors to exit. Toward that end, a firm can be visible about its commitment to be the surviving leader in the industry by engaging in increased promotion or even introducing product improvements. It can encourage competitors to leave by pricing aggressively and by reducing their exit barriers by purchasing their assets, assuming their long-term obligations, or even by buying their business. Kunz, which made passbooks for financial institutions, was able to buy competitor assets so far under book value that the payback period was measured in months. As a result, Kunz had record years in a business area others had written off as all but dead decades earlier.

A problem with the hold strategy is that if conditions change, reluctance or slowness to reinvest may result in lost market share. The two largest can manufacturers, American and Continental, failed to invest in the two-piece can process when it was developed because they were engaged in diversification efforts and were attempting to avoid investments in their cash cow. As a result, they lost substantial market share.

A hold strategy is particularly problematic if a disruptive innovation appears and the strategy prevents a firm from making necessary investments to remain relevant. As a result, firms may be slow to convert from film to digital, to reduce trans fats from packaged goods, or to adapt hybrid technology. The result could be a premature demise of a cash cow business.

PRIORITIZING AND TRIMMING THE BRAND PORTFOLIO

Brands are the face of a business strategy, and getting the brand strategy right is often a route to making the right business strategy decisions. One element of brand strategy is to set priorities within the brand portfolio, identifying the strong strategic brands, other brands playing worthwhile roles, brands that should receive no investment, and brands that should be deleted.

One reason to prioritize brands and trim the brand portfolio is that the exercise provides a good way to prioritize the business portfolio, because the brand will usually represent a business. When the brand perspective is used, the business prioritization analysis can sometimes be more objective and the resulting conclusion more transparent and obvious. The brand is usually a key asset of the business and represents its value proposition. Thus, a recognition that the brand has become weak can be a good signal that the business position is weak. Without prioritization of the brand portfolio, strategic brands will lose equity and market position because marginal brands are absorbing brand-building dollars and, worse, managerial talent. Managers simply follow an instinct to solve problems rather than exploiting opportunities, and too many marginal brands create a host of problems.

A second reason is that prioritizing and trimming the brand portfolio can correct the debilitating confusion associated with overbranding. Most firms simply have too many brands, subbrands, and endorsed brands, all part of complex structures. Some brands may reflect product types and others price-value, and still others customer types or applications. The branded offerings may even overlap. The totality often simply reflects a mess. Customers have a hard time understanding what is being offered and what to purchase; even employees may be confused. The business strategy therefore operates at a huge disadvantage.

A third reason is to address the strategic paralysis created by an overbranded, confused brand portfolio without priorities. It is all too common for a firm to be paralyzed by an inability to commit to how a new offering or new business should be branded. To provide a brand to a new offering or business that will foster success, there needs to be a sense of what brands will be strategic going forward and what their role and image will be. Assigning a brand that lacks a strategic future or whose future is incompatible with that assignment can be a serious handicap to a business strategy.

One partial step to reduce overbranding is to be more disciplined about the introduction of new offerings, new businesses, and new brands. Of course, innovation requires that new directions be introduced, but this does not mean that ad hoc business expansion decisions should be made without a systematic justification process. In particular, any proposed new brand should represent a business that is substantial enough and has a long enough life to justify brand-building expenses, and it should have a unique ability to represent a business—that is, no other existing brands would work.

Controlling the introduction of new brands is only half the battle. There needs to be a objective process to phase out or redeploy marginal or redundant brands after they have outlived their usefulness. The strategic brand consolidation process, summarized in Figure 14.3, addresses that challenge. It involves five distinct steps: identifying the relevant brand set, assessing the brands, prioritizing brands, creating a revised brand portfolio strategy, and designing a transition strategy.

1. Identify the Relevant Brand Set

The brand set will depend on the problem context. It can include all brands and subbrands, of course. However, often the focus will be on a subset, brand groupings of comparable brands. For example, an analysis for GM could include its major nameplates: Chevrolet, Pontiac, Buick, Cadillac, Saturn, and GMC. Another analysis stage could then be subbrands attached to a master brand. Thus, for Pontiac, the subbrands would be Vibe, Aztek, Bonneville, Firebird, Grand Am, Grand Prix, Montana, and Sunfire. When brands are involved that share similar roles, it becomes easier to evaluate the relative strength.

2. Brand Assessment

If brand priorities are to be established, evaluation criteria need to be established. Further, these criteria need to have metrics so that brands can be scaled. A highly

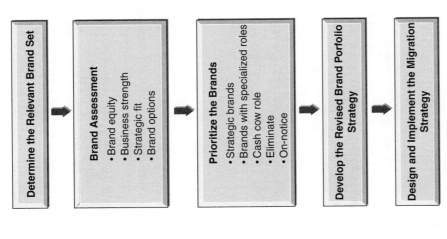

Determine the Relevant Brand Set

Brand Assessment
• Brand equity
• Business strength
• Strategic fit
• Brand options

Prioritize the Brands
• Strategic brands
• Brands with specialized roles
• Cash cow role
• Eliminate
• On-notice

Develop the Revised Brand Portfolio Strategy

Design and Implement the Migration Strategy

Figure 14.3   The Strategic Brand Consolidation Process

structured and quantified assessment provides stimulation and guidance to the discussion and the decision process. There should be no illusion that the decision will default to picking the higher number. The criteria will depend on the context, but in general there are four areas or dimensions of evaluations:

Brand Equity

- Awareness—Is the brand well known in the marketplace?
- Reputation—Is the brand well regarded in the marketplace? Does it have high perceived quality?
- Differentiation—Does the brand have a point of differentiation? A personality? Does it lack a point of parity along a key dimension?
- Relevance—Is it relevant for today's customers and today's applications?
- Loyalty—How large a segment of loyal customers is there?

Business Prospects

- Sales—Is this brand driving a significant business?

- Share/market position—Does this brand hold a dominant or leading position in the market? What is the trajectory?

- Profit margin—Is this brand a profit contributor and likely to remain so? Or are the market and competitive conditions such that the margin prospects are unfavorable?

- Growth—Are the growth prospects for the brand positive within its existing markets? If the market is in decline, are there pockets of enduring demand that the brand can access?

Strategic Fit

- Extendability—Does the brand have the potential to extend to other products as either a master brand or an endorser? Can it be a platform for growth?

- Business fit—Does the brand drive a business that fits strategically with the direction of the firm? Does it support a product or market that is central to the future business strategy of the firm?

Branding Options

- Brand equity transferability—Could the brand equity be transferred to another brand in the portfolio by reducing the brand to a subbrand or by developing a descriptor?

- Merging with other brand—Could the brand be aggregated with other brands in the portfolio to form one brand?

Brands need to be evaluated with respect to the criteria. The resulting scores can be combined by averaging, or by insisting on a minimal score on some key dimensions. For example, a low score on strategic fit may be enough to signal that the brand's role needs to be assessed. Or, if the brand is a significant cash drain, then it might be a candidate for review even if it is otherwise apparently healthy. In any case, the profile will be important and judgment will need to be employed to make final assessments of the brand's current strength.

3. Prioritizing Brands

The brands that are to live, be supported, and be actively managed need to be prioritized or tiered in some way. The number of tiers will depend on the context, but the logic is to categorize brands so that precious brand-building budgets are allocated wisely. The top tier will include the strategic power brands—those with existing or potential equity that are supporting a significant business or have the potential to do so in the future. A second tier could be those brands involving a smaller business, perhaps a niche or local business, or brands with a specialized role such as a flanker brand (a price brand that deters competitors from penetrating the market from below). A third tier would be the cash cow brands, which should be dialed down with little or no brand-building resources invested into them.

The remaining brands need to be assigned descriptor roles, eliminated, placed on-notices, or restructured.

- **Become descriptors.** Those brands that have no equity but serve to describe an offering could be assigned a descriptive role. The Dell Dimension computer, for example, could be judged to have its equity in the Dell brand. The Dimension brand, with no equity, would then be assigned a descriptive role. It could be replaced by the term desktop, but it also could be retained to describe the desktop line of Dell computers.

- **Eliminate.** If a brand is judged to be ill suited for the portfolio because of weak or inappropriate brand equity, business prospects, strategic fit, or redundancy issues, a plan to eliminate the brand from the portfolio is needed. Selling it to another firm or simply killing it become options.

- **On notice.** A brand that is failing to meets its performance goals but has a plan to turn its prospects around might be put on an on-notice list. If the plan fails and prospects continue to look unfavorable, elimination should then be considered.

- **Merged.** If a group of brands can be merged into a branded brand group, the goal of creating fewer, more focused brands will be advanced. Microsoft combined the products Word, PowerPoint, Excel, and Outlook into a single product called Office. The original product brands are now reduced to descriptive subbrands.

- **Transfer equity.** Unilever transferred the equity of Rave hair products to Sauve, and the Surf detergent products to All.

Nestlé has long had in place a system of brand portfolio prioritization. Twelve global brands are the tier one brands on which they focus. Each of the global brands has a top executive that is designated as its brand champion. These executives make sure that all activities enhance the brand. They have final approval over any brand extensions and major brand-building efforts. Peter Brabeck, who became CEO, has elevated six of these brands—Nescafe for coffee, Nestea for tea, Buitoni for pasta and sauces, Maggi for bouillon cubes, Purina for pet food, and Nestlé for ice cream and candy—as having priority within Nestlé. Nestlé has also identified 83 regional brands that receive management attention from the Swiss headquarters. In addition there are hundreds of local brands that are either considered strategic, in which the headquarters is involved, or tactical, in which case they are managed by local teams.

4. Develop the Revised Brand Portfolio Strategy

With brand priorities set, the brand portfolio strategy will need to be revised. Toward that end, several brand portfolio structures should be created. They could include a lean structure with a single master brand, such as Sony or HP, or a "house of brands" strategy like P&G, which has over eighty major product brands. The most promising options are likely to be in between. The idea is to create around two or three viable options, with perhaps two or three suboptions under each.

The major brand portfolio structure options, together with suboptions, need to be evaluated with respect to whether they:

- Support the business strategy going forward
- Provide suitable roles for the strong brands
- Leverage the strong brands
- Generate clarity both to customers and to the brand team

THE CASE OF CENTURION

A large manufacturing firm, which is here labeled as Centurion Industries, went through a strategic brand consolidation process before selecting its portfolio strategy going forward. The process started when the CEO observed that the brand portfolio in a major division was too diffused and that future growth and market position were dependent on creating a simpler, more focused portfolio of powerful brands. The division had grown in part by acquisition and now had nine product brands, only three of which were endorsed by the corporate brand, Centurion. The nine brands served a variety of product markets that could be roughly clustered into two logical groupings. One, the green business group, included five brands. The other, the blue business group, involved four brands. Competitors with less brand fragmentation and more natural brand synergy had developed stronger brands and were enjoying share growth.

In the green business group, a brand assessment supported by customer research was conducted on all five brands. One, Larson, represented the largest business, had substantial credibility in that business, and had high awareness levels. Further, it could be stretched to cover the other four areas even though it had no current presence in any of those areas. It did have a visible quality problem, however, that was being addressed. The decision was made to migrate all of the green business brands to Larson and to make the quality issue at Larson a corporate priority. The first migration stage was to endorse three of the brands with Larson and replace the fourth brand, which drove a small business, with the Larson brand. The second stage, to occur within two years, was to convert all of the brands in the green business group to the Larson name and add an endorsement by the corporate brand.

In the blue business group, the brand Pacer emerged from the brand assessment stage as the strongest, especially in terms of awareness, image, and sales. Because Pacer was in a business area closely related to that of the other three brands, using the Pacer brand for the entire blue business group was feasible. However, one of the four brands in the blue group, Cruiser, was an extremely strong niche brand with a dominant position in relatively small market and delivered significant self-expressive benefits to a hard-core customer base. Thus, it was decided that migrating the Cruiser brand to Pacer would be too risky, but that the balance of the blue group would operate under the Pacer brand. Again, both Pacer and Cruiser going forward would be endorsed by the corporate brand.

The end result was a brand architecture involving three brands rather than nine, with all three consistently endorsed by the corporate brand. The critical decision was making the tough call that in the long run the brand architecture would be stronger if niche brands were migrated into one of two broader brands. There were emotional, political, economic, and strategic forces and arguments against each move. The fact that one exception was allowed made the case more difficult to make and to implement. Critical to organizational acceptance was the use of an objective assessment template, which clearly identified the dimensions of the decision and facilitated the evaluation. It helped that much of each assessment was quantified from hard sales and market research data. Also critical was the strategic vision of the top management, because at the end of the day owners of some of the niche brands were not on board, and without a commitment from the top it would not have happened.

5. Implement the Strategy

The final step is to implement the portfolio strategy, which usually means a transition for the existing strategy to a target strategy. That transition can be made abruptly or gradually.

An abrupt transition can signal a change in the overall business and brand strategy; it becomes a one-time chance to provide visibility and credibility to a change affecting customers. So when Norwest Bank acquired Wells Fargo and changed the name of Norwest to Wells Fargo, it had the opportunity to communicate new capabilities that would enhance the offering for customers. In particular, Norwest customers could be assured that the personal relationships they expected would not change, but they could also expect upgraded electronic banking services because of the competence of Wells Fargo in that area. The name change reinforced the changed organization and the repositioning message. An abrupt transition assumes that the business strategy is in place; if not, the effort will backfire. If, for example, the Wells Fargo technology could not be delivered, the best course would have been to delay the name change until the substance behind the new position could be delivered.

The other option is to migrate customers from one brand to another gradually. This will be preferred when:

- There is no newsworthy reposition that will accompany the change.
- Customers that may not have high involvement in the product class may need time to learn about and understand the change.
- There is a risk of alienating existing customers by disrupting their brand relationship.

KEY LEARNINGS

- The exit decision, even though it is psychologically and professionally painful, can be healthy both for the firm because it releases resources to be used elsewhere, but even for the divested business, which might thrive in a different context.

- A milking or harvest strategy (generating cash flow by reducing investment and operation expenses) works when the involved business is not crucial to the firm financially or synergistically. For milking to be feasible, though, sales must decline in an orderly way.

- Pruning and trimming the brand portfolio provides another perspective on prioritizing businesses, can clarify brand offerings, and can remove the paralysis of not being able to brand new offerings. A five-step prioritization process involves identifying the relevant brand set, assessing the brands, prioritizing brands, creating a revised brand portfolio strategy, and designing a transition strategy.

FOR DISCUSSION

1. Ford in 2006 was faced with large deficits. One contributor was the Jaguar line, which involved over $12 billion in sunk costs, including a purchase price of around $2.5 billion with the rest coming from investments needed to upgrade the line and fix a quality problem. One of the strategic moves was to introduce a low-priced X car, which provided volume but seemed to affect the Jaguar image. What analyses should be conducted to determine whether Jaguar should be sold? Would that differ if the subject was another Ford brand, Volvo, which was profitable?

2. Consider a divestment strategy. Why is it hard to divest a business? Jack Welch divested hundreds of businesses during his tenure. What are some of the motivations that led to these divestitures?

3. Identify brands that are employing a milking strategy. What are the risks?

4. How would you determine if a firm had too many brands?

5. What in your judgment are the key problems or issues in the brand consolidation process?

NOTES

1. Chris Zook, *Beyond the Core,* Boston: HBS Press, 2004.

2. Richard Foster and Sarah Kaplan, *Creative Destruction: Why Companies That Are Built to Last Underperform the Market—And How to Successfully Transform Them,* New York: Currency, 2001.

3. Lee Dranikoff, Tim Koller, and Antoon Schneider, "Divestiture: Strategy's Missing Link," *Harvard Business Review,* May 2002, pp. 75–83.

4. An excellent article that documents these biases and suggests solutions is John T. Horn, Dan P. Lovallo, and S. Patrick Viguerie, "Learning to Let Go: Making Better Exit Decisions," *McKinsey Quarterly,* 2006, No. 2, pp. 65–76.

CHAPTER FIFTEEN

Organizational Issues

All progress is initiated by challenging current conceptions and executed by supplanting existing institutions.
—*George Bernard Shaw*

Structure follows strategy.
—*Alfred Chandler, Jr.*

Those that implement the plans must make the plans.
—*Patrick Hagerty, Texas Instruments*

K orvette's started as a luggage and appliance discounter selling name brands for $5 from a second-floor loft in Manhattan. By 1962, it had become a profitable discount chain with a dozen stores, and its founder was named as one of the most influential retailers of the century by a Harvard retailing guru.[1] Its initial success prompted an aggressive growth strategy, which turned out to be a disaster. The firm dramatically expanded both the number of stores and the number of cities served, expanded its product line by adding fashion goods, furniture, and grocery products, and added more store amenities.

This was a defensible growth strategy, similar to that of other successful discounters, such as Kmart. The problem was its implementation. The strategy was not supported by the right people, structure, systems, or culture. Korvette's personnel lacked the depth to staff the new stores and the expertise to handle the new product areas. The centralized structure did not adapt well to multiple cities and product lines. The management systems were not sophisticated enough to handle the added complexity. The culture of casual management with low prices as the driving force was not replaced with another strong culture that would be appropriate to the new business areas. As a result, by 1966 the firm was near death, and it never recovered.

The Korvette story graphically illustrates the importance of strategy implementation. The assessment of any strategy should include a careful analysis of organizational risks and a judgment about the nature of any required organizational changes and their associated costs and feasibility. Toward that end, this chapter first develops a conceptual framework that will help in analyzing an organization and its link to strategy. The need for achieving congruence among the organization components and strategy is then considered. A third section discusses how a chief marketing officer (CMO) aspiring to affect strategy can get traction, a context that is representative of any efforts to change an organization to adapt to a new strategy. Finally, the book closes with an overview of strategic market management.

A CONCEPTUAL FRAMEWORK

The conceptual framework, shown in Figure 15.1, can be used to identify and position organizational components and their interactions. The heart of the framework is a set of four constructs that describe the organization: structure, systems, people, and culture. The figure includes strategy, which must successfully interact with the four organizational components, and organizational performance. It also includes external and internal analysis, which provides a link to Figure 1.1 and the strategy development process. Consideration of organizational components can help a business identify actual and potential implementation problems, as well as determine how its organization would adapt to a new strategy.

STRUCTURE

Organizational structure defines lines of authority and communication and specifies the mechanism by which organizational tasks and programs are accomplished. A key structural variable is the degree to which authority and responsibility are decentralized.

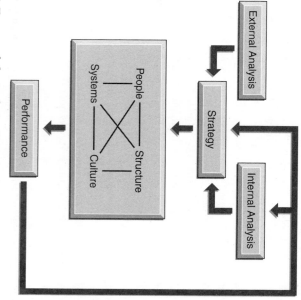

Figure 15.1　A Framework for Analyzing Organizations

Decentralization vs. Centralization

Nearly every organization, from Stanford University to P&G to HP to BofA, prides itself on being decentralized. And with good reasons.

Autonomous groups running distinct businesses have enormous inherent advantages. The managers are close to the market and can therefore understand customer needs. They are also intimate with the product technology and thus can chart the direction of product offerings. Being empowered to act quickly in an environment means no delays in making and implementing strategic decisions, a difference that is vital in dynamic markets. Also, because distinct business units can be held accountable for investments and results, business performance will be known in a timelier and less ambiguous manner. The most impressive feature of decentralization, however, is that it fosters incredible energy and vitality. Managers are empowered and motivated to innovate, to gain competitive advantage by providing superior value propositions to the customers. Nevertheless, there are challenges as well.

One challenge facing a decentralized organization is creating cross-business synergy. Potential synergy is often unrealized because having a host of silos can involve duplication, inefficiencies, and lost opportunities to create value for customers. In addition, it may be hard for a business to support a world-class marketing, IT, or sales function unless it finds a way to combine resources with other units. The failure to achieve synergies can be debilitating when competition for customers is intense and margins are under pressure.

A second challenge is to respond strategically at the firm level to market dynamics. What is strategically optimal for a business unit may not be the best for the firm as a whole. Brand portfolio strategy, for example, is easily undermined if a brand is shared across business units, with each using the brand to its local advantage. Conversely, a technology R&D project that could result in advantage for several business units might not be justified when evaluated at the business level. Resource allocation can be awkward, as successful silo units are reluctant to see resources diverted to new business opportunities.

One way to address these problems is with centralized control, the polar opposite of decentralization. In this model, a centralized team makes all the strategic and tactical decisions and has a strong functional capability to implement them (or at least manage their implementation). Such a group will create business strategy from a firmwide perspective and make sure that synergy opportunities are detected and exploited. To succeed, the central team needs to have credible knowledge of the products and the markets, the necessary resources, and the authority and stature to get things done. It will work best when the business scope is limited or there is a seasoned, knowledgeable CEO who has earned respect throughout the organization. How an organization can centralize some activities and thus mitigate the problems and disadvantages of decentralization is explored in the context of the role of the corporate CMO later in this chapter.

Matrix Organization

A matrix organization allows a person to have two or more reporting links. Several business units could share a sales force by having the salespeople report to a business unit as well as to the sales manager. An R&D group could have a research team that reports both to the business unit and to the R&D manager. As a result, the sales-people and the research team in these examples are each supported by a critical mass of employees and the infrastructure that allows them to excel while still being a part of the business unit. A person might also be attached to a task force (assigned, for instance, to explore a new market opportunity). That person would report to both the task force manager and his or her business unit. The concept of dual reporting requires coordination and communication that can be stressful and costly, but it also provides the flexibility needed to deal with a fast-moving market.

The Virtual Corporation

The virtual corporation is a team of people and organizations specifically designed for a particular client or job. The organizations brought together may be suppliers, customers, and competitors. The people can be drawn from a variety of sources and might include contract workers who are hired only for the project at hand. The virtual corporation can sometimes be formed or modified in a matter of days, which means it is the ultimate response in a fast-moving environment.

Communication firms, for example, are now forming teams tailored to the needs of particular clients. Some members of the team will come from subsidiary firms specializing in corporate design, packaging, direct marketing, and promotions. Others may come from firms that specialize in brochures and the media. The core of the team is likely to be located in a single building, but some team members will be connected via computer workstations that share visual images and in-process advertising.

Skunk Works

Major new business ventures may require separate entrepreneurial units because the slow decision-making process, the resource allocation biases against risky new businesses, and the overhead burden of the core organization are too great a handicap. Small, autonomous groups of people representing all the important functions join together to create a product or a business and nurse it through the early stages of life, often in an off-site garage operation called a skunk works. Used by Nestlé, 3M, IBM, Xerox, and many others, such a group is usually autonomous enough that it can bypass the usual decision process and resist pressures to conform to existing formal and informal constraints. A key to entrepreneurial units is to have a business champion committed to the concept. One firm reviewed fifty new product introductions and found that every failure lacked a voluntary product champion.

Alliance Networks

In the global environment, markets and competitors can change significantly, and it is important to be able to respond quickly. There may not be time to develop needed assets and competencies, and responses that require large commitments to new technologies or distribution channels may be risky, especially for a firm with little relevant background. One way to be able to go online immediately with necessary business changes is to form a network of alliances and joint ventures with suppliers, customers, distributors, and even competitors. With such a network, needed assets can be made available instantly, the firm can focus on what it does best, the risk of failure is shared, and many more opportunities can be funded.

The use of strategic alliances, their motivations, and how to make them work are discussed in detail in Chapter 13 as alliances play an especially important role in global strategy development.

SYSTEMS

Several management systems are strategically relevant. Among them are the information, measurement and reward, and planning systems.

Information System

The information system and the technology, databases, knowledge banks, models, and expert systems on which it is based can fundamentally affect strategy. By providing customer insights, competitive intelligence, and trend analysis, it can drive innovation and strategy creation and adaptation. It can also generate advantage. A retailer that has an ordering and logistical system may be able to deliver lower costs and superior selection compared to competitors. Thus, understanding the current capability and future direction of an organization's information system is a key dimension of strategy development.

Measurement and Reward System

Measurement can drive behavior and thus directly affect strategy implementation. The key to strategy is often the ability to introduce appropriate performance measures that are linked to the reward structure.

One concern is to motivate employees to cooperate, communicate, and create synergy. Rewards that are based too closely on a business unit's performance can work against this motivational goal. As a result, many companies deliberately base a

EASY STEPS TO DESTROYING REAL VALUE
by Henry Mintzberg[2]

1. Manage the bottom line (as if companies make money by managing money).
2. Make a plan for every action. (No spontaneity please, definitely no learning.)
3. Move managers around to be certain they never get to know anything but management well, and let the boss kick himself upstairs so that he can manage a portfolio instead of a real business.
4. When in trouble, rationalize, fire, and divest; when out of trouble, expand, acquire, and still fire (it keeps employees on their toes); above all, never create or invent anything (it takes too long).

portion of their bonuses or evaluations on the results of a larger unit. Prophet, a brand strategy consulting firm with seven offices, encourages cross-office support by making its bonuses conditional on firmwide performance. Another business may focus on divisional performance because synergy across divisions is not realistic.

Another prerequisite is to create measures reflecting a long-term perspective in order to balance short-term financial results. Thus, measures such as customer satisfaction, customer loyalty, quality indicators, new products brought to market, or training program productivity may be useful to gauge the progress of strategic initiatives.

Planning System

Although business strategy development and modification need to be ongoing parts of management, an annual strategic planning process is still useful because it forces managers to take time out to consider strategic uncertainties. Without that impetus, routine tasks will generally absorb management's available time. Workshops and retreats are often crucial elements in dedicating quality time to planning. A planning template, illustrated by the planning forms in the appendix, can provide a common set of constructs and vocabulary that can enable coordination and synergy development.

Creative, out-of-the-box thinking (perhaps aided by formal creative-thinking exercises) is a vital part of any planning system. Too often, strategic planning is nothing but an extrapolation of past strategies, with a financial spreadsheet as the dominant tool. There are two problems with this approach. First, it will not lead to the breakthrough strategies that can reinvent a business when needed. Second, it will not provide the consideration of strategic options that provides the basis for adapting to new events or trends. When Eisenhower said, "Plans are nothing, planning is everything," in part he meant that the process of examining a variety of strategic options makes the manager more capable of adapting or changing when necessary.

Planning should not be separated from the values, culture, and energy of the organization. According to Mintzberg, successful planning is often based on a committing, rather than a calculating style of management: "Managers with a committing style engage people in a journey. They lead in such a way that everyone on the journey helps shape its course. As a result, enthusiasm inevitably builds along the way." Mintzberg paraphrases the sociologist Philip Selznick when he says that "strategies only take on value as committed people infuse them with energy." The output of strategic planning should have soul as well as logic.[3]

PEOPLE

A strategy is generally based on an organizational competency that, in turn, is based on people. Thus, strategies require certain types of people. For each strategy, it is important to know how many people, with what experience, depth, and skills, are needed for:

- Functional areas, such as marketing, manufacturing, operations, and finance
- Product or market areas

- New product programs
- Management of particular types of people
- Management of a particular type of operation
- Management of growth and change

Sourcing: Insiders vs. Outsiders

If the strategy requires capabilities not already available in the business, it will be necessary to obtain them. The two alternative approaches both have risks and limitations.

Looking inside, the organization can access people who are conversant with its culture and systems, have established networks, and have a proven track record. The challenge for them will be to gain the functional skills and expertise and then to earn credibility. One question is whether they have the time and talent to do that. Another is whether they can perform the change-agent role that might be required; they may be too comfortable with the status quo.

Sometimes, team members from outside the firm can be more effective change agents than insiders. The outsider can bring needed functional expertise, experience, and credibility—and, in addition, will not have any perceived emotional ties to existing policies and programs. However, the outsider will not know the organization, especially aspects of the processes, culture, and relationships that are neither formal or visible. As a result, he or she may inadvertently create organizational barriers to initiatives.

STRATEGY AND PEOPLE DEVELOPMENT AT GE

Jack Welch, the legendary former GE CEO, created a system and culture to develop both strategy and people throughout his twenty-year tenure. Five elements were involved.[4]

- Each January, the top 5,000 GE executives gathered in Boca Raton to share best practices and set major business priorities. (In the past, priorities included e-commerce, globalization, and six-sigma quality.) Webcasts of the event were available to the whole organization.
- Each quarter, top executives met in two-day retreats facilitated by Welch and focused on initiatives related to the agenda set in Boca Raton. This was a key place for future leaders to emerge, earn respect, and demonstrate growth.
- Twice a year, Welch and others focused on personnel needs for each business, such as how to handle each unit's top 20 percent and bottom 10 percent of employees.
- In addition, biannual sessions (one in the spring and one in the fall) looked at each business over a three-year horizon.
- The entire effort was supported by the GE social architecture of informality, candor, substantive dialogue, boundaryless behavior, emphasis on follow-through, and making judgments on qualitative business dimensions.

One way to reduce the tensions is to form a blended team of outsiders and insiders, as GE and others have done. An outsider playing a leadership role will be surrounded by insiders, and when an insider is asked to lead change, he or she will be supported by whatever outside talent is needed. Another is to change the culture in order to make a new strategy viable and the task of a change agent more tractable.

Motivation

In addition to the type and quality of people, the motivation level can affect strategy implementation. There are, of course, a variety of ways to motivate people, including the fear of losing a job, financial incentives, self-fulfillment goals, and the development of goals for the organization or groups within the organization, such as teams or quality circles.

Motivation usually is enhanced if employees are empowered to accomplish their goals even when a departure from the routine response is required. People who are inhibited from using their initiative will eventually lose interest and become cynical. Motivation also is enhanced when employees are linked to the corporate culture and objectives. Companies can accomplish these links in part simply by providing titles, such as "host" (Disney), "crew member" (McDonald's), and "associate" (J. C. Penney).

CULTURE

As suggested by Figure 15.2, an organizational culture involves three elements:

- A set of shared values or dominant beliefs that define an organization's priorities
- A set of norms of behavior
- Symbols and symbolic activities used to develop and nurture those shared values and norms

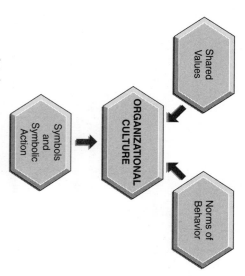

Figure 15.2   Organizational Culture

Shared Values

Shared values or dominant beliefs underlie a culture by specifying what is important. In a strong culture, the values will be widely accepted, and virtually everyone will be able to identify them and describe their rationale.

Shared values can have a variety of foci. They can involve, for example:

- A key asset or competency that is the essence of a firm's competitive advantage: We will be the most creative advertising agency.

- An operational focus: SAS focused on on-time performance.

- An organizational output: We will deliver zero defects, or 100 percent customer satisfaction.

- An emphasis on a functional area: Black & Decker transformed itself from a firm with a manufacturing focus to one with a market-driven approach.

- A management style: This is an informal, flat organization that fosters communication and encourages unconventional thinking.

- A belief in the importance of people as individuals.

- A general objective, such as a belief in being the best or comparable to the best: Komatsu set out to beat Caterpillar; Samsung strove to be a major player in cell phones; Sharp wants to be one of the most innovative in any area in which it competes.

Norms

To make a real difference, the culture must be strong enough to develop norms of behavior—informal rules that influence decisions and actions throughout an organization by suggesting what is appropriate and what is not. The fact is that strong norms can generate much more effective control over what is actually done or not done in an organization than a very specific set of objectives, measures, and sanctions. People can always get around rules. The concept of norms is that people will not attempt to avoid them because they will be accompanied by a commitment to shared values.

Norms can vary on two dimensions: the intensity or amount of approval/disapproval attached to an expectation and the degree of consensus or consistency with which a norm is shared. It is only when both intensity and consensus exist that strong cultures emerge.

Norms encourage behavior consistent with shared values. Thus, in a quality service culture, an extraordinary effort by an employee, such as renting a helicopter to fix a communication component (a FedEx legend), would not seem out of line and risky; instead, it would be something that most in that culture would do under similar circumstances. Furthermore, sloppy work affecting quality would be informally policed by fellow workers, without reliance on a formal system. One production firm uses no quality-control inspectors or janitors. Each production-line person is responsible for the quality of his or her output and for keeping the work area clean. Such a policy would not work without support from a strong culture.

Symbols and Symbolic Action

Corporate cultures are largely developed and maintained by the use of consistent, visible symbols and symbolic action. In fact, the more obvious methods of affecting behavior, such as changing systems or structure, are often much less effective than seemingly trivial symbolic actions.

A host of symbols and symbolic actions are available. A few of the more useful are discussed next.

The Founder and Original Mission

A corporation's unique roots, including the personal style and experience of its founder, can provide extremely potent symbols. The strong culture of L.L. Bean is due largely to its founder's involvement in the outdoors and his original products for the hunter and fisherman. The concept of entertainment developed by Walt Disney, the customer-oriented philosophy of J. C. Penney, the personality of Virgin's Richard Branson and the product and advertising traditions started by the founders of Procter & Gamble continue to influence the cultures of their firms generations later.

Modern Role Models

Modern heroes and role models help communicate, personalize, and legitimize values and norms. Lou Gerstner became a symbol of the new marketing-focused culture at IBM. Other examples are the managers at 3M who tenaciously pursued ideas despite setbacks until they succeeded in building major divisions such as the Post-it Notes division, and the Frito-Lay workers who maintained customer service in the face of natural disasters.

Activities

An executive's use of time can be a symbolic action affecting the culture. An airline executive who spends two weeks a month obtaining a firsthand look at customer service sends a strong signal to the organization. Patterns of consistent reinforcement can represent another important symbolic activity. For example, a firm that regularly recognizes cost-saving accomplishments in a meaningful way with the visible support of top management can, over time, affect the culture.

Questions Asked

An executive of a major bank reportedly shifted concern from revenue to profit by continually asking about profit implications. When a type of question is continually asked by top executives and made a central part of meeting agendas and report formats, it will eventually influence the shared values of an organization.

Rituals

Rituals of work life, from hiring to eating lunch to retirement dinners, help define a culture. One of the early success stories in Silicon Valley was a firm with a culture that was based in part on a requirement that a person commit before knowing his or her salary, and considerable pride in a Friday afternoon beer-bust ritual.

REPRESENTING CULTURE AND STRATEGY WITH STORIES, NOT BULLETS

Research has shown that stories are more likely than lists to be read and remembered. Nevertheless, most business strategists rely on bullet points to communicate both culture and strategy. 3M is one firm that has based its culture on classic stories—how initial failures of abrasive products led to product breakthroughs; how masking tape was invented; how a scientist conceived of Post-it Notes when his bookmarks fell out of a hymnal, and how the Post-it-Notes team, instead of giving up in the face of low initial sales, got people hooked on the product by flooding a city with samples. These stories communicate how innovation occurs at 3M and how its entrepreneurial culture operates.

At 3M, business strategy is also communicated via stories rather than the conventional bullets, which tend to be generic (the goal of increased market share applies to any business), skip over critical assumptions about how the business works (will increased market share fund new products, or result from new products?), and leave causal relationship unspecified (if A is done, B becomes effective). A strategic story will involve several phases—setting the stage by describing the current situation, introducing the dramatic conflict in the form of challenges and critical issues, and reaching resolution with convincing stories about how the company can overcome obstacles and win. Presenting a narrative motivates the audience, adds richness and detail, and provides a glimpse into the logic of the strategist.[5]

OBTAINING STRATEGIC CONGRUENCE

Figure 15.3 lists a set of questions that provide a basis for analyzing an organization and its relationship to a proposed strategy. However, there are also congruence issues to address. A strategy must match the structure, systems, people, and culture of the organization. In addition, each organizational component needs to fit with the others. If an inconsistency exists, it is likely that implementation of the strategy will be affected.

The concept of organizational congruence suggests that interactions between organizational components should be considered, such as:

- ***Do the systems fit the structure?*** Does the compensation system emphasize teamwork rather than individual performance when teamwork and cooperation are required?

- ***Do the people fit the structure?*** Can they operate within the organizational groups and integrate mechanisms to complete the task? For example, creative or entrepreneurial managers may be uncomfortable in a highly structured organization.

- ***Does the structure fit the culture?*** Does the structure complement the values or norms of the organization? For example, a top management group accustomed to controlling dedicated resources may be less effective in a matrix organization, in which persuasion and coordination are more important.

STRUCTURE

- What is the organization's structure? How decentralized is it?
- What are the lines of authority and communication?
- What are the roles of task forces, committees, or similar mechanisms?

SYSTEMS

- How are budgets set?
- What is the nature of the planning system?
- What are the key measures used to evaluate performance?
- How do product and information flow?

PEOPLE

- What are the skills, knowledge, and experience of the firm's employees?
- What is their depth and quality? Do they fit the strategy?
- What are the employees' expectations?
- What are their attitudes toward the firm and their jobs?

CULTURE

- Are there shared values that are visible and accepted?
- What are these shared values and how are they communicated?
- What are the norms of behavior?
- What are the significant symbols and symbolic activities?
- What is the dominant management style?
- How is conflict resolved?

STRATEGY

- Where would the new strategy fit into the organization?
- Would the new strategy fit into the strategic plan and be adequately funded?
- Would the systems and culture support the new strategy?
- What organizational changes would be required for the new strategy to succeed?
- What impact would these changes have? Are they feasible?

Figure 15.3 Obtaining Information about Organizational Components

Corporate Culture and Strategy

Organizational culture provides the key to strategy implementation because it is such a powerful force for providing focus, motivation, and norms. If the culture is congruent with the structures, systems, and people required by a new strategy it can enable and enhance the building of assets and achieving excellence in functional execution. If it is not congruent, however, the culture's motivations and norms could cripple the strategy.

A new strategy's fit with an organization's culture is of greater concern than the strategy's fit with the other organizational components because culture is so difficult to change. An oil company CEO developed elaborate diversification plans that failed because they were incompatible with the firm's oil business culture. The problems experienced by AT&T in its efforts to change from what was a service/production/internal focus to a marketing/external orientation illustrate how powerful and resistant to change a culture can be. AT&T very visibly changed its strategy and even the associated structure and systems (introducing product/market organizations and sales incentives), but was inhibited by the culture. When AT&T hired different types of personnel—MBAs and marketing people—it still found inconsistencies between the new people and the change-resistant culture.

When a new strategy is proposed, it is important to understand the relationship of that strategy to the shared values and norms of the organization. Is it compatible? Will the culture have to be modified? If so, what impact will that have on the organization? Often the worst case develops when a strong positive culture is sacrificed to accommodate a new strategy, and the result is an absence of any positive culture. The Korvette case discussed at the beginning of this chapter illustrates this point.

Hit-Industry Topology

The need for congruence between strategy and organizational components can be illustrated by the three very different types of firms that compete in hit industries.[6] A hit industry is one in which the goal is to obtain, produce, and exploit a product that will have a relatively short life cycle. Examples of such industries include movies, records, fashion, publishing, video games, computer software, venture capital (especially in high-tech areas), and oil. Industries with short life cycles are interesting because many of their organizational problems are more intense and graphic.

The model in Figure 15.4 divides a hit industry into three functions, which are shown as being performed by different organizations, although often two or more

Strategy	Drillers	Pumpers	Distributors
Structure	• Flat, loose • Amorphous	• Centralized • Tight control	• Decentralized • Loose control
Bottom-line Performance Incentives	• High	• None	• Low
People	• Product development	• Production control	• Marketing and distribution
Culture	• Stay loose • Move fast • Take risks	• Disciplined • Cost oriented • Avoid risks	• Promotion-oriented • Control risks
Key Success Factors	• Finding and keeping key people • Idea source • Get products to market quickly	• Exploit the experience curve • Operations • Production • Engineering	• Distribution channels • Inventory • Promotion • Positioning • Pricing

Figure 15.4 A Model of Hit Industries

will coexist within the same organization. An oil industry analogy provides the conceptual framework.

The first organizational type is termed drillers. They are the wildcatters who find oil fields and drill wells, the talent scouts and artists of the music industry the producers and writers in the movie industry, the developers of games, and the editors and authors in the publishing industry. A key success factor is to locate or create the new wells, properties, or projects. An ultimate goal in the music business, for example, would be to get a lock on performing talent and keep the artists happy. Key people tend to be creative, high-energy, decisive risk takers. They thrive in a flat organization with little structure and high bottom-line incentives.

The second organizational type is termed pumpers. They are the well operators and refiners of the oil business, game programmers, movie directors, and production editors in publishing. The key success factors in a pumping organization are operations, production engineering, and an ability to exploit the experience curve. The key people are disciplined, cost and production-oriented, in production and control jobs, and risk avoiders. A centralized organization with tight controls provides an appropriate context.

The third type specializes in distribution. The distributors are the pipeline operators and retailers in the oil industry and the distributors and retailers in the film, game, DVD, and publishing industries. The key success factors in a distribution business usually include marketing, promotion, physical distribution, and access to, or even control over, distribution channels. The key people are in marketing and distribution. A decentralized structure with loose controls and some bottom-line incentives is often effective.

The hit-industry topology shows how the lack of fit between organizational components can develop. Typically, an organization starts as a drilling company. After establishing some products and experiencing rapid growth, the company finds that it desperately needs to control production costs, develop a secure, effective distribution channel, and professionalize the marketing effort. As a result, pumping and distribution people are brought in. The organization then takes the form of either a pumper or a distributor, depending on which function is most critical or which type of person becomes the CEO. In any case, the system, structure, and culture of the organization change, and the drillers who started the business become uncomfortable and leave, perhaps to start a competing business. When the existing wells dry up or are damaged by competition, no one in the organization is available to create new ones.

It is a challenge in any business to keep access to drillers. One approach is to keep the drillers satisfied by financial incentives and organizational mechanisms, such as ad hoc groups with extraordinary freedom and autonomy. However, these special incentives may create inequities and disincentives for others. If entrepreneurial engineers are becoming millionaires, whereas those charged with maintaining existing products are on a fixed salary, tensions are bound to mount. Furthermore, the entrepreneurial groups may need access to the facilities and expertise of the pumpers and distributors, and providing that access may compromise their separateness.

BEYOND INCREMENTAL INNOVATION

A truly paradigm-shifting, innovation—as opposed to incremental improvements—can result in an enormous strategic payoff. Robert Stringer, a strategic consultant, suggests a variety of "breakthrough" or transformational strategies that successful companies can use (in addition to skunk works and decentralization) to reinvent themselves and their markets.[7]

- Make breakthrough innovations a strategic and culture priority, as General Mills has done in the cereal market.

- Hire more creative and innovative people. Citibank once hired packaged-goods marketers in order to vitalize its consumer business.

- Create "idea markets" where the best ideas in the organization compete for funding.

- Become an ambidextrous organization, meaning that the ability to commercialize radical innovation exists in the conventional organization (this solution is efficient, but difficult to implement).

- Use acquisitions, joint ventures, and alliances to bring in innovation. Cisco and Microsoft are case studies on how to do this.

- Participate in a corporate venture-capital fund or internal corporate venturing, whereby new businesses are managed apart from a company's existing business in order to provide entrepreneurs the level of autonomy that they value.

Another way to approach a fit problem is to restrict a business to one function and allow other organizations to perform the other functions. Venture capital firms restrict themselves to being drillers and do not become involved in the other functions. Publishers are largely distribution companies; their production is farmed out and the drillers are actually the authors, who are not part of the organization. A business without in-house drillers may have limited access to new ventures, however, because other firms may successfully contract with the best independent drillers. Also, the price for the proven drillers may become so high that profits are limited.

Problems can also arise when pumpers and distributors share an organization. If one of the two clearly dominates, the problem is minimized. If each is equally significant, however, there could easily be a fit problem.

THE NEW CORPORATE CMO—GETTING TRACTION

A host of firms are developing, expanding, or energizing the role of the corporate chief marketing officer (CMO). One motivation is to generate a more strategic marketing arm that can provide market-driven growth to the firm. Another motivation is to address the inefficiencies and lost opportunities created by product and/or geographic silos that inhibit synergistic programs such as global sponsorships and the effective management of cross-silo brands, including the corporate brand.

The task of the new corporate CMO is representative of any person facing the challenge of changing or adapting a resistant organization to a new or changed strategy. Thus, by studying the CMO context, learnings about the more general problem should emerge.

In a study by the author of this book, some 17 CMOs of major firms were asked to detail the problems they face to bring growth and synergy to an organization characterized by a decentralized structure, and what has worked to address those problems.

One finding is that organizational factors, which differ widely across firms, influence the ability of the CMO to gain traction and what approaches are likely to be effective and even feasible. These factors include the power of silos, especially country silos (some firms like IBM and P&G have reduced the power of country silos, while other firms still have country teams that are very autonomous), the commitment of the CEO to see synergies across silos emerge, the depth of marketing talent both within the CMO's team and throughout the silos, the quality of the CMO's team, and the history of working across silos. With the qualification that firm differences can affect the speed and extent to which a CMO can impact the organization, there are several guidelines as to how a CMO can get traction.

1. Get the CEO on Board

For some CMOs, especially those who are not blessed with a CEO with a marketing orientation and background, the challenge is to gain visible CEO support if not involvement. One approach is to manage the context by talking in terms of the CEO's priority agenda—focusing on growth objectives instead of brand extensions, efficiency and cost objectives instead of marketing synergy or scale, and building assets to support strategic initiatives instead of brand image campaigns. The objective is to reframe marketing as part of strategy, if not the driver, instead of being a tactical management function. Involving top management, particularly in determining the brand vision but also in other forums, will usually translate into support.

2. Get the Right People

The right CMO with the right team can probably make virtually any system work, and the wrong people can make the most optimal system fail. One CMO reported that an advertising manager that lacked competence set back the group a full year by interacting with silo organizations and making naive recommendations. There is danger in having even one weak person on the team if that person is at all visible.

Those in the CMO team as well as key silo marketing people need to be collaborative, especially when the incentives are silo oriented. At IBM, being collaborative is part of the evaluation criterion; the goal is to have people who have a real desire to learn about the products, operations, and programs of other business units and an ability to work across silos. In fact, top central marketing people at IBM evaluate silo-marketing people on this dimension.

3. Cross-Silo Teams

The CMO needs to engage the whole organization. A powerful device to achieve both involvement and buy-in is the use of cross-silo teams of relevant managers, either as task forces or as permanent entities. The minimal goal of such teams is to communicate plans, foster understanding, exchange best-practice experiences, and develop working relationships. Many cross-silo teams do more. Some, for example, manage the brand portfolio, controlling or influencing the introduction of new brands and subbrands and allocating the brand-building budget among them. Others guide cross-silo brand equity and marketing effectiveness-measurement systems.

4. Get Easy Wins

Attempting to address all problems and issues is a recipe for failure, given the realities of limited time, resources, and organizational tolerance. But while important issues need to be prioritized, it is also necessary to build credibility by achieving some visible wins. These early successes often involve identifying organizational units that will support (or at least not oppose) change because they need help to address a meaningful problem or opportunity. They can also involve programs that can be implemented "under the radar." For example, at Cigna, a real estate manager who needed artwork for a building was persuaded to use brand visuals. The CEO of a major division saw the result and promptly decided to extend the idea to all buildings.

5. Don't Try to Control Silo Strategies and Budgets

The CMO and his or her team can take on a host of roles. At one extreme, they can become the silo business strategists, developers of marketing plans and programs, and budget allocators. There are certain situations when an aggressive, proactive CMO with authority and resources is accepted and needed. However, in most cases that approach risks direct or indirect opposition, which can be fatal. Especially in firms without limited organizational support for the CMO, it can make sense to have a reduced role. In Chapter 13, the related context of global brand management facing country silos was addressed and the roles of facilitator (creating and managing the process of developing strategies), consultative (providing information and advice), and service provider (operating common support functions such as marketing research) were introduced. Even the role of facilitator can be a helpful way to build relationships and credibility and to influence what issues and decisions are addressed. And the service provider and consultative roles provide nonthreatening entries into silo strategies.

6. Avoid Arrogance—Engage the Business Units

Relying on authority risks appearing arbitrary and arrogant, and thereby stimulating the natural resentment and avoidance schemes that silos are only too good at. While it is crucial to have the support and delegated authority of the CEO, it is equally crucial to avoid using it, keeping it in the shadows as a silent incentive to cooperate. The CMO still needs to earn legitimacy by insights, actions, and results.

7. Deliver Excellence, Starting with the Brand Vision

It is a lot easier to get cooperation for a brand vision or brand-building program that achieves excellence. Everyone wants to be a part of (indeed, take some credit for) a home run idea. Delivering a successful program is the ultimate driver of credibility, more so than even the best credentials. Achieving excellence is easy to say and hard to do, of course, but the fact is that for a CMO trying to get traction, good is not good enough and mediocre can be terminal. In particular, if a brand vision inspires and fits the strategy, organization support will flow, and the CEO is likely to be out in front.

8. Balance Central Opportunities vs. Local Needs

The CMO charged with creating or enhancing the coordination between the silos must carefully balance the needs of the silo units with the program to be centralized. The silos should have the necessary flexibility to succeed in the marketplace. Decisions as to what should be centralized will be based on questions like:

- What programs or potential programs span markets? To what extent is coordination a key to making them effective? A major sponsorship like the Olympics or the World Cup can be an ideal vehicle to create an acceptance of cross-business teams, because they are so obviously needed and worthwhile in such cases.

- Where is functional expertise best developed? Can redundancy be reduced? It is far better to have one group with a depth of competence in an area like advertising or sponsorships than many with shallow talent and capacity.

- What brands span markets? Does market adaptation compensate for a dilution of the central message? GE Money resisted the "imagination at work" theme at first, then ultimately came to believe that the value of the corporate effort was worth taking advantage of.

- What truly requires local knowledge and management? Are there positions and programs that work across products and markets? Pringles, for example, requires different flavors in different market, but the most of the social and functional benefits work everywhere.

- What deviations in budgets, reporting lines, and authority can be tolerated? What fights are worth winning? In the case of Visa, the integrity of the brand had the highest priority—the energy to fight battles was devoted to avoiding product offerings (such as charging for converting currency) that would compromise the brand promise.

A RECAP OF STRATEGIC MARKET MANAGEMENT

Figure 15.5 provides a capstone summary of the issues raised in both strategic analysis and strategy development/refinement. It suggests a discussion agenda to help an organization ensure that the external and internal analysis has the necessary depth, breadth, and forward thinking and that the strategy creation and refinement process yields winning, sustainable strategies.

CUSTOMER ANALYSIS

- Who are the major segments?
- What are their motivations and unmet needs?

COMPETITOR ANALYSIS

- Who are the existing and potential competitors? What strategic groups can be identified?
- What are their sales, share, and profits? What are the growth trends?
- What are their strengths, weaknesses, and strategies?

MARKET/SUBMARKET ANALYSIS

- How attractive is the market or industry and its submarkets? What are the forces reducing profitability in the market, entry and exit barriers, growth projections, cost structures, and profitability prospects?
- What are the alternative distribution channels and their relative strengths?
- What industry trends and emerging submarkets are significant to strategy?
- What are the current and future key success factors?

ENVIRONMENTAL ANALYSIS

- What environmental threats, opportunities, and trends exist?
- What are the major strategic uncertainties and information-need areas?
- What scenarios can be conceived?

INTERNAL ANALYSIS

- What are our strategy, performance, points of differentiation, strengths, weaknesses, strategic problems, and culture?
- What threats and opportunities exist?

STRATEGY DEVELOPMENT

- What are the target segments? What is the production scope?
- What value propositions will be the core of the offering? Among the choices are superior attribute or benefit, appealing design, systems solution, social programs, customer relationship, niche specialist, quality, and value.
- What assets and competences will provide the basis for an SCA? How can they be developed and maintained? How can they be leveraged?
- What are the alternative functional strategies?
- What strategies best fit our strengths, our objectives, and our organization?
- What alternative growth directions should be considered? How should they be pursued?
- What investment level is most appropriate for each product market—withdrawal, milking, maintaining, or growing?

Figure 15.5 Strategy Development: A Discussion Agenda

KEY LEARNINGS

- Four key organizational components are structure, systems, people, and culture. All must be in sync with each other and with the business strategy.

- The fit challenge between components is illustrated by the hit-industry topology, which contrasts the functions of drillers (who develop products), pumpers (who focus on production), and distributors (who specialize in marketing and distribution).

- Organizational structure defines the lines of authority and communication and can vary in the degree of centralization and formality of communication channels.

- Management systems—including information, measurement and reward, and planning—can all influence strategy implementation.

- People profiles and their motivation provide the bases of competencies needed to support SCAs.

- Because organizational culture—which involves shared values, norms of behavior, symbols, and symbolic activities—is difficult to change, the fit between culture and strategy is particularly important.

- New corporate CMOs hired to stimulate growth and synergy often struggle, but eight paths to gaining traction can help.

FOR DISCUSSION

1. The Korvette concept was started and run by one person and his group of friends. How could its failure have been avoided? Was the problem one of strategy (overexpansion), or was it organizational? Why?

2. What are the advantages of decentralization? Some people argue that more centralization in needed to develop and implement strategy in these dynamic times. Express your opinion, and illustrate it with examples. When would you recommend that the central team use a facilitative role, rather than impose its advice?

3. Evaluate Mintzberg's easy steps to destroying value. Which is the most common step?

4. GE's Jack Welch believes that people are the most important ingredient to success. What are the implications of that belief?

5. Assume that you are CEO of a company like Leapfrog, which sells entertaining, electronic-based learning devices for customers ranging from infants to high school students. Describe the culture you would like to develop and maintain. How would you do that?

6. Evaluate the eight guides to a CMO wanting to get traction if a strong CEO is involved and has made the CMO task a firm priority. Which two a three would you make a priority? What if the CEO has given the charge but has disappeared as a visible supporter?

7. Consider Power Bar, the strategy for which is summarized in the case on pages 110–111. What implications for the culture, structure, systems, and people would you suggest given the nature of the product and the company. Would this change when it was purchased by Nestlé?

8. Pick a bank or other service firm. Evaluate the organizational routes to innovation.

NOTES

1. Robert F. Hartley, *Marketing Mistakes*, 5th ed., New York: Wiley, 1992, Chapter 13.

2. Henry Mintzberg, "Musings on Management," *Harvard Business Review*, July–August 1996, pp. 61–67.

3. Henry Mintzberg, "The Fall and Rise of Strategic Planning," *Harvard Business Review*, January–February 1994, pp. 107–114. Quotes are from p. 109.

4. "GE's Ten-Step Talent Plan," *Fortune*, April 17, 2000 p. 232.

5. Gordon Shaw, Robert Brown, and Philip Bromiley, "Strategic Stories: How 3M Is Rewriting Business Planning," *Harvard Business Review*, May–June 1998, pp. 41–50.

6. The hit-industry topology was developed in discussions with Dr. Norman Smothers.

7. Robert Stringer, "How to Manage Radical Innovation," *California Management Review*, Summer 2000, pp. 70–88.

Strategic Repositioning
HOBART CORPORATION

While Hobart Corporation, a manufacturer of equipment for the food service (restaurants and institutions) and retail (grocery and convenience stores) sectors for more than a century, had developed a solid reputation for high quality and extremely reliable products, it wasn't necessarily seen as an industry leader. It had credentials, however. In addition to being the largest firm in terms of sales, it also had broad coverage of the industry and its product categories and a respected service network, with some 200 locations and over 1,700 service vans. The better competitors excelled in a particular product category (refrigeration, for instance) or were well known in one of the industry sectors but lacked Hobart's breadth of offerings.

Hobart was concerned with less expensive competing products that were made overseas. Most customers were continuing to buy Hobart products, but the threat was growing. Further, it was hard to create advertising and trade show material that would break out of the clutter. Breakthrough products that would attract attention were not easily generated.

In response to these concerns, Hobart sought to establish a different customer-facing brand that would be the "thought leader" in the industry, not just the product leader. It wanted to be known for the best quality, "plus more." The driving idea was to offer solutions to everyday issues its customers faced in their businesses—things like finding, training, and retaining good workers; keeping food safe; providing enticing dining experiences; eliminating costs; reducing shrinkage; and, for some, enhancing same-sales growth. The firm systematically marshaled a knowledge base in order to address these problems.

This driving idea of solving everyday concerns led to a powerful brand-building program around the tagline, "Sound Equipment, Sound Advice." One element was a customer magazine called "Sage: Seasoned Advice for the Food Industry Professional" (now available via the Internet at Sage Online). Sage's in-depth, objective treatment of customer problems and issues made it feel more like a newsstand publication than a corporate promotional tool. At industry trade shows, the Hobart company booth had an "Idea Center" where people could approach industry experts for sound advice about the problems they faced in their businesses. They conducted seminars using leading experts; "The State of Collegiate Dining" was one topic. Internally, the leadership message was reinforced at department and company-wide meetings and through internal newsletters.

Hobart also offered useful content about key issues on its website, hobartcorp.com. Visitors could find papers, question-and-answer sessions with industry experts, briefing documents, and other material updated on a weekly basis. This program has grown to over 100 technical papers on technology, saving labor, reducing shrinkage, productivity, improving food safety, growing sales, and cost management. The brand lived on the Web and in other places as well, thanks to the strategic placement of Hobart content on many other sites frequented by people in the industry. Select elements of this Web content were converted to printed pieces and disseminated broadly.

Hobart shared more sound advice through speeches at key industry shows, events like the Home Meal Replacement Summit, and articles for trade magazines (for example, "Cold War: Smart Refrigeration Arms Restaurateurs Against Food-Borne Illnesses" in *Hotel Magazine*). The goal of public relations became idea placement, rather than product placement. Hobart also changed its approach to new product releases to emphasize how each product helps the customer deal with key business issues. For instance, rather than emphasize specific features like the recessed nozzles on the Hobart TurboWash, the firm communicated how easy it made the task of scrubbing pots and pans, thereby creating happier restaurant and food service employees.

Print advertising, once the prime brand-building tool, played a lesser but still important role, focusing on key customer issues. For instance, one ad showed a sign at a bathroom sink reading, "Employees Must Wash Hands Before Returning to Work." The text underneath the picture asked, "Need a more comprehensive approach to food safety?" and then described the solutions recommended by Hobart.

FOR DISCUSSION

1. Why do chefs buy Hobart for their kitchens?

2. What was the value proposition before the "Solid Equipment, Sound Advice" program? How did it change?

3. What functional strategies did Hobart pursue?

4. The new program soaked up resources, thereby reducing the effort to communicate new product innovations. Was that a wise decision? Which approach is likely to create better support toward a quality position?

5. How could competitors position themselves against Hobart's strategic position? What criteria would be useful in developing this strategic position?

Source: Adapted with the permission of the Free Press, a division of Simon & Schuster Adult Publishing Group from *Brand Leadership*, by David A. Aaker and Erich Joachimsthaler. Copyright © 2000 by David A. Aaker and Erich Joachimsthaler. All rights reserved.

Developing and Countering SCAs, and the Perils of Success
XEROX: THE EARLY DAYS

When Chester Carlson invented xerography in the 1930s, he attempted to market his idea to a host of firms, including Kodak and General Electric. All viewed the rather crude invention as unnecessary in the face of carbon paper and the coated-paper copiers of the day. Finally, in the 1950s, a small firm took the gamble. The result was the Xerox 914, introduced in 1959, which truly revolutionized the copying industry. The first plain-paper copier, it was easy to use and operated at seven copies per minute. The 914 was responsible for the number of copies made in the United States increasing from 20 million to 9.5 billion in only ten years.

The Xerox business strategy through the 1970s involved several pillars. First, the machines were leased at $95 per month, including 2,000 free copies per month to firms who mistakenly felt that their use would never exceed that level. Second, an extensive direct sales and service operation was developed to market the 914 and more expensive models, all of which were relatively complex and needed informed salespeople and responsive service. Third, the R&D focused on the high end of the market, where the best margins were. The low end was virtually ceded to the Japanese, first with coated-paper machines and later with inexpensive plain-paper products. Fourth, international growth was based on a joint venture with Fuji.

The fifth pillar, a major strategic thrust for Xerox in the 1970s, was the "Office of the Future." This concept recognized that the copier was only one instrument of office productivity and business communication, and Xerox wanted to be a leader in the broader playing field. Clearly, the key to the strategy was a computer capability. To fill that gaping hole, Xerox in 1969 purchased Scientific Data Systems, a firm that targeted the scientific community, and changed its name to Xerox Data Systems (XDS). Despite pouring investment into XDS, the firm's products for the business data-processing market never had any success in the office, Xerox's territory. Further, the Xerox organization had too many layers of bureaucracy in too many locations to encourage the integration of computer and copier products. In 1975, after six years of losses, Xerox closed XDS, judging that the computer mainframe market was not part of its core business after all.

Competitors: Savin, Canon, IBM, and Kodak

Savin was a small company obsessed with participating in the copier market and frustrated by the patent chokehold of Xerox. Finally, with the help of an Australian inventor and a consortium of firms from the United States, Germany, and Japan, Savin developed a liquid-toner approach that avoided Xerox patents. Its breakthrough became the Savin 750, manufactured by Ricoh in Japan and introduced in 1975 at $4,999, less than the (then) annual lease price of a Xerox machine. Instead of a direct sales force, Savin sold through dealers who would contact Xerox customers with an attractive alternative when their contracts expired. Dealer service was feasible because the machine was relatively small and reliable; the Savin 750 averaged 17,000 copies between failures. It made twenty copies per minute, the first in less than five seconds, a pace far superior to Xerox efforts at the low end. By 1977, Savin placed more copiers in the United States than Xerox. Meanwhile, Ricoh captured the top market share in Japan, as measured in units.

Canon also avoided the Xerox patents by developing an alternative technology that was licensed to other Japanese firms. Rather than using joint ventures, Canon deliberately decided to market its copiers throughout the world under its own name, even though that would mean relatively slow market penetration in a fast-moving industry. In the long run, keeping control of the brand and operations became a strength. Canon struggled in the United States until 1978, when its NP-80 combined with an aggressive advertising campaign, succeeded in the mid-volume market. By 1979, Canon became a leader among the Japanese copier firms. In 1982, it introduced its Personal Copier, which sold for under $1,000 and had a $65 disposable cartridge. The slower copying speed was unimportant to the target customers, who wanted a small, inexpensive, worry-free machine for the home or office. In 1985, with Savin fading, Canon became the world leader in low-end machines and the second overall company behind Xerox.

IBM attempted through the 1970s to participate in the copier market with a series of products. It was generally unsuccessful, despite its famous name and a large sales force, in part because it was technologically behind and its products were unreliable.

Kodak entered the market in 1975 with its Ektaprint 100, a plain-paper copier that soon became the industry standard for reliability in the mid-volume market. The firm then developed a series of high-end machines that were by many measures the best in the industry. Kodak moved slowly, however, making sure the products were reliable, carefully building a strong service and marketing organization, and avoiding building capacity too quickly. Kodak was still able to move into fourth place in copier sales by 1985 because of its technology, reputation, and resources—and because Xerox was not successful in developing comparable products. A Xerox executive opined that if IBM, with its size and superior marketing skills, had the Kodak machine it would have aggressively captured market share at the middle and high ends, and Xerox would have been severely damaged.

Problems at Xerox

After many years of dramatic success, Xerox faced significant threats in 1980. The firm managed to hold onto its dominance in medium- and high-speed machines, still controlling 60 percent of the market for machines over $40,000 in 1981. Performance at the lower end was much worse, however, and as a result Xerox's share of U.S. copier revenues declined dramatically, from 96 percent in 1970 to 46 percent in 1980. Between 1976 and 1982, Xerox's share of worldwide copier revenues dropped from 82 percent to 41 percent. Why? How did this happen?

One problem was the development of an unwieldy bureaucracy. In 1966, an executive from Ford was brought in to control an undisciplined organization that was expanding at an unmanageable rate. The result was a divisional structure that looked too much like an auto firm, with a painfully complex and slow process of getting a product from design to manufacturing to marketing. Throughout this marathon, the product would be subjected to a system (adopted from NASA) of staged program management, which entailed constant review and criticism.

In part because of this organizational paralysis, Xerox was not able to respond to the Kodak threat at the high end of the market. Xerox had long prided itself on its superior technology, but it actually lagged behind in product development. In the 1970s, it introduced three completely new machines, only one of which was a success—and that one cost more that $300 million to develop. For Xerox to have grown as it did during this decade was more a tribute to its sales force than to the quality of its products.

One of Xerox's major problems in the 1970s was its focus on making the largest, fastest, and fanciest machines. It paid far less attention to reliability, and therefore it was not prepared to compete with machines made by Kodak. Rather than being lean and trim, it became bloated and failed to locate low-cost outsourcing opportunities. When machines like the Savin 750 were introduced, Xerox could not compete in either price or quality.

Despite its large staff, Xerox was weak in customer and market research, even as it transitioned from being a virtual monopoly to a participant in a competitive market. In particular, Xerox gave no thought to the fact that its customers might be willing to trade speed for price and reliability, or that they might prefer to have more smaller, slower machines rather than a few large, faster ones.

Xerox USA ignored the Japanese threat, allowing those firms to get a foothold at the low end of the market that they exploited by moving up. One rationale was that the early Japanese machines were of low quality and priced too high; the Savin 750 was a shock. A second rationale was that the margins at the higher end were much more attractive than those at the low end. Xerox USA, however, failed to recognize that the Japanese firms would use their advantage further down to climb the market ladder. There was also a strong "not invented here" syndrome. After introducing its 2200 model in Japan in 1973, Fuji Xerox offered to export it to the United States, but Xerox USA refused, unable to believe that a Japanese product would be up to Xerox USA standards. It was not until 1979 that Xerox USA finally accepted a Fuji Xerox machine for the American market.

FOR DISCUSSION

1. Identify and evaluate Xerox's strategy in the 1960s. What entry barriers did Xerox create in that decade?

2. Identify and evaluate the strategies of Savin, Canon, IBM, and Kodak. How did each overcome Xerox's entry barriers? Kodak did not aggressively invest behind its equipment at a time when it held a significant technological edge. Why?

3. Why did Xerox lose position in the 1970s? How could that happen? How could a large, successful, admired company be so clueless?

4. What were the strengths and weaknesses of Xerox in the 1980s? What were its strategic imperatives?

5. Xerox had a research think tank in Palo Alto that essentially developed what became the Apple computer. When the Xerox organization was not interested, Steve Jobs and others accessed the concept and started Apple. Why do you think such a blunder happened?

Source: Drawn in part from John Hillkirk and Gary Jacobson, *Xerox: American Samurai,* New York: Macmillan, 1986, pp. 55–57.

DOVE
Leveraging a Brand Asset

In 1955, Unilever (then Lever Brothers) introduced Dove, which contained a patented, mild cleansing ingredient, into the soap category. It was positioned—then and now—as a "beauty bar" with one-fourth cleansing cream that moisturizes skin while washing (as opposed to the drying effect of regular soap). Advertisements reinforced the message by showing the cream being poured into the beauty bar. In 1979, the phrase "cleansing cream" was replaced with "moisturizer cream."

Also in 1979, a University of Pennsylvania dermatologist showed that Dove dried and irritated skin significantly less than ordinary soaps. Based on this study, Unilever began aggressively marketing Dove to doctors. Soon about 25 percent of Dove users said they bought the brand because a doctor recommended it, greatly enhancing the bar's credibility as a moisturizer. By the mid-1980s, Dove had become the best-selling soap brand and commanded a price premium.

The first effort to extend the Dove brand occurred in 1965. The extension, into dishwashing detergent, survives but has to be regarded as disappointing. Because the leading competitor at the time, Palmolive, promised to "soften hands while you do dishes," the hope was that the Dove cleansing-cream message would translate into a competitive benefit. Instead, customers felt no reason to change from the well-positioned Palmolive, and since Dove's reputation for moisturizing and beauty did not imply clean dishes, there was simply no perceived benefit. After receiving weak market acceptance for the extension, Dove lowered the price, creating another source of strain on the brand. Fifteen years after its launch, the brand languished at a rather poor seventh in the U.S. market, with a share of around 3 percent. The dishwashing detergent not only failed to enhance the Dove brand, it also undoubtedly inhibited Dove from extending its franchise further for decades.

In 1990 the Dove soap patent ran out, and arch-competitor P&G was soon testing an Olay beauty bar with moisturizing properties, a product that rolled out in 1993. One year later, Olay body wash appeared and soon garnered over 25 percent of a high-margin product category. Blindsided, the Dove brand team belatedly recognized that theirs was the natural brand to own the moisturizer body wash position. The firm had apparently missed the chance to be a leader in this new subcategory.

In response to Olay, the firm rushed Dove Moisturizing Body Wash into stores. The product did not live up to the Dove promise, however, and a reformulation in 1996 was only a partial improvement. In 1999, though, Dove finally got it right with the innovative Nutrium line, based on a technology that deposited lipids, vitamin E, and other ingredients onto the skin. The advanced skin-nourishing properties provided enough of a lift to allow Dove to charge a 50 percent premium over its regular body wash. Later, Dove introduced a version of Nutrium with antioxidants (which have been linked to reduced signs of aging), which helped Dove to pull even with Olay in the body wash category. By leveraging strong brand equity, pursuing innovative technology, and being persistent, Dove was able to overcome a late entry into the market.

The Dove body wash efforts influenced the brand's soap business, which was flat until the mid-1990s (and, in fact, declined in 1996). The introduction of the body wash corresponded to a 30 percent growth surge in Dove soap from the mid-1990s to 2001, evidence that the energy and exposure of the Dove brand helped even though the product was somewhat waning during much of that period. In addition, the Nutrium subbrand, established in the body wash category, was employed to help the soap business. In 2001, Unilever introduced a Dove Nutrium soap (positioned as replenishing skin nutrients) that was priced about 30 percent higher than regular Dove.

Another battlefield, entered in 2000, was the rather mature category of deodorants—even though dryness, the key benefit, seemed contradictory to the Dove promise of moisturizing, and the target segment was younger than the typical Dove customer. Despite these apparent risks, Dove introduced a deodorant line with uncharacteristically bold advertising (for example, one tag line was "Next stop, armpit heaven"). As it turned out, the deodorants were named as one of the top ten nonfood new products in 2001, garnering over $70 million in sales with close to 5 percent of the market, making Dove the number two brand among female deodorants. The "one-quarter moisturizing lotion" positioning, effectively communicated as protecting sensitive underarm skin, generated a Dove spin on dryness that differentiated the product line.

In spite of this win, P&G's Olay again beat Dove to a new market in the summer of 2000, this time with disposable face cloths infused with moisturizers. It took Dove about a year to respond with its Dove Daily Hydrating Cleansing Cloths. With the body wash success behind it, however, the Dove brand was well suited to compete in this category.

The next product extension was Dove Hair Care, whose moisturizing qualities were directly responsive to one of the top two unmet needs in the category. The product's branded differentiator, Weightless Moisturizers, is a set of fifteen ingredients designed to make the hair softer, smoother, and more vibrant without adding any extra weight. After achieving top-selling status in Japan and Taiwan, Dove Hair Care entered the U.S. market in early 2003 with a massive introduction campaign, joining a product family used by nearly one-third of American families. Two years later it introduced Dove Body Nourishers Intensive Firming Lotion, formulated with collagen and seaweed, intended to give the user firmer skin after two weeks.

These extensions contributed to a dramatic sales success. The brand's business grew from probably around $200 million in 1990 (the bar itself was doing $330 million in 2003) to over $3 billion in 2005. Geographic expansion also contributed. Dove had a presence in eighty countries in 2005, far more than in 1990, with particular strength in Europe (where it gained 30 percent of the cosmetics and toiletries market), Asia-Pacific (25 percent), and Latin America (11 percent).

In 2005, with no major geographic expansion or brand extension in sight, Dove looked to another route to add energy. The result was advertising campaign (first created in the United Kingdom) featuring "real women" with real dress sizes instead of ultra-thin models. Dove branded campaigns to educate and inspire girls to adopt a wider definition of beauty and to achieve a higher self-esteem level supplemented the advertising. The new direction for the brand was based in part on a global study involving 3,200 interviews that revealed that only 2 percent of women thought themselves beautiful, 50 percent of women thought they weight was too high (60 percent in the United States), and two-thirds of women felt that the media and advertising set an unrealistic standard of beauty. The campaign received enormous exposure in the media with over a thousand stories, most but not all positive (some felt it would be ineffective, others pointed out that Unilever was still using models for its other products, and still others thought Dove was promoting obesity). It generated a 10 percent sales boost.

FOR DISCUSSION

1. Why was Dove dormant for so long?

2. What were the keys to the success that Dove achieved in building its brand into a $3 billion business? What was the role of success momentum? The subbrand?

3. What was the role of a vigorous competitor? Would Dove have gotten there without P&G pushing (or, more accurately, pulling) the brand?

4. Why were Dove soap sales affected by the other Dove successes?

5. What does this case tell you about first-mover advantage?

6. What is your opinion of the "Real Beauty" campaign?

Source: Adapted with the permission of the Free Press, a division of Simon & Schuster Adult Publishing Group from *Brand Portfolio Strategy: Creating Relevance, Differentiation, Energy, Leverage, and Clarity,* by David A. Aaker. Copyright © 2004 by David A. Aaker. All rights reserved.

Evaluating and Assessing the Implications of a Transformation Innovation
TRANSFORMATIONAL INNOVATIONS

Business 2.0 nominated several firms with the potential to be game changers with transformational innovations. The magazine noted that the telephone was dismissed in 1876 by Western Union Telegraph (which was offered the technology for $100,000) and by J. Pierpoint Morgan, who called it a novelty with no commercial application. Yet the telephone as we know now transformed the communication industry. Will these firms transform industries as well? Or will they be historical footnotes?

Zopa—Peer-to-Peer Lending

Banking is a highly profitable industry, based in large part on its capacity to lend money provided by savers and in part by its use of credit cards to generate loans at high interest rates. Zopa provides an alternative to banks by enabling people to lend to each other; both the borrower and lender potentially receive better rates than a bank would offer. People join Zopa either as borrowers or lenders. Zopa assesses the credit risk of borrowers using conventional information such as credit reports and verified income, as well as less conventional sources such as eBay ratings. Both borrowers and lenders are pooled so that an individual lender actually is part of a group that will lend money to a group of borrowers, thereby reducing default risks. Zopa processes the payments and receives a 1 percent fee shared by the borrow and lender.

Zopa is established in the United Kingdom. In 2006, it had some 90,000 members, was processing around $100,000 a day (a $10 million a year rate), and was planning to launch in the United States.

Eestor—A New Automobile Power Source

Eestor, formed in 2001, is developing a new solid-state battery in the form of high-power-density ceramic ultra-capacitors called Electrical Storage Units (ESUs). Although the technology is kept confidential by Eestor, reports indicate that an ESU can store over 10 times the energy of lead acid batteries at one-tenth the weight, can be recharged in minutes, has virtually unlimited recharge cycles, and has no overheating risk or hazardous materials.

The automobile market is an important potential application. Eestor's ESUs can run not only small automobiles but even large SUVs. It has been estimated that an Eestor-powered car could drive 500 miles on about $9 worth of electricity and that the engine would cost just over $5,000, where a convention gasoline engine costs from $3,000 to $5,000. A Toronto maker of low-speed electric cars called Feel Good Cars has apparently obtained an exclusive worldwide right to purchase ESUs from Eestor and is expecting to offer automobiles sometime around 2008.

NextMedium

NextMedium facilitates the marketing of brand integration (a term that includes product placement but also brand presence without an actual product) in television shows, movies, and video games. For entertainment companies, NextMedium will help them present their inventory of potential brand integration opportunities, with minimum bids set forth. It will then put that inventory in front of advertisers. When a brand integration opportunity is purchased, there is check-off approval by the creative entertainment professional. For advertisers, this will provide an easy to use way to view and select from the inventory of brand integration options. Advertisers through NextMedium can view or listen to their placement in its context. In addition, NextMedium will also monitor the placement and provide information on the size and composition of the audience exposed to the placement.

FOR DISCUSSION

For each potential transformational innovation, answer the following questions.

1. Who are the industries and firms for which this would be a threat? What is the nature of the threat? How would you go about evaluating it? How can you forecast the impact? What similar examples from history can provide insights? How do they differ? How can you avoid making a decision like the Western Union CEO in 1876? Could this be an opportunity as well for these same firms? What prevents them from participating in the new technology?

2. Will this technology expand the market, bringing in new customers, or will it simply replace the existing business?

3. What are the strategic options for the firms with the transformational technology? What are the pros and cons of each?

4. How would you go about branding and positioning the new product class being proposed? How should it be labeled?

Source: Erick Schonfeld and Jeanette Borzo, "The Next Disruptors," *Business 2.0,* October 2006, pp. 80–96.

Charting a Risky Direction Without Internal Support

SAMSUNG ELECTRONICS

Samsung Electronics, which began in 1972 as a manufacturer of cheap black-and-white television sets, had sales of over $34 billion and a net profit of $5.9 billion in 2002—less than Microsoft's profits, but more than IBM and Nokia (who ranked third and fourth in industry profitability). In part due to its product leadership, Samsung achieved third place in worldwide mobile handset sales (after Nokia, and closing in on Motorola for second), became the second leading seller of semiconductors (after Intel), and was the largest manufacturer of television sets and computer monitors in the world.

The Samsung products delivered function and more. From plasma TV screens to robotic vacuum cleaners to refrigerator-freezers that tell you when you are low on milk to bracelet cell phones, they were cool and had a buzz about them. *Business Week* recognized Samsung as the top information technology company in the world, and its brand was valued by Interbrand at $8.3 billion (ranking thirty-fourth in the world). This performance was astounding, given that only five years earlier Samsung was financially crippled in the face of a Korean economic crisis and some bad strategic decisions.

In some respects, it was the worst of times in late 1996 when Yun Jong Yong became CEO of Samsung Electronics. He addressed the financial crisis in part by cutting some 24,000 employees, shutting factories, and selling business units. But in the face of this adversity, he set the stage for gaining global leadership by enunciating a bold strategy.

The strategy had several components. First, Samsung would change its market position in the United States and Europe from a price-oriented copycat manufacturer to a premium-priced product leader whose wares were sold in the most upscale retail outlets. (Almost no one on Yun's management team agreed with this direction, as it meant walking away from much of the firm's business and would be risky to implement.) Second, Samsung would continue its policy to be vertically integrated and turn its memory and component design and manufacturing into an asset by providing direct access to the latest technology. Nearly all other firms felt that strategic flexibility required moving away from vertical integration. Third, Samsung would be a leader in creating new products designed to be distinctive and cool; the organization would become much faster to market with these products. Fourth, it would build the brand, especially outside Korea, a step that would be crucial in becoming the leader in the near future.

The new course was somewhat aided by the new management initiative launched in 1993 by Lee Kun-Hee, the CEO of the Samsung Group (of which Samsung Electronics is a part). No less than a total change in the way that the group thought, worked, and served customers, the initiative included a focus on quality, listening to markets, creating distinctive advantages, being the best, anticipating the future, creating an organizational environment to foster innovation and growth, and contributing to a better global society. The initiative was relaunched in 1996 after it received little initial traction. As part of the relaunch, Lee in 1996 set up a training center for information-related infrastructure topics.

There were several key aspects to the implementation of Yun's strategy for Samsung Electronics. One was the hiring of Eric Kim to be the global marketing head in 1999. Kim, who left Korea at the age of thirteen, had an engineering and marketing background. He was determined to get the global silos to be on the same page. Toward that end he consolidated the disparate business operations and drove toward a single vision based on the new cool, upscale Samsung brand of technology leadership in digital convergence. He replaced the company's fifty-five advertising agencies with one global agency. In part to emphasize the global future of the firm, Kim made his first big presentation in Korea to four hundred top Samsung managers in English.

Another initiative was sponsorship and advertising. Yun believed that the new Samsung could best be communicated by sports sponsorship. The logic was that sports competition, which involved hard work by athletes striving to achieve their highest potential, suited the industry and the associations that Samsung wanted to nurture. Sports also provided a stage to demonstrate technology. Samsung sponsored several events, including the 1998 Bangkok Asian Games, but the crown jewel was the sponsorship of the Olympics, starting with the 1998 Winter Games in Nagano, Japan. In 1999, Samsung embarked on a $400 million advertising effort around the tag line "DIGITall." This slogan signaled that Samsung was a leader in the digital convergence world, which would apply to all people and all products.

Among the misadventures of Samsung that contributed to the financial crises of 1997 was its experience with AST, which in the early 1990s was among the top four manufacturers of personal computers in the United States. AST was struggling to keep up, however, and began losing money at an alarming rate—in part because its acquisition of the Tandy PC business in 1993 was not managed well, and also because its product development tended to be late (the firm missed a Christmas selling season one year). Meanwhile Samsung, which sold 30 percent of the computers purchased in Korea, tried and failed in its effort to crack the critical U.S. market, a failure attributed to a lack of marketing savvy and distribution clout. Its solution was to invest in AST in 1995, buying the entire company in 1997. A Korean CEO, inserted in 1996, instituted needed manufacturing efficiencies and some co-marketing efforts with Disney. When that did not stem the tide and an effort to focus on the business market failed, Samsung bailed out in December 1998, after having lost well over $1 billion.

FOR DISCUSSION

1. Yun lacked support for his new strategy. How important is organizational buy-in for a CEO's strategy? How valuable is it to have the buy-in be enthusiastic? How can the CEO gain support for a strategy?

2. What are the organizational implications of vertical integration and the new product program? With respect to vertical integration, how would you make sure that the component suppliers have incentives to become efficient even though their customer is captive?

3. How would you change the reward system to reflect the new strategy? In the past, all units were largely measured on sales and market share. How would you change that, if at all? How would you implement any changes?

4. Why didn't Lee's initiative gain traction in 1993? What is needed to make it happen?

5. How should Kim gain acceptance for himself and his ideas? Was it risky to speak in English? In creating a global strategy, would you use a top-down or bottom-up approach?

6. Do you agree with the logic of the Olympic sponsorship? How would you get organizational support for it? How would you decide what sports events to sponsor? Can you recommend a different strategy for communication instead of the sports connection?

7. What was the objective of the AST acquisition? Why did it fail?

Source: Samsung Electronics annual reports, 1997 to 2002; Cliff Edwards, Moon Ihlwan, and Pete Engardio, "The Samsung Way," *Business Week*, June 16, 2003, pp. 56–61.

APPENDIX

Planning Forms

A set of standard forms can be helpful in presenting strategy recommendations and supporting analyses. They can encourage the useful consistency of the presentation over time and across businesses within an organization. They can also provide a checklist of areas to consider in strategy development and make communication easier. The following sample forms are intended to provide a point of departure in designing forms for a specific context. The external analysis in the example is drawn from the pet food industry. The forms are for illustration purposes only.

Planning forms need to be adapted to the context involved: the industry, the firm, and the planning context. They may well be different and shorter or longer given a particular context. Forms for use with other product types—an industrial product, for example—could be modified to include information such as current and potential applications or key existing or potential customers.

THE PET FOOD INDUSTRY

Section 1. Customer Analysis

A. Segments

Segments	Market (Billions)	Comments
Dog—dry	5.5	Largest segment, segmented nutritional offerings, growing
Dog—canned	1.4	Made from dairy products, etc.
Cat—dry	2.6	Second largest segment, nutritional offerings, accelerating growth
Cat—canned	1.6	Made from animal by-products, dairy products, etc.
Dog treats	1.3	Del Monte dominates with Milk-Bone
Pet Specialty	4.6	Large players—Science Diet and Iams, uses vets and pet stores, about 70% dog food, mostly dry, growing at 5%

B. Customer Motivations

Segment	Motivations
Dog—dry	Nutrition, not messy, not smelly, easy to serve, teeth cleaning
Dog—canned	For finicky dogs, taste and nutrition variety
Cat—dry	Nutrition, easy to serve, complement to meal, teeth cleaning
Cat—canned	Taste, cat will like, convenient sizes, easy to serve, finicky cats, variety
Treats	Complement to meal, reward, animal likes it, functional nutritional benefits (e.g., tartar control)
Pet Specialty	Health concern, scientific nutrition, perceived superior ingredients

C. Unmet Needs

Information on pets
Further subneeds of segments (as defined by human nutrition, e.g., allergies)

Section 2. Competitor Analysis

A. Competitor Identification

Most directly competitive: Nestlé Purina Petcare, Del Monte, Mars.
Less directly competitive: Hill Petfood (Colgate Palmolive), Iams (P&G)

B. Strategic Groups

Strategic Group	Major Competitors	Share
(1) Mainstream brands from large consumer firms	Nestlé Purina Petcare	32%
	Mars	11%
	Del Monte	10%
(2) High-end specialty brands	Iams (P&G)	12%
	Hill's (Colgate-Palmolive)	10%
	Other	9%
(3) Private-label brands	Wal-Mart	7%
	Other	4%

Strategic Group	Characteristics/ Strategies	Strengths	Weaknesses
(1) *Mainstream brands from large consumer firms*	*Mainstream products* • *Large portfolio of products* • *Heavy use of advertising* • *Premium/niche products* • *Sell to multiple channels* • *Emphasis on quality improvement*	• *Production scale economies* • *Huge presence in supermarkets, where 35% of industry volume is sold* • *Deep global financial resources* • *Commitment to industry*	• *High-fixed cost commitment to capacity increases competitive pressure on all players to defend share through promotions, etc.* • *Perception as less nutritious than specialty brands* • *Supermarket channel is losing share to other channels* • *Private labeling at Wal-Mart and elsewhere is increasing*
(2) *High-end specialty pet food brands*	• *Narrowly focused, premium-priced product lines* • *High presence in nonsupermarket channels, such as veterinary offices, pet breeders, and specialty stores*	• *Product line focus on health, natural ingredients, and nutrition, resulting in strong consumer demand; high-margin business* • *First-in advantage to high-end specialty segment, resulting in a perceptual edge that supermarket brands find difficult to overcome* • *Sell through alternative channels, which are growing faster and are less competitive and offer limited access to other brands, a barrier to entry*	• *Higher ingredient and production costs* • *Introduction of Iams into grocery and mass merchandise channels narrow differentiation* • *All major national competitors are going after the fast-growing specialty channels*

Strategic Group	Characteristics/ Strategies	Strengths	Weaknesses
(3) Private-label pet foods	• Sell through multiple supermarkets and mass merchandisers under house brand designation	• High volume and low unit costs • Profit margins are attractive to retailers • Power of Wal-Mart as number one retailer (Wal-Mart has 7% of the market) • High-quality offerings with high perceived consumer value	• Little brand differentiation • Low-margin business

C. Major Competitors

Competitor	Characteristics/ Strategies	Strengths	Weaknesses
Nestlé Purina Petcare	• Overall market leader, very broad product line • Increasing emphasis on niche product lines and upgrade of products to premium status • Heavy emphasis on innovative first-to-market new products • Massive advertising and promotional spending to grow share • High commitment to category • Deep financial resources • Company takes long-term view on brand-building efforts; high level of commitment to brands • Global commitment to building brands	• Economies of scale, low costs • Supply-chain efficiencies	• Less developed in nonsupermarket channels • Weak presence in specialty segment • Need to support multiple brands across multiple categories with finite resources

Competitor	Characteristics/Strategies	Strengths	Weaknesses
Del Monte	• *Emphasis on cat food and dog treats, but competes in all segments of market categories* • *Low-cost producer strategy* • *Migrating to a more consumer-centric model with recent acquisitions*	• *Focused on few brands and categories*	• *Relatively weak in brand building* • *Milking strong brands, such as 9-Lives* • *Lack of product innovation in cat food*
Mars	• *Leadership position outside of the U.S.* • *Commitment to building brands* • *Upgrading supermarket brands for premium appeal*	• *Dog food expertise* • *Economies of scale, low costs with acquisition of the private-label supplier Doane* • *Deep financial resources* • *Private firm gives freedom from short-term pressures* • *Packaging renovation*	• *Lack of cat food expertise in U.S.*
Hill's Petfood	• *Leader in specialty and vet markets* • *Entry barriers in vet business for Science Diet brand*	• *Leading recipient of veterinary recommendation* • *Best niche-market product positioning in the industry*	• *No presence in supermarkets, where 35% of industry volume is sold*
Iams (P&G)	• *Traditionally a specialty market brand, with emphasis on specialty-store sales and referrals from pet breeders* • *Moved to grocery and mass merchandise channel which stimulated growth*	• *Deep financial recourses* • *Strong brand equity*	• *Economies of scale* • *Limited market penetration*

D. Competitor Strength Grid

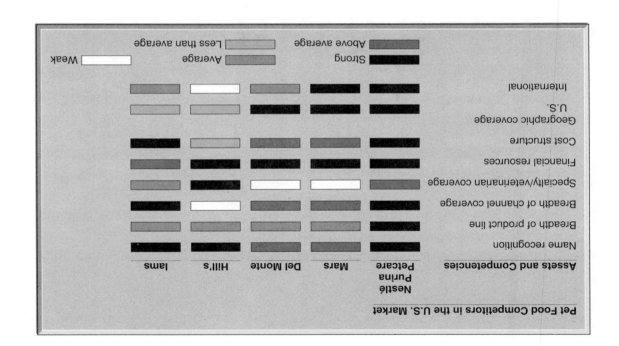

Pet Food Competitors in the U.S. Market

Assets and Competencies	Nestlé Purina Petcare	Mars	Del Monte	Hill's	Iams
Name recognition					
Breadth of product line					
Breadth of channel coverage					
Specialty/veterinarian coverage					
Financial resources					
Cost structure					
Geographic coverage U.S.					
International					

Strong — Above average — Average — Less than average — Weak

Section 3. Market Analysis

A. *Market Identification: The U.S. Pet Food Market*

B. *Market Size*

	1990	1995	2000	2005
U.S. industry sales ($ in billions)	7.7	9.1	11.1	13.9

Emerging Submarkets

- Special diet-based products
- Wal-Mart and other private-label products
- Wellness-focused items (e.g., Naturals)

Market Growth

- Overall pet—growing at 4 percent
- Supermarket—flat
- Specialty store—growing at 5 percent annually
- Mass merchandisers—growing at 4 percent
- Drug—growing at 9 percent

Factors Affecting Sales Levels

- Growth of pet population
- Growth of higher-value products

C. *Market Profitability Analysis*

Barriers to Entry

- Brand awareness, budget for marketing programs, access to distribution channels, large investment required for manufacturing, science, and technology.
- For pet specialty segment—loyalty to Iams and Hill's Science Diet; difficulty of getting recommendations of vets and other influentials.

Potential Entrants

- Other marketing giants, such as Unilever, might enter this industry if they feel it is attractive. However, the probability of new entrants is quite low, because pet food industry is already very competitive, with lots of incumbents, and barriers to entry are high.

Threats of Substitutes

- Human food leftovers
- Food cooked especially for pets

Bargaining Power of Suppliers

- Growing. Raw materials shared with human food markets. Consolidation of suppliers. Quality of raw ingredients requirements growing.

Bargaining Power of Customers

- Grocery stores, warehouse clubs have strong bargaining power over pet food suppliers.
- Specialty stores, veterinarians might have moderate bargaining power.
- Mass merchandisers (especially Wal-Mart, with around 24 percent of the volume in this category) have strong bargaining power.

D. Cost Structure

- Diversified firms have lower cost because of economies in advertising, manufacturing, promotion, and distribution.
- Specialized firms have higher costs.

E. Distribution System
Major Channels

- Supermarkets are dominant in terms of quantity they deal with (35 percent).
- Mass merchandisers handle about 29 percent of market and are growing.
- Pet foods are effective traffic builders in supermarkets and mass merchandisers.
- Farm-supply stores are located in suburbs and local areas.
- Pet stores handle most premium brands and some national brands.
- Veterinarians handle only superpremium brands.

Observations/Major Trends

- Vets' sales are flat and have very high margins both for producers and for themselves.
- Specialty stores' sales are growing at 5 percent.
- These two channels have captured high-involvement customers' needs to feed their pets healthier foods.
- Warehouses have gained footholds in market-leader brands.
- Innovations in packaging have addressed unmet needs.
- Product innovations are creating subcategories.

F. Market Trends and Developments

- Premium and superpremium brands have grown, and most producers are introducing new products in this area.
- Large manufacturers are introducing new products continuously.

G. *Key Success Factors*

Present

- Brand recognition
- Product quality
- Access to major channels
- Gain market share in premium brands
- Introduction of new products
- Breadth of product line
- Marketing program
- Cost reduction
- Awareness or recommendation by specialists
- Packaging
- Capitalizing on relevant human trends (naturals; shift to healthier, higher-quality ingrediants)

Future

- Continue to capture the trends of consumers
- Packaging
- Follow the trends of distributors

Section 4. Environmental Analysis

A. Trends and Potential Events

Source	Description	Strategic Implication	Time Frame	Importance
Technological	New product forms	Limited		Low
Regulatory	Impose standards of content	Limited		Low
Economic	Insensitive to economic changes	Very limited		Low
Cultural	Think of pets as members of families	Growth of superpremium brands	Since the mid-1980s	High
	Demand for new, healthy products	Introduction of healthy products		
	Users' needs have diversified	Multiple specialized segments		
Demographic	Household formation is slowing	Continued innovation of product and communications to keep brands relevant	Since the 1980s	Med–High
	The number of cats is increasing more than dogs			
	The baby boomer is aging			
Threats	High dependence on animal proteins	Risk of animal-borne diseases (BSE) could severely impact ingredient	Current	High
Opportunities	Growing market for premium brands	There is still room for growth in specialized segments	Since the mid-1980s	High
	Expanding market for private labels			

B. *Scenario Analysis*

Two most likely are:

1. Little growth in specialty-store and superpremium segments.
2. High growth in both specialty-store and superpremium segments.

C. *Key Strategic Uncertainties*

- Will growth in demand for superpremium specialty products continue?
- What new subcategories will emerge as significant markets?

Section 5. Internal Analysis

A. *Performance Analysis*

Objective Area	Objective	Status and Comment
1. Sales		
2. Profits		
3. Quality/service		
4. Cost		
5. New products		
6. Customer satisfaction		
7. People		
8. Other		

B. *Summary of Past Strategy*

C. Strategic Problems

Problem	Possible Action

D. Characteristics of Internal Organization

Component[*]	Description—Fit with Current/Proposed Strategy

[*] Structure, systems, culture, and people.

E. Portfolio Analysis

Note: An SBU (strategic business unit) can be defined by product or by segment.

F. Analysis of Strengths and Weaknesses

Reference	Competencies/Competency Deficiencies, Assets/Liabilities, Strengths/Weaknesses with Respect to Strategic Groups
Strategic Group	

G. Financial Projections Based on Existing Strategy

	Past	Present	Projected
Operating Statement			
Market share			
Sales			
Cost of goods sold			
Gross margin			
R&D			
Selling/advertising			
Product G&A			
Div. & corp. G&A			
Operating profit			
Balance Sheet			
Cash/AR/inventory			
AP			
Net current assets			
Fixed assets at cost			
Accumulated depreciation			
Net fixed assets			
Total assets—book value			
Estimated market value of assets			
ROA (base—book value)			
ROA (base—market value)			
Uses of Funds			
Net current assets			
Fixed asset			
Operating profit			
Depreciation			
Other			
Resources Required			

Note: Resources required could be workers with particular skills or backgrounds, or certain physical facilities. A negative use of funds (i.e., profit) is a source of funds. Projected numbers could be for several relevant years.

Section 6. Summary of Proposed Strategy

A. *Business Scope—Product-Market Served*

Product Market

B. *Strategy Description*

- Investment Objective

  ☐ Withdraw

  ☐ Milk

  ☐ Maintain

  ☐ Grow in market share

  ☐ Market expansion

  ☐ Product expansion

  ☐ Vertical integration

Product Market

- Value Proposition

  ☐ Quality

  ☐ Value

  ☐ Focus

  ☐ Innovation

  ☐ Global

  ☐ Other

- Assets and Competencies Providing SCAs

- Functional Strategies

C. *Key Strategy Initiatives*

D. Financial Projections Based on Proposed Strategy

	Past	Present	Projected
Operating Statement			
Market share			
Sales			
Cost of goods sold			
Gross margin			
R&D			
Selling/advertising			
Product G&A			
Div. & corp. G&A			
Operating profit			
Balance Sheet			
Cash/AR/inventory			
AP			
Net current assets			
Fixed assets at cost			
Accumulated depreciation			
Net fixed assets			
Total assets—book value			
Estimated market value of assets			
ROA (base—book value)			
ROA (base—market value)			
Uses of Funds			
Net current assets			
Fixed assets			
Operating profit			
Depreciation			
Other			
Resources Required			

Active dialogue, customer, 32–33
Acura, 155
Adaptability, strategic, 132–134
Adaptation-supporting culture, 133
Adidas, 188
Affinity charts, 30
Aflac, 178, 190
Ajax, 169, 171, 173
Alliances
   instant synergy and, 126
   network of, 262–263
   strategic, 236–239
Alternative industries, analyzing, 215–216
Amazon, 5, 7, 63, 126, 152–153, 155, 163, 165, 184
America Online (AOL), 104, 134
American Express, 171
Ampex, 212
Anarchy in global brand management, 236
Anderson, Chris, 63
Annual planning cycles, 23
Apple Computer, 10, 44, 49, 68, 142–143, 215, 217
Application scope, submarkets and, 60
Applications, product, 28
Argis, Stuart, 182
Arm & Hammer, 180, 181, 198
Armstrong Rubber, 145
Arrogance, avoiding, 275
Asahi Super Dry Beer, 62, 210, 212
Assets
   competitive advantage and, 121–122
   of competitor, 48–51
   core, 126–127
   export of, 44
   leveraging of, 194–195, 213
   protection and strategic alliances, 238–239
   return on, 96–97
   strategic, 7–8
   synergy and, 126–127
   underused, 133
Associations, brand. *See* Brand associations
AT&T, 271
Augmentation, product, 59
Automobile industry innovations, 209
Average costing, 102
Avon, 143, 164, 190

Backward integration, 44
Balance energy bars, 40–41
Banana Republic, 171

Band-Aid, 159
Barriers, exit, 247–248
Bausch & Lomb, 6
Bayer, 60, 139, 161
BCG consulting group, 243
Ben & Jerry's, 85, 143
Benchmarking, 104
BenGay, 181
Best Buy, 184
Big Idea Group, 218
Black & Decker, 35, 97, 127, 163, 195
Bloomingdale's, 147
Blue ocean businesses, 209–210, 214
BMW, 155, 164, 171
Book-of-the-Month Club, 181
Bose, 186
Brabeck, Peter, 255
Brand Asset Valuator, 162
Brand associations, 161–168
   being contemporary and, 166
   brand personality and, 166–168
   breadth of product line and, 163–164
   customer experience and, 165
   emotional benefits and, 164
   global, 165–166, 225
   maintaining relevance and, 162–163
   organizational intangibles and, 164
   product category and, 162–163
   self-expressive benefits and, 165
   specmanship and, 161–162
   trend responders and, 163
Brand awareness, 158–159
Brand customization, 230–233
Brand equity
   brand associations and, 161–168
   brand awareness and, 158–159
   brand identity and, 168–173
   brand loyalty and, 159–160
   conceptualization of, 157–158
   consolidation process and, 253
Brand essence, 170–171
Brand extensions, 196–199
   brand name enhancement and, 198
   endorsed brands, 199
   evaluating viability of, 197–198
   fit of, 197–198
   logic of, 197
   subbrands, 199
   value of, 198

Brand identity, 168–173
  brand essence and, 170–171
  brand position, 173
  core identity and, 169–170
  direct associations and, 169
  extended identity, 170
  multiple brand identities, 173
  proof points and, 171–172
  role of, 172–173
  strategic initiatives and, 171–172
Brand loyalty, 27–28, 99–100, 159–160
Brand personality, 166
Brand portfolio, 251–257
  assessment of, 252–253
  brand elimination, 255
  brand equity, 253
  branding options, 254
  business prospects and, 254
  consolidation process, 252–254
  descriptors and, 254–255
  flexible, 133
  merging brands, 255
  on-notice lists, 255
  prioritizing, 254–255
  revised strategy and, 255–256
  strategic fit and, 254
  strategy implementation, 257
  transfer equity and, 255
Brand position, 173
Brand standardization, 230–233
Brand vision, 275–276
Branded differentiators, 182–184
Branded energizers, 185–191
  branded CEOs, 190–191
  branded programs, 190
  branded promotional activities, 189
  branded sponsorships, 187–188
  characteristics of, 185–186
  endorsers, 188–189
  memorable branded symbols, 189–190
  new branded products, 186–187
Branded programs, 190
Branded promotional activities, 189
Branded sponsorships, 187–188
Branded symbols, 189–191
Brand/firm associations, 100
Branson, Richard, 167–168, 190, 196, 268
Breadth, product line, 163–164
Breakthrough strategies, 273
British Airlines, 141
British Petroleum (BP), 85, 143, 144
Budweiser, 51
Buick, 188–189
Buitoni, 159

Burger King, 153, 163
Burke, Ray, 80
Business portfolio
  brand portfolio strategy, 251–257
  business position and, 246
  confirmation bias and, 246
  divestment and, 245–248
  escalation of commitment and, 248
  exit barriers and, 247–248
  growth-share matrix and, 243–244
  liquidation and, 245–248
  market attractiveness/business position
    matrix, 244–246
  milking strategy, 249–251
  objectivity in divestment decisions, 248
  overview of, 243–245
  psychological biases and, 247
  strategic fit and, 246
Business scope, 5–7
  expansion of, 9
  market definition and, 23
Business strategy
  assets and competencies, 7–8
  customer value proposition, 7
  dimensions of, 4–8
  feasibility of, 10
  functional strategies and programs, 8–9
  future success and, 10
  marketing role in, 14–15
  product-market investment strategy, 5–7
  selection criteria, 9–10
  synergy of, 10
  value propositions and, 139–141
Businesses, new. *See* New businesses
Business-to-business (B2B), 73, 74
Buyer base expansion, 178
Buyer hot buttons, 31
Buyer sophistication, 66
Buzz marketing, 178

Cadbury, 232
Cadillac, 164
Campbell Soup, 29, 44
Canon, 127, 128, 134, 231, 232, 283
Cardinal Health, 199
Castor Motor Oil, 145
Category perceptions, new businesses and,
  213–214
Caterpillar, 49, 53, 227
Cemex, 217
Centralization, 261
Centurion Industries, 261
Charles Schwab, 40, 134
Chase & Sanborn, 249

Checklist of competitor strengths and
 weaknesses, 51–53
Checkout Channel, 80
Chevrolet, 163
Chevron, 184
Chief executive officers (CEOs), branded,
 190–191
Chief marketing officer (CMO), 273–276
Christensen, Clayton, 214–215
Chrysler, 190, 204, 211, 237, 238
Chux, 212
Cigna, 275
Cirque du Soleil, 208, 210
Cisco, 41
CitiGroup, 7, 165
Clairol, 203
Clif bars, 40–41
Clinique, 181
Clorox, 47, 159
CNN, 210
Coca-Cola, 40, 75, 85, 97–98, 135, 195, 213,
 219, 224, 229, 230
Cocooning, 83
Co-creating experiences, 33
Coldwell Banker, 205
Colgate, 63, 178
Collaborative processes, new businesses and, 218
Commitment
 commitment curse, 219
 competitor, 46
 escalation of, 248
Communication system, cross-country, 234
Competencies
 competitive advantage and, 121–122
 of competitor, 48–51
 core, 126–127
 leveraging of, 194–195
 strategic, 7–8
Competition intensity, 67–68
Competitive advantage. *See* Sustainable
 competitive advantage
Competitive entry, superior, 73–74
Competitive overcrowding, 72–73
Competitive strength grids, 53
Competitor analysis
 analyzing submarkets, 53–55
 checklist of strengths and weaknesses, 51–53
 competitive strength grid, 53
 cost structure, 47
 current and past competitor strategies, 46–47
 customer-based approaches, 39–41
 exit barriers and, 47–48
 identification of competitors, 29–44
 image and positioning strategy, 46

Japanese efforts at, 38
 objectives and commitment, 46
 obtaining information, 55–56
 organization and culture, 47
 planning forms, 295–299
 potential competitors and, 44
 profitability, 45
 relevant assets and competencies, 48–51
 size and growth, 45
 strategic groups and, 41–43
 strengths and weaknesses, 48–55
 understanding competitors, 44–48
Components, moving to systems from, 216–217
Confirmation bias, 247–248
Congruence, strategic, 269–273
Consultative model, in global brand
 management, 236
Consumer demand, 74
Consumer trends, environmental analysis and,
 82–87
Contemporary products, 166
Convenience shoppers, 30
Core assets, competitive advantage and, 126–127
Core business, success and leveraging of, 202
Core competencies, competitive advantage and,
 126–127
Core identity, 169–170
Corporate culture, strategic congruence and,
 270–271
Corporate social responsibility, 143–144
Cost advantages
 creation of, 151–152
 sources of, 101–102
Cost barriers, 74
Cost structure. *See also* Profitability analysis
 competitor, 47
 industry analysis of, 49–50
 market, 69
Costco, 155
Country silos, 274
Crayola crayons, 159
Creative thinking
 external analysis and, 22
 methods of, 179
 use of, 36
Critical mass, 229
Cross-country synergy, 234–235
Cross-market exposure, 230–231
Cross-silo teams, 274–275
Cross-subsidization, 226–227
Cultural barriers, 229
Cultural trends
 being alive, 84
 cocooning, 83

Cultural trends (*continued*)
down-aging, 84
environmental analysis and, 83–87
fantasy adventure, 84
green movement and, 84–87
ninety-nine lives, 84
pleasure revenge, 84
small indulgences, 84
tribing, 84
Culture, competitor, 47
Culture, organizational. *See* Organizational culture
Curse of success, 219
Curves, 216
Customer analysis, 24–36. *See also* Customer motivations; Customers
benefits sought from product, 26
changing priorities, 32
creative thinking and, 36
customer as active partner, 36
customer motivations, 29–33
ethnographic research, 35–36
focused strategy and, 28–29
hot buttons, 31
ideal experience and, 36
loyalty, 27–28
multiple segments and, 28–29
planning forms, 294–295
price sensitivity, 26–27
product application, 28
qualitative research, 32
segmentation and, 24–29
unmet needs and, 33–36
user-developed products and, 34
Customer motivations, 29–33, 49. *See also* Customer analysis; Customers
buyer hot buttons, 31
customer as active partner and, 31
customer priorities and, 32
determination of, 30–32
qualitative research, 32
shopper segments and, 29–30
Customer relationship management (CRM), 60, 216
Customer-based approach, in competitor analysis, 39–41
Customers. *See also* Customer analysis; Customer motivations
community mobilization, 33
complaints by, 34
customer value proposition, 7
dialogue with, 32–33
differentiation in global strategies, 228
disinterest of, 66
diversity of, 33

Customer analysis, 24–36. *See also* Customer motivations; Customers

Customization, brand, 230–233

Daimler-Benz, 204
Datsun, 159
Dean Witter, 205
Decentralization, 261
Decision-driven scenarios, 91
Decline, product, 65–66
Defensive strategies, 44
Dell Computer, 42, 121, 130, 152, 155, 215, 255
Demand forecasting, 74
Demographic data
in forecasting growth, 65
segmentation and, 26
trend analysis, 86–87
Dentsu, 126
Deregulation, strategic groups emerging from, 43
Descriptor roles, 254–255
Design appeal, 142–143
Dialogue, customer, 32–33
Differentiation
brand, 182–184
from competitors, 170
Discounts, product, 180
Disinterest, customer, 66
Disney, 51, 143, 149, 196–198, 230
Distribution
capacity, leveraging and, 195
channels and market expansion, 200–201
constraints on, 75
in hit-industry topology, 272
system analysis, 70
Diversity, customer, 33
Diversity, 33
Dolby Laboratories, 141
Dot-com frenzy, 73
Down-aging, 84
Drillers, in hit-industry topology, 272
Driving forces, in growth, 64
Drucker, Peter, 71, 213, 248
Dual organizations, 220

expansion of base, 177–178
fanatical base, 145
improving experiences of, 177
insights of and new businesses, 217
perceived value and, 140
power of and prices, 68
priorities of, 32
product or service relevance to, 140
satisfaction of, 99–100
submarkets and, 62
superior relationship with, 144–145
surveys of, 34
switching costs, 212

DuPont, 231
Duracell, 8, 185
Dysfunctional styles, in global brand
    management, 235

eBay, 62, 63, 212
Ecomagination, 85–86
E-commerce
    adding capacity and, 195
    shakeout of, 67–68
Economic trends, 87–88
Economies of scale, 196, 224, 229, 230
Eddie Bauer, 183
Eestor, 289
Emotional benefits, product, 164
Employee capability and performance, 102
Endorsed brands, 199
Endorsements, 188–189
Energizer, 186
Energizing the business
    branded differentiators and, 182–184
    branded energizers and, 185–191
    creative thinking methods, 179
    customer experiences and, 177
    expanding buyer base and, 178
    home-run marketing programs and, 178
    line extensions and, 178
    loyal customer base and, 177–178
    points of parity and, 177
    product personality and, 178
    product usage and, 178–182
Energy bar industry, 110–111
Enterprise Rent-A-Car, 208, 210
Enthusiastic shoppers, 30
Environmental analysis
    consumer trends, 82–87
    cultural trends, 83–87
    forecasting technologies, 80–81
    government/economic trends, 87–88
    green movement and, 84–87
    impact analysis and, 89–90
    incremental innovations, 81–82
    information technology, 83
    new technology impact, 82
    planning forms, 303–304
    scenario analysis and, 90–93
    strategic uncertainty and, 88–93
    substantial innovations, 81–82
    technology trends and, 80–82
    transformational innovations, 81–82
Environmental programs, 84–87
Escalation of commitment, 248
Essence, brand, 170–171
Esso, 144
Ethnic populations, 87

Ethnographic research
    customer insights and, 217
    customer needs and, 35–36
Excess capacity, strategic alliances and, 238
Exit barriers, 47–48, 247–248
Exit strategies, 245–248
Expansion, repeatable formula for, 228
Experience, brand, 165
Experience curve, 153–154
Extended identity, 170
External analysis, 12, 19–24. *See also*
    Competitor analysis
        analysis objectives and, 20
        as creative exercise, 22
        market definition and, 22–23
        strategic decisions and, 19–20
        strategic uncertainties and, 20–21
        timing of, 23
        uncertainty and, 21–22

Facilitator model, in global brand
    management, 236
Fads, 70–71
Fanatical customer base, 145
Fantasy adventure trend, 84
Fatal biases, new businesses and, 219–220
FedEx, 83, 202
Finance, competitor analysis and, 51
Financial commitment, new businesses and, 213
Financial performance, 96–98
    perceived quality and, 149–150
    profitability and, 96–97
    relative cost and, 101–102
    sales/market share and, 96
    shareholder value analysis and, 97–98
Firm infrastructure, 51
First-mover advantage, 212
Flexibility, strategic, 133
Focused strategy, in customer analysis, 28–29
Ford, Henry, 35
Ford Motor, 4, 8, 60, 153–154, 164, 183, 212, 237
Forecasting growth, 64–65
Forecasting technologies, 80–81
Forms, planning. *See* Planning forms
Forward integration, potential competitors and, 44
Founders, organizational, 268
Frequent-flyer plans, 180
Frito-Lay, 63, 68, 100, 268
Frugal shoppers, 29
Fuji Film, 163
Functional programs, 8–9
Functional strategies, 8–9

Gallo Winery, 13
Gap, 165, 198

Gates, Bill, 190
General Electric (GE), 6, 35, 51, 85, 97, 98, 106, 125, 129, 159, 173, 196, 199, 200, 219, 220, 238, 247, 265
General Mills, 130, 182
General Motors (GM), 20–21, 29, 44, 51, 97, 237
Geographic silos, 15
Geographical expansion, 200
Gerber Products, 186
Gerstner, Lou, 5, 125, 204, 268
Ghost potential, 63
Gillette, 8, 61, 121, 147, 212, 213
Global brand management. *See also* Global strategies
  all hat, no cattle model, 235
  anarchy model, 235
  brand associations and, 165–166
  brand bureaucracy model, 235
  communication systems, 234
  consultative model, 236
  delivering brilliance, 236
  dysfunctional styles, 235
  facilitator model, 236
  managers, 234–235
  planning systems, 234
  service provider model, 235–236
  uninformed dictator model, 235
Global leadership, 232–233
Global strategies. *See also* Global brand management; Strategic alliances
  brand associations and, 225
  cross-subsidization and, 226–227
  expanding global footprint, 227–229
  global brand management, 233–236
  global leadership and, 232–233
  indications for, 226
  innovation and, 225
  low-cost labor or materials and, 226
  market selection and, 228–229
  motivations underlying, 224–227
  national investment incentives and, 226
  scale economies and, 224
  standardization vs. customization, 230–233
  strategically important markets and, 227
  trade barriers and, 227
GM, 133, 224, 237, 238, 245–246, 247, 252
Gold Violin, 145
Goodyear, 227
Google, 63
Government trends, 87–88
Graves, Michael, 143, 187
Green movement, 84–87
Greenpeace, 144

Grids, competitive strength, 53
Grove, Andy, 248
Growth
  competitor, 45
  demographic data and, 65
  disappointing market growth, 65
  driving forces in, 64
  forecasting, 64–65
  high-growth markets, 72–75
  historical data and, 64
  market/submarket analysis and, 64–66, 72–75
  platforms, 3
Growth-share matrix, 243–244

Halberstam, David, 38
Hallmark, 164
Harley Owners' Groups (HOG), 145, 166
Harley-Davidson, 7, 68, 84, 145, 146, 166, 184
Harvest strategy. *See* Milking strategy
Heineken, 230
Heinz, 141, 161
Hewlett-Packard (HP), 4, 8, 34, 42, 131, 153, 196, 255
High-growth markets
  competitive overcrowding and, 72–73
  risks of, 72–75
High-risk markets
  changing key success factors and, 74
  changing technology and, 74
  disappointing market growth and, 74
  distribution constraints and, 75
  price instability and, 75
  resource constraints and, 75
  superior competitive entry and, 75
Historical data, in forecasting growth, 64
Hit-industry topology, 271–273
Hobart Corporation, 280–281
Hold strategy, 250–251
Home Depot, 7, 61, 144, 155
Home markets, strong, 228
Home-run marketing programs, 178
Honda, 127, 135, 173, 195, 232
H&R Block, 196
Human resources management, 50

Iacocca, Lee 190
IBM, 34, 55, 61, 66, 68, 125, 163, 186, 196, 200, 204, 225, 230, 268, 274, 283
Ideal experience, conceptualization of, 36
Identity, brand. *See* Brand identity
Ikea, 155
Image, competitor, 46
Immelt, Jeff, 6
Imperatives, strategic, 172

Implementation barriers, 129
Inbound logistics, 50
Incentives, product usage and, 180
Incremental innovations, 81–82
Incumbent curse, 219
Indirect competitors, 39
Industry economics, global strategies and, 228
Industry trends, 108–109
Information systems, 263
Information technology, 83
Infrastructure, firm, 51
Inland Steel, 237
In-N-Out chain, 146
Innovations, 2
   analysis of, 102
   competitor analysis, 51
   global, 225
   low-end disruptive, 214–215
   new businesses and, 210, 211–213
   new-market disruptive, 215
   technological, 81–82
Insiders, organizational analysis and, 265–266
Instability, price, 75
Intangibles, organizational, 164
Intel, 35, 248
Intent, strategic, 134–136
Internal analysis, 12
   benchmarking, 104
   brand loyalty, 99
   brand/firm associations, 100
   customer satisfaction, 99
   financial performance and, 96–98
   innovation, 102
   long-term profitability measures, 98–102
   manager/employee capability and performance, 102
   planning forms, 304–306
   product and service quality, 100
   profitability, 96–97
   relative cost, 101–102
   sales and market share, 96
   shareholder value analysis, 97–98
   strengths and weaknesses, 102–103
   structuring strategic decisions and, 105–106
   threats and opportunities, 103–105
Internet
   competitor information and, 55
   customer communities and, 33
   industry shakeout, 67–68
   information updates on, 181
Intimacy, product, 145
Investment
   national incentives and, 226
   overinvestment, 141

   patterns of, 6
   product-market strategy and, 5–7
   programmatic strategy and, 141–142
   return on, 9–10
   strategic alliances and, 238

Jaguar, 142–143, 161
J.B. Kunz Company, 102
J.C. Penney, 268
Jell-O, 159, 180, 181
Jobs, Steve, 190
John Deere, 199
Joie de Vivre, 166
Joint ventures, 239. *See also* Strategic alliances
JVC, 237, 238

Kaizen, 128
Kao Corporation, 51
KC Masterpiece, 183
Kelleher, Herb, 190
Kentucky Fried Chicken (KFC), 153, 163, 200
Key success factors (KSF), 58–59, 71–72, 123
Kingsford Charcoal, 122
Kirin Beer, 62, 212
KitchenAid, 63
Kleenex tissue, 159
KLM Cargo, 216–217
Kmart, 173
Knowledge, buyer, 66
Kodak, 61, 212, 215, 283
Korvette, 259–260
Kraft, 189

Labor, low-cost, 226
Lafley, A.G., 6
Lane Bryant, 166
Lead countries, in globalization strategies, 231
L'eggs, 70, 212
Lenox, 196
Level of analysis, 22–23
Leveraging
   brand extensions, 196–199
   core business success and, 202
   economies of scale and, 196
   expanding scope of offering, 199–200
   geographical expansion, 200
   implementation of, 194–195
   manufacturing skills and, 195
   marketing skills and, 195
   mirage of synergy, 203–206
   new markets, 200–201
   option evaluation, 201–202
   product-market attractiveness, 201
   repeatability and, 203

Leveraging (*continued*)
  research and development skills and, 196
  sales and distributions capacity and, 195
  stretching core business and, 202
  success potential and, 202–203
Levi-Strauss, 83
Levitt, Theodore, 9, 230
Lexus, 7, 59, 123, 145, 147, 155, 171, 217
Line extensions, 178
Lionel trains, 159
L.L. Bean, 163, 268
Lmart, 165
Logistics, in-bound and out-bound, 50
Long John Silver, 153
Low-cost culture, 155
Low-cost labor, 226
Low-cost manufacturing, 238
Low-cost materials, 226
Low-end disruptive innovation, 214–215
Lowe's, 7
Loyalty, brand, 27–28, 159–160
Loyalty programs, 177–178
Luna energy bars, 210

Male shoppers, 27
Management. *See also* Global brand
  management; Strategic market
  management
  competitor analysis and, 51–52
  human resources management, 50
  manager capability and performance, 102
  managerial pride, 247
  new businesses and, 212
  total quality management, 148–149
Manufacturing
  competitor analysis and, 51
  leveraging skills, 195
Market access, strategic alliances and, 237–238
Market attractiveness, exit strategy and, 246
Market attractiveness/business position matrix,
  244–245
Market definition, external analysis and, 22–23
Market expansion, potential competitors and, 44
Market growth, disappointing, 74. *See also*
  High-risk markets
Market research
  competitor information and, 55–56
  finding new product uses and, 181–182
  globalization strategies and, 232
  market share analysis, 96
  planning forms, 300–302
Market size
  ghost potential, 63
  global strategies and, 228

  potential, 62–63
  small markets, 63
Market trends. *See* Trends, market
Marketing
  chief marketing officer (CMO), 273–276
  competitor analysis and, 52–53
  growth strategy and, 15
  home-run programs, 178
  myopia, 9
  product dysfunction and, 15
  role in strategic analysis, 15
  role in strategy development, 15
  strategic role of, 14–15
Marketing skills, leveraging and, 195
Market/submarket analysis, 53–55
  brand relevance and, 61
  competition intensity, 67–68
  competitive overcrowding and, 72–73
  cost structure, 69
  customer power and, 68
  decline detection, 65–66
  dimensions of, 59
  disappointing market growth and, 74
  distribution constraints and, 75
  distribution systems, 70
  emerging submarkets, 59–62
  ghost potential, 63
  growth, 64–66
  key success factors, 71–72, 74
  market trends, 70–71
  maturity detection, 65–66
  objectives of, 58–59
  potential competitors, 68
  potential market size, 62–63
  price instability and, 75
  profitability analysis, 66–69
  resource constraints and, 75
  risk in high-growth markets, 72–75
  small markets, 63
  substitute products and, 68
  superior competitive entry and, 73
  technological changes and, 74
Marriott, 35–36, 133, 199
Materials, low-cost, 226
Matrix organizations, 261–262
Mattel, 204
Maturiteen, 27
Maturity, product, 65–66
Maytag repairman, 189–190
McDonald's, 126, 153, 161, 163, 197, 200, 219,
  230
McKesson, 83
Measurement systems, 263–264
Media spillover, 230

Mercedes, 123
Merging brands, 255
Merrill Lynch, 61
MetLife, 178, 190
Metrosexual, 27
Michelin, 189–190, 227
Microsoft, 2, 44, 165, 255
Milking strategy, 249–251
  conditions favoring, 249–250
  hold strategy, 250–251
  implementation problems, 250
Miller Beer, 51
Mintzberg, Henry, 263
Misreading trends, 134
Mitsubishi, 196, 238
Mizrahi, 143
Mobil, 63
Mobility barriers, 42
Moore, Gordon, 248
Morton salt, 159
Motivation
  customer, 49
  strategy implementation and, 266
Motorola, 239
Mr. Clean, 189–190
MTV, 164
Multiple brand identities, 173
Multiple businesses, 2
Multiple segment strategies, 28–29
MySpace, 145

Name awareness, 158–159
Name dominance, 159
Names, global appropriateness of, 233
National investment incentives, 226
Nestlé, 153, 195, 255
Net present value, 98–99
Netflix, 63
NetJets, 216
New branded products, 186–187
New businesses
  alternative industry analysis and, 215–216
  asset leverage and, 213
  attractive financial returns of, 210–211
  blue ocean businesses, 209–210
  category perceptions and, 213–214
  collaborative processes and, 218
  from components to systems, 216–217
  concept of newness and, 210
  customer insights and, 217
  fatal biases and, 219–220
  financial commitment and, 213
  first mover advantage and, 212
  from ideas to market, 218–220

  innovation and, 211–213
  lower price points and, 214–215
  managerial persistence and, 212
  market trends and, 217–218
  relentless innovation and, 213
  successful traits of, 212–213
  viability in established organizations, 220
  vision and, 212
New markets
  geographical expansion into, 200
  new segment expansions, 200–201
New segment expansions, 200–201
Newbie shoppers, 29
New-market disruptive innovations, 215
NextMedium, 289–290
Niche offerings, viability of, 63
Niche specialists, 145–146
Niches, market, 59
Nike, 26, 131, 143, 159, 165, 203
Nippon Steel, 237
Nissan, 159, 231
No-frills products/services, 152
Nordstrom, 144, 147, 164, 165, 171, 212
Norms, 267
Norwest Bank, 257
Nuclear family, 87
Nucor, 134

Objectives, competitor, 46
Ocean Spray, 181
Offbrand, 186
Ogilvy & Mather, 205
Ohmae, 101
One-stop shopping, 205–206
On-notice lists, 255
OnStar, 142, 183
Operations-based cost efficiencies, 152–153
Opportunism, strategic, 130–132
Opportunity analysis, 103–105. *See also* New
  businesses
Oral B, 184
Organizational analysis
  alliance networks and, 262–263
  chief marketing officers and, 273–276
  conceptual framework and, 260
  corporate culture and strategy and, 270–271
  decentralization *vs.* centralization, 261
  external, 12
  hit-industry topology and, 271–273
  information systems and, 263
  internal, 12
  management systems and, 263–264
  matrix organizations and, 261–262

Organizational analysis (*continued*)
measurement and reward systems and, 263–264
motivation and, 266
norms and, 267
organizational culture and, 266–268
organizational structure and, 260–263
people and, 264–266
planning systems and, 264
shared values and, 267
skunk works and, 262
sourcing and, 265–266
strategic congruence and, 269–273
symbols and symbolic actions and, 268
virtual corporations and, 262
Organizational culture, 266–269
founder and, 268
norms, 267
rituals and, 268
role models and, 268
shared values, 267
symbolic actions, 268
symbols, 268
Organizational intangibles, 164
Organizational structure, 260–263
alliance networks, 262–263
decentralization vs. centralization, 261
matrix organizations, 261–262
skunk works, 262
virtual corporations, 262
Orville Redenbacher, 198
Outbound logistics, 50
Outsiders, organizational analysis and, 265–266
Outsourcing
core competencies and, 127
design appeal and, 143
as global strategy, 238
Overcapacity, 65–66
Overcrowding, competitive, 72–73
Overinvestment, in value-added activity, 141

Paradigm shifts, 129–130
Parity, brand identity and, 170
Partnership programs, 153
Past strategies, competitor, 46–47
Patent protection, 141
People development, 265
Pepsi, 2, 40, 41, 75, 203, 213, 229
Perceived quality, 149–150
Perceived value, 154–155
Personality
brand, 166
product, 178
Personalized experiences, co-creation of, 33

Peugeot, 227
Philadelphia cream cheese, 159
Philip Morris, 195, 213
Pillsbury, 189–190, 198
Pizza Hut, 153
Planning forms, 294–308
competitor analysis, 295–299
customer analysis, 294–295
environmental analysis, 303–304
internal analysis, 304–306
market analysis, 300–302
strategy summary, 307–308
Planning systems
global brand, 234
strategic planning and, 264
Pleasure revenge trend, 84
Points of differentiation (POD), 123
Points of parity (POP), 123, 177
Political problems, 74
Political uncertainties, 229
Popcorn, Faith, 71, 83
Porter, Michael, 50, 66
Portfolio analysis. *See* Brand portfolio;
Business portfolio
Portman Hotels, 145
Positioning strategy
of brand, 173
of competitor, 46
Potential competitors, 44
Potential customers; profitability analysis
and, 68
Potential market size, 62–63
Potential synergy, leveraging and, 203–206
PowerBar, 40–41, 59, 110–111
Preempted positions, 232
Presto shoe, 187
Price incentives, 180
Price instability, 75
Price points, 214–215
Price pressures, 65–66
Price sensitivity, 26–27
Pringles, 122, 141, 230
Priorities, customer, 32
Problem research, 34
Procter & Gamble (P&G), 5, 6–7, 8, 35, 47, 63,
122, 153, 196, 200, 212, 218, 225,
229, 233, 236, 255, 268
Procurement, 50
Product line breadth, 163–164
Product usage, 178–182
ease of use, 179–180
finding new uses, 181–182
frequency of use, 179
positioning for frequent use, 181

providing incentives for, 180
reducing undesirability and, 180
reminder communications and, 180
Product-market investment strategy, 5–7
Products. *See also* Product usage
applications and segmentation, 28
benefits sought from, 26
copying of, 229
customer associations and, 162–163
differentiation of, 65–66
expansion and potential competitors, 44
quality analysis of, 100
relevance of, 162–163
substitute, 66
superior attributes of, 141–142
Product-use associations, 41
Profitability analysis, 96–97. *See also* Cost
  structure
  of competitor, 45
  customer power and, 68
  existing competitors, 67–68
  market and submarket, 66–69
  potential competitors, 68
  substitute products and, 68
  suppler power and, 68–69
Programmatic investment strategy, 141–142
Programs
  branded, 190
  functional, 8–9
Promotional activities, branded, 189
Proof points, 171–172
Psychological biases, in analyzing business, 247
Pumpers, in hit-industry topology, 272

Quaker Oats, 165, 204
Qualitative research, in customer motivation, 32
Quality
  perceived, 149–150
  superior. *See* Superior quality
Quality Function Deployment (WFD)
  program, 30
Questions
  to structure competitor analysis, 39
  to structure market analysis, 60
Quin, James Brian, 246

Raikes, Jeffrey, 199
Ralph Lauren, 143, 165
Raymond Corporation, 146
Real value, 263
Recognition, name, 159
Reebok, 203
Related sales, in forecasting growth, 65
Relative cost, 101–102

Relentless innovation, 213. *See also* Innovation
Relevance
  brand, 61
  product, 162–163
Reluctant shoppers, 29
Reminder communications, 180
Repeatability, leveraging and, 203
Repositioning
  campaigns, 181
  product class, 60–62
Research and development (R&D) leveraging,
  196
Resource constraints, 75
Retailing trends, 108–109
Retaliatory strategies, potential competitors
  and, 44
Retrosexual, 27
Return on assets (ROA), 96–97
Return on investment (ROI), 9–10
Reward systems, 263–264
Rheingold Brewery, 213
Rituals, 268
Role models, 268
Ronald McDonald House, 143, 186, 190
Rossignol, 44, 165
Rough Guides, 36
Royal Crown Cola, 75, 213

Sales analysis, 96
Sales capacity leveraging, 195
Samsung, 135, 159, 178, 188, 291–292
Samuel Adams, 200
Saturation, 66
Saturn, 59, 145, 217
Savin, 135, 282
Scale economies
  cost advantages and, 153
  global strategies and, 224
  strategic alliances and, 237
Scenario analysis, 90–93. *See also* Strategic
  uncertainty
  categories, 91
  decision-driven scenarios, 91
  identifying scenarios, 91–92
  relating to strategies, 92–93
  scenario probabilities, 93
  strategy-developing scenarios, 90–91
Schlitz, 149, 150
Schwab, 163, 196
Schweppes, 162
Schwinn, 70–71, 199
Scope, application, 60
Sears, 143, 205
Seasonal reminders, 180

Segmentation, 24–29
  brand loyalty and, 27–29
  customer characteristics and, 25
  definition of, 25–26
  demographics and, 26
  focused strategy and, 26
  multiple segment focus and, 28–29
  price sensitivity and, 26–27
  product-related approaches, 25
  strategy dimensions, 24–25
Self-Expressive Benefits, product, 165
Selznick, Peter, 264
Service provider model, in global brand
  management, 235–236
Service quality analysis, 100
Shared values, 267
Shareholder value analysis, 97–98
Shell, 144
Shoppers
  convenience, 30
  enthusiastic, 30
  frugal, 29
  newbie, 29
  reluctant, 29
  strategic, 30
Short-term financial pressure curse, 219
Shouldice Hospital, 146
Siebel, 60, 162, 216
Siemens, 196
Silos, 274–276
Sirius, 35
Size, competitor, 45
Size curse, 219–220
Skunk works, 262
Sky Roadster, 186
Small indulgences trend, 84
Small market investing, 63
Snapple, 204
Social programs, corporate, 143–144
Sony, 51, 125, 127, 143, 145, 159, 196, 204, 255
Sophistication, buyer, 66
Sourcing, 265–266
Southwest Airlines, 120, 152, 155, 215
Specmanship, 161–162
Sponsorships, branded, 187–188
Sprite, 231
Standardization, brand, 230–233
Starbucks, 9–10, 144
Strategic adaptability, 132–134
  adaptation-supportive culture and, 133
  misreading trends and, 134
  strategic flexibility and, 133–134
  trend identification and evaluation and,
  132–133

Strategic alliances, 236–239
  accessing name or customer relationship, 238
  excess capacity and, 238
  forms of, 237
  investments and, 238
  low-cost manufacturing and, 238
  motivations for, 237
  nature of, 236–237
  product line components and, 237
  scale economies and, 237
  strategic market access and, 237
  technology access and, 238
  trade barriers and, 237
Strategic assets, 7–8
Strategic business units (SBU), 12
Strategic commitment, 128–130
Strategic competency, 7–8
Strategic congruence, 269–273. *See also*
  Organizational analysis
  corporate culture and strategy, 270–271
  hit-industry topology, 271–273
  organizational interactions and, 269
  questions for analyzing, 270
Strategic decisions
  external analysis and, 19–20
  structuring of, 105–106
Strategic drift, 131–132
Strategic fit
  brand portfolio and, 254
  exit strategy and, 246
Strategic flexibility, 133–134
Strategic groups
  competitor analysis and, 41–43
  conceptualization of, 42–43
  emerging from deregulation, 43
  mobility barriers and, 42
  projection of, 43
Strategic imperatives, 172
Strategic initiatives, 171–172
Strategic intent, 134–136
Strategic market management
  adapting strategy, 12–13
  characteristics of, 10–14
  creating strategy, 12–13
  external analysis and, 12
  implementing strategy, 12–13
  internal analysis and, 12
  objectives of, 14
Strategic necessities, 71–72
Strategic opportunism, 130–132
  benefits of, 130–131
  economies of scope and, 131
  entrepreneurial culture and, 130

information gathering and, 130
strategic drift and, 131–132
Strategic philosophies, 127–136
strategic adaptability, 132–134
strategic commitment, 128–130
strategic intent, 134–136
strategic opportunism, 130–132
Strategic planning, 264
Strategic strengths, 71–72
Strategic stubbornness, 129–130
Strategic uncertainty, 88–93. *See also* Scenario analysis
external analysis and, 20–21
immediacy of, 90
impact analysis and, 89–90
management of, 90
Strategic value, 238–239
Strategically important markets, 227
Strategy, functional, 8–9
Strategy-developing scenarios, 90–91
Strengths and weaknesses
competitor, 48–55
internal analysis of, 102–103
Stringer, Robert, 273
Structure, organizational, 260–263
Stubbornness, strategic, 129–130
Subbrands, 199
Submarkets, emerging, 59–62. *See also* Market/submarket analysis
Substantial innovations, 81–82
Substitute products, 66, 68
Substitute technologies, 66
Superior attributes, 141–142
Superior customer relationships, 144–145
Superior quality, 146–150
customer definition of, 247
dimensions of, 147–148
financial performance and, 149–150
signals of, 149
total quality management, 148–149
Supplier power, prices and, 68–69
Sustainable advantages, 140–141
Sustainable competitive advantage (SCA), 120–136
alliances and, 126
assets or competencies and, 7–8
business strategies and, 10
creation of, 2–3
key success factors and, 123
product market served and, 122
role of synergy and, 125–127
strategic intent and, 134–136
value proposition and, 122
Symbolic actions, 268

Symbols
branded, 189–191
business strategy and, 268
global appropriateness of, 233
Synergy
alliances and, 126
benefits of, 126
competitive advantage and, 125–127
core assets and competencies and, 126–127
cross-country synergies, 234–235
leveraging and, 203–206
meaning of, 125
product market, 8
Systems
communication, 234
distribution, 70
information, 263
measurement, 70
moving from components to, 216–217
planning, 234
reward, 263–264
solutions, 143

Taco Bell, 153
Taglines, external, 170
Target, 103, 143, 147, 187
Target product market, 122–123
Technical superiority, product, 146
Technology
changing, 74
development, 50
environmental analysis and, 80–82
forecasting technologies, 80–81
incremental innovations, 81–82
new technology impact, 82
overevaluation of, 74
strategic alliances and, 238
submarkets and, 62
substantial innovations, 81–82
substitute, 66
transformational innovations and, 81–82
Tesco, 202, 228, 229
Texas Instruments, 161
The Body Shop, 85, 143, 144
The Learning Company, 204
Thinking out of the box, 36
ThinkPad, 186
Thomson Corporation, 78
Threat analysis, 103–105
3M, 7, 52, 82, 127, 131, 145, 159, 164, 268, 269
Tide, 184
Time Warner, 134
Timex, 212
Tommy Hilfiger, 163

Toshiba, 159, 239
Total quality management (TQM), 148–149
Toyota, 2, 8, 26, 61, 85, 103, 128, 133, 143, 164, 165–166, 213, 233, 237, 238
Trade barriers
dodging, 227
strategic alliances and, 237
Trade-off questions, 31
Transfer equity, 255
Transformational innovations, 81–82, 289–290
Transformational strategies, 273
Trends, market, 70–71
identification and evaluation of, 132–133
misreading, 134
new businesses and, 217–218
responders, 163
submarkets and, 62
vs. fads, 71
Tribing, 84
Turner, Ted, 80

UBS, 153
Unaided recall, 159
Uncertainties, strategic. *See* Strategic uncertainty
Underused assets, investing in, 133
Unilever, 153, 255, 286–288
Uniqlo, 153
Unmet customer needs, 33–36
communication of, 33–35
creative thinking and, 36
ethnographic research and, 35–36
ideal experience and, 36
problem research and, 34
Upshaw, Lynn, 172
User-developed products, 34

V-8 vegetable juice, 159
Value, 150–155
creating cost advantages, 151–152
experience curve and, 153–154
low-cost culture, 155
no-frills products/services, 152
operations efficiency and, 152–153
perceived value, 154–155
scale economies, 153
successful competition and, 151
Value chains
components of, 50
primary value activities, 50
secondary value activities, 50–51
Value propositions
corporate social programs, 143–144
cost advantages and, 151–154

design appeal, 142–143
feasibility of, 140
low-cost culture and, 155
niche specialists, 155
perceived value and, 140, 154–155
product or service value, 150–155
relevance of, 140
strategy challenges and, 139–141
superior attribute or benefit, 141–142
superior customer relationships, 144–145
superior quality, 146–150
sustainability and, 140–141
sustainable competitive advantage and, 122
systems solutions, 143
Values, shared, 267
Valvoline, 187
Vanguard, 215
Venture capitalist industry, 246
Victoria Secret, 145–146, 166
VideoOcart, 80
Virgin Atlantic Airlines, 145, 163, 167–168, 196, 268
Virtual corporations, 262
Visa, 9, 164, 165, 188, 200, 230
Volkswagon, 142, 232
Volvo, 142, 161, 164, 173

W Hotels, 142–143
Wal-Mart, 5, 7, 28, 68, 85, 86, 113–115, 120, 121, 144, 153, 155, 161, 163, 199, 229
Walt Disney, 268
Walton, Sam, 113–115
Weaknesses. *See* Strengths and weaknesses
Web sites. See Internet
Welch, Jack, 199, 245–246, 265
Wellness trend, 84
Wells Fargo, 2, 206, 257
Westin Hotel Chain, 182–183
Whole foods, 217
Williams-Sonoma, 5, 31, 145, 146
Woods, Tiger, 188

Xerox, 61, 135, 211, 282–284

Yahoo!, 68, 126
Yamaha, 209
Yoplait, 210
Young & Rubicam, 182, 205

Zandl Group, 71
Ziff Davis Communications, 131
Zopa, 289